Damned Nation

DAMNED NATION

Hell in America from the
Revolution to Reconstruction

———◆———

KATHRYN GIN LUM

OXFORD
UNIVERSITY PRESS

OXFORD
UNIVERSITY PRESS

Oxford University Press is a department of the University of Oxford.
It furthers the University's objective of excellence in research, scholarship,
and education by publishing worldwide.

Oxford   New York
Auckland   Cape Town   Dar es Salaam   Hong Kong   Karachi
Kuala Lumpur   Madrid   Melbourne   Mexico City   Nairobi
New Delhi   Shanghai   Taipei   Toronto

With offices in
Argentina   Austria   Brazil   Chile   Czech Republic   France   Greece
Guatemala   Hungary   Italy   Japan   Poland   Portugal   Singapore
South Korea   Switzerland   Thailand   Turkey   Ukraine   Vietnam

Oxford is a registered trademark of Oxford University Press
in the UK and certain other countries.

Published in the United States of America by
Oxford University Press
198 Madison Avenue, New York, NY 10016

CIP data is on file at the Library of Congress.

ISBN 978–0–19–984311–4

1 3 5 7 9 8 6 4 2
Printed in the United States of America
on acid-free paper

To Mom, Brian, and Nick
and to the memory of Daddy

Contents

List of Illustrations

Acknowledgments

TO THOSE WHO have facilitated and accompanied me on this journey through hell, I cannot thank you enough.

I am grateful for the support of the Beinecke Rare Book and Manuscript Library, the Huntington Library, the Howard R. Lamar Center for the Study of the American West, the Bill Lane Center for the Study of the American West, and the Richard J. Franke Fellowship at Yale.

This project could not have been completed without the sage advice, close edits, critical encouragement, and generous mentorship of Jon Butler, who introduced me to Benjamin Abbott, *Sin and Fear*, heretical histories, and (though I haven't always implemented it) the value of concision. My deep appreciation also goes to Skip Stout, who helped me understand the New Divinity, reminded me what to (and what not to) prioritize, and challenged me to think about the big picture. I also want to thank Johnny Faragher for reminding me that the nuts and bolts of history mattered when my head was too far in the clouds, and Carlos Eire for letting me float back up during conversations about death, the afterlife, and the problem of evil. Thanks too to Katie Lofton, who challenged me to interrogate the terms I took for granted, introduced me to new ways of thinking about old subjects, and always knew just when to email or call with much-needed moral support. David Blight encouraged my attempts to "nail jelly on the wall" practically from day one of graduate school; Joanne Freeman helped me to organize my excitement over the discovery of the three Murrays.

George Miles at the Beinecke and Peter Blodgett at the Huntington have been beyond helpful with their tips on sources, enthusiastic discussions about manuscript materials, and shared excitement over research finds. Olga Tsapina at the Huntington, Greg Eow at Sterling Memorial Library, and John Barker at the Hawaiian Mission Children's Society Library also pointed me toward important materials. Thanks are also due to Thorin

Tritter, who taught me the intricacies of archival research during my summer with the Gilder Lehrman Institute, and to Carl Brasseaux, who revolutionized my research methodology by insisting that I use Filemaker Pro and guiding me through the transition.

Many thanks to my editor at Oxford University Press, Cynthia Read, who wrangled my writing and arguments into much sharper form, editorial assistant Marcela Maxfield, who patiently fielded all manner of questions along the way, and Lynn Childress, for her careful copyediting. My deep gratitude also goes to my readers, Peter Thuesen and Edward J. Blum, whose close readings, careful comments, constructive criticisms, and encouragement made this a much better book.

Richard White and Jack Rakove have encouraged me since my undergraduate days at Stanford and continue to be models of scholarly generosity. I am so grateful. Thanks to Richard for challenging me to refine my argument and for making it possible for me to work at Stanford in my last year of graduate school. David Holland introduced me to the field of American religious history; this book is in some ways an exploration of questions first sparked in his seminar on the subject. Thanks too to my colleagues at Stanford for their support in the final stages of revising.

Special thanks to Judith Weisenfeld for her incisive comments on the manuscript as a whole, Wallace Best for his enthusiasm about the project, Elaine Pagels for her encouragement and advice, Jessica Delgado for her critical feedback and constant support, and Jeff Stout for asking a question during my job interview that has stuck with me ever since. Princeton graduate students Leslie Ribovich and Caleb Maskell read revisions with eagle eyes and offered invaluable suggestions. Thanks, too, to my writing and revising group at Princeton (DOPE! it works)—Judith Weisenfeld, Jessica Delgado, Nicole Kirk, Annie Blazer, Grace Yukich, Manu Radhakrishnan, Michaela DeSoucey, John Millhauser, and Janet Vertesi. My Princeton and Stanford "Religion and War in America" students provided a critical undergraduate perspective on chapter 6, for which I am grateful, and members of the Religion in the Americas Workshop at Princeton helped me to refine the argument and structure of chapter 3.

Special thanks are also due to Paul Harvey for reading and commenting on the penultimate version of the manuscript. I have also benefited from feedback on various chapters and ideas from Ramón Saldívar, Sylvester Johnson, Edward Curtis, Sally Promey, Tisa Wenger, Garnette Cadogan, Sang Ngo, the American Religious History Workshop at Yale, the History

Colloquium at Princeton Theological Seminary, and the American Studies Colloquium at Princeton. All mistakes that remain are fully my own.

To my friends and colleagues at Yale, I couldn't have done this without you. Robin Morris kept me sane with midnight diner runs, incomparable humor, and late-night phone calls. Carmen Kordick read and commented on all my chapters and encouraged me through the ups and downs of graduate school. Catherine McNeur provided close reads of chapters and generously shared her brilliant archival finds. Many thanks for scintillating conversations, thoughtful edits, and good times also go to Julia Guarneri, Alison Greene, Molly Worthen, Sarah Hammond, Dave Walker, Francesca Ammon, Helen Curry, Sara Hudson, Sam Vong, Bronwen McShea, Taylor Spence, Charlie Edel, Sarah Koenig, Jason Ward, Grace Leslie, and from our time at the Huntington, Jennifer Vanore and Sarah Keyes, and from Gilder-Lehrman, Nick Osborne.

Last but hardly least, this project was built on the love and support of the people back home. Thanks Paw and Gung for the unconditional love; the Lew family for always calling to check up on me and for stress-releasing vacations; the Lee family (Palo Alto) for letting me stay at your house and for stress-busting games of Monopoly; the Lee family (Orange County) for much-needed weekend escapes during my time in Pasadena; and Auntie Helen and the Yuens for your constant support. Salina has become a good friend through the years. Thanks to Anita Gilbert-Lum, who read the final manuscript with eagle eyes. Thanks too to the members of Holy Cross Lutheran Church, the neighbors on Turtle Rock Lane, and the dog park people (and dogs!—especially Willie, Yoyo, and Jessie).

And finally, to Mom and Nick (who read everything), Brian (who knows everything), and to the memory of Dad (who believed I could do anything): thank you isn't enough. This is for you.

K.G.L.

A Note on the Text

I HAVE SOUGHT to transcribe quotes exactly as they appear in the sources without correcting for spelling or grammar. I have decided not to include the common "[sic]" to indicate spelling choices different from contemporary standards, as it would hopelessly clutter the text and detract from the flavor of antebellum writing. I have only included "[sic]" to indicate obvious typos in original texts. For handwritten manuscripts where words are sometimes impossible to decipher, I have included question marks "[?]"; strikethroughs and additions "[^]" are also indicated for handwritten manuscripts to convey the creative writing and editing process these texts often went through. All mistakes and omissions are entirely my own.

Damned Nation

Introduction

DAMNED NATION?

"ETERNAL HELL! NO man does and no man can believe it," scoffed philanthropist and abolitionist Gerrit Smith in an 1859 lecture in Peterboro, New York. "Were such a belief possible it would be fatal.... The whole nation would be struck with paralysis, and frozen with horror.... every step in that direction is a step toward the madhouse." To the heterodox Smith, antebellum Americans who professed worry about the life to come were dupes at best who did not fully understand the implications of their belief, or insincere fakers at worst who manipulated the masses through appeals to fear. Smith saw hell as a nonsensical doctrine that people in their right minds could not possibly believe, for if they did, they would do nothing but sit on their haunches and quake at the prospect.[1]

Peter Paul Simons, an African American porter in New York City, saw another possibility for engagement with hell beyond dupe, faker, and paralyzed lunatic. In an 1839 speech before the African Clarkson Association, Simons urged that belief in the afterlife could and should generate active involvement with the world's problems, especially the pressing outrage of slavery. "We seem to have lost all sight of the splendid mirror of immortality, we act like when this miserable life is ended, it will be to an eternal nonentity," he bemoaned. But "what boots this miserable life since it is to pass away, even if it is lost by disease or strife?" The consequences of inaction would redound beyond the current generation to the next, and into the life to come: "Remain inactive, and you will be the cause of rearing children for an eternal torment, for they in an ecstacy of despair will curse their maker for suffering such bitter oppression to be practised upon them." Unlike Smith, Simons held that taking the afterlife seriously necessitated defiance, especially for the enslaved and others who wanted to end the "peculiar institution." "Remain inactive," he warned, "and the almighty himself will spurn you, for lack of courage and not using properly your agency. No, we must show ACTION! ACTION! *ACTION!*"[2]

Far from debilitating all nineteenth-century Americans as they waited in fear of eventual doom, the prospect of damnation excited believers like Simons to intense engagement with the world around them. Historians have tended to focus on political concepts like republicanism, liberalism, and democratization as the primary ideologies motivating Americans in the first century of nationhood, implicitly agreeing with Smith that belief in eternal damnation could not possibly have spurred action. But the driving threat of damnation reached beyond the white male electorate and past the shifting borders of the nation as missionaries tried to save the world from hell's terrors. Even as doubters like Smith spurned it, evangelicals who focused on the importance of immediate rebirth proclaimed that eternal torments loomed near for all who failed to change their hearts, from children to the elderly, women to men, Euro-Americans to indigenous people and African American slaves. As evangelicals proselytized, the ranks of those touched by their warnings skyrocketed. In just one measure of their reach, the nation had only 668,000 church members (17 percent of the population) in 1776; by 1850 that number stood at 7.8 million (34 percent of the total population). Not all of these were evangelicals, but the statistics also do not reveal the full extent of their influence, leaving out laypeople who attended evangelical churches sporadically, heard revival sermons, and read tracts without becoming full-fledged members.[3]

This book privileges the perspective of neither believers nor doubters, but instead seeks to understand how they influenced, interacted with, and unsettled each other in the new nation. The prospect of damnation had the power to extend beyond the pulpit into people's everyday lives because it laid bare the essential interdependence between right and wrong behavior and true and false belief. The threat of hell influenced prescriptions for what it meant to be both a good Christian and a good American in an age of nation-building, territorial expansion, and debates about whether the nation's labor force should be slave or free.

The Question of Survival

Gerrit Smith's perspective lived on the fringes of religious respectability in antebellum America, but he was hardly the first to critique the concept of eternal damnation. Attacks against hell picked up steam in the United States in the late eighteenth century and even earlier across the Atlantic. Hell's survival in the young nation was never assured and its uses to spur action in the sociopolitical sphere even less so.

Several factors tested the concept's significance. Seventeenth- and eighteenth-century Enlightenment thinkers across the Atlantic and in the colonies began to suggest that human nature was fundamentally innocent and perfectible rather than inherently depraved and deserving of hell. They challenged the Calvinist view that heaven and hell existed for and by God's pleasure and that He could put whomever He pleased in either place. In questioning God's absolute sovereignty and human depravity, some turned to the promise of universal salvation and rejected the concept of hell entirely. Scholars writing about this rejection tend to portray it as a natural result of human progress away from the ignorant, pessimistic, and close-minded, and toward the more enlightened and tolerant.[4]

The First Amendment—"Congress shall make no law respecting an establishment of religion, or prohibiting the free exercise thereof"— might also have been expected to diminish the presence of hell-talk in the socio-political sphere. Threats and warnings of individual and corporate punishment and calls for communal prayer and fasting had long resounded from colonial pulpits on occasions ranging from executions to elections to colonial wars.[5] If Revolutionary-era Deists like Thomas Paine had had their way, disestablishment, though not implemented all at once, would have ended the influence of such corporate jeremiads.[6] As Paine wrote in *The Age of Reason*, "All national institutions of churches...appear to me no other than human inventions, set up to terrify and enslave mankind, and monopolise power and profit." Dubbing the idea that the majority of the world was damned through Eve's "eating of that apple" as both "absurd" and "profane," Paine claimed that "it is impossible to conceive a story more derogatory to the almighty, more inconsistent with his wisdom, more contradictory to his power, than this story is." He looked forward to the day when "a revolution in the system of government would be followed by a revolution in the system of religion."[7]

But despite the revolutionary hopes of Enlightenment thinkers and the apparent "decline of hell" in contemporaneous Europe, the concept of hell did not just survive in antebellum America: it thrived. It saturated private and public discourse. The American case suggests that hell was not an archaic concept destined to disappear once people became educated and enlightened. Antebellum Americans did not uniformly relinquish belief in damnation but vigorously debated the meanings and implications of the concept. How and why did hell survive the onslaughts that diminished its power elsewhere? What was the significance of its survival? And why did so many Americans frame their concerns about themselves and their friends, families, nation, and world in terms of divine punishment and everlasting torment?

Damned Nation?

Some have seen Americans' anxieties over their potential salvation or damnation as little more than economic and sociopolitical angst that believers channeled into a disciplined religious faith. Alexis de Tocqueville suggested as much when he wrote that American preachers "always show [their congregations] how favorable religious opinions are to freedom and public tranquility; and it is often difficult to ascertain from their discourses whether the principal object of religion is to procure eternal felicity in the other world, or prosperity in this."[8] Evangelical leaders who sought to establish moral hegemony over the new nation and its citizens did indeed argue, against their critics, that the threat of hell was necessary to ensure peace and virtue in the new republic. They maintained that nothing but hell could prevent people from committing murder or behaving licentiously, since even capital punishment would otherwise just usher them into oblivion or a better world.[9]

But hell was never just a top-down tool for social control. To reduce it to a prop for capitalist democracy or a mere reflection of this-worldly anxieties is to overlook the critical role hell played in the worldviews of many Americans. Hell was never distant. It underlay conceptions of justice and equality. It haunted dreams and waking visions. As absorbed as they seemed in the affairs of this world, after all, Americans were also ever close to the next in a pre-antibiotic age when death still seemed to strike all with impunity. In 1800 the US population's average age was sixteen; the average American could expect to live to the ripe old age of forty. Americans circulated and read a German physician's intimidating computations, "that there are on the earth 960,000,000 human beings, and that the average deaths are 29,000,000 annually, 80,000 daily, nearly 3,700 hourly, and fifty-five every minute." Since death could neither be controlled nor avoided despite the era's emphasis on human ability and improvement, Americans sought to at least control their own eternal outcomes.[10]

Instead of diminishing the influence of religious threats in the new nation as Deists like Paine had hoped, disestablishment fostered intense competition between religious groups, bringing to the fore the question of what would happen at death to followers of different faiths. Although ministers had been warning of hell's horrors for generations, late eighteenth- and nineteenth-century evangelicals increasingly made its punishments more the responsibility of humans to avoid than the prerogative of a sovereign and arbitrary God to invoke. They declared that making the "right" choices in belief and behavior was a matter of eternal bliss or misery, even as other voices challenged their presumed cultural dominance. For laypeople sorting through a bevy of sermons, printed texts, and speeches, determining whom and what to believe and how to act was at once a most common experience and one with extraordinary implications for the life to come.[11]

Nor were individuals only worried about their own eternal welfare. Tocqueville puzzled over Americans' civic-mindedness when he sought to understand how a nation of striving and self-interested individuals could simultaneously be teeming with voluntary reform organizations (not a few of which were designed to save the bodies and souls of the "fallen"). Even as individuals feared that their own spiritual choices would have lasting repercussions for themselves, their worry over the eternal fates of others was harder to explain. The older Puritan idea of the nation as a corporate "City on a Hill" that God would providentially bless or punish could hardly ensure communal identity and patriotic concern as territorial ambitions expanded the nation's reach, the population grew from natural increase and immigration, and different religious groups jostled for adherents. The question of what constituted "America" and "Americans" was not easily answered in the early national era, and getting individuals to feel invested in the eternal welfare of their fellow citizens was no simple task when hundreds or even thousands of miles separated them. A nation strung loosely together of individual believers worrying about their own afterlives might indeed have led to Gerrit Smith's paralyzed polity. Although he admitted that Americans "do not affect a brutal indifference to a future state" and "no puerile pride in despising perils which they hope to escape from," Tocqueville could hardly believe that the afterlife could actually drive social concern: "I have known zealous Christians who constantly forgot themselves, to work with greater ardor for the happiness of their fellow-men; and I have heard them declare that all they did was only to earn the blessings of a future state. I cannot but think that they deceive themselves; I respect them too much to believe them."[12]

But what if we took their claims about hell seriously?[13]

Individuals did not only want the "blessings of a future state" for them-selves but also wanted to be reunited with their loved ones after death. Of course, this desire was hardly new to the nineteenth century. What was new was that families could no longer be counted on to worship in the same churches and often did not even stay in the same locales. Death had once been an insular, communal affair with the dying one surrounded by friends and family at the home, followed by the body's procession to the village church to be buried. By the nineteenth century, though, this model was becoming a vestige of the past. Individuals could no longer assume that their friends and family believed the same things they did or that they would end up in the same place before and after death. Nor could they rely on ministers to follow their flocks and ensure that they stayed in the fold.[14]

The solution was embedded in the problem. Since there were hardly enough ministers to keep up with the growing and transitory population, evangelical leaders told laypeople that they shared responsibility for con-verting their fellows—that, given the agency to change their own hearts, it behooved them to convince others to do the same, saving them from eternal torments in the life to come. In other words, where ministers had previously claimed primary authority for disseminating the Word's warnings, now they spread more responsibility to laypeople. They also spread blame, telling listeners that their own salvation and the welfare of the nation rested on their ability to persuade family and friends. "True" believers were not to hope or strive for salvation in solitude. Antebellum evangelicals connected their own eternal destiny with others' everlasting fates, believing that they themselves would be held culpable if they failed to curb the sinfulness of unrepentant neighbors, whether they were drink-ers, gamblers, Sabbath-breakers, slaveholders, or radical abolitionists.

As older social hierarchies refigured amidst revival fire, economic chaos, and political disorder, then, antebellum Americans assessed and tried to influence who was bound for heaven and hell in an effort to monitor the otherworldly state and this-worldly concerns. Laypeople, as well as ministers, identified themselves and others not only by their race, class, and gender but also by the status of their souls, which could both reinforce and cut across these other identities. The very insta-bility of the meanings of "America" and "American" contributed to a desire for clarity; the categories of "saved" and "damned" moved be-yond the level of the individual's relationship with God to become crit-ical markers of social segregation and communal identity in the new, heterogeneous nation. The threat of damnation encouraged and discouraged certain kinds of behavior, identifying those Americans who complied as redeemed members of a redeemer nation, while painting those who refused as menaces to their neighbors' and nation's welfare and eventual inheritors of hell.

As transportation and publication technologies improved, making the world itself seem smaller, the definition of "neighbor" also expanded to include one's metaphorical "neighbors" across the continent and globe. Believers conceived of themselves as bound together in an imagined community of the saved. They sought to extend this community to encompass their fellow, unconverted Americans, and then to use a virtuous America as a springboard from which to eventually convert the rest of humanity, bringing about the millennial peace. The process of identifying who was in need of missionizing could result in swathing entire nations—the "perishing heathen" of the Americas and the world—with the "darkness" of eternal damnation if believers did not intervene or the "heathen" did not respond appropriately.

But American evangelicals were not always confident about their own abilities to redeem the rest of the world, much less themselves. They feared that if they failed in their task, they might become enmeshed in webs of culpability with the unsaved that threatened all their dreams of creating a righteous nation and world, sending all to hell instead. Americans are famous for their millennial optimism, but the evangelicals' fear of being exposed as not much better than the world they were trying to redeem lurked ever near.[15] As clear as the binary between saved and damned might seem theoretically and theologically, after all, it was hardly so in real life. For one group to declare some behaviors and beliefs hell-worthy was for this group to claim superiority and power over others, whether it was ministers over laypeople or missionaries over the so-called "heathen." But no single group could ever declare absolute ownership of the threat of damnation.

The categories of "saved" and "damned" shifted as some laypeople questioned the authority of ministers to dictate what beliefs and behaviors might send a person to hell. Not many went as far as Gerrit Smith. Still, laypeople increasingly found extenuating factors that might absolve a loved one from damnation. When faced with eternal separation from their friends and family, it became much easier for many Euro-Americans to apply the prospect of hell to the distant "heathen" or the clearly sinful "other" than to a loved one dying without clear indication of having experienced conversion.

The so-called "heathen," for their part, hardly accepted this rendering of their afterlife status without complaint. As much as the categories of saved or damned seemed to override racial distinctions—since conversion or backsliding could presumably usher someone from one group into the other regardless of skin color—they were also inextricably bound with white missionaries' and evangelicals' notions of racial and cultural superiority. Aware of this conflation, some missionized people refused a heaven supposedly populated by saved white Christians and declared their intention to join their ancestors after death. "Hell" to white Americans was not a hell to nonwhites, they argued. Others, who converted to Christianity, turned the prospect of hell back on a hypocritical and oppressive white society, challenging their monopoly over the keys to salvation. In so doing, they tapped into white evangelicals' greatest fears about failing in their task of redemption and damning their own nation instead of saving the "damned nations" of the world.

Sources and Structure

To tell this story of hell's survival and significance in the young nation, *Damned Nation* weaves from the pulpits of eastern elites to the graves of lonely western wanderers, from the journals of missionaries to the visions of Native American prophets, and from the plantations of the southern slavocracy to the insane asylums of the North. Hell permeated the cultural landscape and there is no single timeline in its American evolution between the Revolution and Reconstruction. Different people believed different things at different times in different places. Belief in and uses of hell were never simply epiphenomenal; tradition and context interwove to produce both continuity and change.[16]

This book is organized, then, to show how the doctrine was adapted and contested not only over time but also across society and space. Three parts broadly take us from the Revolution to Reconstruction while focusing on different kinds of sources and people: (1) Doctrine and Dissemination, (2) Adaptation and Dissent, and (3) Deployment and Denouement. Part One focuses on theologians and ministers to see how they debated the social repercussions of hell in the early years of the republic (chapter 1), and how they disseminated damnation to produce immediate repentance, conversion, and action on behalf of others in antebellum sermons, religious newspapers, and missionary reports (chapter 2). Part Two looks at how laypeople dealt with the terrifying injunction to convert and convert others or be damned. Some adapted ministerial warnings to shape themselves and their communities as saved (chapter 3). Others spurred new beliefs as they pushed back against evangelical dominance and justified their hearts and habits for themselves (chapter 4). Part Three addresses hell's application to the sociopolitical arena in the slavery controversy (chapter 5) and the Civil War (chapter 6). The scale of death in the war intensified Americans' longings for future reunion with their loved ones, even as the threat of hell to solidify group identity and condemn certain behaviors never fully disappeared.

Through it all, doubts about hell and fervent belief in it energized considerable controversy, personal anxiety, and civic concern in America's first century of nationhood. The lurking possibility of damnation brought together matters of the most far-reaching and personal nature, encompassing the infinity of the cosmos and the intimacy of the family, the seriousness of conversion and the ordinariness of day-to-day behavior. The fear of damnation underlay the morality politics that some scholars have started to highlight as a significant force in American political life.[17] The threat of ultimate punishment awaiting misbehaving and unbelieving members of the community, as well as those who failed to curb the bad behavior and change the hearts and minds of others, underlay revivals, missions, and social reform movements at least as much as the promise of a thousand years of peace. The two went hand in hand: to bring about the millennium required converting as much of the world as possible, which in turn rested on an assumption that the nations of the world were damned without American intervention. But what if the "damned nation" was America instead?

PART ONE

Doctrine and Dissemination

I

"Salvation" vs. "Damnation"

DOCTRINAL CONTROVERSIES IN
THE EARLY REPUBLIC

AMONG THE MANY congratulatory letters George Washington received after assuming the presidency was one from "the Convention of the Universal Church, assembled in Philadelphia." "SIR," it began, "Permit us, in the name of the society which we represent, to concur in the numerous congratulations which have been offered to you." The letter reassured the president that "the peculiar doctrine which we hold, is not less friendly to the order and happiness of society, than it is essential to the perfection of the Deity." One of its signers, Universalist minister John Murray, had known Washington since serving as a chaplain in the Revolutionary War. The minister and his second wife, Judith Sargent Murray, had even stopped to dine with the Washingtons on their way to the Convention. Thanks in large part to their efforts, universal salvation was no longer an obscure creed espoused by a scattered few. Now the Convention sought to establish Universalism as a recognized, socially responsible faith.[1]

Washington responded favorably. "GENTLEMEN," he began, thanking them for their well-wishes, "It gives me the most sensible pleasure to find, that in our nation, however different are the sentiments of citizens on religious doctrines, they generally concur in one thing: for their political professions and practices, are almost universally friendly to the order and happiness of our civil institutions. I am also happy in finding this disposition *particularly* evinced by your society."[2] Such affirmation of the Universalists' civic friendliness, from none other than the first president of the newly United States, must have gratified the Convention. They were well aware that other Protestant clergy, especially the Calvinists, disdained their "peculiar doctrine."

One of Universalism's harshest critics was a Presbyterian minister also named John Murray and close in age to the other. To distinguish the two, their followers dubbed the Universalist "Salvation" Murray and the Presbyterian "Damnation" Murray.[3] While "Salvation" preached the eventual redemption of all humanity, "Damnation" treated congregants and readers to vivid depictions of a hell gaping wide for sinners of every stripe. Universalism, he argued, offered license to sin without fear of consequences and undermined the justice of God by making Him a weak and ineffective ruler. "Salvation" and Judith Sargent Murray, for their part, believed that the promise of heaven for all presented a more perfect and rational view of God as loving and merciful rather than vengeful and arbitrary. Such a God, they hoped, would do more to inspire virtue and good works in the new nation's citizens than a tyrannical deity who could arbitrarily condemn a significant part of His creation to eternal perdition.

The controversy over the justness and necessity of eternal hell took off in the aftermath of the revivals that swept New England and spread through the colonies in the mid-eighteenth century. Out of these revivals came intense debates over predestination, human nature, and the character of God, which dovetailed into the arguments over damnation. These debates did not stay hermetically sealed within a vacuum of theological speculation but traveled into the social and political realms as Americans worried about the success of their national experiment. In a new republican society, where disinterested virtue seemed the only check on unbridled power and tyranny, the choice to reject or retain belief in eternal damnation was much more than an arcane doctrinal dispute. Universalists and their opponents alike suggested that their beliefs represented not only the safest religious faith for the individual but also the best moral glue for the new nation.[4]

Each group, in attacking the other, defined itself further. Those who rejected damnation had to explain how the promise of heaven for all would promote morality in the here-and-now. And attacks on Calvinism by Universalists and others new to the scene, including the early Methodists, prompted some Calvinist theologians to defend their traditional faith by reshaping it for a new era. In so doing, they helped to revitalize the idea of damnation for a new generation and ensure that Universalism would remain marginalized through the antebellum years. But in the early decades of the republic, Universalism seemed poised to blossom beyond the hopes and fears of damnation's detractors and defenders alike.

Awakening Controversies

The religious ferment precipitated by the New England awakenings that had begun in the 1730s did not go uncontested and formed the essential backdrop to the Universalist controversy. Supporters of the revivals, including Jonathan Edwards and his followers, found themselves defending the legitimacy of the passionate religious experiences they had inspired, the necessity of spiritual rebirth for salvation, and the continued validity of the Calvinist doctrine of predestination. Predestination did not square easily with revivals: if God had already determined who would be saved, what could revivals do but instill anxiety and despair in those who lacked the ability to repent and be reborn? Meanwhile, English intellectuals across the Atlantic had been questioning the justness of hell since the seventeenth century. They mostly wrote for each other, worried about the possible consequences of letting their ideas reach the masses. But educated Americans like Edwards were aware of their doubts and arguments.[5]

Edwards warned that "the very principal reason of such thoughts arising in the mind is a want of a sense of the horrible evil of sin."[6] All were born wicked after Adam's fall, and God was justified in letting any individual plunge into the "bottomless gulf" of hell without forewarning. But this did not mean that humans had no agency and therefore no responsibility for their fates. Instead, said Edwards, all sinners had a natural ability to repent, since nothing physical or external, like pain or paralysis, hindered their doing so (at least in a Christian society). Individuals had no excuse for the depravity of their hearts and their warped wills. It was their duty to heed God's call, especially in a revival setting where everything was calculated to facilitate a change of heart and nothing but their own intransigence and moral failure prevented them from doing so.[7]

While defending the natural freedom of the will, Edwards also reaffirmed predestination and God's ultimate, even inscrutable, sovereignty. Although all sinners had a duty to repent and hence escape the terrors of hell, God only elected certain people, for reasons unknown, to receive a new spiritual sense. This godly infusion enabled the elect to direct their warped moral inclinations toward repentance, rebirth, and love for "Being in general." The damned were so not by external factors but by their own fallen free wills, which God had not chosen to redeem.[8]

Believing that humans had the physical if not the moral ability to repent and be saved, Edwards and his fellow revivalists exhorted them with fire and brimstone discourses like the infamous 1741 "Sinners in the Hands of an Angry God." After the initial revival in Northampton had subsided following the suicide of Edwards's uncle, Joseph Hawley (who was convinced that he was damned), Edwards had realized that "hell, in all its fury and torture, would have to be enlisted if heaven were ever to be gained." He had an "explicitly—at times excruciatingly—physical conception of hell's torments," drawing from observations of nature.[9] His "Sinners" sermon compared fallen humanity, in the eyes of God, to a "spider, or some loathsome insect," suspended by God's mercy "over the fire." Edwards ended the sermon with a powerful altar call:

> And now you have an extraordinary Opportunity, a Day wherein CHRIST has flung the Door of Mercy wide open, and stands in the Door calling and crying with a loud Voice to poor Sinners.... Many that were very lately in the same miserable Condition that you are in, are in now an happy State, with their Hearts filled with love.... How awful is it to be left behind at such a Day! To see so many others feasting, while you are pining and perishing!... How can you rest one Moment in such a Condition?

The sermon provoked intense physical and emotional reactions. One congregant observed that "there was a great moaning and crying out throughout the whole house." Similar ecstasies and terrors were reported throughout New England in the early 1740s and in other regions where the revivals spread.[10]

Calvinist opponents of the revivals, including the Congregationalist "Old Lights" led by Boston minister Charles Chauncy and the Presbyterian "Old Side," believed that the intense experiences such sermons produced were at best mere enthusiasm and at worst the work of the devil playing on the minds of the overwrought and excitable masses. They were particularly alarmed by the license such enthusiastic experiences seemed to give laypeople to criticize staid ministers as "spiritually dead." They saw the attempts of Edwards and his followers to square predestination with free agency as impenetrable and unconvincing metaphysical speculation. These opponents believed that revivals, where sinners were suddenly convicted of their depravity and impending damnation to the point of fainting and crying, would not result in true rebirth. They held that real conversions should and would come about through membership in the church community and diligent use of the traditional means appointed for the reception of saving grace: prayer, Bible study, attendance at services, and

Holy Communion. Ultimate salvation required a life of obedience and not just sudden rebirth produced by terror. Through such gradual means and holy living the elect would come to know of their election, while those who were not elect would at least conform to the external ordinances of Christian behavior.[11]

These anti-revivalists were not uniform in their opposition. Some saw themselves as conservatives shoring up the traditional faith of their Puritan forbears against the novelty and disruption of Edwardsean revivalism; others veered in a more liberal direction, repudiating attempts to create a "consistent Calvinism" that would square free will with the sovereignty of God. The more these increasingly liberal ministers emphasized the church as the means of saving grace, the less they hewed to the doctrine of predestination. They stressed the importance of moral living over a change of heart. They also emphasized the ethical example of Christ rather than the traditional Calvinist doctrine that Christ's death on the cross saved the elect alone. Some of these theologians and ministers, receptive to the encroachments of Enlightenment rationality and optimism on the Calvinist tenets of original sin and partial election, formed the vanguard of American Unitarianism. Even Chauncy himself would turn to universal salvation by the 1780s, though he published his defenses of the doctrine anonymously, testament to the incendiary nature of rejecting damnation in the early republic.[12]

The "Insanities" of Calvin and Hopkins

By the second half of the eighteenth century, then, the Calvinist idea that damnation resulted from inherent and inherited depravity and from God's selection of only a few for salvation was coming under attack from within. At the same time, external threats to the doctrine of predestination were filtering into the colonies from religious movements with overseas roots, like Universalism. Methodists were also beginning to make incursions, doing away with unconditional election in favor of emphasizing free will and ability to strive for salvation (a theological position known as Arminianism). Not all early Americans were Calvinists, but Calvinism was the dominant theological tradition against which most other groups defined themselves and which received the most fire from freethinkers in the late eighteenth and early nineteenth centuries.[13] They accused Calvinism of painting God as an arbitrary dictator who randomly chose whom to save and whom to damn. No less than Thomas Jefferson decried

Calvin as "indeed an Atheist... or rather his religion was Daemonism....
It would be more pardonable to believe in no god at all, than to blaspheme
him by the atrocious attributes of Calvin." Likening an American theologian, Samuel Hopkins, to Calvin, Jefferson wrote that both propounded
"insanities.... The straight jacket alone was their proper remedy."[14]

This Samuel Hopkins was famed (and reviled) for his declaration
that sinners should be willing to be damned for the glory of God. A New
England native, Hopkins considered himself the direct heir to Jonathan
Edwards and likewise sought to defend the consistency of Calvinism
against external and internal onslaughts. Hopkins wrote his major works
after Edwards's death in 1758, as the excitement generated by the revivals continued to spin out in theological debates. His own conversion had
occurred in the midst of the awakenings in New England while he was
a student at Yale in the late 1730s and early 1740s. His classmate David
Brainerd, later a missionary to the Native Americans, was keen on ascer-
taining Hopkins's spiritual state. Although Hopkins initially resisted,
Brainerd soon succeeded in frightening him out of his apathy. After weeks
of agony and guilt, Hopkins "had a sense of the being and presence of
God, as I never had before.... I was greatly affected, in the view of my own
depravity, the sinfulness, guilt, and odiousness of my character; and tears
flowed in great plenty."[15]

Hopkins set his energies to systematizing Edwards's thought. He
drew on Edwards's distinction between natural ability and moral inability to battle against the incursions of liberals like Charles Chauncy and
Jonathan Mayhew. Hopkins thought they had veered in an alarmingly
Arminian direction, putting more emphasis on good behavior and personal agency than on God's sovereignty and man's fallen state. Hopkins
believed uncompromisingly in the depravity of human nature. He argued
that the traditional means of opening oneself to saving grace—devotions,
communion, prayer—only further condemned those who practiced them
but continued in unbelief. God was beholden to save no one who used
these means, since "there are no promises of saving mercy made to sinners, upon any condition short of faith in Jesus Christ."[16]

According to Hopkins, true holiness consisted in spiritual rebirth
marked by the transformation of self-love, which he considered the essence of sin, into selflessness or "disinterested benevolence." Edwards had
discoursed on benevolence as primarily an aesthetic notion. To Hopkins,
it was a moral and social imperative. He criticized what he saw as the
selfish individualism of Yankee merchants and businessmen like those in

the bustling port town of Newport, Rhode Island, where Hopkins became minister of the First Congregational Church in 1770. His attack against selfishness made him one of the earliest opponents of the African slave trade that greatly added to the wealth of Newport's merchants and seafarers. In the midst of the Revolution, Hopkins maintained that America could not expect deliverance if it continued in the "crying sin" of "enslaving the Africans," for which God might "yet punish us seven times more." Half a century later, abolitionists would echo the idea that Americans as a whole could be punished for the sin of slavery.[17]

Hopkins's famous statement that true converts must be willing to be damned for God's glory also grew from his assault on selfish individualism: "He therefore cannot know that he loves God and shall be saved, until he knows he has that disposition which implies a willingness to be damned, if it be not most for the glory of God that he should be saved."[18] In other words, to argue that it was cruel and arbitrary for some to be eternally damned and others saved was to think of one's own good instead of the eternal and higher good. Rather than agonize over their own eternal destiny, people should spend their energies trying to ameliorate moral and social ills and better their society. Fear of hell from self-love could not be a person's sole motivation to repent: the true mark of regeneration was the alignment of your will with God's for the good of all, even if you yourself were to be damned for reasons that were inscrutable to humans, but made perfect sense in the all-knowing mind of the all-wise and ultimately benevolent Creator.

Hopkins was not a popular preacher; he was known more as a theologian than a dynamic figure in the pulpit.[19] His defense of innate depravity and the justice of God in choosing whom to damn went consciously against the grain of Enlightenment optimism and the emerging sense of the self as an individual, and not just a cog in society, that characterized the western transition to modernity. Still, despite his unpopularity with some, Hopkins's call for self-sacrifice for the sake of the greater good resonated in the new nation, where virtue seemed to be the only glue holding society together.[20]

John "Salvation" Murray (1741–1815)

While Hopkins was defending his view of the nature of God, man, and eternal damnation, the two John Murrays landed in America. "Salvation" was the elder by a mere five months. The best source that we have of

FIGURE 1.1 Frontispiece to *Life of Rev. John Murray, Written by Himself, New ed., with a continuation, by Mrs. Judith Sargent Murray* (Boston: Universalist Publishing House, 1896).

Photograph by author.

his personal religious history is his own autobiography. First published in Boston in 1816, a year after his death, the volume reminded Universalists of Murray's important role in founding the denomination in America.[21] It also served as an apologetic, explaining to non-Universalists why a Calvinist would choose to abandon his faith. Murray portrayed himself as an erstwhile persecutor of Universalists who had had a change of heart and became one of the movement's biggest supporters, much like Paul with the early Church (fig. 1.1).

The son of a respectable but far from wealthy Calvinistic Anglican father and Presbyterian mother, Murray painted his childhood in England and Ireland as austere and filled with "the doctrines, taught by that gloomy Reformer.... hence my soul frequently experienced the extreme of agony." The threat of eternal damnation was never far from his mind and the more the "naturally vivacious" child chafed against his father's strict ordinances, the more "Religion became a subject of terror." His father was so strict that he would not allow Murray to seek a college education, "trembling for [his] spiritual interest, if removed from his guardian care."[22]

In his late teens, after his father died, Murray took care of the family and then traveled to London, where he let loose and lived a "life of dissipation" for a year. Soon after, in debt and deeply embarrassed, he fell in with followers of the famous revivalist George Whitefield. Feeling himself to be accepted and forgiven, his "bosom swelled with the most delightful sensations." Yet even still, Murray was troubled that, while he might be saved, countless others would suffer eternal damnation. He "exclaimed, Lord, why me? Why take me, and leave these poor, unfortunate beings to perish in a state of sin and misery?" In response to such anxieties, he comforted himself that "such was the sovereign will and pleasure of God; he would have mercy, on whom he would have mercy, and whom he would he hardened."[23]

Murray married another follower of Whitefield, the pious Eliza Neale, and thought about entering the ministry himself. While attending Whitefield's Tabernacle, he became aware of the teachings of one James Relly, whose fame rested on a piece entitled *Union: Or, a Treatise on the Consanguinity and Affinity between Christ and His Church*. This publication laid out Relly's central contention that Christ and humans are joined with Christ as the head and humanity as the body. Because of this union, all of humanity suffered with Christ on the cross, just as the death of the head causes the death of the body. According to the traditional Calvinist view, Adam's original sin affected all humans, but Christ's sacrifice was effective only for the elect.[24] Relly's doctrine of union modified the last part of this formula so that, just as all individuals were condemned through Adam, so all were saved through Christ's suffering.[25]

Murray initially viewed Relly's teachings—and even Relly himself—with undiluted animosity. He even claimed a willingness to murder Relly if God saw fit, again in keeping with his self-portrayal as a Paul-like convert to Universalism.[26] It was only when he and his wife actually read a copy of Relly's *Union* and then listened to him give a sermon that he had a change of heart. The effect of the doctrine was nothing short of a conversion experience. It altered his entire outlook on life: "I regarded my friends with *increasing affection, and I conceived, if I had an opportunity of conversing with the whole world, the whole world would be convinced.*"[27]

Within the Whitefieldian religious community of London, Murray's embrace of Rellyan doctrines was not to be tolerated. When his changed views became clear, the community promptly excommunicated him.

A host of woes followed: his infant son died, followed by his wife of consumption. Unable to pay his wife's medical bills, Murray found himself in debtors' prison contemplating suicide. The prospect of leaving England for America to "avoid, if possible, a part of [his] misery" ultimately raised him from his despair. Released from prison, Murray boarded a ship, the *Hand-in-Hand*, to the colonies. The ship beached off the New Jersey shore in 1770. In an origin story that has become almost mythical among Universalists, Murray happened upon a certain Thomas Potter, who had already been exposed to ideas about universal salvation from various frontier sects that professed different versions of the doctrine. Potter had built a meetinghouse but was awaiting a preacher. He made a pact with Murray: if the wind changed and Murray's ship was able to sail off, he would let him go; if not, it would be a sign that Murray was destined to preach in America. The wind did not change, and Murray agreed to stay.[28]

In telling this story, Murray probably wanted to convince his opponents that he had had no designs in crossing the Atlantic other than securing his own peace of mind. This would make his subsequent mission seem more providential and organic than if Relly had sent him to America for the express purpose of spreading his doctrines. But spread them he did. He not only filled Potter's pulpit but also itinerated along the Northeastern seaboard, encouraging his audiences to conclude in favor of universal salvation without always using the terms explicitly. As he gained the support of those who found his doctrines congenial, he eventually preached a basically consistent Universalist theology that included some Calvinistic tenets along with Relly's doctrine of the consanguinity of Christ and humanity.[29]

Murray never denied human depravity nor did he argue for a temporary, remedial hell, as did Charles Chauncy and Baptist minister Elhanan Winchester, who also turned to universal salvation.[30] Rather, Murray argued that God intended hell only for the fallen angels and that at the final judgment all humanity would be cleansed of sin and ushered into heaven for eternity. Murray was less than forthcoming about what would happen between death and the final judgment, suggesting that unbelievers would suffer because of their own anxieties and fears. He refused to call this suffering "purgatory," instead applying that word derogatorily to the temporary hell espoused by other believers in universal salvation ("There are some... who will have it that, tho' all Mankind will finally be saved, they have much to do, or to suffer, in order to *satisfy divine justice*... before they can see God, in Glory, they must pass through a Purgatorial

Fire"). In Murray's estimation, this took saving power away from Christ and put it in the hands of sinners to save themselves through purgatorial penance: those who advocated for such a hell "do not conceive that it is the Blood of Jesus Christ *alone* which cleanseth from all sin." Murray's concessions to Calvinism were deep.[31]

Not that the Calvinist clergy cared. "Salvation" Murray was not well-educated, but his ability to reach ordinary people and non-theologians through "far-fetched" reasoning greatly disturbed the Calvinists, no matter the internal divisions that already plagued them since the mid-century revivals.[32] Murray was a popular and dynamic preacher, drawing audiences from as far as twenty miles away, inviting comparisons to George Whitefield, and even filling staunch Congregationalist Ezra Stiles's pulpit at the request of some of his parishioners (though unbeknownst to Stiles himself). He proved so popular that, within the first few years of his arrival in America, he had received invitations to fill many other pulpits too and preached in Philadelphia, New York, Newport, Providence, Boston, Newburyport (home to "Damnation" Murray), Portsmouth, East Greenwich, and New London. Along the way, he even debated eternal punishment with Samuel Hopkins himself. For the Northeast's Calvinist ministers, struggling to fill their pews and offering plates in an era of "low and erratic levels of church adherence," Murray threatened to draw potential congregants to what they saw as a dangerous and heretical doctrine.[33] As Andrew Croswell, a Boston minister, complained in 1775, "He can put on a bold face, and make his hearers *laugh* and *giggle*; and while he is able to do this, he may be sure of a train after him, in all populous places." Philadelphia minister John Stancliff even likened Murray's power to a contagious disease, which he satirically dubbed "the putrid Murrinitish plague," prescribing a remedy of sprinkling the victim's head with the ashes of Sodom and Gomorrah, and surrounding the patient with pictures of the suffering of the damned.[34]

John "Damnation" Murray (1742–1793)

Another of Murray's opponents probably resented him all the more because he shared the same name and age, was also born overseas, and could easily be mistaken for him in a pre-photographic age.[35] Although he did not leave behind a detailed autobiography, we can piece together enough details of the Presbyterian Murray's life to shed some light on his quite different religious trajectory (fig. 1.2).

The Rev. JOHN MURRAY, A.M.
late Paſtor of the Presbyterian Church, in
NEWBURY-PORT.
Born 22 May 1742 Died 13 March 1793.

FIGURE I.2 Portrait of John Murray engraved by Samuel Hill. Misc. front matter, in James Miltimore, "A Sermon, preached in the Presbyterian Church, in Newbury-port, April 7, 1793, occasioned by the much lamented death of Rev. John Murray, A.M..." (Exeter: Printed and sold by Henry Ranlet, 1793). *Early American Imprints*, Series 1, no. 25824.

Courtesy of American Antiquarian Society.

John "Damnation" Murray was born in Antrim County, Ireland, and raised in the Presbyterian Church. Unlike "Salvation" Murray, he received an extensive education: first at a school not far from his birthplace, then with a private tutor, and finally at the University of Edinburgh. At the age of 15, he entered into full communion in the Presbyterian parish of his birth.[36] Whether he experienced the same anxieties as the other Murray over his election is unclear. Since he never forsook his childhood faith, he likely felt no need to leave behind an autobiographic apologia. In fact, he was so doctrinally rigid that he became embroiled in a controversy because he refused to be licensed by a Presbytery that he "charged... with doctrinal defections."[37]

In the midst of this controversy, which escalated into an attack on his character, he decided to come to America. The year was 1763, seven years before the other John's arrival, and his pretext was an invitation from an uncle in Boothbay, Maine, to fill that town's Presbyterian pulpit. Although the licensure controversy never fully subsided even in America, "Damnation" was nevertheless able, like the other Murray, to acquire a reputation for Whitefieldian prowess in the pulpit.[38] He actively strove to ensure that his training would not be forgotten, especially in contrast to "Salvation"'s lack thereof. He remarked on the latter's "entire want of learning or education" and noted that "Salvation" had "lately been imported from England": a likely reference to the belief that Relly had sent the Universalist to America in order to spread his insidious doctrines. The reference also suggests an attempt to link himself with the established Calvinist clergy against someone who was only seven years more "foreign." The Universalist Murray was far from an "illiterate leader," as "Damnation" dubbed him, but the fact that he was perceived as such, and as a "Stranger" by many native-born clergymen, reflects the prejudice of the educated clergy against him and other ministers from rapidly growing populist denominations like the Methodists and Baptists, who lacked formal theological training.[39]

"Damnation" also linked himself to American supporters of revivals, expressing hope that the awakenings that had begun in America would be the start of a global phenomenon that would usher in the millennium. Although he arrived after the mid-century heyday of the revivals, smaller, local seasons of awakening continued even as the controversies kindled by Edwards and his followers still swirled. "O Lord arise," prayed Murray in a 1764 letter, after witnessing and preaching in a series of Long Island revivals, "and visit all Nations with thy all-powerful Grace. Amen. Come Lord Jesus!" Murray's successes in Gilbert Tennent's Philadelphia pulpit, where he brought in many new members, Boothbay, where he led an "extensive revival," and Newburyport, where he eventually settled, earned him a reputation as a potent revivalist and eloquent preacher.[40]

If "Damnation" Murray's printed sermons are any indication of his revival style, he used his Whitefieldian eloquence very differently from the other Murray, to impress his audience with the horrors of eternal damnation. "Where now is the sparkling poison of the wanton eye?" he asked in a 1768 sermon describing "The Last Solemn Scene":

Altered into the baleful image of horror and despair—the very picture of the ugliest fiend below: whenever they roll their eye-balls, their ghastly looks are telling all within them. The very visage of the sinner points out the favorite passion of his soul, as strongly as if you saw the drunkard rise rolling in his vomit—the lascivious taken in the adulterous moment—the prophane lips just stretched open with their usual blasphemies.[41]

This hair-raising sermon was apparently quite popular as it was reprinted at least four times, as late as 1824, more than thirty years after Murray's death. His views were hardly novel; the graphic imagery is reminiscent of Edwards's "Sinners in the Hands of an Angry God."

Judith Sargent Murray (1751–1820)

Judith Sargent and her family would have undoubtedly heard sermons like this from ministers like "Damnation" Murray, who still dominated New England pulpits in the 1760s and 1770s. But they had also been introduced to James Relly's writings by an Englishman in their hometown of Gloucester, Massachusetts, even before "Salvation" Murray's arrival. They found Relly's ideas congenial but were not sufficiently convinced to leave the town's Calvinist First Parish. They were not theologians or ministers, but wealthy merchants and seafarers—the kind of people Samuel Hopkins condemned as self-interested—whose roots in the port town of Gloucester ran deep. Descendants of Puritans, they were far from provincial and were frequently exposed to new ideas and people from across the Atlantic.[42]

Judith was the eldest of the Sargent children (fig. 1.3). At the age of 18, she married another wealthy Gloucesterian sea captain, John Stevens, who was also intrigued by Relly's writings. Judith was better educated than most women of the time, due in part to her privileged upbringing. From an early age, she was a prolific writer and staunch advocate of women's ability and right to earn a living on their own. She looked up to Mercy Otis Warren and hoped to also attain celebrity through her pen.[43] Still, her education did not include theological training. The arrival of "Salvation" Murray in America was a godsend. Here was a man who had met Relly in the flesh and would be able to explain to her and her family the complexities of his doctrines.

In 1774, four years after "Salvation"'s arrival, Judith initiated correspondence. She wanted "with the strictest propriety," she wrote, to "mingle souls upon paper." In her very first letter to him, she expressed her admiration and gratitude for his teachings. She had decided to embrace his version of Universalism and told him why: "I acknowledge a

FIGURE I.3 Portrait of Mrs. John Stevens (Judith Sargent, later Mrs. John Murray). 1770–72. Oil on canvas, 50 × 40 in. (127.0 × 101.6 cm) by John Singleton Copley (1738–1815).

Daniel J. Terra Art Acquisition Endowment Fund, 2000.6; Terra Foundation for American Art, Chicago, IL, U.S.A. Photograph courtesy of the Terra Foundation for American Art, Chicago/Art Resource, NY.

high sense of obligations to you, Sir, I have been instructed by your scriptural investigations, and I have a grateful heart.... You have enlarged my views, expanded my ideas, dissipated my doubts, and led me to anticipate, and with sublime, and solem pleasure, the mystery [?] of the resurrection." Murray seems to have responded favorably, asking Judith to "show [him] what the God Man hath revealed to [her] soul." She answered modestly, suggesting that she was at a loss for words to explain her feelings: "I can much better meditate on the blissful vision, than impress my sense of the immensity.... When I contrast my days of ignorance with those on which the sun of Righteousness hath dawned, I am wrapt in pleasure."[44] Their correspondence continued, and in 1776 Judith and her family stopped attending the First Parish of Gloucester. In 1778 they formed a society of Christian Independents with some other defectors and appointed "Salvation" Murray as pastor. Judith never repented of her choice to accept the doctrine of universal salvation. She published a Universalist catechism in 1782, defended the faith in public writings, and subtly infused her other publications with Universalist ideas. And in 1788, a year after her first husband's passing, she married John Murray himself.[45]

Judith's letters to John suggest that her acceptance of Universalism was based on her conviction that the faith was more "reasonable" and less "inconsistent" than Calvinism. It supported her belief in the ultimate equality of all mankind and importantly, womankind, since it posited that everyone, regardless of "sect, age, country, or even sex," in her own words, belonged to "one grand, vast, and collected family of human nature."[46] The promise of universal salvation also helped Judith to cope with the uncertainties of life in the eighteenth century, where the austere doctrines of men like Samuel Hopkins and "Damnation" Murray did not provide much solace. Her letterbooks, poetry, and essays are filled with reports of deaths, sickness, and sorrow, coupled with her assurance that there would be a final restoration. In an essay entitled "Death of an Unbeliever," for instance, she consoled an unbelieving dying friend with the promise of universal salvation: "The record which God hath given of himself, proclaims the universality of his love, and of his power, the restitution of all things, the wiping of every tear from every eye." Judith noted that "those individuals who were, upon this occasion, assembled in the chambers of death, continued silent, they tacitly consented that the Heretic, if in her power, should soothe the agonized mind of their departing friend, nay their countenances were descriptive of approbation."[47] To Judith, even these non-Universalists seemed to concede the comforting power of the "heretical" idea that all might be saved.

The Virtues of Hell

A number of factors influenced the religious trajectories of the three Murrays, then, from divergent upbringings, to childhood fears of damnation, belief in gender parity, and the vicissitudes of eighteenth-century life. But the intensity of the controversies over universal salvation in the early republic cannot be explained by such factors alone. The choices these Murrays presented to the wider public had import for more than individual believers.

All three Murrays considered themselves to be, or at least presented themselves as, American patriots. Before the Revolution, the Sargents were politically active leaders who had served in colonial administrations.

Although they initially opposed independence from England for financial reasons, they later changed course in response to England's progres-
sively heavy-handed governance.[48] The two John Murrays also supported
independence and served as chaplains in the war. Their positions on hell
may not have been explicitly influenced by political factors, but all three
Murrays were conscious of the potential sociopolitical repercussions of
their views on the nascent nation on which they had staked their futures.

A monarch could wield force and engender fear in his or her subjects, but in a republic, virtue became the watchword that would prevent
power from developing into tyranny and corruption. Virtue was also at
the forefront of the debates over universalism. As the nation settled un-
easily into independence, the question of how to ensure its survival fed
into the question of what role, if any, religion should play in its society and
governance. The Protestant clergy had not always seen republicanism as
compatible with their creed, because republicanism focused on this life
instead of the next and seemed to emphasize humans' ability to govern
themselves without acknowledging their depravity before God. However,
astute clergymen soon saw they could argue that their religion was essential to republicanism. It could inspire virtue not only in potential political
leaders but also in ordinary women and men, preventing them from laps-
ing into anarchy and licentiousness. Even Benjamin Franklin, whose private beliefs were anything but conventional, worried that "talking against
religion is unchaining a tiger; the beast let loose may worry his liberator."
Something had to keep the masses in line.[49]

In a republic, fear of the sovereign could be replaced by fear of God,
driving inherently depraved people to virtuous behavior in the effort to
avoid future punishment. Late eighteenth-century Calvinists were not the
first to link fear of hell to the avoidance of sinful acts; Edwards's grandfather Solomon Stoddard had written that although "'the fear of the displeasure of parents, the justice of rulers,' and 'divine vengeance in this
world' all helped restrain sin… 'the fear of hell' was 'much more powerful.'"[50] Revolutionary-era Calvinists emphasized this link further as they
battled Universalists and made their peace with republicanism. Christian
republicans defined virtue, according to a recent scholar, as "the ability or
willingness of individual citizens to submit to the moral law of God as revealed in the Old and New Testaments."[51] Although submission to moral
law never ensured salvation in the eyes of most Calvinist clergy, failure to
submit was an almost certain guarantee that one was not actually regenerated. Even the Edwardsean revivalists, who argued for the necessity of

a change of heart, believed that spiritual rebirth also produced a shift toward moral living or "disinterested benevolence," to use Hopkins's words.
Although Hopkins did not believe fear of hell to be a sufficient motive to
virtue, the lurking possibility of damnation was essential to his theology,
as it forced people to realize that their lives were not their own but part of
a grander scheme.

The link between religion and morality appears clearly in "Damnation"
Murray's 1783 Bath-Kol: A Voice from the Wilderness. Illustrating Murray's
identification with the American experiment, Bath-Kol (the title refers to
a heavenly voice proclaiming God's judgment) is a 371-page religious history of America that ends in Murray's present with a scathing depiction
of the dangers of deism and universal salvation. Written anonymously
on behalf of the Presbytery of the Eastward, the book presented a united
front of Calvinist orthodoxy against these threats. Murray based Bath-Kol
on the premise that individuals' faith or apostasy could directly affect the
well-being of the nation, just as it had done for the ancient Israelites. God's
providential hand had been present in everything the early colonists, and
now American citizens, had gone through as a people.[52] God had already
visited the Americans with such "scourges" as droughts, the growing tyranny of the British crown, and losses in war.[53] He had also shown mercy
to His backsliding people, ultimately delivering them from British rule.
But, in this typical jeremiad, Murray accused Americans of ingratitude
and failure to "purg[e] the irreligious elements" from society. America had
better be prepared for another scourge from God's hand, Murray implied,
if the people did not quickly act to combat the "present low state of vital
religion in this country, the great and general declension in the practice
of piety and virtue; the alarming progress of vice and immorality of every
kind, and the growing defection from the pure doctrines of grace as they
are laid down in the scriptures."[54]

In this atmosphere of apparent declension, with the national experiment seeming as or more likely to fail as to succeed, "Damnation" Murray
saw "Salvation"'s Universalism as dangerous: it was not "vital religion" because it could lead people in an Antinomian direction, encouraging them
to ignore the law and sanctioning all kinds of untoward behaviors with no
threat of future punishment. As he put it in Bath-Kol, "Religion and morality are divinely connected together: no man can put them asunder: in
our better times they lived happily in concert, and now we see that religion was no sooner proscribed and banished from any people or place,
than morality and virtue took wing and followed her."[55] Murray did not

just mean any kind of religion, of course, but his kind of religion, which affirmed the eternality of future punishment.

Regardless of the controversies that roiled their doctrinal unanimity, the denial of eternal hell was something the Calvinist clergy could band together to oppose because it shook the very foundations of their faith and, as they saw it, the social order. "Damnation" Murray wrote:

> No doctrine has ever been advanced under colour of a christian name, that more directly strikes at the root of all virtue and religion. It stops not at restoring us to the arms of popery, in one of its grand fundamental articles, viz. that of Purgatory; it rushes headlong down the precipice of Deism—dashes its blindfold votary on the rocks of Manicheism and Stoicism in his fall; and, as with a mill-stone tied about his neck, it plunges him into the deep of infidelity and Atheism in the end.[56]

In the early republic, the charge that Universalism led to Atheism had political overtones. John Locke had famously noted that religious tolerance should be extended to all religious groups except atheists, because "Promises, covenants, and oaths, which are the bonds of human society, can have no hold upon an atheist. The taking away of God, though but even in thought, dissolves all."[57] Even if Universalism was not immediately harmful, Murray likewise suggested, it led down a slippery slope to the dissolution of social bonds and should not be tolerated.

Other writers and clergymen concurred. Sounding much like Locke, Boston minister Andrew Croswell compared Universalism unfavorably to Catholicism: while Catholics might not respect an oath of loyalty because of their primary allegiance to the Pope, Universalists had no reason to respect any oath whatsoever, because even liars would ultimately end up in heaven. They would make dangerous political leaders. Furthermore, Croswell argued, Universalism would encourage societal menaces ranging from drunkards to "whoremongers and adulterers" and murderers. "As such preaching is so evidently inimical to all vertue, and productive of all vice," he wrote, "no one can be a consistent friend to morality, who is *not* an enemy to it." He urged his readers to stay away from "Salvation" Murray. God had allowed him into the land to test the people: "that it might appear who would be carried away with every wind of doctrine, and embrace another gospel; and who would hold fast the form of sound words delivered to us, and be like mount Zion that can never be moved."[58] A pamphlet published in 1785 by the First Parish of Gloucester, where the Sargents had once been members, also accused Universalists of undermining the sanctity of oaths and endangering civil society, going so far as to say that "this man, and his pernicious doctrines, have been more damage to this town, than the late war; for while this destroyed our interest, those have corrupted our morals in their first principles."[59]

The controversy flared up in the 1780s, once "the late war" had settled down and the question of governance and the maintenance of social order rose to the fore. In this decade of heated constitutional debates and weak federal government under the Articles of Confederation, politicians argued over the limits and extent of religious liberty. In Virginia, Patrick Henry famously opposed James Madison's broad *Memorial and Remonstrance against Religious Assessments* with a plea for specifically Christian liberty and not the individual's right to believe anything he or she wished without governmental oversight. "The general diffusion of Christian knowledge hath a natural tendency to correct the morals of men, restrain their vices, and preserve the peace of society," he maintained in a 1784 bill brought before the Virginia legislature.[60] These were exactly the things "Damnation" Murray and other anti-Universalists warned that the doctrine of universal salvation could not do. The 1780s was also the decade when Charles Chauncy published his anonymous *Salvation for All Men* (1781) and Hopkins opined that the true believer should be willing to be damned. Hopkins also published a direct attack on Universalism in 1783, the same year as the publication of *Bath-Kol*.

Newspapers joined the fray over Universalism. One 1784 article stated that "the issue of such a system is that man may live as they chuse, and be as wicked as they please, without fear of punishment." The article continued sarcastically, "An excellent design for which mankind, and human society have great reason to thank *Universalists*. The same arguments by which these benevolent men, have expelled all punishments from a future state, with equal force will banish all punishments from the present state."[61] A 1787 poem reprinted in a number of New England papers depicted the licentiousness and immorality Universalism would encourage:

> Blest are the clam'rous and contentious crew,
> To them eternal rest and peace are due.
> Blest all who hunger and who thirst to find
> A chance to plunder and to cheat mankind.[62]

By parodying the Beatitudes, the poet sought to show just how topsy-turvy was Universalism's promise of blessings to all, including liars, thieves, cheaters, and the disorderly.

Universal Morality

But Universalists had counterarguments for why the promise of universal redemption was conducive to morality. One was that unbelievers would still suffer before the final restitution, though they disagreed about how. As we saw, the Murrays refused to countenance any "purgatory," though they acknowledged that sinners might still inflict pain upon themselves. Even supporters of a temporary, punitive hell, like Charles Chauncy, characterized the Murrays' theology as "very like an *encouragement* to *Libertinism*."[63] Their arguments influenced such members of the founding generation as John Adams, who noted that "I believe too in a future state of rewards and punishments too; but not eternal," and Benjamin Rush, who grew up Calvinist, but "never doubted upon the subject of the salvation of all men" after reading writings by Chauncy and Elhanan Winchester.[64]

Punishment after death was never central to the Murrays; instead, they used ideas about the character of God and the duties of humans to each other to defend the positive social effects of their version of universal salvation. In a 1790 letter to her parents, Judith described her husband's response to the serious charge "that he denied the ability of Virtue!!" John pled, "Not Guilty.... Nay we establish the Law, rendering it honourable."[65] God's Law did require punishment for sin, but that punishment had already been exacted in the death of Christ. As John explained in an undated letter, "God, instead of clearing the guilty, exacted the uttermost farthing, hence he is a *just God*, and a Saviour."[66] The Murrays attempted to deflect critiques of their version of Universalism as dangerously blasé about sin's seriousness. Knowing what God had done to His own son for their sake should inspire people to good behavior.

Where "Damnation" offered a jeremiad in *Bath-Kol*, the Murrays instead saw the atmosphere of the early republic as particularly conducive to virtue. Judith wrote, in a 1798 essay in *The Gleaner*, that "at no period since the lapse of Adam, was the world in so high a state of improvement, as it is at this very instant...the augmentation of its virtues is rapid." She applauded America's "admirable Constitution" and "*order of Virtue*," which supplanted a hereditary nobility. This "order of Virtue," she wrote, "is alone ennobling; and since the career being open to all, we may with democratical equity pursue the splendid prize."[67] For Judith and John, America's openness was to be celebrated, not feared, because it allowed for doctrines like their own to flourish. They still professed the depravity of humankind but contended that anyone who adopted belief in universal salvation could rise above it. They even sometimes suggested that depravity might not be inherent to human nature, as when John wrote that "vices, of many sorts, are unnatural—they are *solely* the Effect of Habit."[68] This optimism about humanity and society contrasts strikingly with *Bath-Kol* and could explain why Universalism appealed to a number of the nation's freethinking and confident new political leaders.

In a 1791 pamphlet, John Murray exhorted fledgling Universalists to "Do right—as Men—as members of civil Society—and as Christians."[69] He defined morality as "the Duty we owe to Ourselves—our Families— our Brethren in the same Faith—our Enemies, the Community of which we are a Part, and all Mankind."[70] This definition highlights the "social and communal" nature of salvation in the early Universalists' beliefs.[71] Like Samuel Hopkins, Murray believed that virtuous behavior should not depend on selfish fear of future punishment. But unlike Hopkins, Murray argued that virtue should derive from one's sense of fellowship with the rest of saved humanity, and not from self-abasement before a sovereign God: "The *consistent Universalist* views *all mankind* as they are viewed by their everlasting Father—and this *Father* he is persuaded is *no Respector of persons*—he dare not, therefore, *injure* any of his *Father's children*." Although Christ had already paid the price for *"all mankind,"* said Murray, Universalists should not think that they "have *nothing at all to do*." They should do good works not for their own salvation or for God's sake alone, but "because *profitable* unto men." If one had to spend eternity with one's fellows, treating them well in the here-and-now made sense.[72]

In a 1790 letter to her niece, Sarah Sargent Ellery, Judith invoked similar themes of communalism, benevolence, justice, and morality. "The sons and daughters of mortality," she wrote, "are ushered into being precisely in one mode—We are all subjected to similar casualties and death with undistinguishing hand, closes the scene—If I admit that the God who made me, possesseth all power, all wisdom, all mercy, and all goodness—I cannot suppose he hath called me into being, to plunge me into irreme- diable, and comfortless despair." God's infinite mercy to all humanity in His just plan for redemption, she told Sarah, "is a sufficient reason why I should be solicitous ... to acquaint myself with the things that belong to my peace, why I should be careful, by a life of innocence, usefulness, and integrity sustaining in the sight of Men, a blameless character, to adorn that doctrine, which I verily believe originated in the bosom of Deity."[73]

In his autobiography, "Salvation" Murray elaborated further on God's character as revealed in the plan of universal redemption. "Ah, sir!" he said to one detractor, "man, poor, fallen man, who in his present state is enmity against God, is ever measuring the love and compassion of Deity by his own scanty rule.... I have frequently said that there is not a person of character upon this continent who would bear to be delineated, whatever character he sustains, as he thinks and speaks of the Most High."[74] John and Judith's Deity was beneficent, averse to the sight of suffering, rational and fair in the sense that He did not create humanity for the purpose of random destruction, and just because He made sure the Law against sin was fulfilled by His son.[75] The Murrays tried to persuade others that such a Deity was a rational choice not only for them but also for the new nation, because of His ability to inspire virtue and gratitude in His subjects.

Monarch or Moral Governor?

But to "Damnation" Murray, such a Deity was too weak to be legitimate. The Universalists' God was akin to a ruler who lets murderers loose on society: "Turning conspirator with the worst enemies of society, he supports the individuals whom it is his business to crush—and virtually proclaims hostilities against the whole body of the community, which he is bound to protect." Such a God possessed a "feminine sort of goodness, which Origenism fancies for its deity! Which constrains him, for his own happiness, to keep all sinners from pain. And we must return and caress the offender, whether he cease his rebellion or not!"[76] Just as the Universalist Murrays had done, so "Damnation" deployed the rhetoric of community. But in his pessimistic view of human nature and society, there would always be enemies and offenders to be rooted out: religion theoretically produced morality, but there were inevitably some it would never touch, for whom punishment would always be necessary.

"Damnation" Murray's use of gendered language to describe the Universalists' Deity is striking. While writing Bath-Kol, he had consulted Judith's 1782 Universalist catechism, because John had not given "the world his system from the press, under his own signature."[77] Judith had made no attempt to conceal her gender in the document. The first line of her Preface reads: "When a Female steps without the Line in which Custom hath circumscribed her, she naturally becomes an Object of

Speculation." But, she continued, "If there is any Thing that ought, for a Moment, to take Place of those exquisite Sensations, which we boastingly term peculiarly feminine, it is surely a sacred Attention to those Interests that are crowned with Immortality." Although women were denied education in science and other "male" pursuits, they could "freely expatiate" on the "Page of Revelation." Nor could women be politicians, but their religious views could still have political ramifications. Judith's arguments reflect the notion that women should be spiritually and morally upright "republican mothers" by shaping the "Minds of [their] young Folks" for the good of society.[78]

Perhaps unable or unwilling to allow that a woman could have written a theological text on her own, even one defending a "spurious" theology, "Damnation" Murray described the catechism as primarily the work of John and "his preachers in this and a neighbouring state"—"any pretences to its being the work of his Landlady alone, notwithstanding." Murray may have been using the term in its archaic connotation as a "mistress" rather than referencing joint living arrangements.[79] As one of Judith's biographers points out, some onlookers surmised that John and Judith's friendship was already becoming romantic by 1779, when Judith was still married to John Stevens. She apparently saw the friendship as purely chaste but made no secret of her admiration for the minister.[80]

Although "Damnation" Murray dismissed her as author of the catechism, his reference to the Universalist God's "feminine" goodness was no compliment, implying that Universalism was feeble and soft regardless of the gender of the person espousing it. Women were thought to be easily swayed by their emotions and sympathies; "Damnation" instead held forth a vision of divine justice meted out by an impartial, uncompromising, judge-like, and masculine God. "Far be it from the Most High," he wrote in *Bath-Kol*, "that it should fare with the righteous and wicked alike! The Judge of all the earth will surely do right. He will by no means clear the guilty."[81] Injustice consisted of unequal portions in this world (the prospering of the wicked and the suffering of the righteous), as opposed to the salvation of some and damnation of others in the next. Temporal inequality was perhaps "necessary for a state of probation," but had to be amended in a future state in order for God's justice to be meaningful:

If there is a God, he is the moral governor of the world.—If he is such a governor, he is just. If just in his nature, he is so in his administrations. And if so, he must give to every thing its due. Doing thus, he will not fail to manifest his approbation of virtue in his subjects, by distinguishing it with proper marks of his favour; and much less can he ever neglect to signify how far he judges vice to be in the wrong, by inflicting upon it the punishment fit.[82]

Here "Damnation" Murray held God to rules of human justice—rewarding virtue and punishing vice—that He must follow or else not be worthy of worship. This contrasted with the more arbitrary, all-sovereign God of the Puritans, who could do as He pleased, choose whom to save from the justly damned multitude, and command the respect of all His creatures for doing so. Unlike Samuel Hopkins, who felt that everyone should be ready for damnation as their deserved lot, Murray inched toward the externalization of damnation to only the clearly vicious, a trend that became more pronounced in the next century. Hell was not a place to which he was afraid to go: it was a place to which the wicked should be afraid to go, for the benefit of virtuous believers.

Yet Murray did not go all the way toward binding God by rules of human justice and benefit, as when he wrote that "whatever rewards are promised by the Creator to the obedience of a mere creature, are promised by an act of grace, which is altogether arbitrary."[83] Murray also indicated the need for God to serve as "monarch" for a monarchless America. He deplored the fact "that we should venture on a solemn renunciation of all subjection to the crown of England, without setting apart so much as one day to implore the countenance of Heaven on the measure, and invite him to the CROWN OF AMERICA."[84] In Murray's worldview, a monarchical and powerful God was especially necessary to a nation founded on republican principles because, without an earthly king to mete out punishments and instill fear, only a heavenly monarch could keep human depravity in check. Such sentiments reflect a still-uneasy relationship between the Calvinist clergy and the new government in the 1780s, and the apprehension about republicanism still felt by the clergy in the early years of nationhood.[85]

For the most part, though, "Damnation" Murray assumes in *Bath-Kol* that God must be rational and understandable to His creations, denying the Universalists' claim that the Calvinists' God was tyrannical. Murray urged that believing in a not-quite-monarchical but not-quite-democratic God—and acknowledging Him in the political sphere—offered the only safe option not only for the individual, who might end up eternally damned if he or she chose to believe in Universalism, but also for the new nation, which might end up in its own sorry state of decline, chaos, and anarchy if its people embraced heretical and dangerous doctrines.

The New Divinity and the Meaning of the Atonement

Controversies over the necessity of rewards and punishments, the efficacy of hell for social cohesion, and the relationship between God and humans continued to resound well into the nineteenth century. Universalism thrived on the western frontiers and Southern revivalists found themselves battling its allure as they sought to increase their ranks among a population, black and white, that had only recently and incompletely felt their influence. One scholar notes that as the Southern gentry became increasingly educated, they and "even a few men and women of lower rank" found Universalism persuasive: "Around the turn of the century, churches were occasionally obliged to expel the stray brother or sister who became tinctured by Universalism, and one Baptist fellowship even took the precaution of forbidding any member to 'countenance or encourage any man to preach, who preaches the doctrine of redemption from hell.' "[86]

But despite the fears of the orthodoxy and the hopes of its followers, Universalism did not grow into a numerically dominant movement.[87] Internal disagreements over just how universal salvation would occur continued after "Salvation" Murray's death in 1815, with "restorationists" believing in a temporary hell and "ultra Universalists" in no hell at all.[88] Universalists faced a difficult task persuading people to abandon the faith of their forebears. As some Calvinist clergymen observed, if Universalism was wrong, its adherents would end up in hell; if not, everyone would go to heaven anyway, so what was the sense of adopting such an unorthodox faith?[89]

But hell's defenders were not able to shut down the movement entirely. Even if the major Protestant denominations—the older Congregationalists and Presbyterians, and the newer but burgeoning Methodists and Baptists—rejected universal salvation, the Universalists' conception of God as loving and benevolent eventually became more mainstream.[90] The God of *Bath-Kol*, occupying a middle ground between arbitrary sovereign and moral governor, can be seen as a step in this direction.

"Damnation" Murray was no theological innovator, but he was also transitional in his defense of the related Calvinist doctrine of imputation.

In a series of three sermons preached in 1788, several years after the publication of *Bath-Kol*, Murray supported the traditional notion that the atonement paid a debt for the sins of the elect and directly imputed Christ's righteousness to them.[91] As in *Bath-Kol*, Murray was ever concerned to prove God's moral governance, stressing that imputation not only "satisfied the law" but also "magnified it and made it honorable." But he skirted the issue of how imputation to the elect alone could translate into a revival call to everyone. He ended his last sermon of the series with an uneasy appeal to sinners to both repent at peril of eternal damnation and wait for the Holy Spirit to enable them to do so:

> There is no peace, saith my GOD, to them [who are not justified by Christ]. Awful words! Methinks I see them stand shivering on the brink of the dreadful gulph—their hearts throbbing—their eyeballs rolling—their teeth gnashing—and their trembling voices beginning the eternal shriek! whilst the lip of justice is pronouncing their final doom—and the hand of vengeance is chaining them to the rock of never—never—never ending torment and despair!

Murray told his listeners (and readers) that they still had time to avoid this doom, "since that dreadful hour is not yet arrived with you.... Awake! Awake! what meanest thou, O sleeper! Behold, the Judge is at the door! O make haste, for heaven's sake, haste! flee from the wrath to come!" Murray then turned this appeal to activity (Awake!) into a paradoxical combination of free will and inertia: "This faith must be your act:—though an act performed by strength not your own. It is the result of free sovereign grace. It is the hand of the HOLY SPIRIT that must change your hearts—and make you willing in the day of his power. O wait on him, then, for this high favor!" Readers might have been forgiven for wondering how they were to simultaneously awake and await awakening. This was the same conundrum Edwardseans presented when they tried to square predestination with free agency by arguing that sinners had the moral inability and natural ability to repent.[92]

Arminian opponents already found that formulation unconvincing. They also rejected imputation, holding that "Salvation [was] a cooperative effort with God" available to all who wanted it.[93] Late eighteenth-century Edwardsean supporters of revivalism, known as the "New Divinity," responded to their critics by modifying the doctrine of imputation and developing a "governmental" model of the atonement that "Damnation"

Murray anticipated but never quite reached. Samuel Hopkins's contemporary, Joseph Bellamy, had introduced this idea in the 1750s but it did not catch on with the New Divinity until the 1780s, in response to the Universalist controversy and the growing presence of Methodists and liberal Calvinists in the new United States. According to Bellamy, Christ's sacrifice did not pay a literal debt for the elect, but "honored God's moral law, just 'as the perfect obedience of Adam, and of all his race, would have done.'" Because Christ, fully human yet also divine, willingly took on the punishment humanity deserved, God could "pardon the whole world...consistently with his honor."[94] Bellamy did not believe that all would actually seek pardon but that the ultimate ratio of saved to damned by the end of the millennium would more than justify God's benevolence. In 1758 he speculated that, since most of the world's population had not yet been born, and since the (presumably Protestant) population was quickly rising in Europe and America, "above 17,000 would be saved, to one lost" by the end of Christ's thousand-year reign. Even Hopkins, despite his unwavering belief in humanity's depravity and selfishness, nevertheless agreed with Bellamy that in the end, "many more of the human race will be happy than miserable" because of God's ultimate benevolence.[95]

A new generation of New Divinity ministers, many of whom had studied with Hopkins and Bellamy, developed the governmental theory of the atonement further. These theologians and ministers were hardly immune to the critiques of Calvinism hurled by Arminians and Universalists.[96] Jonathan Edwards the Younger even noted that the traditional Calvinist doctrine of imputation had left him "exceedingly perplexed and embarrassed."[97] The New Divinity expanded on Bellamy's idea that Christ's voluntary death on the cross satisfied the demand for justice in God's moral government. They argued that Christ's sacrifice did not apply literally and only to the limited and seemingly random elect, but showed all sinners the power of God's wrath against sin as a clear warning of what would happen to them should they continue in unbelief and wrongdoing. This did not mean that predestination no longer held meaning for the New Divinity, who continued to develop Edwards's distinction between natural and moral ability. But not only did the intransigent have the natural ability to repent: now they could also clearly see the consequences of sin through the example of Christ's death.[98] As Stephen West, a Connecticut native and Yale graduate who became an Edwardsean after discussing theology with Samuel Hopkins put it,

Christ's death served as "a visible discovery of the anger of God against sin." If sinners heeded the discovery and repented immediately, God could pardon them with the integrity of His moral government intact.[99] If not, they had only themselves to blame.

Equality of Opportunity or Outcome

Immediate repentance would become the altar call of the evangelical revivals of the Second Great Awakening.[100] To the New Divinity, moral governance in the here and hereafter required punishment for sin; their modifications to Calvinism simply made punishment more the result of human willfulness than of God's arbitrariness, an important concession to the Enlightenment faith in human ability that nevertheless shied away from the possibility that all would ultimately be saved. In sociopolitical terms, the New Divinity gestured toward equality of opportunity for salvation but drew the line firmly at equality of outcome, because they believed that the latter would undermine social welfare by making individuals irresponsible and unmotivated, with no consequences to fear for their sins. Such thinking was actually more in line than the Universalists' with the Founders' pursuit, rather than guarantee, of happiness.

In changing their God from absolute monarch to moral governor, and in laying emphasis on the natural ability of all humans to repent and be saved, the New Divinity brought their version of Calvinism closer to other nascent evangelical groups like the Methodists, even while distancing themselves further from the doctrine of universal salvation. Protestants first adopted the term "evangelical" during the Reformation, to distinguish their doctrine of salvation through faith alone, by grace alone, in the Bible alone, from Catholicism. In the antebellum American context, the loose term "evangelical" embraced pro-revival Calvinists, Arminian Methodists, and Freewill Baptists among others who hoped to spur voluntary submission to Christ and emphasized the change of heart as the only way for sinners to stay out of hell. Their calls to sinners to repent immediately or shoulder blame for the punishment they might otherwise have avoided was a departure from strict predestinarianism.[101]

This is not to say that theological differences between evangelicals ever disappeared. The former Presbyterian turned Methodist itinerant Benjamin Abbott, for instance, noted that the New Divinity's theology "so confused my mind, that I threw it by, determining to read no more in it, as my own experience clearly proved to me, that the doctrines it contained

were false."[102] But as much as the New Divinity might try to finesse the theology surrounding free agency and predestination, and as much as they
still battled against the Benjamin Abbotts of the early republic, these fine
doctrinal details were increasingly blurred in the practice of preaching
damnation.

"His Blood Covers Me!"

DISSEMINATING DAMNATION IN THE SECOND GREAT AWAKENING

LEGEND HAS IT that Jonathan Edwards delivered "Sinners in the Hands of an Angry God" in a bland monotone so that listeners would not be distracted by an overly theatrical delivery.[1] Famed antebellum revivalist Charles Finney took a different approach. From singling out individual congregants by name, to sending them to the notorious "anxious bench," where concerned but unconverted sinners sat in full discomfiting view of the congregation, Finney stocked an arsenal of methods to induce shame and spur conversion.

The content of Finney's carefully calibrated sermons worked in tandem with his methods. Trained as a lawyer, Finney had little patience for dense theological explications. Instead, he used the pulpit to build a compelling case for conversion, appealing to people's deepest interests and personal ties. "It will be vastly affecting," he cautioned in a typical 1835 sermon, "for persons who have stood in a near relation to each other here, to be not only spectators but witnesses in each other's final trial before God." Husbands and wives will have to testify against their spouses. Parents will see their unsaved children swept to hell for reasons "directly chargeable to themselves." " 'Alas!' they will exclaim, 'My son is lost, for eternity lost, and his blood covers me!' " Finney closed by speaking directly, as if to each individual: "Will you hear? Will you have mercy on your own soul? Will you come to Jesus and be saved, or will you reject him and be damned?"[2] He may well have followed this exhortation with a dramatic gesture toward the anxious bench.

Those not so fortunate as to partake of Finney's preaching in person could read this sermon in the *New York Evangelist*. The explosion of religious publishing swept such rhetoric beyond the pulpit, into neighboring towns and villages, down canals and roadways, and into people's homes.[3] Older fire-and-brimstone texts like Michael Wigglesworth's "The Day of Doom," Edwards's "Sinners," the *New England Primer*, and Richard Baxter's *Call to the Unconverted* were reprinted well into the nineteenth century. Newer print resources available to antebellum Americans also grew exponentially between the late eighteenth century and the Civil War. One scholar estimates that "by midcentury, 400 publishing firms, 3,000 booksellers, and over 4,000 printing offices made texts available across America." The number of titles circulating between 1820 and 1850 almost equaled the total number published between 1639 and 1791. And the number of newspapers increased from forty during the American Revolution to over two thousand by the time of the Civil War.[4]

Evangelical leaders of the Second Great Awakening used pulpit and press to emphasize each individual's natural ability and responsibility to escape hell, befitting the antebellum celebration of the can-do, self-made man.[5] Their stress on individual agency obscured the evangelicals' increasingly hierarchical and paternalistic leadership structures and the coerciveness of their tactics (how free could conversion be at peril of eternal punishment?).[6] But to read this emphasis as a veil that evangelical leaders drew over their ever-tightening control of the masses would be to miss the complexity of their motivations and laypeople's responses. Many who disseminated the threat of damnation actually feared it for themselves and believed that they could and should do something to save people from it.

Hellfire preaching and penny-press publishing could only reach so many. Ministers also tugged on familial and peer ties to urge laypeople to spread the warning themselves, as in Finney's threat that parents would feel responsible if their "wayward children" were damned. They also tried to extend this sense of responsibility: if ordinary people could be held accountable for the fates of their literal brothers and sisters, then why not also for the eternal welfare of the whole brotherhood of man? "His blood covers me!" could apply to more than one's immediate family.

Evangelical leaders' pleas—for the responsibility of ordinary Americans to save themselves, their communities, their nation, and their world from everlasting torment—highlight the social divisions and hubris that the concept of damnation could foster. If conversion meant the difference between heaven and hell, then those who heeded the warnings to repent would be part of an eternal "in" crowd, forever separated from the damned. Yet the notion that converts were responsible for the eternal welfare of others could also give rise to profound anxiety and pessimism. In the evangelicals' burdensome calculus, the weight of the world lay ponderously on the shoulders of the few, whose own eternal salvation depended on their ability to warn others away from the fires of hell.

The Conversions of Preachers

Ministers did not ask laypeople to take responsibility for the souls of others without modeling such action themselves. In memoirs published in the nineteenth century, they explained that the fear of hell prompted their own conversions and desire to share the warnings and promises of Scripture with others. In publishing such reminiscences, they stood in a tradition stretching back to the English Puritans, whose conversion narratives informed the later memoirs of exemplary Americans like David Brainerd and Sarah Osborn. As one scholar puts it, these texts modeled the "incessant spiritual warfare against the self" that "promised that only by descending into the depths of despair could the believer hope to ascend into the heights of assurance of salvation."[7] But where the Puritans had emphasized the individual's inability to do anything in the face of God's sovereignty, evangelicals more typically recognized their own paradoxical ability and responsibility to submit to God's sovereign grace.

The memoirists typically began by describing their former hardness of heart. Born on Long Island in the early eighteenth century, Benjamin Abbott wrote that for the greater part of his early life, he "lived in sin and open rebellion against God, in drinking, fighting, swearing, gambling, &c." Abbott's wife was a Presbyterian and he often followed her to meeting, where "many times the Spirit of God alarmed my guilty soul of its danger; but it as often wore off again."[8] The eccentric Lorenzo Dow, born to poor farmers some forty-five years later in Coventry, Connecticut, had similarly been exposed to Calvinism in his youth, seesawing between serious concern and neglect over the state of his soul.[9] Jarena Lee, later licensed as the first woman to preach in the African Methodist Episcopal Church, replicated this pattern in her spiritual narrative. As a child in the late eighteenth century, Lee told a lie that soon overwhelmed her with feelings of guilt. "The Spirit of God moved in power through my conscience," she recalled, "and told me I was a wretched sinner. On this account so great was the impression, and so strong were the feelings of guilt, that I promised in my heart that I would not tell another lie. But notwithstanding this promise my heart grew harder."[10]

Even Finney, born in 1792 in Warren, Connecticut, claimed to have been a virtual "heathen" by the time he reached adulthood. When he was a child, his parents had moved the family to the backwoods of Oneida County, New York, and then to Lake Ontario, where preachers were few and far between, "ignorant," and often mocked. As a young adult he attended services at a settled church in Adams, New York, but found the preaching of the town's conservative Calvinists confounding. The minister "seemed to take it for granted that his hearers were theologians.... But I must say that I was rather perplexed than edified by his preaching." Finney later suggested that intellectual pride had stood in the way of conversion: he wanted to understand the Bible with his head rather than accept its promises with his heart.[11]

Each of these preachers next told how the Lord alarmed their guilty consciences with the fear of hell. Abbott described a dream where he saw "devils and evil spirits," "scorpions with stings in their tails," and the lake of fire, which "appeared like a flaming furnace" where the "screeches of the damned were beyond the expression of man." Nor was he a mere spectator: he was there to be tortured with a "vice" that left his body "in a gore of blood" and scorpion stings that "stuck fast." Just as he was about to be thrown into the lake, he awoke: "But O! what horror seized my guilty breast! I thought I should die and be damned."[12] Dow also recorded vivid dreams of devils dragging him to hell, where he heard the terrible shrieking of demons and the damned.[13] In the depths of anxiety and despair, thinking they were already doomed, both men recalled attempting suicide. Abbott stopped when he thought he heard a voice saying, "This torment is nothing to hell,"[14] and Dow when he realized that "if you end your life, you are undone for ever; but if you omit it a few days longer, it may be that something will turn up in your favor."[15] Both converted with the guidance of Methodist ministers, who convinced them of their ability to escape from hell and be saved.

Jarena Lee also claimed a suicide attempt prompted by anxiety over the state of her soul. In her case, a foreboding vision overwhelmed her after the unsuccessful attempt. "The awful gulf of hell seemed to be open beneath me," she recounted, "covered only, as it were, by a spider's web, on which I stood. I seemed to hear the howling of the damned, to see the smoke of the bottomless pit." Lee interpreted her vision, which recalled Jonathan Edwards's famous sermon, as proof of "eternal damnation" since "this language is too strong and expressive to be applied to any state of suffering in *time*." She cycled between anxiety and reassurance as she wrestled with a call to preach without approval of the male leadership. A vision of Christ finally gave her a sense of peace that, she said, never again left her and that, by inclusion in her memoir, served to legitimize her work as a female evangelist.[16]

He did not recount such terrifying pre-conversion dreams, but Charles Finney also recalled feeling "that I was by no means in a state of mind to go to heaven if I should die." The more he read the Bible, the more he was convinced of the danger of delaying repentance. One night, "a strange feeling came over me as if I was about to die. I knew that if I did I should sink down to hell; but I quieted myself as best I could until morning." When he awoke, Finney skulked into the woods near the law office where he worked, battling with his pride. Finally, he realized that intellectual belief in the Bible was not enough and that immediate and voluntary trust was more powerfully transformative.[17]

After experiencing a change of heart, each of these preachers recalled feeling overwhelmed by a sense of responsibility for the salvation of others. The very day of his conversion, Abbott urged his family and neighbors to "flee from the wrath to come"; in response, "some laughed and others cried, and some thought I had gone distracted." By nightfall, a rumor swirled around the neighborhood that he was "raving mad." Abbott, though, was far from fazed: he even gained a reputation for "preaching *hell* and *damnation* to the people."[18] He later became a Methodist itinerant and saw it as his calling to spread the word that hell was very real but salvation available to all who asked for and accepted it.

Dow too felt a keen sense of responsibility for saving his fellow humans from the wrath to come. In late 1795, he had a dream that harkened back to the Methodist sermon that had started him on the road to conversion and to Edwards's "Sinners":

> I thought I saw all mankind in the air suspended by a brittle thread over hell, yet in a state of carnal security. I thought it to be my duty to tell them of it, and again awaked: and these words were applied to my mind with power: "there is a dispensation of the gospel committed unto you, and woe unto you if you preach not the gospel."[19]

For Edwards, it was God alone who could save the spider from the yawning pit below, though sinners could improve their chances by putting themselves in the way of God's mercy. For Dow, the duty to save "all man-kind" was his. Not only did he have the ability to pull himself from the pit; he also had the agency and responsibility to warn others to do the same. Dow's account of his conversion, his habitually unkempt dress, and his use of homespun logic and emotional pleas to excite his audiences into repentance, led some to doubt his authenticity. Yet in a measure of how close Methodists and revivalistic Calvinists would become by mid-century, in 1849 New York Baptist John Dowling, the editor of Dow's autobiog-raphy and collected works, noted that although he disapproved of Dow's vituperations against the Calvinists, he nevertheless held his conversion to have been true. Dowling's reasoning recalls Samuel Hopkins's argu-ment that, to be truly saved, one must be willing to be damned: "There is no greater evidence of the genuineness of conviction for sin, than when it is accompanied by a heartfelt sense of the justice of God in the condem-nation of the sinner. This Lorenzo seems to have felt in a high degree."[20]

Lee's call to preach was so strong that she challenged restrictions against female preaching with spontaneous exhortations, claims to have brought about deathbed conversions, and petitions for recognition to the leadership of the African Methodist Episcopal (AME) Church. In the mid-dle of a male preacher's sermon on Jonah she got up, "as by altogether supernatural impulse," she recounted. "I told them I was like Jonah, for...I had lingered like him, and delayed to go at the bidding of the Lord, and warn those who are as deeply guilty as were the people of Ninevah." Lee seemingly chastised herself for not exhorting as much as she felt the Lord was calling her to, but also chastised the male leadership for not allowing her to preach without fear of reprimand. This bold move paid off: rather than deny her call, the Bishop affirmed that "he now as much believed that I was called to the work, as any of the preachers present."[21]

Like the others, Finney entered a lifelong quest for the salvation of his fellows: "Nothing, it seemed to me, could be put in competition with the worth of souls." Throughout his ministerial career, Finney would apply the lessons learned in his own experience as a parishioner. In keeping with his emphasis on the practice of preaching rather than the doc-trinal debates that theologians so enjoyed, he was unafraid to join with Methodists and Baptists in promoting revivals, even holding them up as examples of how a direct and earnest pulpit style could more readily per-suade than the discourses of learned men.[22]

This is not to say that doctrine did not matter to these laypeople-turned-preachers. Abbott's, Dow's, and Lee's experiences with the paralyzing fear that they were among the eternally reprobate led them to oppose predestination. They certainly did not oppose the evocation of fear, but they did oppose it when preachers offered no clear way out. Dow famously summed up the homespun Arminian understanding of Calvinism as follows: *"You can and you can't—You shall and you shan't— You will and you won't—And you'll be damned if you do—And you will be damned if you don't."*[23] In his memoir, Finney also tried to style himself as a self-made theologian who followed his own path in departing from traditional Calvinism, but scholars have pointed out that Finney's ideas actually drew heavily from Jonathan Edwards's successors, and especially from Congregationalist minister Nathanael Emmons (1745–1840).[24] In a famous 1812 sermon, "The Duty of Sinners to Make Themselves a New Heart," Emmons argued that sin lay in the exercise of sinful acts and not in an inherent sinful disposition, or taste, over which individuals had no control. Conversion, or making oneself a "new heart," simply consisted in "the exercising of holy instead of unholy affections," which everyone had the natural ability to do.[25]

Where Emmons left sinners with the Edwardsean paradox of unhindered natural ability and predestinated moral inability, however, Finney softened the paradox and tried to explain how the call to repent immediately could coexist with predestination, contrary to what Methodists might claim. In a series of "doctrinal sermons" in the mid-1830s, Finney argued that God did not arbitrarily choose whom to save and damn, but instead chose those He knew would convert without detriment to others. In other words, God was not partial but eminently practical:

> Suppose a man in this city has a peculiar difficulty in regard to the Christian religion which not a man here knows how to remove.... But suppose it was known that there was a man in England who was qualified to teach him and bring him right.... But it was found that to take that man from his present post of responsibility would be a greater injury to the universe than it would to let this infidel go to hell. Would God do right to send the man from England here to save this sinner? Certainly not.

Finney then brought the example to its logical conclusion: "He [God] does not go out of his way, and give up the salvation of a greater number to save an individual.... if individuals place themselves where the great moral interests of the universe will not allow him to reach them with the means of salvation, they must be lost."[26] Although one could argue that God's election of the most easily reached still made Him unfair or at least partial (what of the so-called "heathen" overseas?), Finney here basically ignored the issue of unequal access. Instead, he focused on those people in the regions where he and other revivalists preached—especially the "burned-over" western districts of New York and Ohio—who, he argued, had no excuse not to place themselves in the way of saving grace. By finessing predestination to make it fit with the sinner's own responsibility, Finney spoke to denominational distinctions that faded in his practical preaching. Predestination simply became another spur to sinners to attend Sabbath services and revivals, read the Bible, repent, and make their salvation sure.

While the differences between these preachers—in education, gender, socioeconomic status, and denomination—are certainly significant, then, their similarities are more striking.[27] Abbott, Dow, Lee, and Finney all described their pre-conversion selves as obstinate, experienced the fear of hell prior to their change of heart, and used that fear in their own ministerial careers as an impetus to exhort others to flee from hell. Despite legitimate theological disputes, all four also held that, in not opening themselves to saving grace or acting righteously, sinners had no one to blame but themselves for eternal damnation. Given these similarities, we might wonder whether they deliberately tailored their narratives to fit accepted norms. Since each recorded their experiences long after the fact, memory intertwined with keen awareness of older patterns and current expectations to establish their authors' experiences as models of genuine conversion. One George Peck (born 1797) remembered that as a boy he and his family would read such narratives together: "What a glorious time we had reading the Life of Benjamin Abbott!" When read aloud over the flickering candlelight, Abbott's vivid visions of hell must have made a strong impression. Peck would later become a preacher himself.[28]

Instructing Preachers in the Uses of Hell

Where revivalists' memoirs helped to establish an ideal pattern of conversion, advice manuals and newspaper articles written for ministers instructed them in the right manner of preaching for converts. In the eighteenth century, ministers had disagreed on how to discern the "true" change of heart, with anti-revivalists looking for external conformity to the Christian lifestyle and pro-revivalists plumbing the depths of the soul. By the 1810s and beyond, the convergence of evangelicals in a united desire to convert the rapidly expanding American population gave rise to texts that taught a professionalizing male clergy how to discern and provoke both external and internal signs of conversion.[29] Abbott, Dow, Lee, and other populists exhorted emotionally and extemporaneously.[30] Advice texts tried to standardize the practice of preaching for younger Presbyterians, Congregationalists, and Episcopalians, and for Methodists who were becoming ever more genteel as their adherents began to enter the middle class.[31] Ministers wanted to know how to replicate the successes, without the excesses, of earlier revivalists. In the wake of disestablishment they sought sources of authority that were neither state-supported nor simply charismatic. They turned to institution building, founding seminaries, societies, and religious journals; male preachers also embraced an emerging model of masculinity. As one scholar puts it, a pastor no longer enacted the role of "stern patriarch" or "kindly father," but instead sought to "be an enterprising competitor in the masculine public sphere," an "expert manager who carefully cultivated and grew his flock, diagnosed and treated their individual spiritual ills, and skillfully guided them through this world to the next."[32] Leaving no stone unturned, advice texts not only laid out the essentials of ministerial labor but also specified why, how, and when to use the threat of hell.

These texts urged ministers to connect their own eternal welfare to that of others. Eighteenth-century ordination sermons had also warned ministers that they would be held accountable for "Souls that perish through their neglect."[33] Antebellum advice texts made sure ministers did not forget the lesson. Methodist Timothy Merritt warned, in a sermon to the New England Conference, reprinted in *Zion's Herald*, that ministers "will remember that if the wicked are not warned, their blood shall be required at their hands. *Knowing, therefore, the terror of the Lord they will persuade men.* The heaviest curses in all the word of God await those who see the sword coming, but give not warning."[34] An 1849 preacher's manual written for seminary students at Alexandria by William Meade, Bishop of the Protestant Episcopal Church of Virginia, similarly stressed the higher responsibility preachers bore for the souls of others. "We have to give an account not of ourselves only, but of other souls unto God," he wrote. "The severity of the trial and the weight of the penalty will be proportioned to the trust reposed. The witnesses against us will be lost souls, and perhaps they also will be among our executioners and tormentors."[35] The torments of hell might not actually be equalizing, Meade implied: some would suffer more than others and "lost souls" could serve as both punishers and punished.

Meade classified the whole of humanity according to eternal status. While some Calvinists were still hotly debating the question of infant damnation into the nineteenth century, the Episcopalian Meade believed that infants could not be held responsible for their fates. God would surely "not refuse them a place in some of the many mansions of heaven," he suggested. But everyone who had reached the "age of accountability" would be categorized according to their choices in this life: "As there is but one heaven for the righteous, and but one hell for the wicked, so we find all men divided into two classes." In a veiled acknowledgement of the growing numbers of Catholics migrating to the United States by mid-century, Meade explicitly noted that there is "no third place," neither a "limbus infantum, or place for unbaptized children," nor "a purgatory for the half-converted, half-justified adults."[36] Fates were decided at the moment of death, so people needed to be warned from hell in life. Meade dramatized just how high the stakes were for Protestants. Americans' anxieties surrounding the state of their souls, and the terrible feelings of responsibility that weighed on their ministers, suggest the continued repercussions of purgatory's "death" centuries after the Reformation.[37]

In order for preaching to be effective, the authors of these advice texts noted, it must "embrace all the fundamental doctrines of the gospel," in the words of Presbyterian Heman Humphrey, president of Amherst College. In his 1842 handbook, *Thirty-Four Letters to a Son in the Ministry*, Humphrey explained that the pastor was not "at liberty to select such topics as you think will please your hearers best, and leave out those which are most obnoxious to men of 'perverse and reprobate minds.' "[38] For, he noted, "the most awful threatenings in the Bible are found in the New Testament, and many of them were uttered by the Savior himself." After quoting a choice selection of particularly fiery verses, Humphrey acknowledged that, in preaching such texts,

> You may be told that you entirely miss your aim; that nobody was ever frightened to heaven or ever will be, and much more to the same effect. But let Paul answer for you. "Knowing therefore the terror of the Lord, we persuade men." Let Jude speak to the same point. "And others save with fear, plucking them out of the fire." Remember, my dear son ... "he that judgeth you is the Lord."[39]

That Humphrey felt the need to justify the preaching of hell suggests that discomfort in the pews dissuaded some ministers from dwelling on its punishments by mid-century. Some scholars have suggested that the preponderance of women in antebellum churches led to a "feminization" of theology as ministers toned down the fire and brimstone rhetoric. But this was not the case across the board. Instead, we might read the prevalence of hell in these advice texts as pushback against perceived softening.[40]

Humphrey was hardly alone in urging preachers not to shy away from talking about hell.[41] In fact, he sounded much like the more famous Finney who, in his 1876 *Memoirs*, recalled that Old School Calvinists "used to complain that I let down the dignity of the pulpit...that I said 'hell,' and with such an emphasis as often to shock the people; furthermore, that I urged the people with such vehemence, as if they might not have a moment to live; and sometimes they complained that I blamed the people too much."[42] Revivalist newspapers also exhorted preachers not to sugarcoat their sermons or eschew due warnings to sinners. An article in the *American Revivalist, and Rochester Observer*, for instance, approvingly noted that all the great revival preachers, from Whitefield to Edwards to Finney, shared a common trait: "They preached much terror." For antebellum evangelicals, such direct language could frighten people out of their sinful complacency into reliance on God alone.[43]

Having established that the Bible sanctioned hellfire preaching to awaken fallen humans from a path to ultimate ruin, the ministerial guides addressed how best to deliver the threat of hell. Be *"bold and earnest, my dear E., in your preaching, as one 'who must give account,'"* wrote Humphrey. But also be "tender," since "nature itself teaches us" that compassion "ought always to be felt for those who are ready to perish, however much they may deserve to perish."[44] These seemingly opposed qualities also defined the ideal antebellum Christian man, who should be compassionate in the domestic sphere and stern in the competitive marketplace.[45] The minister had to walk a fine line between boldly terrifying sinners out of their hardness of heart and callously shocking them into the belief that they were certainly damned. Rather than give the impression that "he is almost willing they [sinners] should be" lost, the preacher should instead convey serious concern for his flock and his earnest desire that they be saved.[46]

Even if a minister followed this kind of advice, ensuring that "true" conversions actually happened remained a tricky business. The fine line between compassion and callousness was particularly difficult to negotiate when a potential convert was in a state of extreme anxiety. Should the minister encourage the anxious with the hope of heaven or continue to pummel them with the threat of hell? Was anxiety a sign of the Spirit striving with the hardened heart, or merely a sinner's selfish and carnal fear of death and the excruciating punishments that would follow? Humans bore direct responsibility to humble themselves and accept salvation, but this required a paradoxical combination of self-renunciation and self-interest.[47]

To achieve this difficult balance and ensure that the anxious sinner came to Christ out of true repentance and not fear alone, advice texts warned ministers not to offer reassurance or hope too quickly. Brooklyn Presbyterian Ichabod Spencer suggested in his 1850 *Pastor's Sketches* that anxiety could be a sign of the Holy Spirit striving with the sinner, but prolonged anxiety could mean that the sinner was resisting. He recounted a conversation with an anxious young woman: " 'How long have you been in such deep trouble of mind?' 'For three weeks,' said she, sobbing aloud." Rather than comfort her, Spencer retorted, " 'Then, *for three weeks you have done nothing but resist the Holy Spirit!*' "[48] The next week, the young woman told Spencer that his harsh words had cut to the quick and she was now hopefully converted. Spencer styled himself a diagnostician of souls and presented his book as a kind of physician's manual that showed other ministers how they too could diagnose and treat almost any kind of spiritual malady that stood in the way of conversion.[49]

A writer for the *New York Evangelist* who went by the initials "A.R.A." similarly warned that, until the sinner repented and submitted to God's will, it did not matter "however anxious he may be": "if impenitent, he is *not in the good* way, but *in the way to ruin.*" Even if anxiety produced despair, the minister should not stop warning that hell awaited the unrepentant. For despair was, at base, selfish and prideful: the sinner wanted to save herself, realized that she could not, and gave into immobility rather than submitting to and believing in the sufficiency of Christ's sacrifice. "This despair then is his excuse for neglecting present duty," concluded A.R.A. "He must be driven out of this shelter—driven from self-dependence— must give up his self-will, and despair of saving himself, or he must perish! There are no means like a pressure of duty, and deep conviction, and the thunders of damnation *to chase away such despair.*"[50] The threat of damnation, then, could frighten a sinner both into and out of despair and into a dutiful reliance on God alone.

This advice was especially applicable at the deathbed. Ministers vacillated between accepting that the dying could truly convert and warning that last-minute conversions could not necessarily be trusted. Heman Humphrey advised against reassuring the dying sinner too quickly: "beware that you do not encourage him to hope that his sins are pardoned, before he has cast himself upon the mercy of God, through a crucified Redeemer. Many, I fear, have been thus prematurely encouraged to their eternal undoing."[51] Time was short at the deathbed, but calming the dying before real repentance had occurred could be eternally perilous. Better to make their last moments on earth hellish than to usher them into eternal hell.

Using the threat of hell at funerals was also tricky, though no less important. Not all funerals required lengthy sermons, Humphrey instructed, but "there will doubtless be favorable opportunities, for bringing the awful realities of death, judgment and eternity to bear upon individuals, who never attend church, and whom you can never hope to reach at any other time." The minister must exercise caution in describing the character of the deceased, since relatives and friends would likely desire a sermon suggesting heaven as their final resting place. "This is treading upon very delicate ground," Humphrey warned; "Most men are too imperfect to be held up as models even in that hour when their virtues are most vividly remembered. And when you have once begun to praise the dead, where will you stop?" But "Say what you will...you cannot alter the condition of the dead. It is too late. Their account is sealed up to the day of judgment." And what of the "notoriously wicked"? Should the minister "tell the people you have no doubt that he has gone down to the world of despair"? In such instances, the minister had to decide on a case-by-case basis. If the "respectable family connections" of the dead were present, "It would be wrong to inflict the torture upon them, unless ministerial fidelity clearly requires it." But if the equally vicious companions of the dead man were also present, "it may be your duty...to say, that such was his character you have no hope of him, and to beseech them not to plunge into the same place of torment."[52]

We cannot know exactly how many inexperienced young ministers these advice texts reached. Available publication numbers for Ichabod Spencer's manual show that nearly a quarter of the ministerial population owned a copy by mid-century.[53] New generations of evangelical ministers who read these manuals would have been groomed in similar habits of thought about the divisions of humanity into the saved and damned, the importance of converting the latter into the former, and the appropriate uses of the threat of hell to do so.

That said, the texts did allow that faithfulness to the Scriptures did not mean ignoring the comforting doctrines of salvation, grace, and Christian living. Humphrey noted that American preachers perhaps overly emphasized the moment of conversion rather than how to live as a Christian, while their British brethren did the opposite, focusing "upon the hopes, privileges, and glorious prospects of believers in this world, and upon the blessedness of the heavenly state." He wrote, "Their ordinary preaching is, as I apprehend, much better adapted than ours to 'edify the body of Christ,' as ours is better suited than theirs, to awaken sinners and bring them to repentance."[54] He concluded that American preachers should strive for greater balance, advice with which anti-revivalists who followed an older model of ministerial oversight and care would likely have agreed. Significantly, though, Humphrey never argued that the British model was better than the American. Nor did he suggest that revivals aimed at saving sinners from hell were any less important than Christian living. On the contrary, he devoted nearly sixty pages toward the end of his 352-page manual exclusively to the subject, noting that "there is not, within the whole range of ministerial and pastoral duty, a more important topic." The many antebellum articles and books on the subject suggest that he was hardly the only minister who felt this way.[55]

But what accounts for this American focus? The rapidly expanding population and geographic and religious mobility of antebellum Americans—moving not only from country to town or East to West but also from church to denomination to different religious group entirely—suggests a possible explanation. The population of the new nation grew from 5.3 to 9.6 million between 1800 and 1820, and shifted from almost 95 percent living in the Atlantic states to nearly 25 percent living west of the Appalachians. By 1850, as American expansionism swelled the nation's territorial reach, the proportion living west of the Appalachians increased even further, to more than half the total population of over 23 million.[56] Even though the number of ministers expanded three times as fast as the rest of the population, there were still only 27,000 serving the population by mid-century, translating to an average of 852 people per minister.[57] Meanwhile, the urban population jumped from 7 to 20 percent between 1820 and 1860.[58] Congregations experienced greater turnover than those in Western Europe, such that American ministers were not always able to keep track of their parishioners' daily lives.

Nor did they necessarily want to. One scholar has noted that ministers increasingly forsook rural and poor urban parishes that could not afford to pay them a steady salary. Instead, they angled for the "more lucrative and powerful positions created by the professionalization of the ministry," using less prestigious positions as springboards to pulpits with more prominence.[59] Thus, in the western regions to which many Americans migrated there was a dearth of religious leaders and even the cities had far fewer than could serve their burgeoning populations. In such a fluid atmosphere, trying to terrify people into repentance before either they or the minister took off was not an unreasonable strategy.

From Pulpit to Print to Peer Pressure

Evangelicals put great stock in the booming print industry as a means of extending their influence where their numbers were small. The American Bible Society, founded in 1816, and American Tract Society, founded ten years later, were among the first publishing companies to install steam-powered presses in the United States, greatly facilitating the rapid dissemination of religious literature.[60] One estimate suggests that the American Tract Society "was distributing five million pages of printed material annually" by the late 1820s. Most of its publications were pamphlets between four and sixteen pages long, meant to have ecumenical appeal across Protestant denominational lines. In addition to tracts and Bibles distributed by colporteurs and through the mail, antebellum Americans could also read ever more religious newspapers and books.[61] Images could also be more easily reproduced.

The messages in texts that aimed at saving readers from damnation echoed what ministers were urging from the pulpits—directly so, of course, when sermons were reproduced for print consumption.[62] The multidenominational 1824 *The Southern Preacher: A Collection of Sermons, from the Manuscripts of Several Eminent Ministers of the Gospel, Residing in the Southern States*, for instance, was compiled by the Rev. Colin McIver for the "edification of his readers," who may have resided at a distance from regular ministers. McIver selected sermons that aimed to "instruct and persuade their hearers, to accept of salvation through Jesus Christ, on the terms proposed in the Gospel." The sermons' titles and authors' affiliations bespeak the regional and denominational commonality of raining terror from the pulpit: for instance, "On the Character and Doom of the Wicked" (Rev. Adam Empie, Episcopalian of Wilmington, North Carolina), "On the Necessity of Preparation for Death" (Rev. John Capers,

Methodist from South Carolina), and "On the Consequence of Unbelief" (Rev. Benjamin Palmer, Congregationalist of South Carolina).[63]

Another of Empie's sermons, "On the Guilt and Danger of Delaying to Keep God's Commandments," cautioned readers not to think that a deathbed conversion could wipe away a lifetime's worth of sin, much as Humphrey warned in his manual. Putting off repentance until the "last stages of life, though it lifts you above Hell, will leave you among the lowest grades in Heaven," Empie explained. Like the southern Meade, Empie posited a not-quite-equal afterlife. He continued, "Could we put the question to those miserable exiles from happiness, who dwell among the Apostate damned; could you ask them, what brought them to that state of misery; millions of voices, from the infernal pit, would rise in peals of thunder, roaring out delay! delay! delay!"[64] In the early republican South, where evangelicals were starting to outnumber Episcopalians, we can see the influence of their call for immediate repentance on Empie's sermon.

An early temperance sermon by Ebenezer Porter, "The Fatal Effects of Ardent Spirits," also highlighted the dangers of delay and connected it to the ill consequences of alcohol. Porter preached it after "a transient man perished in the snow, with a bottle of spirits at his side, about a mile from the meetinghouse"[65] and published it at the request of his ministerial brethren. The sermon described the slippery slope to eternal perdition that began with the first sip of "ardent spirits." "With slow, but steady progress," Porter cautioned, "the habit becomes inwrought into the constitution: the man reels in the street; is callous to shame and remorse; loses the use of his limbs, his tongue, his reason—in one word, he is ruined:—health, estate, character, body and soul ruined." To Porter, drunkenness impaired the sound judgment that was necessary to ready the soul for the afterlife. It "renders men totally unprepared for that hour [of death].... During actual intoxication he is as really incapable of repentance, or any other religious exercise, as a brute or a stone; and therefore is utterly unfit to die. Let this be remembered while it is added,—he is peculiarly exposed to die, and to die suddenly." Porter deemed alcohol consumption the "prevailing sin of our day," "so fatal to the morals, the lives, and the souls of my fellow men, and so threatening to the welfare of my native country."[66]

Even children were not immune from the evangelical warning to flee immediately from the fires of hell in case of sudden death. The *New England Primer*, first printed in the seventeenth century and reprinted multiple times in the eighteenth and nineteenth centuries, gave children easily memorized verses like these:

Tho' I am young yet I may die,
And hasten to eternity:
There is a dreadful fiery hell,
Where wicked ones must always dwell:
There is a heaven full of Joy,
Where godly ones must always stay:
To one of these my soul must fly,
As in a moment when I die. . .

Many reprints of the *Primer* included the Shorter Catechism, which espoused a predestinationist theology that newer revivalist texts dodged. "All Mankind by the Fall, lost communion with God, are under his wrath and curse, and so made liable to all miseries in this Life, to death itself, and to the pains of hell forever," the Catechism explained. Thus was the child introduced to the concept of innate depravity and next to the concept of election: "Did God leave all Mankind to perish in the State of Sin and Misery? God having out of his mere good Pleasure, from all eternity, elected some to everlasting Life, did enter into a Covenant of grace, to deliver them out of a state of sin and misery, and to bring them into a state of Salvation by a Redeemer."[67]

Where the Catechism focused on God's "mere good Pleasure," the 1832 "Who Will Go to Heaven?" in the "Children's Department" of the *American Revivalist and Rochester Observer* vested agency in children themselves. Rebirth, the article instructed, "is to become a Christian—to become holy, like God." Should a child fail to be born again, danger could ensue:

O! Reader, how can you live one day longer the enemy of God? How can you lie down and sleep to-night without first giving your heart to God, and becoming a Christian? Should you suddenly be called to die, as many children are every day, remember you would immediately sink down to the world of woe.[68]

Of course, not all antebellum children's literature was so terrifying. Still, evangelicals justified the dissemination of damnation to the sentient of all ages because they saw it not as cruelty but as an act of mercy that could save the sinner from much worse to come.[69]

Ministers also extended the warnings they gave themselves to lay disseminators of the faith. In the "Sunday School Department" of the *New York Evangelist*, a "Superintendent" exhorted Sabbath School teachers to exercise more prayerful concern for their charges. Though young, they were nevertheless "God's enemies." "The thought that immortal souls are depending on him [the teacher] for spiritual instruction," the article warned, "ought to drive him to the throne of grace in agony.... A teacher, who feels so little for the souls of the children that he will not unite in coming together to pray, is in danger of being called to a reckoning; and for his unprofitableness, cast into outer darkness."[70]

An 1837 article in the *New York Evangelist* went further still, telling not only Sunday School teachers but *every*one to keep a watchful eye on their family and friends. "The natural state of all men is but an extension of the domains of the pit," the article explained:

> The fixtures of mercy, the cords of truth and forbearance, are cast around the invited sinner. He is prevented by them from the hopeless plunge. One after another of these cords are broken.... There is a friend—a relative: he is gone! just gone! but gone forever!

The article reads like a sermon—it is again reminiscent of Edwards's "Sinners in the Hands of an Angry God." "The Living in the Pit" was brief, however, occupying less than a single column on one page of the newspaper. Such succinct but gripping printed texts functioned as quick conscience-prickers for a mobile society. Where Edwards had focused on the individual before a sovereign God, "The Living in the Pit" moved the reader's gaze from the anonymous "sinner" to "a friend—a relative" also suspended over the pit. "They [the damned] are binding weights around the necks of their children, relatives and friends, to accelerate and secure their fall. Abandoned themselves, they are leading others away from the haunts of soliciting angels of mercy," the article warned. "Their presence is pollution." The subtext for the already-converted was clear: curb the "pollution" or risk sliding into the pit yourselves along with everyone you love.[71]

This appeal to the laity to take responsibility for the souls of others picked up on a theme in English Puritan Richard Baxter's *A Call to the Unconverted*. The American Tract Society reprinted this piece numerous times in the nineteenth century. "If your eyes were so far opened as to see hell," Baxter had written more than two centuries earlier, "and you saw your neighbors that were unconverted dragged thither with hideous cries: though they were such as you accounted honest people on earth, and feared no such danger themselves, such a sight would make you go home and think about it, and think again, and make you warn all about you."[72] Baxter's theology anticipated the New Divinity's: rather than a limited atonement, he suggested that Christ's sacrifice made salvation possible for all. Because of this theological perspective, Baxter could urge people to take note of their neighbors' states and warn each other to convert or face the prospect of hell. His text resonated in an era when personal agency and responsibility to save others became the order of the day. By appealing to lay converts' stake in the eternal welfare of others, ministers North and South were able to deflect blame from themselves when they failed to save as many as they hoped and when their congregants took off for parts west.[73]

An article written for the *Western Luminary* appealed to the individual's responsibility for family members, posing a set of questions. One through four asked if the reader truly believed "every text of God's word." For those who answered in the affirmative, the questions continued:

5. Have you, then, a father, or mother, or brother, or sister, or husband, or wife, or child, or friend, you tenderly love, who has not been born again—who does not believe?

6. How often, believer, do you, with an aching heart, plainly warn them of their tremendous danger, by telling them what you believe—viz.—"that they every moment, yes, every moment, asleep or awake, are most certainly exposed to the unutterable horrors of eternal damnation in the fiery lake, where the despairing sufferer, though crying in intense agony for one drop of water to cool his parched and scorching tongue, cries and cries in vain?"[74]

Evangelicals pulled on the heartstrings and consciences of the already-converted to spread the word to their loved ones. Ministers embellished biblical teachings about the continuity of this-worldly relationships in the life to come. Christ had taught that "in the resurrection they neither marry, nor are given in marriage, but are as the angels of God in heaven," and one scholar suggests that "neither heavenly recognition nor fellowship of the saints was a major theme during the years from 1770 to 1840, especially among leaders of the Second Great Awakening." Yet revivalists' appeals to earthly ties and familial responsibility suggest that this was a transitional period.[75]

New Haven minister Elisha Cleaveland directly addressed the duty of husbands and fathers in an 1849 sermon "Published by Request." Cleaveland targeted those who had caught California gold fever and were itching to strike it rich out West. This was a sermon precisely calculated for the mobile milieu of mid-century America. "Take into view not merely your present life, which is but a vapor, but the whole of your unending existence," he implored. "Look at the subject as from the shores of eternity...look at it as from the depths of everlasting perdition!" Cleaveland enjoined the men to consider the lasting consequences of an impulsive move: "Is there no danger that in consequence of your absence they [your children] may be tempted away from the path of virtue, and lay the foundation of ultimate ruin? And will you imperil their souls, their temporal and eternal welfare, for the doubtful chance of gaining a few pounds of gold?" The slim chance of prosperity was not worth the big risk of eternal damnation—not only for men themselves but also for their families. In suggesting that a man's departure could spell his loved ones' ruin not only temporally but also eternally, Cleaveland downplayed the personal agency of women and children and appealed to men's paternalistic sense of responsibility for their families.[76]

By contrast, the American Tract Society's pamphlet, "To Mothers," impressed upon them their solemn duty to save their children from hell. "The noise and tumult of the active world often drown the 'still small voice' of the Gospel," the pamphlet noted. "But this Tract is designed for a different situation in life; for those who do not mingle in the bustle and hurry of the world; who are retired to a more quiet, though not to an unimportant space."[77] The pamphlet spoke to the developing middle-class ideology of separate spheres, according to which men left the house for employment while women were supposed to tend to domestic affairs.[78] To the housebound woman who felt herself "*unknown*," "*obscure*," and "*secluded*," the tract assured her to the contrary. She was not an "unknown" in the house; in fact, her "influence with [her] child is greater than that of a Legislator or General." Nor was she "obscure": "*You* are *immortal*. You must go to the *judgment*; and every whisper of your life will be exhibited, before an assembled universe! *Secluded!*—What if the eye of the world does not follow you into the domestic circle? Is it not restraint enough that your *child* is there? That child has a *soul*, worth more than a million globes of gold."[79] Since child or mother might die at any moment, "The time for your exertion is very *short*": "Let this golden opportunity pass...and the precious immortal is trained for some other state than the paradise above."[80]

Evangelicals also coded a feeling of responsibility for the eternal welfare of others as a harbinger of revivals. "All who would aid this work," noted an 1830 article in the *New York Evangelist*, "must possess a deep sense of the guilty and dangerous condition of impenitent men, and exhibit a consistent and holy life.... It is vain to expect that they, who know little of the power of truth, and have never seriously thought of their guilt and danger, will be very solicitous for *themselves*, while the professed disciple of Christ show no anxious solicitude for them. The power of solicitude or of indifference to produce the same effect upon the minds of others, we all know to be very great." Peer pressure, in other words, could be a powerful means of exciting the unconverted to serious concern over their eternal state. "It is then the first and most imperative duty, on the part of Christians," the article concluded, "if they would hope for a revival, and ever see their friends escaping the fires of the eternal pit, to rouse themselves from *lethargy*, and to *feel deeply*, and to act *consistently*."[81] This would not only benefit the unconverted, but would also vouchsafe the authenticity of the convert's own change of heart. Joshua Bradley concluded his *Accounts of Religious Revivals in Many Parts of the United States from 1816 to 1818* with "Questions" meant to allow lay readers to evaluate their own heart. "Do you feel a love to mankind—such as you did not feel before you became religious?" he queried. "Have you a great desire that the souls of men should be saved, by being brought to a genuine faith and trust in the Redeemer?"[82] Affirmative answers to these questions would show the prospective convert that her conversion was in fact "genuine."

Saving the "Heathen" from the "Shadow of Death"

If the responsibility to save others extended beyond ministers to their flocks, and from their flocks to their friends and family, where did such responsibility end? Significantly, Bradley asked if converts felt a love to mankind and not just to their immediate neighbors. And the tract "To Mothers" attributed global and even eternal significance to the raising of a pious child in the domestic sphere: "That child who now prattles on your knee, or sports around your dwelling, may yet tell some perishing heathen of Jesus of Nazareth; may yet be an able soldier in the army of Immanuel, and may plant the standard of the cross on the shores of Greenland, or under the burning sun of Africa."[83] The failure to produce godly children might have consequences even for the distant "heathen." The Great Commission, after all, applied to all nations, not simply Americans.[84]

American missionary efforts to save the world from the devil's snares and claim it for Protestantism took flight in the second decade of the nineteenth century, with the establishment of the interdenominational American Board of Commissioners for Foreign Missions (ABCFM) in 1810. Puritan divines like John Eliot and David Brainerd had attempted to missionize native peoples both by sequestering them in praying towns and by living and preaching among them, and the British Society for the Propagation of the Gospel in Foreign Parts, established in 1701, had sought to spread Anglicanism not only among colonial settlers but also among Native Americans and African slaves. Still, the creation of the ABCFM marked the first organized effort by the young United States to send missionaries both overseas and to the indigenous peoples of North America.

Antebellum evangelicals saw practically the entire world as a mission field. At the beginning of his 1854 *A Manual of Missions: Or, Sketches of the Foreign Missions of the Presbyterian Church*, John Cameron Lowrie, corresponding secretary of the Presbyterian Board of Foreign Missions, included a map of the world roughly color-coded by religion (figs. 2.1 and 2.2). The map depicted much of the world as gray (Heathen), red (Roman Catholic), and yellow (Mohamedan), while only small portions were blue (Protestant). Even in North America, only the East Coast, Texas, and parts of the Pacific Coast were blue. This was wishful thinking, since Texas and the Pacific Coast were hardly majority Protestant by 1854.[85]

The map did not just show the geography of different religious traditions as a matter of neutral fact: it showed them to incite action, urging Americans to spread the blue of Protestantism across the globe, saving the "heathen" and other "benighted" peoples from the fires of hell. The choice of gray for "heathendom" was hardly arbitrary: it suggested that "heathenness" was a cultural void that would eventually be colored in by one of the other major religions—for evangelicals, that had to be Protestantism. Conveniently, this aim coincided with American dreams of territorial expansion. The extent to which missionaries self-consciously contributed to expansionist goals is debatable, but their efforts certainly assisted the spread of American Protestant culture as they sought to remake other societies to look more like their own.

In his 1849 *Dr. Scudder's Tales for Little Readers about the Heathen*, published by the American Tract Society, medical missionary John Scudder

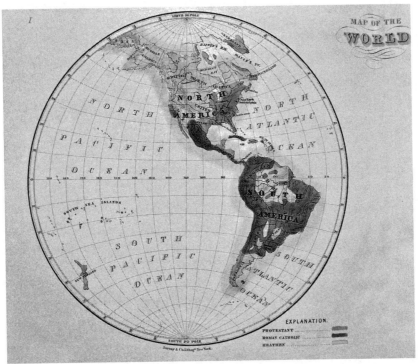

FIGURE 2.1 Frontispiece (L) in John Cameron Lowrie, *A Manual of Missions, or, Sketches of the Foreign Missions of the Presbyterian Church* (New York: Anson D. F. Randolph, 1854).

Photograph by Nicholas Lum.

called children's attention to maps like these. "MY DEAR CHILDREN," he wrote:

> I want you to look at the red spots on it, and think how many millions of people embrace the religion both of the Greek and Roman Catholic churches—a religion which is nothing more nor less than paganism.... After this, I want you to look at the green spots, and think of the hundred and twenty millions of Mohammedans.... I want you also to look at all the dark spots, where, with comparatively a few exceptions, the people are in pagan darkness.... And in view of all this darkness...I want you, my dear boys, to ask yourselves whether it may not be your duty, after you grow up, to become ministers, and go and preach the Gospel to them.[86]

Scudder was adamant that the "heathen" could not be saved without Christian intervention. "It is a charity which has no foundation," he

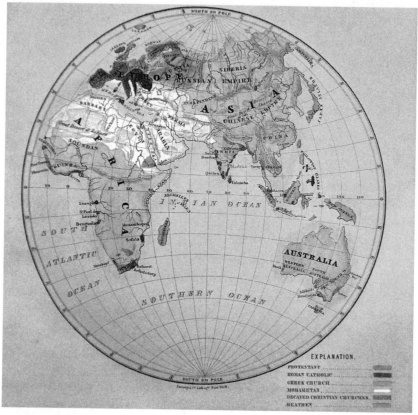

FIGURE 2.2 Frontispiece (R) in John Cameron Lowrie, *A Manual of Missions, or, Sketches of the Foreign Missions of the Presbyterian Church* (New York: Anson D. F. Randolph, 1854).

Photograph by Nicholas Lum.

declared, "to suppose that the heathen can go to heaven. I have preached the Gospel to tens of thousands of them, but I never saw one who had the least atom of a qualification for that holy place."[87]

According to Scudder, the "heathen" on their own would never be able to "relish" the "pure joys" of heaven.[88] Saving them involved not only transforming their belief systems but also how they lived their lives, from their relations with their ancestors, to their marital and sexual practices, to the food and drink they consumed. Consider Walter Macon Lowrie's *Sermons Preached in China*. Walter, John Cameron's brother, included only one sermon explicitly aimed at a Chinese audience (the rest were intended for English speakers in China). This "Sermon to the Chinese" was on "THE PUNISHMENT OF HELL." "The torment of hell is endless and unceasing," Lowrie warned, "so that we should greatly fear it." He continued:

> The people of this place say that in the seventh month all the spirits in hell are allowed to come forth, and that we should at that time spread tables and prepare food for them to eat. All this is the doctrine of the Buddhist priests and is wholly destitute of proof; it deserves no attention, and is unworthy of your belief.

This sermon, preached in Ningpo in 1847, typifies the scorn white missionaries felt for the cultural practices and religions of the peoples they were attempting to missionize. Lowrie dismissed Chinese ancestors as "spirits in hell." For him and many other American missionaries, not only did the "heathen" lack the gospel, they also frequently held "perverted" forms of religiosity that negatively influenced their entire cultures and made them guiltier than if they practiced no discernible form of religion at all.[89]

What other characteristics defined the so-called "heathen"? Or as another Presbyterian missionary to the Chinese, William Speer, put it, "What are 'heathen'?" The "what" rather than "who" in Speer's question may seem somewhat derogatory or at least dehumanizing. At the same time, Speer's use of the word "what" suggests that he saw "heathenness" not as an innate identity defining who a person was, but as a temporary title that could be lost once the "heathen" converted. "We apply it ['heathen'], to all the races of man who are without the Bible; to those who are wanderers from the way of life," Speer wrote. "They see the dim light of nature and of their traditions from the patriarchal age; they hear the still small voice of natural conscience; but they are without the clear light of the revelation which we enjoy." To Speer, "heathen" was a designation connected to an ancient divergence of races, applying to entire peoples who were spiritually and intellectually stunted, and therefore damned, by having lived in the "darkness" for so long. The term implied a moral and paternalistic imperative to save them from themselves by changing their hearts and habits.[90]

A sermon by another evangelist to the Chinese, Rev. Ira Condit, provides a window into the urgency driving foreign missionary work. The handwritten manuscript dates from 1867, but Condit's views show little change from earlier generations. "Will the heathen, without the gospel, perish?" he asked. It was, Condit assumed, "one of the most solemnly important questions" to "every follower of Christ," because if the answer was affirmative, everyone would be under "the great—the dreadful—the tremendous responsability...to do what he can to send them the gospel & save them as speedily as possible." The "heathen" "are possessed of minds & immortal souls," he wrote:

> So every Christian should realize this unavoidable conclusion, that the heathen are sinking to eternal misery as fast as the scythe of death mows them down.... The 400 millions of China_ the 100 millions, or more, of India_ the tens of millions of Africa & of the islands of the sea, are daily marching in dark & terrible columns down through the gates of death, to join the vast hosts that crowd the caverns of hell.

Condit determined that "more than one-half of the population of the whole globe" was potentially doomed and urged Christians to do all they could to halt these millions from their death march.[91]

As confident as they were that God would bless their efforts, missionaries still worried about why their labor often seemed so unsuccessful on the ground. One way to explain their difficulties was to blame the "heathen" themselves. In an 1836 volume on *The Heathen Nations: Or Duty of the Present Generation to Evangelize the World*, members of the Sandwich Islands Mission grappled with their feelings of failure after more than a decade and a half of work. They listed a series of attributes that made the "heathen" difficult to save. The first, they suggested, was hard to express: "For want of better terms, we call it apathy, listlessness, imbecility of mind, torpitude of intellect, vacuity of thought, inability to reason, and the like." Second was "a destitution of ideas, and a consequent destitution of words on the subject of true religion and pure morality." And third, "minds...pre-occupied with false notions, which have grown with their growth and strengthened with their strength."[92]

Religious and racial difference became interchangeable when "false notions" were framed not as individual choices but as inherent and inherited qualities of mind perpetuated by generations of stunted and vacuous "heathens" in the "dark" regions of the world. Some scholars have suggested that racism as a full-fledged ideology required the decline of older religious categories like "Christian" and "heathen," which could ostensibly be transformed through conversion and backsliding. But to antebellum evangelicals, religious and racial categories could be mutually reinforcing.[93] Although religious status was supposed to be changeable, racial characteristics were supposedly permanent and could be used to explain why the missionaries had such a hard time converting the "heathen." "To understand correctly the feature of mind we refer to," the Sandwich Islands missionaries explained, "it is necessary to witness, as we do, the vacant and unmeaning stare of a dark and chaotic intellect."[94] If the "heathen" were innately "imbecilic" and possessed of "dark intellects," missionaries could excuse themselves when the "heathen" failed to convert. The implication was that some were simply not savable.

An 1859 image of "The Sacrifice to the Goddess Pele" in *Harper's Weekly* suggestively illustrated these assumptions (fig. 2.3). The picture showed a pit of molten and steaming lava, indigenous Hawaiians dancing in nearby kayaks, and what appears to be a person falling into the flames.[95] But for a burning palm tree to the right of the frame, it might have passed for a picture of hell. Travelers were not shy about comparing volcanoes to their imagination of hell. One described the appearance of Pele's fires in terms no less striking than Edwards's: "Here was the real 'bottomless pit'—the 'fire which is not quenched'—'the place of hell'—'the lake which burneth

THE SACRIFICE TO THE GODDESS PELE.

FIGURE 2.3 "The Sacrifice to the Goddess Pele," *Harper's Weekly*, April 16, 1859, 249. Photograph by Nicholas Lum.

FIGURE 2.4 The Massachusetts Bay Colony Seal (seventeenth century).
Courtesy of Massachusetts Archives, The Commonwealth of Massachusetts.

with fire and brimstone'—the 'everlasting burnings'—the fiery sea whose waves are never weary."[96]

Depicting the sacred sites of Hawaiians as hellish and their practices as demonic implied that some were willingly hurling themselves into the clutches of Satan despite missionaries' best efforts. This move from confidence in Americans' ability to evangelize the "heathen," to demonization of the "other," mirrored the trajectory of Puritan attempts to convert Native Americans in the colonial era. From the paternalistic optimism of the Massachusetts Bay Colony Seal ("Come over and help us"!) (fig. 2.4) to the brutality of King Philip's War, demonization of indigenous people facilitated violence no less than assuaging colonists' feelings of guilt.[97]

But antebellum missionaries realized that they could not just blame the "heathen" for their lack of success. The "heathen" might have characteristics that made their conversion difficult, yet missionaries also blamed Euro-Americans for failing to contribute enough money and volunteers to the cause. Just as revivalists urged lay converts to take responsibility for the conversion of loved ones, so missionaries urged lay converts to invest in the souls of the "heathen." American Christians, they noted, put too much emphasis on sending Bibles and tracts to mission fields, which did no good if the "heathen" could understand neither the religious ideas in such texts, nor the words used to convey them. The missionaries warned:

> You must go YOURSELVES and teach the Bible to the heathen. YOU CAN NOT CONVERT THE WORLD BY PROXY—YOU CAN NOT DO IT BY THE PRESS.... You can not be guiltless, dear brethren, till you go forth in person to the perishing heathen. We beseech you, therefore, quiet not your consciences by sending forth Bibles and tracts. THAT WILL PROVE A FALSE QUIETUDE. THE DAY OF JUDGMENT WILL TEAR IT FROM YOU.[98]

The Sandwich Islands missionaries had imported a printing press to the islands and devoted much effort to creating a written Hawaiian language, publishing tracts as well as a massive translation of the Bible. But warm American bodies were needed to make the arduous voyage to the islands and other mission fields in order to learn and teach their languages and spread the gospel of salvation. Missionaries warned that Americans' lack of monetary and bodily investment in the cause had repercussions not only on the eternal welfare of the "heathen," but also on Americans themselves: on them the "blood of the heathen" would rest, imperiling their own eternal welfare at the final judgment.

Antebellum evangelical missionaries are often remembered for proclaiming that their efforts to convert the world would bring about the millennium. But not all of their accounts were triumphalist, as early optimism yielded to disappointment. In their private writings and in public pleas for more laborers, money, and prayers, missionaries expressed misgivings about their capacity to save what they believed to be a dying world, condemned to the fires of hell without their intervention. "If we look at the heathen *numerically*, they are six hundred millions," the Sandwich Islands missionaries lamented, "and the missionaries from the United States to whom their salvation is committed, one hundred—one man for six millions." Like Lowrie in his *Manual of Missions*, these missionaries color-coded the world, though for them the gradations of "heathen," Catholic, and "Mohammedan" gave way to stark black and white: "If we look at the earth *geographically*, the maps are almost black on which are designated the population of the land and the sea still under the dominion of the prince of darkness. For one square mile with light flashing on it,

there are thousands spread with the pall of death." Without more investment by American Christians, they concluded, "It is impossible that the
few missionaries from the American churches should convert the world.
They could not *explore* it."[99] And the price of their failure would redound to
America itself: "As often, nearly, as the clock ticks, one of the heathen goes
to an undone eternity...for want of the means of life, which Christians in
the United States possess and do not impart. Will not God remember to
make inquisition for blood? Will not his soul be avenged on such a nation
as ours?"[100] Would the damned nation be our own?

"The Heathen among Us"

Foreign missionaries were not the only evangelicals asking American
Christians for men and money to save the unsaved and usher in the millennium. Other evangelical leaders focused on the unchurched within
America. These evangelicals styled themselves as city and home missionaries and called attention to the poor and destitute within American cities,
as well as Euro-Americans who migrated from the eastern seaboard to the
Pacific coast.[101]

At times missionaries seemed to be competing. "The poor pagans are
to be pitied," wrote New York Presbyterian Ezra Stiles Ely in a typical passage from 1810, the same year as the founding of the ABCFM, but

> Christians, you are more to be pitied...you, who pray that God
> would bring the heathen into his Church...but take no trouble to
> diffuse knowledge among the ignorant within your own sphere of
> influence.... Will it not be more tolerable in the day of judgment,
> for the heathen, than for you?

Ely devoted his ministerial career to serving those he called the "Pagans in
Christendom," preaching in the New York City Hospital and Almshouse,
and pioneering early city missions in the 1810s. He believed that the totally "ignorant"—specifically, the unmissionized "heathen"—had less to
fear than those who had received the gospel light but failed to share it.
Whether the "heathen" might have a second chance during or after the
final judgment, he did not say. But those "pagan" Euro-Americans who
lived forgotten in the midst of a so-called Christian nation would not be
let off the hook so easily, because they would presumably have encountered the gospel in some form or other. Even worse off would be the

professed Christians who should have worked with and for these "Pagans in Christendom" by preaching the gospel to them, printing tracts, and contributing money for the distribution of Bibles.[102]

Like the Sandwich Islands missionaries, city ministers invested in the salvation of the "Pagans in Christendom" also used numbers to make their case. In his Prefatory Address to Ely's published journal Philip Milledoler noted that, of the 1,409 people in the hospital and almshouse, 800 were capable of receiving religious instruction, 1,000 more were admitted each year, and 200 died annually. For these many ill, destitute, and near-death souls, there was only one minister: Ely. "There are doubtless some, who enter these institutions with minds shrouded in ignorance, and hearts hardened in sin," Milledoler wrote, "to them, how necessary is it that divine instruction should be communicated, and one more effort made to snatch them from perdition. Such an attempt is intercepting them on the very borders of destruction." He continued:

> Whilst we explore far distant regions of missionary labour, shall we pass over our own fields, which are whitening to the harvest?...The soul of a pauper in the Almshouse of New-York, is as valuable, as the soul of an Indian on the banks of the Ganges.[103]

The term "whitening" here, to refer to the unsaved on American soil, contrasts suggestively with the notion that Americans should not invest so much energy on nonwhite foreigners overseas.

Another New York minister, Samuel Irenaeus Prime, painted the city's gambling dens, saloons, and brothels as gateways to hell in his 1846 *Life in New York*. Prime was an Old School Presbyterian who edited the *New York Observer*, a competitor to the pro-Finney revivalist newspapers. *Life in New York* was based on a series of sketches he wrote for the *Observer* in a long-running column titled the "Irenaeus Letters." While Prime did not share Finney's fame, he nevertheless reached thousands through his column and books, popularizing a conservative response to Finney's revivalism. Prime believed that conversions that resulted from dramatic tactics could only be short-lived and superficial.

Yet he did not shy away from scare tactics himself in his depiction of the city as hell. To Prime, heaven and hell were never abstract places but always connected to this-worldly realities. His Old School ideal was inspired by his childhood in the country, where small congregations were served by fatherly ministers who followed the seasons of their parishioners' lives,

awakening them through intensive seasons of prayer, but not then aban-
doning them to find other souls to save. His was not unlike the colonial
Old Side and Old Lights model, or Heman Humphrey's description of
Great Britain's ministers, who focused on "edifying the body of Christ."

Prime's ideal depended on a small and stable society where no one
moved, neither pastor nor parishioners. Still, he was not immune to the
demographic changes that spurred his revivalist counterparts: he himself
had relocated to the city for employment when poor health put an end to
his ministerial career. But even as he joined thousands of other Americans
on the move, he noted that a primary purpose of *Life in New York* was
that "the young in the country may learn the dangers that lurk in the city,
and keep away from their reach."[104] Prime bemoaned the selfishness of
city-dwellers and the anonymity that living in the city afforded, such that
people could go about their daily lives without knowing or caring what was
happening to their neighbors or neighborhood. "Look at the throngs of the
young," he lamented, "flocking in the broadest and slipperiest road that
leads to the bottomless pit. You can not step into Broadway after nightfall
without seeing them. They are tripping it down to the rayless dungeon of
eternal wo, as lightly and madly as if it were not the dance of death!... But
who cares! Who of the uncounted Christians of this proud city has the
burden of these wretched candidates for judgment on his conscience?"[105]
The self-absorbed, impersonal, vice-filled city was the polar opposite of the
intimate, communal, and wholesome countryside. Where one was a fore-
taste of heaven, the other was the very entry to hell.

Prime's description of a "Nocturnal Subterranean Excursion" offered
a lurid account of a visit to an underground dance hall. Prime drew on
the experiences of a friend and police officer to paint the scene in hellish
terms, as if he had been there himself. "On being informed that we were
on a pleasure excursion through his dominions," he wrote, the proprietor "threw open his infernal ballroom door" to reveal a "motley multitude of men and women, yellow and white, black and dingy, old and
young...there they were, a set of male and female Bacchanals dancing
to the tambourine and fiddle; giggling and laughing in a style peculiar to
the remote descendants of Ham"—a reference to the supposed "curse of
Ham" used to justify racial slavery. Like Ely and Milledoler, Prime then
compared these "Bacchanals" to the traditional targets of overseas missions, suggesting that the racially mixed "motley" in the demonic un-
derbelly of New York was as much, if not more, in need of missionary
efforts: "Talk of the degradation of the heathen; of savage pow-wows, and

pagan carnivals; and stir up sympathy for the slaves of sin in the depths of Africa and Asia," he wrote:

> Here we were...in the centre of the first city in the most Christian country on the earth.... and as the drinking and fiddling went on, the fury of the company waxed fiercer, until the scene was as unreal and bewildering as if we had been suddenly ushered into the revelling halls of the prince of darkness.[106]

Apologizing for going on at such length, Prime made clear his motive: "I wish to impress those who read, with the power of the truth, that there is beneath this city a mass of moral putrefaction, sufficient to bring out the worst plagues in the store of an offended God.... This picture ought to compel support, and greatly augmented support, for CITY MISSIONS."[107]

In addition to monetary contributions, what Prime wanted was for white country folk to be happy with their lot and stay in their villages where they were closed off from the "motley" temptations of the city. The problem that Finney and his followers addressed by itinerating and scaring people into conversions before they moved away, Prime tried to solve by telling them not to move in the first place. "Providence has a place for each of us," he affirmed, "and it is well if we have grace to find our place to keep it."[108]

Similar themes permeated Ned Buntline's popular 1848 *The Mysteries and Miseries of New York*. Buntline (the penname of Edward Z. C. Judson) was deeply enmeshed in the popular culture of his time.[109] In his brief stint as a reformer, he wrote this volume both as an exposé of the dirty underworld of the city and as a salacious and voyeuristic piece of popular entertainment, fictionalizing in gritty detail extreme poverty, gambling, prostitution, the plight of the "fallen" woman, and even abortion.

Buntline's Preface might have come straight from the pen of Ely, Milledoler, or Prime (though embellished as only an accomplished penny-press writer could):

> Should christians, those good and devout people who supply the sun-scorched Hottentots with woollen blankets...and send their missionaries there at an expense of millions to convert them to our ways...shudder at pictures which they see in the following chapters...I pray them to seek out the spots which I describe, and see for themselves whether missionaries are not more needed

here; aye, in the very centre of this great city, than in the far off
lands of India, or the isles of the South, where the heathen are
children in vice and degradation, when compared to the heathen
among us.[110]

That even Buntline weighed the "sun-scorched" "heathen" overseas
against the "heathen among us" is a measure of just how widespread
such comparisons had become by mid-century. Buntline's work reached
a large audience, and the success of the *Mysteries and Miseries of New York*
spawned sequels and imitations in other cities.

Western Ladders to Heaven and Hell

Still other ministers and organizations sought funding for western missions. Formed in 1826 to provide financial assistance to Presbyterian,
Congregational, and other Reformed denominations in the West, the
American Home Missionary Society (AHMS) soon expanded its vision,
making explicit the link between home missions, the welfare of the
nation, and the salvation of the world. As immigrants arrived not only
from Europe but also from Latin America and Asia, missionaries became
hyperaware of the immense opportunities and dangers awaiting them in
the West.

"The West is destined to be the great central power of the nation, and
under heaven, must affect powerfully the cause of free institutions and
the liberty of the world," wrote Lyman Beecher in his 1835 *Plea for the West*.
Sounding much like the Sandwich Islands missionaries but calling for
more than money and men, he continued: "Nor is it by tracts, or Bibles, or
itinerating missions, that the requisite intellectual and moral power can
be applied. There must be permanent powerful literary and moral institutions." Beecher and the American home missionaries hoped to create
stable western societies, including churches and educational institutions,
replicating what they saw as the best qualities of eastern life. Then, if the
pressures of industrialization and immigration adversely affected the
East, the virtue that supposedly flourished there in earlier times would not
be lost forever, but would instead thrive in western communities where
Easterners could reclaim what they had lost.[111]

Beecher and members of the AHMS fully realized that they were
not missionizing a blank and uninhabited frontier. They were trying to

impose Protestant institutions and cultural patterns on regions where Catholic missionaries had often already proselytized native populations and where newer Catholic immigrants were settling with their priests, who could wield the threat of hell as effectively as any Protestant.[112] In the 1850s Redemptorist and Jesuit priests brought the "parish mission" model from Europe, spending eight to fourteen days in local Catholic communities where they held morning and evening services that included masses, songs, and sermons on heaven and hell, reminding their hearers of the importance of confession.[113]

Anti-Catholic memoirs deplored the use of hell by Catholic priests, as if Protestants did not do likewise. Born Catholic in Charlesburg, Quebec, François Pepin moved to Detroit, Michigan, where he later converted to Methodism. In his memoir, Pepin noted that the threat of hell, as deployed by priests, had kept him Catholic for longer than he inclined. "I knew no other way," he wrote, "Protestantism I believed, was devil's religion; mine was the only true church, and all without her pale were hereticks and would surely go to hell. Where then could I go? What else could I do, but cleave to the Church of Rome?"[114] After his conversion, Pepin painted his former beliefs as just so much ignorance and superstition. The sensationalistic, widely discredited, but still wildly popular *Awful Disclosures, by Maria Monk, of the Hotel Dieu Nunnery of Montreal* (1836) likewise suggested that the threat of hell functioned to keep Catholics from leaving the fold: "Among the instructions given us by the priests, some of the most pointed were those directed against the Protestant Bible. They often enlarged upon the evil tendency of that book, and told us that but for it many a soul now condemned to hell, and suffering eternal punishment, might have been in happiness."[115] Although the memoir's authenticity was questioned almost from the start, it sold 300,000 copies in its first twenty-five years in print and shaped many readers' ideas about Catholicism.[116]

Catholic and Protestant damnatory polemics also took visual form. Catholic trappers and traders had lived among the indigenous peoples of the Pacific Northwest since the mid-eighteenth century. In 1838 Father Francis Norbert Blanchet and Father Modeste Demers arrived in the region from eastern Canada. To teach the basics of Catholicism to native and métis (the offspring of native women and French men) inhabitants speaking different languages, Blanchet devised a visual aid that came to be known as the Catholic ladder (fig. 2.5). The ladder, first constructed on a wooden stick and then on large paper sheets, showed the chronology of

FIGURE 2.5 Fr. Francis Norbert Blanchet, *Catholic Ladder* (detail), ca. 1840. 6 1/2 ×
58 in. Section from middle of ladder, showing the Crucifixion to the Protestant
Reformation.

Courtesy of The Oregon Historical Society, Image Number OrHi 89315.

sacred history from beginnings to the present through a series of bars and
simple pictures representing sacred events. There is no sign of heaven or
hell in the earliest extant Catholic ladder. The Reformation simply figures
as a wilted branch off the main course of sacred history, with three bars
standing for Luther, Calvin, and Henry VIII. Native people curious about
the religious practices and beliefs of their French Canadian relatives and
trading and trapping partners found the ladder helpful, and versions of it
remained in use until the 1880s.[117]

Protestant missionaries arrived in the region around the same time as
Blanchet. As winning native converts became a competitive enterprise, ex-
planatory ladders became more elaborate and polemical. A mere branch
representing the Reformation was hardly enough for another famous
Catholic missionary, Father Pierre-Jean de Smet. In 1843 he published
his own version of the Catholic ladder that was more explicit about the
Protestant/Catholic split. In the lengthy text accompanying his ladder, de

Smet wrote, "Jesus Christ comes to conduct us into the right road, and enable us to keep it by the grace of redemption. The devil is enraged at the loss he suffers; but he succeeded in the following ages, by inducing men to walk in a new, bad road, that of the pretended Reformation."[118]

Reacting against the Catholic depiction of the Reformation, two Protestant missionaries in present-day Idaho, Henry and Eliza Spalding, produced a ladder of their own sometime between 1840 and 1846 (fig. 2.6). Henry did not shy away from depicting their ladder as a direct response to the Catholics' in an 1846 letter to the Secretary of the American Board:

> They tell the people that Luther laid down his black gown & cross together & went off in the Road to hell after a wife & never returned & that all American preachers, *i.e.*, all Protestants are on the same road to destruction.

FIGURE 2.6 Henry H. and Eliza Spalding, *Protestant Ladder* (detail), ca. 1845. Section from top of ladder, showing Martin Luther on the "right" (directionally/morally) and narrow path to heaven, and the Pope on the wider, leftward path, falling into hell at the top of the image.

Courtesy of The Oregon Historical Society, Image Number OrHi 87847.

> To meet this attack I have planed & Mrs. S. has drawn & painted
> a chart about 6 feet long & 2 wide containing 2 ways, one narrow &
> one broad.[119]

Eliza drew the ladder with ink and colored dyes made from berries and natural pigments, and made multiple copies for Henry and native preachers to use. The right side of the ladder showed Martin Luther on a narrow path to heaven, while the Pope and his followers occupied the wider leftward path to a fiery hell where the Pope would eventually fall. Significantly, the Spaldings did not include Native American beliefs as a possible path leading to heaven or hell. To the Spaldings, the only options Native people had were to convert to Catholicism (and end up in hell), or Protestantism (and be saved for heavenly bliss). Their ladder is more detailed than Blanchet's, and the Spaldings noted that, when used by indigenous preachers, bigger crowds gathered: hardly a surprise, given the greater visual excitement it offered.[120]

An even more visually impressive ladder came from Canadian Catholic priest Albert Lacombe in the early 1870s, showing the roads to heaven, hell, and even purgatory in still greater drama and detail in a scroll measuring nearly six feet long and one foot wide (fig. 2.7). In contrast to the Spaldings' vision of the Pope falling into the fires of hell, this ladder showed the Pope sitting on a throne, pointing out the right path to heaven. Purgatory appeared on this ladder as a smaller version of hell, but on the path to heaven rather than a dead-end. By this point, lithography techniques had improved, allowing Lacombe to produce a ladder more sophisticated and comprehensive than previous missionary visuals. The Pope even endorsed the ladder, which was printed in tens of thousands of copies worldwide.[121]

As cultural contact and competition became more pronounced in the Pacific Northwest, then, missionary visuals evolved from a basic chronology to sacred directives showing the paths to misery or bliss. In their use of such images, Protestant missionaries borrowed from the Catholics against whom they were competing. Catholics had long relied more on the power of images, orality, and sacred drama than on the power of text alone.[122]

Our Country

Protestant missionaries in the West also had to contend with freethinking and unorthodox groups like the Deists and Universalists, who continued

FIGURE 2.7 Reverend Albert Lacombe, O.M.I., *Tableau-catéchisme/Pictorial cate-chism* (detail), 1874. Purgatory to the left, hell to the right, heaven above. Original at Missionary Oblates, Grandin Province Archives at the Provincial Archives of Alberta. Printed on four pasted panels glued together and backed with linen, at-tached to a stick, and rolled like a scroll.

Electronic image courtesy of the Department of Special Collections and University Archives, Marquette University Libraries.

to persuade, as well as with Campbellites, Mormons, and Millerites. As an AHMS correspondent put it, in the appropriately titled 1842 pamphlet, *Our Country; Its Capabilities, Its Perils, and Its Hope. Being a Plea for the Early Establishment of Gospel Institutions in the Destitute Portions of the United States,* "Many of the immigrants from Europe are the disciples of Hume and Voltaire.... Clubs and associations are found in almost all our towns on the rivers, and often elsewhere, zealous and active, and so well skilled in the arts of delusion as to lead many unwary and foolish youth astray."[123] How could missionaries hope to Christianize the West if infidelity and the "arts of delusion" seduced even those Americans who migrated there? European "disciples of Hume and Voltaire" were supposed to fall under the sway of well-behaving and correctly believing Protestant Americans, not the other way around.

The success or failure of missionaries in the West also had implications for missions abroad. As an article in *The Home Missionary* put it, "We are often reminded that *Foreign Missions* are dependent upon *Home Missions*."[124] America was supposed to set a good example for other countries and peoples to emulate, especially as those people began flocking to its western shores. Observing the California gold rush in the mid-nineteenth century, Reverend Isaac H. Brayton found the "assemblage" of men who came to the new state to be "a promiscuous one," including "men of every character" from the United States, all manner of European and Latin American immigrants, Sandwich Islanders, and "from China, thirty thousand idolaters." In the missionaries' worldview, Protestants could either save them from hell, or find themselves swept along to the eternal pit instead.[125]

In the pamphlet *Our Country*, the Executive Committee of the AHMS dramatized the "URGENCY OF THE PRESENT CRISIS IN THE WEST" and the responsibility of Easterners to defuse it. At the moment, the East wielded the greatest influence: "Here are the seats of science, and the schools of the prophets. And the Spirit of God is here, raining down righteousness upon our churches and literary institutions, and preparing many laborers for his harvest. Now, it is with us to give shape to the moral character of this country." But if the East failed to quickly convert the West, its influence would just as quickly decline. As the unchristianized (read: non-Protestant) populations of the "new and rising communities of the West and South" grew beyond those of the "older states," the Executive Committee warned, "they will roll back upon the East a tide of vice and irreligion; and who then shall plant anew her overwhelmed and desolated institutions? Our country is in danger, and the souls of present and unborn millions are in danger, while Christians all over the land, and Christian ministers, are suffering everything but Christianity to take root, and spring up and bear fruit on the fertile soil of the West. If, then, *we* do not now mould the West, it will soon mould *us*."[126] It was the fear of pollution writ large—from unbelieving neighbors, to dens of iniquity in the cities, to a vast and "irreligious" West and back again.

Underlying the temporal danger posed to the nation by an unchristian West was the eternal danger to the "souls of present and unborn millions"—the threat of hell not only for Americans in this and future generations but also for the "heathen" overseas, since the AHMS argued that the West would be the staging grounds for a missionary push to the rest of the world. Just as Finney had claimed that God elected those individuals who would be most easily converted and most influential in spreading Christianity, so the AHMS Executive Committee contended that God had chosen America first, to convert the rest of the world:

> To neglect the moral renovation of our own country is, therefore, a fraud upon a dying world.... How long shall the tribes of the earth move before our eyes, in sad procession, down to the shades of eternal death, because the hearts and the treasures of this land, which should be devoted to their rescue, are themselves, for the most part, yet unredeemed from the power of Satan?[127]

The idea that saving "heathens" depended on converting "pagans" within a Christendom that American evangelicals were attempting to extend from East to West revealed not only the evangelicals' chauvinism but also the anxious burden of their self-imposed responsibility to save their fellow Americans, and then the world, from the fires of hell. The question of whether oneself and one's fellow human beings would escape hell tied together the closeness of the city's poor and the remoteness of the "heathen" to the West and overseas. It empowered converts with great responsibility and threatened them with terrible punishment should they fail. This is what ministers and missionaries tried to convey to their flocks. And this is what laypeople responded to in shaping their lives around the doctrine.

PART TWO

Adaptation and Dissent

3

"Oh, Deliver Me from Being Contentedly Guilty"

LAYPEOPLE AND THE FEAR OF HELL

IN OCTOBER 1854, 12-year-old Mary ("Minnie") Corinna Putnam of New York City (fig. 3.1) sat down to pen a letter to her "Dear Grandmamma." A leader in the Baptist church, her grandmother had been encouraging Minnie to turn her thoughts to "salvation and eternal life." "You said for me to tell you how I first came to think on that all important subject," Minnie wrote. "It was three years ago. I began by making kind of experiments upon the power of God.... I presumingly prayed for anything almost that my own sinful heart dictated." But then Minnie came across some books "that were just the things for me": "It was as if the finger of Providence pointed them out to me.... They contained warnings, threats, denunciations of sin, fearful foretellings of the wrath to come. They aroused me out of my dangerous apathy."[1] On young Minnie, the fire and brimstone texts had the awakening effect that evangelical ministers desired.

Yet although the texts frightened her into "a habit of prayerfulness," this "tranquility of mind brought with it a fancied dangerous security." For, Minnie explained, "the books, though perhaps the right things for me, struck at the flowers, not at the root. They made me fear damnation, but not love Heaven, nor Christ, nor seek salvation through him." Minnie here showed her awareness of the distinction ministers drew between carnal fright and appropriate awe. Realizing that she had veered too far toward the former, "I began to apply the proofs of salvation to myself," and now "I know that my desire is not the selfish desire of which you speak, merely to be saved! I know it's the desire to love God and have eternal

FIGURE 3.1 Portrait of Mary Putnam Jacobi and her brother, George Haven Putnam, ca. 1847–49. 4 × 5 in. Mary Putnam Jacobi Papers: Photographs of MPJ. Courtesy of The Schlesinger Library, Radcliffe Institute, Harvard University.

life.... It seems strange to see people talking unconsciously of other affairs, instead of seeing the danger of waiting any longer."[2]

Minnie's letter illustrates the doctrinal awareness shared by lay believers, even the young: far from being passive dupes sitting in the pews, they discussed with each other, and for the most part understood, the nuanced distinctions between self-abnegation and self-effort, striving for heaven and striving to escape hell. Minnie's fear of damnation gave rise to a deepening sense of religious awakening; her concern that this fear was selfish impressed upon her the need for humility and repentance. She interpreted this humility, in turn, as a sign that she was finally oriented toward heaven. Still, her insistence that she was not interested in religion "merely to be saved" but to "love God and have eternal life" could be read as simply another way of phrasing the desire to escape the torments of hell.

That Minnie's "Grandmamma" served as her spiritual confidante highlights the communal concern laypeople shared for each other's souls. The idea that ordinary people could be responsible for their own and others' conversions empowered them to construct saved selves and communities that both reinforced and crossed boundaries of race, class, and gender. The categories of "saved" and "damned" complicated other shifting identities for Americans who listened to sermons, read evangelical texts, and applied the "proofs of salvation" to their hearts and habits. Theoretically, anyone could belong to the ranks of the saved, but in practice, middle-class conventions dominated evangelical directives. A woman's responsibility was to ensure that her family kept to the straight and narrow path. Men were to avoid worldly temptations while earning a living that enabled their wives to oversee the family's domestic and religious affairs.[3] Minnie's father was the publishing scion George Palmer Putnam; as a white child in a well-to-do family, she had the guidance of her grandmother, the benefit of literacy, and the luxury of time with which to read and ponder the state of her soul.

Some who did not fit the white middle-class ideal claimed salvation on their own terms. Not everyone could afford the time to scrutinize the state of their souls, and not everyone could successfully walk the line between anxiety and despair, hopeless guilt and excessive self-confidence. The evangelicals' often-paradoxical injunctions—apparent in Minnie's insistence that she sought salvation alone but did not seek merely to be saved—made the process of conversion difficult for some. While biological or other causes for mental distress were undoubtedly involved, records of insanity and suicide due to "religious anxiety" document the price that the fear of damnation could also extract. The celebrated antebellum religious marketplace was not an equal playing field. Although the separation of church and state meant that different religious groups had to compete for converts, evangelicals wielded a powerful weapon in the threat of hell.

Constructing Saved Souls

Evangelical leaders preached that only a change of heart could keep the sinner out of hell, but the shaping of the heaven-bound subject did not end at the moment of conversion.[4] Strict predestinarians held that the elect could never backslide, but the Arminian Methodists argued that backsliding was absolutely possible, and in practice most other evangelicals taught that the perceived experience of backsliding could mean that one had never truly converted in the first place. For laypeople, the avoidance of damnation was a matter of sustaining right belief and behavior throughout the seasons of life.

This was no easy task. One scholar has suggested that texts like John Bunyan's *The Pilgrim's Progress* and American imitators that took readers on didactic journeys through sins and their consequences worked to "inoculate" sinners against life's many temptations. The gritty realism of books like Samuel Prime's *Life in New York* and Ned Buntline's *Mysteries and Miseries of New York* sought not only to spur contributions to city missions but also to turn laypeople away from the vices they described. An early board game, the New Game of Human Life, taught explicit moral lessons: "Parents were instructed to play with their children and '...contrast the happiness of a Virtuous & well-spent life with the fatal consequences arriving from Vicious & Immoral pursuits.'" Laypeople could journey into depravity and taste its consequences imaginatively so they would not have to actually make the same mistakes in order to learn from them.[5]

Performative and visual aids played a similar didactic role. A long-running "Infernal Regions" exhibit in Cincinnati's Western Museum dramatically portrayed the hellish consequences of sin. The exhibit featured rotating wax figures with actors voicing the demons and Satan; its purveyors advertised the "good moral and religious purposes" it served. The actor portraying the devil warned audiences that "unless they behaved themselves properly he should have to claim them at some future time." The exhibit also displayed the real skeletons "of Malefactors Executed in Ohio, within the last 20 years, for their criminal offences." While the masterminds behind the exhibit (sculptor Hiram Powers and author Frances Trollope, mother of novelist Anthony) actually scorned evangelical revivalism's emphasis on fire and brimstone, a visitor recollected in 1854 that "it was, every evening, crammed by people who liked to be frightened and feel bad on purpose." Like Buntline's volume, the exhibit could be at once entertaining and instructive.[6] The same might be said of an undated and anonymous nineteenth-century folk carving of the "Flames of Judgment," a detailed wood sculpture that presumably served as both decoration and moral lesson (fig. 3.2).

Along the same lines, colorful and intricate temperance maps depicting the "Ocean of Life" (fig. 3.3) trained viewers to see that the path to damnation was hardly just a slippery slope—it was a veritable riptide towing the sinner from the first sip of grog to the channel of destruction. The apparent innocuousness and swift danger of water made it a potent metaphor for life's temptations in an era when waterways were primary transportation routes, and accidental drownings and shipwrecks not uncommon. The maps vividly showed that "Religion Channel" was just one strong current away from "Misery Regions" and the "Reprobate Empire," not only for seasoned tipplers but for all on the "Ocean of Life."

Taken together, sermons, tracts, temperance maps, missionary ladders, board games, and exhibits showed the many different consequences

FIGURE 3.2 *Flames of Judgment*, Artist Unidentified, Northeastern United States. Mid-nineteenth century, paint on wood. 11 1/8 × 7 1/4 × 2 1/4 in. Photographed by John Bigelow Taylor, New York ©2000.

Photo courtesy of Sotheby's.

of sin. But laypeople were never just passive consumers of this material. Ordinary people tried to navigate the twists and turns of their daily lives with careful precision. The more anxious prospective converts felt about the state of their soul, the more they hoped that salvation was on the way. And the more they acknowledged their guilt and hellworthiness, the more they took comfort in knowing that pride would not bar the entry to heaven. Feeling anxious and acknowledging sin were not simply passive states but exercises that evangelical laypeople could actively pursue as agents in their own salvation process.[7]

Like Minnie Putnam, many turned to the practice of writing to reflect on whether they belonged to the category of "saved" or "damned." They read exemplary memoirs like those penned by the ministers in the last chapter and sought to shape their lives in similar ways. That laypeople could adopt and circulate the same textual forms used by ministers signaled a theoretical openness to the "priesthood of all believers," though ministerial oversight put limits on spiritual equality.[8]

FIGURE 3.3 *Map on Temperance* (Boston: Howe's Sheet Anchors Press, 1846). Created by William Meacham Murrell; lithographed by Ephraim W. Bouvé.
Courtesy of John Hay Library, Brown University.

Martha Laurens Ramsay of Charleston, South Carolina, kept a diary that, like Minnie Putnam's letter, reveals her careful navigation of the currents of her soul. Ramsay, daughter of former Continental Congress president Henry Laurens, was well-read and counted Richard Baxter and John Locke among the authors she studied. In early June 1795 she wrote, "I can no longer say the skies are darkening, for they are so darkened that I see no light; and I am ready to call myself desolate, forsaken, cast off by God: yet, I dare not murmur, I am not in hell, where I deserve to be."[9] While we might take her feelings of desolation as a sign of evangelical "psychomachia" ("a psychological pilgrimage of incessant warfare against the self," as one scholar defines it[10]), her Hopkinsian resignation suggests that Ramsay took heart in feeling forsaken, reading it as a sign that she was not actually doomed since she was not guilty of presumption.

Ramsay also recorded her responses to the sermons she heard. Far from scoffing at fire and brimstone rhetoric, she at one point desired even more guilt-inducing oratory than the preacher offered. "I felt my heart so bowed down under a remembrance of past sins, and more especially of sins recently committed," she wrote on an August Sabbath in 1795, "that

I was ready to set myself down as a vile hypocrite, fit only for damnation, ripe for Hell, and so utterly unworthy of eating with the children of God, that I thought I must have staid at home in sorrow, and tears, and despair." Still, Ramsay went to service, where "Dr. Hollinshead's sermon was a very excellent and extensively encouraging one; but, alas, I fear I have more need of having my heart broken, than of having it comforted." In a veiled critique of the sermon, which she felt might lull her into a dangerous complacency, she concluded, "Oh, deliver me from being contentedly guilty." For Ramsay, acknowledging her guilt and resting in the conviction that she deserved hell provided more comfort than a comforting sermon.[11]

The pressure of sitting in the pews and acting outwardly Christian while inwardly tormented troubled another diarist, Mary Morton of Massachusetts. On October 23, 1810, she wrote, "What a solemn and awfully dangerous state is that of one, who has a name to live in the church of Christ, while destitute of true religion. Certainly the state of gospel hypocrites will be the most wretched of any of the inhabitants of the dark world of despair." Morton was not judging others but worrying about herself. "I think I have been this day near the borders of despair," she continued, "and have had a faint view of the anguish of the awakened hypocrite. I am as it were chained down by the sin of unbelief. My transgressions stare me in the face. I am undone completely as to any remedy in myself, and must eternally perish, unless sovereign mercy prevent." As the minister who edited and compiled Morton's writings approvingly noted, "The above extract . . . discovers great lowliness of mind; great fear of self-deception; and great sensibility to the evil of sin. . . . These expressions were not the mere effusions of her feelings in a moment of darkness and gloom."[12]

Ramsay's and Morton's diaries served as models for other laypeople to examine their spiritual lives. Just as ministers' manuals taught them how and when to disseminate the threat of damnation, so accounts of laypeople's conversions and religious lives published in books, tracts, and newspapers (often with much editorial intervention) provided patterns of appropriate belief and behavior for lay readers, especially women, most of whom could not aspire to the ministry.[13] Dr. Hollinshead, whose sermon Ramsay had found insufficiently guilt-inducing, explicitly noted his hope that her diary would "contribute much to the establishment and comfort of many pious exercised christians who walk in fear and darkness, for want of knowing how others have been affected in scenes of trial like their own.' "[14] Ramsay, Morton, and other models of female piety would likely have been pleased that their writings could serve a useful and salvific purpose for others after their deaths. Their diaries suggested that guilt did not simply disappear overnight. Although ministers could not always follow them through the ups and downs of their daily lives, laypeople could and should keep track of themselves, reenacting their conversions on a smaller scale as they ritualistically mortified themselves in order to feel comforted in their humility and to construct their souls as saved.[15]

Pious women were not the only ones navigating between anxiety and confidence. The 27,000 men who became ministers by mid-century reflect only a fraction of male investment in American Christianity. Theodore Dwight Weld, later a prominent abolitionist, did not become a minister but was nevertheless deeply influenced by evangelicalism. Groomed for the ministry, he left Andover Seminary due to ill health in 1820, just one year after starting. Even while at the seminary, he had not yet experienced a change of heart. It would take another six years and much opposition before none other than Charles Finney converted him. Weld had heard of Finney and scoffed at his dramatic measures, but his aunt one day tricked him into attending a sermon on how "One Sinner destroyeth much good." Feeling that Finney was referring to him and had "held [him] up on a toasting-fork before that audience," he reacted with overt hostility. But the guilt he felt on publicly abusing Finney the day after the sermon led, finally, to the breaking of his pride, his wholehearted conversion, and the complete reversal of his feelings, even to the point of becoming the foremost lay promoter of Finney's revivals.[16]

But Weld still worried over the state of his soul. He was luckier than most: while Finney often elicited conversions and then left, Weld could continue to communicate with his mentor directly. In an April 22, 1828, letter to "My dear father in Christ," he complained that "I make slow headway beating up against the wind and tide of my wicked heart. My easy besettings are strong besettings. Pride you know is one of the chiefest with me. It makes dreadful havoc in my soul. It would lay it in ruins every day, but for Christ's strengthening." In an age when masculine self-sufficiency could lead to success in the marketplace, manly pride over one's merits and accomplishments was not necessarily considered sinful. But for the Christian convert, pride could suggest dangerous self-sufficiency rather than ultimate reliance on God. Weld feared falling into the trap of attributing revival successes to his own efforts.

He warned Finney, too, not to become so confident in his ability to spark revivals that he treated them almost as a "trade," "machinery," or "formality." He asked Finney to ponder his own state: "Has no sin any dominion over you?...My dear father in Jesus, you are in such a maddening whirl of care, responsibility and toil, I do dreadfully fear that you neglect the culture of personal holiness." He urged Finney to "retire alone at least for an hour...and enter into the secret chambers [of] your soul and solemnly debate this matter with your conscience in the fear of God. Oh break up the fallow ground of your heart and desist not from effort till satan is bruised under your feet."[17] The devil could still tempt the convert, and even one as important as Finney could backslide.

Shaping Saved Women and Men

In addition to the practice of reflecting and writing on their guilt and repentance, evangelical laywomen and men also shaped their identities as "saved" through the use of guidebooks that explained how best to behave.[18] Just as ministers' manuals harnessed the energy of earlier revivalists for a professionalizing clergy, so lay advice texts channeled the emotional exuberance of the conversion experience into the day-to-day steps necessary to live as "saved" women and men. While fire and brimstone did not feature as prominently in these guides as in those intended for ministers, readers primed by hellfire sermons and conversionist pamphlets and newspapers might nevertheless discover ominous warnings between the lines.

Catharine Beecher's influential *A Treatise on Domestic Economy for the Use of Young Ladies*, for instance, encouraged women to treat their "peculiar responsibilities" in the domestic sphere as serious business. First published in 1841, Beecher's *Treatise* saw multiple reprints over the next several decades. As Americans began to adorn their homes with imported goods and to emulate the latest fashions from Europe,[19] Beecher warned women not to fritter their time away on clothing and appearance, "household furniture and ornaments," and fancy foods. "No woman has a right to put a stitch of ornament on any article of dress or furniture, or to provide one superfluity in food," she instructed, "until she is sure she can secure time for all her social, intellectual, benevolent, and religious, duties." Beecher encouraged her readers to pursue "*a habit of system and order*" following "*general principles*" "based on Christianity, which teaches us to 'seek first the kingdom of God,' and to place food, raiment, and the conveniences of life, as of secondary account." The saved woman ordered her life not only because it was domestically pleasing but also because she would be judged for it: "for the right apportionment of time," Beecher explained, "we are to give an account at the final day."[20]

Some women and girls took such warnings to heart. In his children's book on the "heathen," missionary John Scudder cited the testimony of a little girl who "used to think a great deal about having nice clothes, before I thought so much about the heathen." The girl wrote to Scudder:

> My mother told me some time ago, that she thought she would get me a white dress when I was ten years old. I am now ten years old, and this evening mother gave me two dollars to get the dress, or dispose of it in any way I thought best; and I wish you would take it to have the poor heathen taught about the Saviour. If I live, and it is the Lord's will, I hope I shall come and help you teach the poor heathen about the Saviour.[21]

Scudder hoped that other readers would follow the exemplary child's lead and renounce finery in favor of saving the "heathen."

Similarly, in his *Memoirs*, Finney recounted the exemplary conversion of a "Mrs. Gillett" during a revival in Rome, New York. As the sister of a missionary, she had been exposed to evangelical precepts prior to Finney's arrival and already felt "that she was not one of the elect, and that there was no salvation for her." Finney described her as "a woman of refinement, and fond of dress... nothing, however, that I should have thought of as being any stumbling-block in her way, at all." According to Finney, Mrs. Gillett cast all her anxieties on him when he came into town: "She was evidently going fast to despair; but I could see that she was depending too much on me; therefore I tried to avoid her." One scholar has interpreted such interactions of avoidance and discomfort as evidence that antebellum women were basically "without benefit of clergy."[22] Finney, though, portrayed his avoidance of Mrs. Gillett as a purposeful strategy to make her stop relying on him and seek conversion for herself. That is exactly what she did. While Finney had seen her fondness for ornaments as innocuous, Mrs. Gillett decided on her own that it was keeping her from conversion. "I thought... God did not care about such trifles," she told Finney. "This was a temptation of Satan."[23] Mrs. Gillett embodied the discipline Catharine Beecher called for in her *Treatise*. The saved woman was supposed to be industrious, efficient, and plain; by contrast, her damned counterpart was indolent and flashy.

Advice guides warned men against falling for the seductive wiles of the painted woman.[24] Catharine's famous brother Henry Ward Beecher, in his *Seven Lectures to Young Men* (1844), described the "Strange Woman" as adorned in "Silks and ribbons, laces and rings, gold and equipage; ah! how mean a price for damnation." Henry's generic "Strange Woman" was already beyond salvation; his warning focused on men. The youth foolish enough to be enticed by her superficial glamor entered none other than the "Chariot of Death,—drawn by the fiery steeds of lust which fiercely fly."[25] Men could also be tempted by finery for themselves: the character of the dissolute, foppish dandy was a staple of popular literature and advice guides alike. The villain in Royall Tyler's 1787 play, *The Contrast*, for instance, was "a flippant, pallid, polite beau, who devotes the morning to his toilet."[26]

Minister John Todd's bestselling *The Student's Manual* (1835) taught young men who were leaving home for the first time how to exercise self-control in order to stay on the straight-and-narrow path. Todd told students how to eat ("It is the *quantity*, rather than the kinds of food, which destroys students"), how to exercise ("It must be regular, and daily"), and even how to take care of their teeth to avoid bad breath and premature decay ("cleanse them with a soft brush and with water, in which a little common salt is dissolved").[27] All of this, Todd noted, was but prelude to the "most important" work: the "Discipline of the Heart": "bringing it into subjection to the will of God." Citing the youthful resolutions of Jonathan Edwards and a pious young college man, Todd urged his reader to vow to "make religion my chief concernment" and determine "never to lose one moment time, but to improve it in the most profitable way I possibly can."[28]

Young minds, he warned, were particularly susceptible to "skepticism and infidelity"; the proliferation of Deist and other "infidel" texts made it all too easy for them to fritter away their time reading "bad books" and endangering their souls.[29] "I do entreat my young readers never to look at one—never to open one. They will leave a stain upon the soul which can never be removed," he wrote. "And if you have an enemy, whose soul you would visit with a heavy vengeance...and whose damnation you would seal up for the eternal world, you have only to place one of these destroyers in his hand."[30] Todd went on to list some of the questions posed by "infidel writers," apparently negating his own injunction never to even open such a book: "'Why was sin permitted?—What an insignificant world is this to be redeemed by the incarnation and death of the Son of God!—Who can believe that so few will be saved?'" These were the same kinds of issues raised by "Salvation" Murray and others who questioned the justness of predestination and eternal hell for so many. A student might easily have read Todd's book and agreed that these were, in fact, difficult questions. But Todd dismissed them as unworthy of consideration, "jejune and refuted," and raised only by inferior men.[31]

"What sort of men are infidels?" he asked. "They are loose, fierce, overbearing men. There is nothing in them like sober and serious inquiry. They are the wildest fanatics on earth."[32] The saved man, by contrast, exercised admirable self-control and made good use of his time in order to direct his energies—intellectual and physical—toward a single goal. "*Let it be your immediate and constant aim to make every event subservient to cultivating the heart,*" Todd exhorted. "Every thing, every circumstance in our condition, is designed by Infinite Wisdom as part of our moral discipline.... Every indulgence of vice, every neglect of duty, strengthens the habits and propensities to do wrong and to go astray."[33] Here, in a nutshell, was the reason why the convert had to keep examining himself throughout the ups and downs of daily life: to shape himself into a self-made and disciplined Christian man and to shun the many vices that continued to imperil his eternal welfare, from opening an infidel book, to tasting a sip of grog or failing to control his carnal inclinations.

Nor was it only the writings of freethinkers that advice texts warned against. ATS Tract No. 493, "Beware of Bad Books," cautioned readers that "books of fiction, romance, infidelity, war, piracy, and murder" "*are one of the most fruitful sources of eternal destruction....* Foundations of morality are undermined. The fatal arrow is fixed in the soul, while the victim only sees the gilded feather that guides its certain aim. He is lost, and descends to a hell the more intolerable, from a contrast with the scenes of fancied bliss with which the heart was filled by the vile, though gifted destroyer." Instead of whiling away their time reading novels, the tract urged readers that time is more than money—it "is *eternity!*...The Holy Spirit has not bestowed upon us the book divine, that we might flit from flower to flower like the butterfly, neglecting all the ends of rational and immortal being, and go to the judgment mere triflers."[34]

Seeking Saved Families and Communities

Self-control and diligence also enabled saved individuals to direct their extra time toward the salvation of their families and communities, as ministers repeatedly urged. Catharine Beecher tied a woman's domestic economy to the welfare of the nation: "The success of democratic institutions, as is conceded by all," she wrote, "depends upon the intellectual and moral character of the mass of the people. If they are intelligent and virtuous, democracy is a blessing; but if they are ignorant and wicked, it is only a curse."[35] Where "Damnation" Murray had warned that the health of the nation depended on its citizens' constant awareness of the threat of hell, Beecher suggested that the success of American democracy depended on women's ability to ensure the virtue of their families and communities. She did not wield hell's horrors with as heavy a hand, but the final judgment was still an essential part of her framework. Just as women would be held accountable for the "right apportionment of time" at an individual level, she wrote, so they must also "use [their] influence and example to promote the discharge of the same duty by others.... If, by late breakfasts, irregular hours for meals, and other hinderances of this kind, she interferes with, or refrains from promoting regular industry in others, she is accountable to God for all the waste of time consequent on her negligence."[36] Even the most mundane affairs took on eternal import when viewed through the lens of accountability. Families, communities, and even the nation were to be formed along the same industrious lines as the saved individual. Antebellum Protestants did not emphasize discipline for the sole purpose of molding good workers, even if that was not an unwelcome side effect. Discipline freed the time needed to devote to their own and others' salvation in the midst of their busy lives, an ever more important necessity as "religion" was coming to seem increasingly separate from the "secular" world of commerce and politics (even as religious discipline underlay the same).[37]

Women were often at the forefront of lay efforts at saving souls. Even as Martha Ramsay daily struggled to find personal peace, she also worried that the cares of everyday life imperiled her loved ones' eternal welfare. In September 1795, she asked God for "the thorough conversion of a very near and dear friend" and "that my dear husband may be preserved from worldly entanglements, and enabled so to manage his earthly affairs, that they may never interfere with his heavenly business."[38] Ten years later she continued to express similar concerns:

> My husband is under trials and straits, which make my heart ache for him, and for myself.... My children, though in many respects, sources of great delight to me, cause me also much anxiety for their souls, and for their future temporal welfare.

She ended the entry with an expression of the longing for communal salvation that provided believers in hell with spiritual relief: "Let me cry for nothing importunately but salvation. Salvation for myself and for those who are near and dear to me as my own soul; and O Lord! let the joys and the hopes of this salvation, keep thy poor servant from being desolate."[39]

Mary Morton also tried to encourage those around her. "How can it be that christians, who have themselves been made partakers of the blessings of the gospel, can be indifferent about the souls of others," she marveled in a diary entry. "Sure it is a very unfavorable mark."[40] If she could not become a minister, Morton could marry one, and in 1812 she became the second wife of the Reverend Elijah Dexter. Shortly before her marriage, in a letter to "Miss S.H.," a recent convert, she sought to subtly pass on her understanding of the Christian's responsibility. "I sometimes hope I have some small discoveries of the glory of the gospel salvation, and am filled with astonishment that I can live so amazingly stupid," she wrote. Imagine the check on the new convert's joy when she read that even a soon-to-be pastor's wife experienced continued spiritual "stupidity." Morton went on:

> Yet I feel that it is important for others [to be converted], even if I myself should be a castaway. The souls of others are of equal value, and eternal life will be to them equally precious; and their superior talents for usefulness perhaps makes it more desirable that they should embrace the gospel.... Nothing will shut the soul out of heaven but persevering impenitence. Whom then will the condemned sinner find to accuse as the cause of his damnation? Will not his mouth be stopped by a consciousness that he has been his own destroyer?[41]

Morton here showed her Hopkinsian willingness to be damned. She also anticipated Finney's suggestion that God elects those who are most easily converted and most useful in helping to save others. The implication for "Miss S.H." was to compare herself to the professedly "stupid" Morton and not become overly prideful in her own apparent conversion. Constructing a saved community required that individual members constantly remind themselves that "the souls of others are of equal value," never resting on their own laurels in their attempt to extend the community from self to family to friends.

Some women looked beyond the immediate circle of their loved ones. Such a one was Elizabeth Willard, whose early religious career focused on the evangelization of the near and dear and progressed to distributing tracts to wider audiences by the 1860s. Elizabeth was in her late twenties with two young children when she took up her husband's old account book "for the purpose of treasureing up some of the dealings of God with my Soul."[42] Unlike Morton's and Ramsay's devotional diaries, Willard's was never published. Still, she recorded her thoughts, feelings, and religious exercises in at least as much detail.

Willard's early entries record her interactions with neighbors in Oswego, Indiana. She and husband Rowland, a western adventurer and physician, had relocated there from Covington, Kentucky, where they had helped found Western Baptist Theological Institute. In her first entry, dated July 30, 1842, Elizabeth noted that she had conversed with a neighbor over "her soul's condition." She had sought to persuade the neighbor of the "reasonableness" of the Ten Commandments and the consequences of "the sin of breaking them," and believed that her words had had at least some saving effect. A few months later she worried that, of the many children in the Deacon's family, "not one gives evidence of a change of heart. The father and mother are esteemed very pious. This I have thought a very strange thing. I have tried to be faithful with two of them. They seem rather disposed to hear yet no disposition to do. O Lord my hope is in thee. Work thou! or they perish soul and body in hell." Since the parents' influence was apparently ineffective, Willard herself intervened. She found the children willing to listen, but not to act on the warnings she gave. "Lord I pray thee let it not be thus with my dear Children," she concluded the entry.[43]

The following year, Willard expressed interest in the teachings of erstwhile Baptist William Miller, who predicted that Christ's return was imminent (a theological position known as premillennialism). If this was true, people must be saved before Christ came to take His own and leave the rest. "I have not considered this subject much until lately," Elizabeth wrote on New Year's Day 1843, but

> I rejoice in the thought that he may speedily appear to end this scene of suffering and take his people to be ever with him. but O when I look around me, and over the earth, my heart sinks within me. O the untold number that ~~will~~ would, by such an event, be swept (^as) by the a besom ~~of~~ to destruction. ~~to endless woe!!~~[44]

The insertions and strikeouts in this passage were made with a writing implement different from that used for the original entry; someone (likely

Elizabeth herself or Rowland) may have tried to tidy the manuscript for publication. That the besom *of* destruction, sweeping the sinner "to endless woe," became a besom *to* destruction was no accident. Rowland would eventually abandon his belief in hell as an eternity of torment in favor of the complete destruction of the wicked, a position known as annihilationism. Elizabeth's own views are less clear; she seems to have wavered between annihilationism and eternal damnation.[45] In the early 1840s, however, both still believed that Christ's coming would speed the descent of unbelievers into hell. As Elizabeth later recalled, "I did what I could to persuade all my acquaintances, and every one, over whom I had any influence to prepare to meet our Blessed Lord."[46]

Although Miller's prophecies failed to come true, Elizabeth was hardly fazed. Her continued belief in premillennialism solidified her confidence in her own escape from "certain ruin." As she became ever more committed to her faith, her concern for the eternal welfare of others spread to wider fields. In late 1852 she wrote an obituary for a young Mrs. Smith, published for the benefit of the "RESPECTED FRIENDS OF OSWEGO" in the *Kosciusko Republican*:

> As I stood by her suffering couch and witnessed her utter inability to reason or reflect, or even to express her desires, I felt, as I never felt before, the importance of a life of holiness, as a preparation for such a dreadful hour.
>
> In view of such scenes, who among us can remain indifferent while unreconciled to God! My spirit has been stirred within me to try to be more faithful; and this is my humble apology for thus addressing you at this time....
>
> O let not such loud calls be unanswered by us! Let us not procrastinate the GREAT WORK OF LIFE, in the vain hope of doing it in a few fleeting dying breaths![47]

Any antebellum evangelical minister might have written this rather terrifying eulogy. Heman Humphrey would certainly have approved. That its author was a premillennialist laywoman in a small town in Indiana shows how prevalent was the idea that sudden death could lead to hell for the unprepared and unconverted. Laypeople did not just quietly receive ministers' warnings. A marginalized woman like Elizabeth Willard could not easily aspire to the ministry, but she could act on her feelings of responsibility for others by publishing an altar call to cease procrastinating in eternal affairs.

By the 1860s Willard's zeal for saving souls had become so great that some considered her "crazy in religion." The responsibility to save as many as possible weighed as heavily on her as on any minister. While continuing to evangelize family and friends, Elizabeth (who now lived in Hammonton, New Jersey, with Rowland) passed out religious tracts at the local depot and to people she encountered along the way. Despite these efforts, she never felt completely satisfied that she had done enough. Random strangers slipped through her grasp, as she could not always muster the courage to hand out tracts to them. Her laments ring through her journal—from "big tears of penitence" that she would not wipe away in order to "witness to my grief that I had not done all I could to win souls to Christ,"[48] to anxiety over her feeling that still more work awaited her. "O I do feel if I can do my duty to my fellow men," she wrote in April 1862, "& clear my skirts of the blood of souls, I will not faint at the road by which I am to accomplish it."[49] By 1863 she had begun to distribute tracts amongst "Afric's sable sons" in Egg Harbor, New Jersey, a train ride away. Willard also exhorted the free black population directly, reminding them that "Those who have done good" would be raised to "the resurrection of life & those who have evil to the resurrection of damnation."[50]

Willard could be considered a religious zealot whose premillennialism set her apart from the nation's more numerous postmillennialist evangelicals, but her trajectory was hardly unique for a serious lay believer in the convert's responsibility to save others from hell. In the antebellum evangelical worldview, the work of women like Ramsay, Morton, and Willard was not just sentimental or compensatory. Their belief that unrepentant sinners were destined to fiery torment gave their lives a real sense of urgency and purpose, a cause that sanctified their domestic economy and "deliver[ed them] from being contentedly guilty." While male revivalists increasingly styled themselves as professional doctors of souls, women provided much of the behind-the-scenes influence that made the conversions of men possible in the first place, by ordering their domestic lives to leave them time for religious affairs, praying for their salvation, handing them tracts, and serving as essential partners in mission work.

Even Theodore Dwight Weld, whose conversion so famously happened at the hands of Charles Finney, had been primed for the occasion by his mother. In a letter dated February 26, 1826, Elizabeth Weld modeled for him the convert's struggle with pride and submission. "When adverse breezes fan us, may we quietly submit," she wrote. "Whatever my appearance or conversation may indicate at times...still I have seasons when I hope my proud heart can say 'it is well.'" Elizabeth then noted that she had "heard of the revival at Utica—hope our friends there will be sharers." Of course, she was most concerned about her own son, using soft but firm pressure to encourage his conversion: "We hope and pray too that our dear Theodore may not be left to witness, to wonder, and perish. You have not forgotten the counsel of your dying Uncle—'Theodore it is a great thing to die, think of it.'"[51] Finney's preaching might have been the turning point for Weld, but his family's concern had prepared him to receive it.

If women's care lay behind the drama of immediate conversions spurred by male revivalists, both united in seeking communities of the saved that included an equal balance of the sexes. Men were prime targets of antebellum evangelical concern.[52] In his *Accounts of Religious Revivals in Many Parts of the United States from 1816 to 1818*, Joshua Bradley noted that a Fair-Haven congregation had "only four males, and twenty five females" in 1816. The arrival of a revivalist from Georgia ignited some religious excitement, and a "leading man" of the town persuaded his fellow residents to join him in investigating its promises. This man had recently witnessed a revival in New York that "he observed was not confined to women and children, and men of weak minds: but men of the first characters, and talents."[53] Bradley may well have embellished here to emphasize to readers that revivals were not just women's work or child's play.

The "leading man" admitted that he "had doubts respecting the divinity of the scriptures, and the truth of religion," but

> said he would unite with [the townspeople], and make a thorough inquiry. If after a faithful, impartial and thorough examination, they should find that religion was a farce, heaven an imaginary good, and hell a bug-bear, they would give themselves no more trouble about it. But if they found those things to be realities . . . they would give all diligence to obtain an interest in them. If they were important to one, they were to all. And if they were any thing, they were every thing.

Whether the "leading man" actually uttered these exact words, Bradley clearly wanted his readers to see how the promise of heaven and threat of hell could take on communal importance. Just as women were to encourage their families to convert so they could all be saved, so Bradley's "leading man" used his influence to encourage his community to examine the claims of religion jointly. The questions he suggested they focus on pertained to the "immortality of the soul," "man's accountability," the "truth of the scriptures," and the "future state of retribution." After some investigation, "They found," Bradley claimed, "that it was high time to attend to the concerns of eternity, and secure the salvation of their immortal souls."[54]

The "leading man" was especially worried about his own soul. According to Bradley, he felt that God might be "making an instrument of him" for the salvation of others, but feared that "he himself should be cast down to hell." To whom did he turn in his anxiety but a neighbor's pious wife, "and requested her to pray for him," another case of how a woman's quiet example could influence the men around her. But she refused: "She told him that he must pray for himself. He said, he was so wicked he could not pray." In refusing, she acted like male revivalists who turned away from the struggling in order to force them to submit to Christ alone. After his own wife held a well-attended prayer meeting at his house, the "leading man" finally experienced a sense of calm, and the next morning "felt reconciled to [God] through Jesus Christ." Bradley shaped the account at Fair-Haven into an exemplary narrative. The "leading man"'s conversion and the reported impact of revival on his village demonstrated an idealized interplay of women's and men's religious labors. Male clergy and laymen had more public influence and opportunities to travel and network, and thus were able to spark general interest in revivals across towns and churches. But in the depths of their own anxiety they turned to women for prayer and spiritual sustenance.[55]

Struggling for Salvation in the West

Antebellum communities were hardly ever stable and it was not possible for all laypeople with evangelical aspirations to participate in the ideal revivals described by Bradley. Some had to move in search of work or simply preferred amusement over constant self-scrutiny and anxiety in their spare time. The values the Beechers, Todd, and others sought to inculcate came most easily to middle-class families who could afford for women to stay at home and whose men labored in steady occupations that allowed them to leave their work behind in the evenings and on the Sabbath.

A lower-class white layman seeking his fortune out West might nevertheless try to shape himself into a self-controlled middle-class man in community with like-minded evangelicals. Born in the mid-1830s, Frederick Niles could not become a minister or missionary because of his "weak" eyes (so he said) and probably also because of his familial and financial situation: his absentee "poor impenitent" father had sought his fortune in the California Gold Rush, only to establish another family there and never return. Niles's mother and sister Ellen lived in a small log cabin in Indiana; Ellen's husband had set off for Pike's Peak in search of gold and she labored to support the family. When he visited after a five-year absence, Niles was shocked to see how much she had aged. (Catharine Beecher's decorous manual would have meant little to this impoverished woman—she had lost her front teeth and could hardly have afforded to waste time or money on fine clothes and ornaments.) Instead of acting on his ministerial aspirations, Niles worked a variety of odd jobs to make ends meet, from pruning plants in a nursery to teaching at a boys' school in the Pennsylvania area. In mid-1859 he followed in his father's and brother-in-law's footsteps, heading first to Pike's Peak and making it as far as California before eventually returning to New York.[56]

Although he could not become a minister or even join a church permanently during his wanderings, Niles filled his diary with approving comments about sermons he heard, disapproving observations about his unbelieving neighbors, and worries about the eternal salvation of his family members, particularly his father. On March 6, 1859, before he left home, he reported that he had "heard an excelant sermon from the text 'Be not weary in well doing for in due time you shall reap if you faint not' By Elder Henbrick_ it very much encouraged me to continue in striving with God, to have mercy upon my poor impenitent Father, and his family." Niles believed that he could help save his father's soul through prayer. "O," he continued, "...that I may yet be blessed with the happy_ news that my Father is borne again, & have the blessed privilige of uniting with the Angels in heaven, in rejoicing over a new-born soul." He feared that his father might die an unbeliever in far-off California, making a future reunion impossible not only in this world but also in the next.[57]

Niles was well aware of unbelievers around him and welcomed sermons that applied the threat of future punishment to their unsaved souls. On March 13, 1859, while he was still teaching school, he recorded his impressions of a sermon by a "Rev. Mr. Blakeslee":

It was just such a[^n] one as I have long been desirous of hearing _ a doctrinal one. Showing how some were elected by God, to be his

chosen people; while others were as vessels of wrath fitted to destruction—made so by their owne obstinacy and hardness of heart_
and their rejection of Gods mercies sent to warn them of sin, of
righteous[^ness], & [^of] a judgment to come.

This was just the kind of sermon Martha Ramsay might have welcomed to
arouse her from "contented guilt." Niles wrote more about religion than
most ordinary laymen but he was hardly an elite theologian with seminary
training. He was an equal opportunity evangelical congregant, listening
to Baptist, Methodist, Presbyterian, Congregationalist, and Episcopal sermons. He still clearly understood the doctrinal content of this one, with
its distinctive New Divinity-esque modifications to the concept of election.
He concluded:

> It was a very solemn and heart searching sermon, & it does not
> seem possible that any one could listen to it unmoved. I sincerely
> hope and pray that it may be the means under God of rousing up
> more than one, who heretofore has sought security in his sins._
> For, seeking security in ones sins, is like hiding in that which will
> eventually be the fuel for the fire that is unquenchable_ and food,
> for the worm that dieth not.[58]

Although he hoped for the salvation of sinners in the abstract, Niles
also at times depicted himself as a persecuted believer and those around
him as unruly antagonists whose behavior jeopardized their future welfare. He rejoiced when he closed his school "for good" on March 26,
1859, because he would "now no more [be] the object of the malice, of
wicked boys." These "young rowdies," as Niles called them, tormented
the young 23-year-old teacher even after he closed the school by "slam-
ming the benches about the house, kicking the doors, & throwing sticks
against the house." They enacted an active and unrestrained masculinity
that ran counter to Niles's evangelical self-control. "May God have mercy
upon them," Niles closed the entry, "before, they shall become so hardened in sin that they will be beyond the reach of mercy. _ _"[59] Perhaps
Niles did sincerely wish for the conversion and eventual salvation of these
"rowdies," but he also seems to have taken some pleasure in contemplating the ultimate punishment they would face unless they curbed their
boisterous behavior. The boys' lack of respect for his pious authority
should not be taken as a sign that evangelicalism and its threats of doom

for the unbelieving and misbehaving were on the outs by mid-century. Unruly schoolboys were hardly a new phenomenon in 1859. We might instead read Niles's discussion of the "young rowdies" as an example of the success of an evangelical philosophy that divided the world into the saved "us" versus the unsaved "them." Rather than indulging them as typically rambunctious adolescents, Niles saw the schoolboys as potentially hellbound.

If Niles thought that he could escape rowdiness and impenitence by traveling West, he was wrong. Although he reveled in the mildness of the western weather, thoroughly enjoyed the rolling prairie landscapes, and admired the plainspoken sermon of a "real Backwoods man" at a packed Methodist Episcopal quarterly meeting in Indiana, he also bemoaned the infidelity he witnessed among his peers. "Our Bible class turned_ into a warm debate, on doctrinal subjects_ nothing good came out of it, I fear,"[60] he wrote in December 1859, soon after heading to Kansas and Nebraska Territory for the gold rush. A temperance man, Niles also railed against drunken passersby: "O what an argument against this place _ when will the time come when those who robb. their fellow men of their money their, c[^h]arachter & their souls eternal welfare be justly delt with, & what will man not do for the sake of Mammon." He saw the suppliers of alcohol as greedy thieves and soul-murderers, just as deserving of eternal punishment as the drinkers themselves: instead of spreading salvation, as the convert was supposed to do, they spread hell in a bottle (for Niles, not just a figure of speech!).[61] And he also looked with horror upon the violence with which western men sometimes resolved their differences. "O what is this world coming to when men can thoughtlessly send their fellows trembling before their Maker, with all their sins and iniquities upon their head," he wrote after a double homicide over illegal voting in Nebraska.[62]

Niles missed the regularity of church services in the West, vowing to remain steadfast despite the lack of religious infrastructure.[63] Like the home missionaries who worried that the West might succumb to bad influences, so Niles worried that the West might turn him and other fortune-seekers for the worse. "I have just been listening to the sad history of a fellow mortal who has once stood high in the church," he noted at the end of May 1861, and "...who is now, as he says, hopelessly in the clu[^t]ches of Satan." Business, it seems, got in the way of religious observance: "he marked his first step, from the fold of god, as being taken when he neglected the prayer meeting on plea of business, next the class meeting, next the preached word then family & secret prayer._ _ _ then all was gone." Many men who traveled west did not have the company of a wife like Martha Ramsay to encourage them not to let their earthly affairs interfere with heavenly priorities. Although this "fellow mortal" tried to return to the fold, "the darkens [*sic*] appears the cloud that hangs between his Soul & his maker & he expects to go on down the hill of destruction until he has gained its base," Niles wrote. "O what a dreadful state of mind is their no peace, no happiness in any nook or corner of the earth for him. a hopeless despare has settled upon him- and he awaits his doom ~~like one~~ and ta[^l]ks of it with the hardened calmness of ~~one going to the scaffold.~~[^a desperado]."[64]

The ease with which this backslider tumbled down the "hill of destruction" made Niles anxious about the state of his own soul. He concluded, "O may I take timely warning _ and watch my life lest I like him _ begin the downward career by neglecting my christian duties _ _ which I have been very strongly tempted to do—and fear—in some instances have in part yielded...to the voice of the tempter _ _....."[65] The trailing dashes and dots evoke the anxiety aroused by the thought that the saved could yield to the power of temptation and be damned. As much as Niles tried to differentiate himself from hellbound "young rowdies," drunkards, murderers, and mammon-chasers, he also worried that he might become like the very people he condemned.[66] The year before he had already noted "how dead and cold is religion in the West." "My owne heart has grown cold in a measure, from surrounding influences," he admitted, describing how weary he had grown in the "Heavenly race" though he had once thought he might easily persevere until the end. "How true it is that man cannot worship God & mammon."[67]

Niles sought consolation and reassurance in private devotions and whatever Sabbath services he could attend, and tried to disseminate the gospel's warnings and promises himself. When populist Christians (with roots in the Cane Ridge revivals of early nineteenth-century Kentucky) made inroads into Nebraska, Niles jumped aboard and tried to create a Sunday School. "I do hope I may succeed in starting or helping to start a S.S. that will be the means of saving the precious youth of this town from the vortex of ruin that is just before them," he wrote, "& from ^[following] the examples of some of their parents—."[68] As he journeyed further westward, he continued to seek out worship services and assist in Sunday School efforts aimed at saving youths from the "vortex of ruin." Niles also continued to make note of those sermons that warned of the wrath to come.[69]

Niles's frequent observations on the "infidelity" he saw around him and the many souls he believed were heading to hell could mean that many of his fellow western journeyers were indifferent to evangelical Protestantism's threats, but Niles also found kindred spirits along the way. Not all like-minded men kept such detailed diaries, but the tendency to discriminate between a believing "us" versus an unbelieving "them" was hardly unique to Niles. The concept of a final judgment dividing believers from unbelievers, and the notion that the "living in the pit" could be detected this side of the grave, fostered a separationist mentality among antebellum evangelicals. This mentality helped to create a sort of "imagined community" that stretched from this world to the next, comprising all who followed the same codes of conduct and belief and who could recognize each other even as they journeyed far from their childhood homes.[70] For believers, the stakes involved in such membership were high: life or death, salvation or damnation, heaven or hell. But the distinction between these binaries was not always clear-cut or inflexible. Believers were supposed to evangelize nonbelievers and extend the community of Christians, but they also worried that the reverse might occur. Niles was not alone in fearing that he might lose his faith by failing to prioritize his eternal welfare, even as he sought the worldly gain that might help him to become the solidly middle-class man living in a stable Christian community that he wanted so desperately to be.

Shaping a Saved World

If the saved were supposed to be efficient, disciplined, self-reflective, self-controlled, and plain, then the damned could be defined in opposite terms: inefficient, lazy, unreflective, uncontrolled, and frivolous. Not coincidentally, the latter were terms white evangelicals frequently applied to all variety of people they viewed as damned "others." The terms recall the traits assigned by the Sandwich Islands missionaries to the local "heathen," which ostensibly explained the difficulty of effecting their conversions. The same or similar terms were also applied to slaves who deliberately worked slowly as a form of resistance, and to Native Americans who resisted white attempts at "civilizing" them.[71]

White lay evangelicals harbored hopes of remaking the world along the same lines they used to shape themselves and their communities, joining with clergy and missionaries to establish schools that tried to teach discipline by the clock, separate children from ancestral customs, and urge (and sometimes force) them to dress in plain attire. Eliza Fairbanks of Franklin, Massachusetts, was profoundly concerned about "the eternal welfare of my fellow creatures" and, despite the misgivings of her mother and sister, applied for a position with the American Board of Commissioners for Foreign Missions. She was sent to the Mississippi Choctaw in December 1827, and soon after married a fellow missionary, William Hooper. Like Elizabeth Willard, Hooper still worried that she was not doing enough to save the "heathen" even after committing herself to the missionary effort. She feared that her own sins and "awful stupidity" might jeopardize her work with her mission students. "This day must set down lost," she wrote in her diary on December 14, 1827. "And however much I may suffer for it, O do not permit other souls to become partakers of the punishment due only to myself." She bemoaned her failure to make use of every opportunity to evangelize and save the souls of her mission wards: "Two young ladies with me all the evening, and not a word for God. Not a word to promote their eternal welfare. O should they be called before another morning in their present state, how must I forever condemn myself for the sins of this evening." Hooper's diary was never published, but she expressed the hope that if she should die, it might prove useful to others. By constantly belittling herself and lamenting her misuse of time and evangelizing opportunities, Hooper, like Mary Morton, suggested that if even a missionary was so hyper-aware of her shortcomings, her readers should be even more so.[72]

That evangelicals presented white middle-class values as models for the "heathen" to emulate did not, of course, preclude alternative formulations by the people they missionized. Indigenous people responded to Christian evangelization and education in different ways and always with an eye toward practical benefits.[73] Tribes in the Northeast, for instance, had already experienced several waves of evangelization by the nineteenth century. Famed Pequot minister William Apess (1798–1839) was drawn to Methodism through the influence of his aunt, Sally George, a tribal leader, preacher, and healer. She and other Native Christian leaders who had converted during the awakenings of the mid-eighteenth century sought to both minister to their people and defend them from the encroachments of white American society.[74] Apess followed in their footsteps. The title of his 1833 volume, *The Experiences of Five Christian Indians: or the Indian's Looking-Glass for the White Man*, suggested to white audiences that they should reflect about their own purported Christianity in light of the accounts contained therein.

Among the narratives Apess included was that of his aunt, who recounted taking the threat of hell so seriously that she considered suicide. "One day as I was passing by a large deep brook, the enemy of my soul tempted me to destroy myself in that place, by casting myself in," George explained.

> But I strove to raise my little heart to God, that he would have mercy upon my soul and save me.... I fell to the earth as one dead, under the power of God. And while in this situation, I saw the pit of destruction opened for poor sinners; it was no imagination either—it was a solemn reality—it was plain before me. My soul was in sore distress, and I expected nothing but hell for my portion forever.... The Lord heard prayer and sent down his melting grace into my soul; and before I arose from the ground I was translated into the kingdom of God's dear Son.[75]

George's account recalls the archetypal conversions of Benjamin Abbott, Lorenzo Dow, and Jarena Lee not only in her self-destructive thoughts but also in her forceful claim to have had a "solemnly real" vision of the "pit of destruction." The report of suicidal thoughts on par with those recorded by iconic ministers lent authenticity to George's account of conversion in the face of persecution and discrimination.

The Hawaiian youth Henry Obookiah, who inspired the mission to the Sandwich Islands, also left a memoir that made him perhaps the best-known antebellum paragon of the "heathen" convert. The nephew of a Hawaiian holy man, Obookiah became a sailor following the violent deaths of his father, mother, and brother in the upheavals leading to the unification of the islands in 1810. In 1809 he landed in New Haven, where he wondered at the importance of the written language he saw around him and sought instruction in the same. Of course, in an evangelical college town like New Haven, lessons in the English language went hand in hand with proselytizing. In his memoir, Obookiah recounted his initial opposition to such ministrations: "On account of my ignorance of the true God, I do not wish to hear them [ministers] when they talk to me.... I was told by them about Heaven and Hell, but I did not pay any attention to what they say; for I thought that I was just as happy as the other people, as those who do know about God much more than I do." Obookiah's defenses did not last long, however: "This thought, as I see to it now, was the most great and dangerous mistake."[76]

Soon, the teenager recounted a conversion process much alike in language to the exemplary Anglo-American narratives:

> Many thoughts come into my mind that I was in a dangerous situation. I thought that if I should then die, I must certainly be cast off forever.... I fell upon my knees and looked up to the Almighty Jehovah for help. I was not but an undone and hell-deserving sinner. I felt that it would be just that God should cast me off whithersoever he would—that he should do with my poor soul as it seemed to him fit.[77]

In addition to demonstrating Obookiah's Hopkinsian sense of God's justness in damning him, the memoir also testified to the genuineness of his conversion by showing that he subsequently felt a deep concern for the eternal welfare of the souls of others. In a letter to a Mrs. A–, he instructed:

> We must be born again and have a new spirit before we die. As soon as we shall be dead, all we must stand before the judgment seat of Christ. Friend, perhaps you have not done any thing wicked, so that God can punish you. I hope you have not.—But if we are not his friends and followers he will cast us into Hell, and we shall be there for ever and ever. I hope you will think upon all these things. Friend to you,
>
> Henry Obookiah.[78]

And in 1812 Obookiah expressed his worries about the Hawaiian people to a "Christian friend":

> I hope the Lord will send the Gospel to the Heathen land where the words of the Saviour never yet had been. Poor people worship the wood and stone and shark, and almost every thing their gods; the Bible is not there, and Heaven and Hell they do not know about it.[79]

Compiled by the ministers who worked with him in New Haven, Obookiah's purported words conveyed the ideal adoption of the concept of hell by a missionee. His memoir was hagiographic and, following his premature death in 1818, fired up subsequent generations of missionaries to send the "Gospel to the Heathen Land."

As we saw in chapter 2, the Sandwich Islands missionaries readily blamed Hawaiian "heathens" when their efforts seemed less than successful, but their warnings resonated with some. A student at Lahainaluna Seminary on Maui, formed to train young Hawaiian men to become teachers and preachers themselves, referenced the idea of two roads in an 1838 essay. The student, named Makaiheekona, wrote: "On our graduation, there are two roads on which we can go—a crooked road and a straight road, to make plain the way we should go. On my opinion we should go on the one road, so we can enter the glory we can see and hear of it. This is our one road."[80] Another anonymous seminary student wrote:

> The man who harbors sins will cause the body to perish. Here are the sins that cause death: worship of idols, adultery, thievery, covetousness, bearing false witness. There are many sins that cause death to us if we harbor these sins in Satan's name. The result will be death everlasting in the fires of Gehenna.[81]

Under missionary oversight, the Lahainaluna seminarians also produced a temperance map in English and a simplified version in Hawaiian, showing the reach of the idea that humans were paddling on the dangerous "Ocean of Life" toward safety or doom (fig. 3.4). The visual had particular relevance in an island world where alcohol was already a significant problem.[82]

We cannot know the extent to which the students were simply parroting what was expected of them and to what extent they believed what they produced. We need not automatically dismiss their professions as insincere. But it is not easy to understand why some missionees would accept the belief that they would be damned if they did not convert to an alien set of beliefs and practices. Generalizations inevitably gloss over regional and temporal particularities and changing affiliations over time in individual lives.[83] In the case of Obookiah, a possible explanation might take into account his youth, orphaned status, and separation from his homeland. Meanwhile, continued violence, disease, and religious upheaval on the islands he left behind may have made some of his Hawaiian compatriots more receptive to the missionaries' message. Similar factors may have been at play for Native Christians in the Northeast. Many Pequots had been brutally slaughtered and survivors dispersed by land-hungry Puritan colonists in the 1637 Pequot War. Those who continued to live on the eastern seaboard were often impoverished and had frequent contact with white

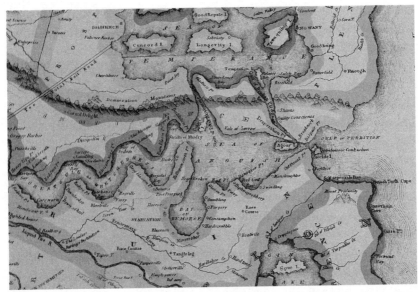

FIGURE 3.4 *Temperance Map* (detail). By C. Wiltberger Jr.; Lahainaluna Engraving, map, in English: 16 1/2 × 18 1/2 in. Published by L. Andrews, Lahaina, Maui, mid-nineteenth century. Republished in 1972 by the Hale Pa'i Printing Museum of the Lahaina Restoration Foundation, Lahainaluna, Lahaina, Hawaii, 96761. Detail shows the "Sea of Anguish" in the center and the "Sea of Temperance" above it, connected by the "Strait of Total Abstinence" and the "Gulf of Broken Pledges," which also leads to the "Gulf of Perdition" to the right.

Photograph by author from personal copy.

society, sometimes serving as indentured servants or in other domestic capacities, all the while being exposed to on-off efforts at evangelization in schools and at local revivals. As with Obookiah, their isolation and prolonged immersion in the society that had dispossessed their ancestors may help to explain their receptivity to that society's dominant evangelicalism, especially in the face of eternal threats against the unconverted.[84]

Still, we must not attribute all such receptivity to destitution and isolation alone. Indigenous people could find the tenets of evangelical Christianity persuasive even while seeking its practical benefits and recognizing (with clear-eyed acuity) white hypocrisy. William Apess noted that many white Americans committed the sin of neglect: "We were represented as having no souls to save, or to lose; but as partridges upon the mountains. All these degrading titles were heaped upon us." For Apess, to claim conversion was to resist this dehumanizing representation. Apess also turned condemnation on whites for bringing alcohol to his people. "And we little babes of the forest had to suffer much on its account, O white man!" he wrote. "How can you account to God for this? Are you not afraid that the children of the forest will rise up in judgment and condemn you?"[85]

For her part, Hannah Caleb, also featured in Apess's book, "felt a great enmity to the christian religion" prior to her change of heart, even "wishing...I had been left like the rest of my kindred, ignorant and unknown." Not only did so-called Christians behave hatefully toward each other, backbiting and arguing, she observed, they also treated "the poor Indians, the poor Indians" with contempt, "merely because we were Indians": "with the same abilities, with a white skin, I should have been looked upon with honor and respect.... These pictures of distress and shame were enough to make me cry out, O horrid inconsistency—who would be a christian?" Yet Caleb was able to separate the truth claims of evangelicalism from the way it was practiced by white Americans. Damnation and salvation knew no color lines; she prayed to "be saved from hell, and everlasting destruction," and rested assured that "the Lord heard prayer and spared me." Apess noted that she died at the age of 40 and "fell asleep in the arms of Jesus...while her soul was wafted upon the wings of angels to the spirit land, to dwell around the throne of God forever and ever."[86]

For Apess, Caleb, and other nonwhite Christians, the idea that all humans could end up in hell if they did not curb their pride and repent, and that all might prosper in heaven if they did, could be an attractively equalizing prospect.[87] It meant that white American Christians were just as endangered as the "heathen" they sought to evangelize if they treated them with disrespect and dishonesty. African American slaves and free blacks also drew on the equalizing potential of the afterlife, as we shall see in chapter 5. Even as white middle-class evangelicals tried to shape the world to look like themselves and their own communities, then, missionized people pushed back with their own vision of a just cosmos with a heaven and hell that reinforced the ultimate equality of all humans before God. The saved communities they envisioned crossed racial boundaries, as did their identification of who counted as the "living in the pit."

Insanity and the Medical Response to Hell

The exemplary narratives of nonwhite as well as white converts depicted a suicide attempt as an expected outcome of contemplating the possibility that the unconverted self might be destined for eternal hell. Thoughts of suicide may have seemed real to sufferers at the time, but in the narratives they also served the rhetorical purpose of conveying the depths of self-abnegation—the metaphorical death—that true converts should experience prior to spiritual rebirth. Obviously, none of these converts actually committed suicide. True converts were not to act on their despair but to throw themselves on God's mercy for salvation. But not all were able to keep their fears of eternal damnation from overwhelming their hopes for eventual salvation. Ministers' and doctors' reports of mental breakdowns and successful or attempted suicides related to religious anxiety testify that some were unable to safely navigate the movement from anxiety to assurance.[88]

By the late eighteenth century, some physicians were starting to see the treatment of mental illness as their responsibility, but antebellum ministers still believed that the causes of insanity—and hence, its prevention—could fall within their purview.[89] Ezra Stiles Ely, the city missions advocate who served the New York City Hospital and Almshouse beginning in the second decade of the nineteenth century, wrote extensively on the cases he encountered there. He attributed insanity in general to the Fall: "Would any of our race have exhibited such a spectacle, had not sin, deformity, imbecility, mental disorder, and idiotism, entered the world by the first transgression?" he asked. "Of all the disorders, to which humanity is subject, that of insanity is the most dreadful; because, in almost every instance, it puts the patient beyond the reach of the Gospel."[90] To evangelical ministers like Ely, the insane were like the perishing "heathen," unable to comprehend the promises or perils of the gospel because of their lack of reason. While the Fall explained the original entrance of insanity into the world, Ely also listed more immediate causes of madness: "vicious company," "avarice," "disappointments" (in business or love), "drunkenness," "novels" (beware of bad books!), "slavery," and "incontinence" (unchastity).[91] Ely differentiated between those who became insane as a result of factors outside their control (e.g., slavery or business failure not due to one's avarice), and those who became insane as a result of sin (e.g., intemperance, greed, and skepticism). Ely thought the former might still have a chance at salvation: "if piety exists previously to insanity, we ought not to suppose that the severe judgment warrants any unfavourable conclusion concerning the soul's condition in the future life."[92] But for those whose insanity was the direct consequence of their sins, it marked the point beyond which conversion was impossible, and hence the earthly entrance to hell.

Ely recounted the case of a Deist named H----n. Titling this story "The Punishment of Infidelity," Ely noted how H----n scorned his Presbyterian upbringing after encountering the works of Voltaire "and other infidel writers"—exactly what John Todd warned against in his guidebook for young students. The deaths of his mother and of a Deist friend (who renounced his "infidelity" on his deathbed), however, sent him into great torment of soul. Although once a prosperous and adventurous merchant who made his living from voyages to the West Indies, H----n soon "became habitually gloomy. He felt himself guilty and wretched, but did not believe in Christ, the way to pardon, peace of conscience, consolation in tribulation, and everlasting fidelity." H----n's unbelief, said Ely, soon gave way to insanity and the conviction that he was damned. He "stabbed his niece, whom he tenderly loved," and three times attempted suicide by hanging and once by slitting his throat before coming to the asylum, where he "was prevented, for a time, from intruding into the presence of his Judge."[93]

Here Ely encountered him. By this time, H----n had apparently rejected his former Deist beliefs. Although he agreed with Ely that "God is able and willing to save unto the uttermost all who come unto him," he viewed himself as incorrigibly damned. "God is a sovereign," he told Ely, and "he will not save me: for, I have been such a sinner, that God is miserable while I am out of misery. I ought to suffer. It is my duty to suffer for ever." Ely concluded that "if there is any such thing as a desire to be damned for the glory of God,"—that famous Hopkinsian notion again—"H----n certainly possessed that grace, but it was only in a state of insanity, and indescribable misery." While at the asylum he attempted suicide again, this time by starvation, "and from day to day, proclaimed that to-morrow he should be in hell." When his Deist friends came to visit him and attempted to cheer him up by mocking his religious fears, he instead warned them against infidelity. "My present agonies are unutterable, and what must damnation be to a guilty sinner?" he asked his friend Ben. "You cannot laugh me out of my present condition. You know that I am miserable now, and I tell you that my false ideas of religion have produced all that suffering which you witness. Ben, I am in hell! O be warned by me!" Ely editorialized: "His were the agonies of one already damned." Soon thereafter, while no one was paying attention, H----n did in fact commit suicide by strangulation. "But, alas!" Ely concluded, "Who, that being often reproved hardeneth himself, can escape everlasting burnings? Must we not say concerning many who imagine that they must choose the most favourable alternative, 'in preferring death by your own hands, to present anguish, you become secure of hell?' "[94]

Ely clearly intended H----n's suicide to serve as a cautionary tale: infidelity left people with no defenses against death and at its worst could cause insanity, which could lead to suicide and eternal damnation. Ely's didactic voice dominates this narrative. H----n and other suicides, who reportedly repented of their sins but still feared for their eternal well-being, represented only a tiny minority but one that ministers exploited to the hilt.[95] As much as ministers tweaked and embellished their stories for didactic purposes, they are still suggestive of the effect fire and brimstone could have on ordinary people. In an age when lectures were still considered entertainment, laypeople's imagination of the life to come could be kindled by dramatic pulpit performances as well as printed texts and visuals. Dissenters might thumb their noses at the fear of hell, but even without attending an evangelical church they would have encountered a barrage of warnings that could settle into the mind's recesses and emerge with devastating power in the face of death or other trauma.[96]

By the 1830s, some medical experts were starting to argue that religious excitement itself, and not the ravages of sin, was causing people to lose their reason.[97] In 1833, the year the State Lunatic Hospital at Worcester, Massachusetts, opened, Superintendent Samuel B. Woodward listed one of the institution's notable patients as "No. 142," a married man who had been admitted on November 13 at the age of 75. The diagnosis? "Dread of Future Punishment." Reportedly, the man had languished in this state for three weeks before his friends committed him to the Hospital. Woodward assessed the sufferer's state as "Stationary," and after only seventeen days of observation he declared the patient "Incurable."[98]

By the time of his Fourth Report (1835–36), Woodward was tabulating the diagnosed causes of insanity among his patients in more detail, even sorting them by gender and "curability." The leading causes of insanity were "Intemperance" (primarily affecting men), "Domestic afflictions" (disproportionately affecting women), "masturbation" (men), and "ill health" (women). Religious reasons represented the fifth leading cause, affecting 41 patients. More men than women (26:15) fell into this category, divided about evenly between the "curable" and "incurable." Woodward knew that some would find this surprising: "It is a very common observation by the unreflecting," he noted, "that females become insane more frequently than men from religious causes, and this is often spoken reproachfully of religion. The facts here recorded shew a different result."

Woodward acknowledged that religious reasons for insanity could range widely; he gave as examples "high excitement" and "exaltation," but also "fear of future punishment...fear of the displeasure of the Deity," and a "sense of guilt."[99] Later studies from New York also found religious anxiety to be a leading cause of insanity irrespective of gender. A report of the New York State Asylum reproduced in Ned Buntline's 1848 *Mysteries and Miseries of New York* found 152 insane from religious reasons, split evenly between 76 men and 76 women, while an 1849 report noted 178: 87 men and 91 women. By contrast, in these two reports intemperance only affected 50 and 67, respectively, and only 8 women total.[100]

In labeling religious anxiety as a cause of insanity, Superintendent Woodward and the authors of the New York reports may have been influenced by the publication, in 1835, of Doctor Amariah Brigham's *On the Influence of Religion upon the Health and Physical Welfare of Mankind*, which concluded that religious excitement was dangerous to both physical and mental health (fig. 3.5). Brigham, who was one of the founders of the *American Journal of Insanity* (now *Psychiatry*), and the precursor to the American Psychiatric Association, saw religious enthusiasm and anxiety as the products of overly wrought and excited nervous systems "magnetized" by protracted and mesmerizing (or hypnotic) preaching. "If, therefore, a number of people be kept for a long time in a state of great terror and mental anxiety," Brigham wrote, "no matter whether from vivid descriptions of hell, and fears of 'dropping immediately into it,' or from any other cause, the brain and nervous system of such a people is as liable to be injured, as the stomach and digestive organs are from the frequent use, during the same length of time, of very stimulating food and drink."[101]

Brigham also addressed the problem of suicide due to religious "melancholy," noting that the despairing fear of impending damnation "is not unfrequent in this country." "Of all kinds of insanity, it is the most deplorable," he wrote:

> Many in this country believe they have committed "the unpardonable sin," and abandon themselves to despair; while others become so on being told from the pulpit...that if they have ever had their minds much excited on religious subjects,—or "awakened" as they express it,—and have not encouraged these feelings, and obtained a "hope," then in all probability, their day of salvation is passed. These become religious melancholics, and not only often attempt to destroy themselves, but also their friends and dearest kindred.[102]

FIGURE 3.5 Amariah Brigham (1798–1849). Engraved by H. B. Hall from a Daguerreotype.

Images from the History of Medicine, the National Library of Medicine, Portrait no. 791.

Brigham cited "above *ninety cases* of suicide from religious melancholy," and "thirty cases" where the "unhappy sufferers" attempted "to kill...their children or dearest relatives, believing they should thereby ensure the future happiness of those they destroyed."[103] Instead of viewing a suicide attempt as a laudable step on the path to conversion, Brigham saw it as pathological. The sense of responsibility for the souls of others that ministers sought to inculcate, he argued, could instead backfire as murder of the near and dear (as H----n had tried with his niece). Revivalists' attempts to break the pride of prospective converts could lead to their "conversion" not to Christianity but to insanity. Unconsciously echoing Weld's 1828 complaint about his mentor Finney's "machinery," Brigham wrote:

> Now whoever will carefully and without prejudice examine this subject, and call to mind the immense amount of *machinery* in operation in this country, to excite the minds of men, women and

children, and to keep them excited, by numerous meetings,—by exciting and alarming discourses, respecting "sinning away the day of grace," "committing the unpardonable sin," "dropping into hell immediately," &c. &c.... will not be surprised at the number of the insane being so great, *but rather that it should be so small*.[104]

Brigham argued that it was particularly important to avoid terrifying women and children. His concerns primarily related to the womb. He believed that acquired insanity could be passed on: "Females, whose minds have been for a considerable time greatly excited, may, in consequence, transmit to their offspring a tendency to nervous disease and to insanity."[105] Children with this tendency could in turn easily be affected by the preaching of fear: "Descriptions of the terrors of hell, accounts of the devil or satan, &c., often cling to them through life, with a pernicious potency and influence." Brigham buttressed his case by citing European experts, who noted that "it is very dangerous to work on the young imagination with descriptions of the torments of hell. This is not the method to educate children to be pious; it is the way to render weak minds superstitious, and strong minds incredulous."[106]

Just as Heman Humphrey had noted that revivals and conversion preaching were more common in America than in Europe, so Brigham was keenly sensitive to the fact that insanity seemed uniquely prevalent in the United States and especially in the North, where more records were kept. Brigham explained that "insanity is a disease that always prevails most in countries where the people enjoy civil and religious freedom, and where all are induced, or are at liberty to engage in the strife for wealth, and for the highest honors and distinctions of society. We need therefore to be exceedingly careful not to add other causes to those already existing, of this most deplorable disease." He suggested, in other words, that insanity was related to the apparent freedom of choice and economic anxiety in a capitalistic society, which could then be exacerbated by the dissemination of terror, "probably" the most powerful "of all the passions of the mind."[107]

The anxiety, depression, and suicidal thoughts and actions described in these texts might indeed be attributed to the upheavals caused by the new nation's expanding market society, its increasingly individualistic culture, failed business transactions, social isolation, and/or chemical imbalances in the brain.[108] But we cannot entirely discount the power of religious terror. Social and biological causes notwithstanding, people *believed* the fear of hell could send a person to the asylum. The reports did not merely tally the opinions of official superintendents or insanity "experts." As the 1849 New York Report put it, "It is a record of what we have been informed by the friends and acquaintances of patients, was the exciting cause of the attack."[109] The theory that insanity could be caused by religious excitement was even codified in the national census by the 1860s.[110]

While some have suggested that "psychiatry and the social sciences have from the beginning played roles in eroding religious faith,"[111] we might instead see antebellum proto-psychiatrists' arguments against the preaching of religious terror as part of the evolution of a gentler strain of American religiosity. This strain never superseded but existed in creative tension with the fire and brimstone rhetoric that was thought to lead to religious insanity. The threat of hell could be used as a counterbalance against sentimentality, while a softer interpretation of biblical dictates could be used to combat terror-inducing preaching.[112]

Brigham and Woodward did not blame Christianity per se for their patients' problems. They distinguished between "pure" Christianity and the version espoused by evangelical clergy. Although "religious excitement...may cause insanity and other diseases," Brigham clarified, "the religion of Christ condemns that excitement, terror and fanaticism which leads to such effects; 'For God hath not given us the spirit of fear; but of power, and of love, and of a sound mind.' 2 Tim. i. 7."[113] This verse that speaks to love and mercy starkly contrasts with those cited by the likes of Heman Humphrey to prove that the Bible sanctioned, and indeed demanded, the preaching of hell. Woodward similarly contended that "the genuine principles of christianity have no tendency to distract the mind." He also claimed that "few individuals are so completely insane as to be beyond the reach of moral instruction, and perhaps I may add moral responsibility. If so, it may be doubted whether it be right to incarcerate men, and deprive them also of that instruction upon which their future wellbeing may depend." He and other advocates for the insane suggested that what they needed was not dramatic preaching about their danger, but gentle and calm religious services and instruction that could alleviate their suffering and perhaps even rehabilitate their minds.[114]

"But There is a Point Where the Doctrines Shrivel"

The alleviation of suffering rather than the condemnation of its sinful causes brings us back to Minnie (now known as Mary) Corinna Putnam,

FIGURE 3.6 Untitled portrait of Mary Putnam Jacobi, in "Two portraits of Jacobi; in one she is reading," ca. 1860–1865. 2 1/4 × 3 1/2 in. Bogardus, n.d., New York, New York, United States, photographer. Mary Putnam Jacobi Papers: Photographs of MPJ.

Courtesy of the Schlesinger Library, Radcliffe Institute, Harvard University.

the 12-year-old child whose letter to her "Grandmamma" opened this chapter. Just five years after her hopeful conversion, Mary "began questioning and investigating concerning the truth of the Calvinistic theology."[115] Fresh out of a girls' school in 1859, Mary set her heart on becoming a doctor. She attended the New York College of Pharmacy in 1861, graduated from the Female Medical College of Pennsylvania in 1864, and the Parisian École de Médecin in 1871. Today she is renowned under the name "Mary Corinna Putnam Jacobi," having married Jewish pediatrician Abraham Jacobi, as the first woman to join the American Academy of Medicine (fig. 3.6).

Her religious trajectory has received less attention. In April 1863, while attending medical college, the 21-year-old Mary informed a Reverend Dr. Anderson that the questioning she had begun four years earlier, "in full faith and expectation that my doubts would speedily be settled, and my faith grounded anew," had instead taken her in the opposite direction.

"Today finds me a total disbeliever in the distinctive tenets of the technically called orthodox system of divinity," she asserted, requesting formal separation from the church. Perhaps Putnam, like the medical "experts" on insanity, was beginning to question whether illnesses could be explained by external factors, rather than as judgments or tests from God that needed to be borne and that demanded speedy repentance in case of sudden death. She summed up her reasons for rejecting the "orthodox system of divinity":

> If one cannot believe in the mystery of God without the Trinity, in the mercy of God and the vicariousness of pure love without the Atonement, in the hatefulness of sin without eternal punishment, why then I suppose it is best that men should believe these partial symbols of the vast ideas which would escape them. But there is a point where the doctrines shrivel.[116]

While hell raised the stakes for some believers and gave meaning to their decision to convert and seek the conversions of others, the difficulty of balancing the hope of heaven with the fear of punishment, and trust in God's mercy with faith in His justness, gave pause to others, especially in the face of suffering and death. The notion that the threat of hell was too terrifying for ordinary people and that the insane might not be responsible for their sufferings was part of a wider backlash against the idea of damnation. After all, if external factors, like being terrorized by ministers who preached damnation for hours on end, could account for what once seemed a terrible judgment from God (insanity), then why could not mitigating factors also explain other sins that were supposed to condemn a person to hell?

4

"Ideas, Opinions, Can Not Damn the Soul"

ANTEBELLUM DISSENT AGAINST DAMNATION

IN AN 1852 article entitled "The Instinct of Progress," Spiritualist James Richardson, Jr. wondered how his fellow Americans could be so committed to progress in the "world of action and of business," but so retrogressive in their religious affairs. Americans celebrated "our Manufactories, our gigantic Steamers, our Railways and our Telegraphs" but were "mere children, infants, ignoramuses, in morals, religion and theology." Richardson claimed to be different. He saw existing denominations as steps along the way to higher understanding: "Calvinism was my book of A B C's. Among the Baptists I perhaps was taught to spell. Unitarianism was my School Reader.... They are but the cast-off skins of the caterpillar and *the soul grows at every moulting.*"[1]

In trying to explain why more Americans did not follow such a path, Richardson suggested that the fear of hell hampered serious thought and inquiry. But he told his readers not to worry: "*Ideas, opinions, can not damn the soul, even should they prove false. Slavery, confinement, the repression of thought, the destruction of mental activity,—of mental and spiritual life—that is damnable; its free growth and progress—that is saving.*" Richardson rejected eternal damnation in a hell of fire and brimstone as irrational, unjust, and exclusionary. He redefined damnation as the unwillingness to explore and question and claimed Jesus as a spiritual seeker too: "'This is the damnation,' says Jesus, 'that light hath come into the world, and men love darkness rather than light, because their deeds are evil.'" Richardson and other antebellum spiritual seekers sought community outside the ranks of the evangelical saved and rejected the authority of evangelical ministers to diagnose the state of their souls.[2]

Hell was a polarizing concept that mobilized some to action because they feared it, while mobilizing others to religious innovation against it. Opposition to the evangelical deployment of hell took many forms. It did not always have to involve absolute acceptance or rejection of the doctrine. For those unwilling to go as far as Richardson, a common compromise allowed hell for one's antagonists or the distant or obviously sinful "other" to coexist with the rejection of hell for one's self, kith, or kin. In a rapidly expanding nation, where geographical separation could easily become permanent due to accidents or the ravages of disease, resistance to the concept of a personal hell could exclude the possibility of eternal damnation for one's own through the ever-powerful desire for communal salvation and future reunion. But reunion could also be racialized. Many nonwhites rejected a heaven populated by white evangelicals, while some white laypeople rendered themselves as "saved" and the nonwhite "other" as doomed through the application of static racial classifications that paralleled missionaries' complaints about the "incorrigible" (and hence unsaveable) "heathen."

Separate Afterlives for Separate Peoples

A prime early example of pushback against the use of hell in a missionary context comes from a 1710 "Indian Speech in Answer to a Sermon, preached by a Swedish Missionary, at Conestogo, in Pennsylvania." First recorded in Latin by Jonas Aurén, the "Indian Speech" was reprinted multiple times in late eighteenth- and early nineteenth-century newspapers and a nineteenth-century tract. By 1929 it had become the stuff of legend, surfacing again in the *Reading Eagle*.[3] The speechmaker began by noting that "our fathers were under a strong persuasion (as we are) that those who act well in this life, will be rewarded in the next, according to the degree of their virtues; and, on the other hand, that those who behave wickedly here, will undergo such punishments hereafter, as are proportionate to the crimes they were guilty of." To the speechmaker, such persuasion could only have come from direct and divine revelation. A series of pointed questions to the missionary followed:

Does he believe our forefathers, men eminent for their piety, constant and warm in the pursuit of virtue, hoping thereby to obtain eternal happiness, were all damned? Does he think that we, who are zealous imitators of them in good works, and influenced by the same motives as they were...are in a state of damnation? If these be his sentiments, they are surely as impious, as they are bold and daring.[4]

These difficult questions spoke to a persistent problem faced by missionaries: asking people from other cultures to convert was asking them to abandon eternity with their ancestors.

The speechmaker also took on the idea that the "heathen" had enough natural light to be condemned even if they had never received the gospel: "But supposing our understanding were so far illuminated, as to know it to be our duty to please God, who has yet left us under an incapacity of doing it; will this missionary therefore conclude, that we shall be eternally damned?" By making the question seem preposterous, the speechmaker made the relativistic possibility that God gave different revelations to different peoples seem all the more rational: "It is our opinion, that every man is possessed with sufficient knowledge for his own salvation.... And to say, in a matter so necessary, [God] could not at one and the same time reveal himself to all mankind, is nothing less than a denial of his omnipotence." This case for God's power advanced the possibility of, if not universal salvation, then at least universal means of salvation, as long as people abided by the rules God gave them.[5]

The speechmaker closed with a powerful statement about his people's view of the Almighty, their place in His creation, and their ill-treatment by those who claimed to have received His only true revelation:

To say the Almighty has permitted us to remain in a fatal error, through so many ages, is to represent him as a tyrant. How is it consistent with his justice, to force life upon a race of mortals without their consent, and then to damn them eternally, without ever opening to them the door of salvation....

In a word, we find the Christians much more depraved in their morals than we are; and we judge of their doctrine, by the badness of their lives.[6]

The speechmaker reversed white proselytizers' moral calculus by suggesting that they might be "more depraved" than those they sought to convert. The missionary apparently had such a hard time refuting the speech that, "upon his return to Sweden, [he] published his sermon, and the Indian's answer, in Latin. He dedicated them to the university at Upsal, and desired them to furnish him with arguments to confute such strong reasonings of the Indians."[7]

The speech's re-publication numerous times suggests its appeal to American freethinkers as an Enlightenment-era critique of Christianity. Unlike Native Christians, who accepted the evangelical hell for its equalizing potential, this speechmaker challenged the idea that evangelicalism's promises and threats could apply the world over. Instead of a single saved community set over against all the damned, the Conestogo speechmaker posited separate afterlives for separate peoples, broadening the possibilities of who might be rewarded in the afterlife while keeping cultural boundaries intact. The notion that God gave different revelations to different peoples also appeared in the teachings of Native American revitalization prophets whose names, unlike this speechmaker's, survive: the Delaware Prophet Neolin, the Seneca Prophet Handsome Lake, and the Shawnee Prophet Tenskwatawa.[8] These men told their followers that respecting instructions given specifically to their people would be more conducive to future rewards than converting to Christianity.

In the 1760s Neolin, a member of the Lenni Lenape, created a cosmological map based on visionary conversations with the Master of Life (fig. 4.1). The four-part rectangle at the base of the map represented the earth and its various good and bad inhabitants. Those on the right side of the rectangle would go straight to heaven, those on the upper left would undergo various purgation processes (represented by the roads A, B, and C), and those on the bottom left would go straight to hell.[9] The map came from a region near the Great Lakes where French, English, and Indians commingled and sometimes clashed. Neolin was likely influenced by Catholic missionaries preaching the doctrine of Purgatory; his map also recalls the Catholic ladders discussed in chapter 2.[10]

For Neolin, though, sinful acts were not those decreed in the Bible or by priests, but the adoption of certain European ways (like excessive alcohol consumption) and failure to resist European encroachment ("as to those who come to trouble your lands,—drive them out, make war upon them"). But he also adopted some European customs: Indians were no longer to take more than one wife, for instance, nor engage in medicine dances. He reassured the Lenni Lenape that the Master of Life would reverse their suffering if they listened to his prescriptions: "Ye have only to become good again and do what I wish, and I will send back the animals

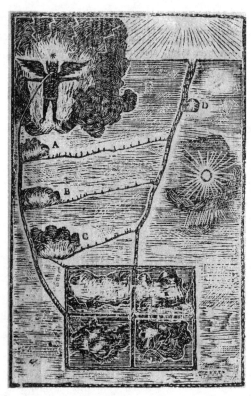

FIGURE 4.1 "Mah-tan'-tooh, or the Devil, standing in a flame of fire, with open arms to receive the wicked." In Archibald Loudon, *A selection, of some of the most interesting narratives, of outrages, committed by the Indians, in their wars, with the white people...* (Carlisle [Pa.]: From the press of A. Loudon (Whitehall), 1808–1811). Monroe Wakeman and Holman Loan Collection of the Pequot Library Association, on deposit in the Beinecke Rare Book and Manuscript Library, Pequot L92.

Courtesy of the Beinecke Rare Book and Manuscript Library.

for your food." Nowhere did he tell them to convert to Christianity in order to escape everlasting punishment.[11]

Like Neolin, Handsome Lake and Tenskwatawa had visions that affirmed their followers' special status with a culturally specific Creator. The 1794 Pickering Treaty and the 1795 Treaty of Greenville had not ended disputes over land cessions for either the Iroquois or the Shawnee. Both men experienced the grief of dispossession, both had been alcoholics prior to their visions, and both forwarded syncretistic plans for revitalization. Handsome Lake's visions began in 1799; he urged his people to avoid alcohol (to which he himself had been addicted), witches, and medicine bundles, and to adopt an agricultural way of life, build houses, and keep livestock in imitation of "our younger brethren" (the whites). At the same time, he had a vision in which Christ instructed him to "tell your people that they will become lost when they follow the ways of the white man."[12]

An otherworldly "Journey over the Great Sky Road" included more expansive visions about the life to come: "The narrow road leads to the pleasant lands of the Creator and the wide and rough road leads to the great lodge of the punisher." Messengers of the Creator showed him the punishments awaiting those who did not repent and follow his Code, known as Gai´wiio'. Handsome Lake also predicted an apocalyptic end to the world around the year 2100 that only his followers would avoid. The "earth will be destroyed by fire and not one upon it will escape," he declared, but before that happened, the "faithful" would "enter into a sleep" during which the "Creator [would] withdraw their lives" painlessly so that they would avoid the tribulations to come. Handsome Lake also made provisions for those who died before his revelations:

> Now it is said that your fathers of old never reached the true lands of our Creator nor did they ever enter the house of the tormentor, Ganos´ge'. It is said that in some matters they did the will of the Creator and that in others they did not. They did both good and bad and none was either good or bad. They are therefore in a place separate and unknown to us, we think, enjoying themselves.

This was Handsome Lake's way of responding to the thorny problem of what happened to ancestors, recalling the Conestogo speechmaker's pointed question: "does he believe our forefathers...were all damned?" As a number of scholars have pointed out, Gai´wiio' was an Iroquois alternative to Christianity that still drew from its precepts. Handsome Lake's Code spelled out the difference between the Seneca and whites as well as their special position with the Creator: to the Seneca specifically had He revealed Gai´wiio', and only the followers of Gai´wiio' would be translated to heaven at death and escape the horrors of the end times.[13]

Tenskwatawa's 1805 vision was even more expansive: he claimed that it authorized him to "instruct all the red people the proper way of living," not just members of his own tribe.[14] As then-President Thomas Jefferson reported, Tenskwatawa taught that "[the Indians] must return from all the ways of the whites to the habits and opinions of their forefathers." Yet like the other prophets he too attacked shamans and medicine bundles (perhaps to shore up his own authority), and instituted ritualistic practices possibly borrowed from Catholicism.[15]

Tenskwatawa told his followers that two guides had allowed him to look at heaven and hell. The heaven he saw was like an idealized pre-white America: "a rich, fertile country, abounding in game, fish, pleasant hunting grounds and fine corn fields," where the dead "plant, they hunt, play at their usual games & in all things are unchanged."[16] He predicted a future apocalypse that similarly restored the bounties on earth. Channeling the Great Spirit, Tenskwatawa instructed: "If you hearken to my Counsel, and follow my instructions for <u>Four Years</u>, There will then be two <u>Days of darkness</u>, During which I shall travel unseen through the land, And cause the animals, such as they were formerly, when I created them, To come forth out of the Earth."[17] If heaven and the endtimes spelled the restoration of a pre-European America, hell was similar to the Catholic purgatory, where sinners were tortured with undying fire until they repented and were finally able to enter heaven.[18] While Indians were the favored peoples of the Great Spirit and had even been created separately (whites having been made by an evil "white spirit"), Tenskwatawa targeted tribal opponents in wide-ranging witch-hunts that sometimes ended in executions.[19] His more famous half-brother Tecumseh is renowned as the mastermind behind early nineteenth-century pan-Indianism, but Tenskwatawa's teachings were just as important in shaping a sense of pan-tribal community and articulating a promise of restoration here and in the hereafter if Indians followed the Great Spirit's prescriptions.[20]

Although they did not reject a hell after death, then, these native revitalization prophets nevertheless rejected hell as a place to which those who did not follow the words of the Bible or the prescriptions of priests would go. Like Euro-American Christians, they used the threat of future punishment as a means of shoring up group identity and patterns of appropriate and inappropriate behavior, and as a place to which to consign their enemies. However, although evangelicals allowed (albeit grudgingly and often contradictorily) that nonwhites could become Christian, these prophets, like the Conestoga speechmaker, were understandably less than eager to share their revitalized afterlife with those who taught that their forefathers were damned.

As famous as were Neolin, Handsome Lake, and Tenskwatawa in the colonial and early national periods, less prominent native laypeople espoused similar ideas well into the nineteenth century. Although they did not leave their own written records, the views of the anonymous women and men in Presbyterian Augustus Ward Loomis's 1859 *Scenes in the Indian Country* can be discerned between the lines of his narration. The Creek and Cherokee had been renowned for their adoption of "civilized" ways prior to their forcible removal west of the Arkansas along the Trail of Tears, but Loomis soon learned that "a portion of the nation have always been desperately opposed to schools, and to the improvements urged by our government, and by the missionaries."[21] Loomis acknowledged that the Creek and Cherokee resented being *"driven"* from their native land in Georgia "as they express it," not least because they had been forced to leave behind the "graves of their kinsmen and their braves." But unlike missionaries who had worked among the Creek and Cherokee prior to their removal, many of whom were conflicted about the actions of the Jackson government, Loomis, whose primary experience had been among the Chinese, was less than sympathetic. He wrote that "they now have a goodly land, if they improve, and are disposed to enjoy it."[22] He did not connect the dots between their removal and hostility toward Euro-American encroachments, which extended beyond the things of this world to the life to come. "With some of the Indians," he noted, "there appears to be a belief that the red men and the whites will have separate places assigned them after death; therefore not unfrequently when we ask a person where he expects to go when he dies, he will answer, quite unconcernedly, 'Oh, where other Indians go, I suppose.'"[23]

On one memorable day, Loomis and his fellow missionaries "received this answer at two or three houses in succession." One lodged a "mother with several children around her." According to Loomis, "She reckoned they would be about as well off in the next world as most Indians; they would be found in the biggest crowd at any rate"—a vision of enduring cultural community that breezily dismissed the evangelicals' community of the saved. An "old warrior" a few houses down gave a similar response to the question of whether he felt ready to "leav[e] this world." "That's not a matter that troubles me at all," he retorted. "I'll go where the other Indians do, I guess." Meanwhile, "two little Indian boys, brothers" at the mission's Kowetah school, who were slow to learn their lessons and the English language, "said that their parents had strictly charged them not to worship the white man's God, for none of their relatives had gone to the white man's heaven; and unless they wished to be separated from their parents and kindred after death they should not learn the white man's religion, nor pray to the white man's God."[24] What Loomis interpreted as "indifference" and "unconcern" we might instead see as purposeful rejection of missionaries' attempts to further divide indigenous people not only in this world but also the next. The desire for future reunion ran perhaps even deeper for the Creek and Cherokee Loomis interviewed because of their forced separation from the sacred resting places of their ancestors.

Accepting the Christian hell, furthermore, meant rejecting cultural practices they had shared with their forefathers but that missionaries denounced as sinful and hellworthy. In a visit with a Mekko, or chief, for instance, Loomis encountered angry opposition. According to the Mekko, the government had promised that if his people moved west of the Arkansas, they would not face continued intrusion by the whites. But, he protested, "now you are on after us again." The missionaries countered that they did not intend to interfere in political affairs, but the Mekko pressed, "Ah, but...our customs, our busks, dancing, ball-plays, races, drinking, card-playing, and such things; if you come here to preach, will you preach that they are all right? or will you even promise to say nothing at all about them, one way or the other?" These customs represented a syncretistic blend of older traditions with newer adoptions. "We like all these things," the Mekko continued, "Our fathers taught them to us, and the Great Spirit taught the same to them. We are bound to perpetuate them, and we *wish* to perpetuate them; indeed we like them, and we mean to practise them." As much as Loomis sought to persuade him that "with that determination you will not expect to go to heaven" and that if he converted he would lose interest in these activities, the Mekko rebuffed all his testimonies.[25]

The Mekko's son-in-law similarly rejected the claims and threats of the missionaries. "As for myself," he told Loomis, "there are some customs which your kind of people say are wrong, but which I like, and I don't intend to give them up; and if I must be sent to hell for even a few sins, why then, for ought I see, I might as well take a full swing in all of them and enjoy myself as much as possible; for with one sin I would be sent to hell, and with ten thousand sins I couldn't any more than go there." Loomis, not surprisingly, met these arguments with all the more fire and brimstone and somewhat hopefully recorded at the end of the meeting that "before we had finished this short conversation he was beginning to look very serious; his eyes were riveted on the ground, and in that posture he was standing, still leaning against the door-post until we were out of sight. I never saw him afterwards."[26] Of course, the apparent "seriousness" that Loomis saw may well have expressed nothing more than the man's desire for Loomis to stop talking and leave him in peace. Although they could not keep land-hungry white settlers, speculators, and sermonizers from their lands, these Creek and Cherokee laypeople sought to keep a separate afterlife that they would share with their ancestors, living as they pleased, untroubled by the incursions of whites.

"This Is Really a Sad Picture"

Native Americans were aware of differences of opinion among Euro-Americans. "I can't read," the Mekko told Loomis, "and I don't know anything about the Bible, but some of your own white men tell me that it's only a 'pack of lies.' "[27] Euro-Americans were likewise aware of Native arguments against their vaunted superiority. "Our people and our government have sinned alike against the firstborn of the soil," wrote Margaret Fuller in *Summer on the Lakes, in 1843*. Fuller laid out the Indian's "simple creed" in terms strikingly similar to those of the anonymous Conestogo speechmaker: "there is a God, and a life beyond this; a right and wrong which each man can see, betwixt which each man should choose; that good brings with it its reward and vice its punishment." She, too, flipped the tables on Euro-American virtue: "all unprejudiced observers bear testimony that the Indians, until broken from their old anchorage by intercourse with the whites, who offer them, instead, a religion of which they furnish neither interpretation nor example, were singularly virtuous, if virtue be allowed to consist in a man's acting up to his own ideas of right."[28] Fuller here echoed a central claim of the speechmaker: to each his/her own (leave us alone). It is hardly surprising that a Transcendentalist would have found this attractive.

Fuller's was not the only pen lending support to this idea. By the mid-nineteenth century, the opinion that some people should not be held responsible for their supposedly unsaved state and that missionaries should leave them alone was spreading. Changing medical views of insanity played a role in this shift. If the insane were not necessarily responsible for their conditions, could not the same be said of the "heathen" who lived beyond reach of the gospel? Amariah Brigham made exactly this leap in his book on religion and health. Taking on "the works of Edwards, Sprague, and Finney," which he dubbed "illogical," Brigham mocked the notion that "unless it [the Holy Spirit] is imparted, no human being can escape indescribable torments in hell forever." He was particularly offended by the idea "that this influence of the Holy Spirit is not constantly imparted to men, but only occasionally; and then not to mankind scattered

through various countries, but to the individuals of one country; and not
to all the inhabitants of a country, but only to the members of some one
religious congregation; and not to all of them, but only to a few." Just as
missionaries listed the numbers of "perishing heathen" over all the earth
(and even visualized them, as in Lowrie's color-coded map), so Brigham
cited his own figures, showing that "only from forty to fifty millions" of the
world's 700,000,000 population "are Protestants, and these are divided
into innumerable sects," while a full half "are Polytheists." Evangelicals
used such numbers to persuade American converts to take responsibility
for a "dying" world, but Brigham wanted to show how preposterous such
narrow truth claims were: "To those who believe that the Protestant is
the only pure and acceptable religion," he opined, "this is really a sad
picture."[29]

Brigham did not advocate Universalism as a cure. But latter-day
"Salvation" Murrays did. Such a one was Abel Thomas, a Universalist minister who debated the justness of eternal damnation in a series of published letters with the ubiquitous Ezra Stiles Ely in the 1830s.[30] Thomas
also recounted conversations in which he tried to convince people of the
truth of universal salvation in his 1852 *Autobiography*, a Universalist version of the colloquial evangelical ministers' memoirs. In an exchange with
a Methodist farmer, Thomas argued that even after death a change toward
belief in Christ was possible. How else, he asked, can "any of the countless myriads of the heathen, so living and so dying...be saved? You dare
not contend that they will *all* be damned; and if you admit that any of
them will be saved, on Gospel principles, you open a door for the salvation
of all mankind." Thomas did not note the farmer's response other than
that they parted with "mutual respect and good wishes," but he proudly
declared that some years later a man by the same name had become a
Universalist.[31]

Despite evangelicals' theological modifications to make damnation a
result of avoidable failings in belief and behavior rather than an immu-
table decree from on high, then, arguments for universal salvation continued to make inroads. The question of why God would allow so many
millions in historically non-Christian nations to be damned became ever
more pressing as Americans became more aware of the distant "heathen"
through the writings of travelers and missionaries. By mid-century, the
concept of election had lost its terror for many American churchgoers,
who believed that they had the natural ability to repent.[32] But in the evangelical schema, election still seemed to apply to the world at a macro-level,

because God had supposedly given some nations the responsibility to spread salvation while consigning others to wait in "darkness." Much as individual election had called forth heated debates about God's fairness and justice, so too did the idea that huge swaths of humanity might be damned simply because of the regions and religions into which they had been born.

Herman Melville's first novel, *Typee: A Peep at Polynesian Life* (1846), presented a bestselling fictional challenge to the missionaries' perception of the world as hellbound without evangelical intervention. The first-person narrator, Tommo, leads the reader through his own journey from fear of Polynesian natives as cannibals, to growing appreciation of them as noble savages. The narrative is an inversion of the didactic guides that led readers into the pit of hell. Tommo describes the Typees' landscape as the opposite of what he expected and indeed, a virtual Eden. But he worries that this Eden might become corrupted, pointing to the effects of missionaries on Hawaii: "Let the once smiling and populous Hawaiian islands, with their now diseased, starving, and dying natives, answer the question. The missionaries may seek to disguise the matter as they will, but the facts are incontrovertible; and the devoutest Christian who visits that group with an unbiased mind, must go away mournfully asking—'Are these, alas! the fruits of twenty-five years of enlightening?' "[33] Tommo then turns the tables on the supposed saviors of the dying "heathen" to suggest that their "civilization" is much worse: "The fiend-like skill we display in the invention of all manner of death-dealing engines...distinguish the white civilized man as the most ferocious animal on the face of the earth." Where missionaries depicted the "heathen" as shrouded in darkness and gloom, Tommo also suggests that for the Typee, who "are either too lazy or too sensible to worry themselves about abstract points of religious belief," "all was mirth, fun, and high good humor. Blue devils, hypochondria, and doleful dumps, went and hid themselves among the nooks and crannies of the rocks."[34] How stark the contrast to the religious melancholia described by Amariah Brigham.

"The Parrot Twaddle of Presumptious Dogmatists"

Of course, such melancholia did not touch all Americans. Just as the Mekko and his brother-in-law vowed to continue cultural practices that missionaries condemned, so others also defiantly continued their pursuit of pleasures in this life that evangelicals denounced as hell-worthy.

Some liquor salesmen, prostitutes, and gamblers rejected the notion that hell could be so bad as to make them pursue alternate livelihoods or recreational activities. An "obdurate offender" told Ezra Stiles Ely, for instance, that

> he should melt no sooner than his companions in the focus of divine wrath; and a man whom I have often reproved, has told me repeatedly and with solemnity, too, "that he expected to go [to?] hell; but this was his consolation, that he could endure the fierceness of God's wrath as well as any man, for he was tough as any damned being." A woman, (yes, a woman!) of this description I have seen to-day, who is infected, but says that "she has been seven years in the professional business, has never been caught before, and, since she took up her trade to get a living, she is determined to die in it."[35]

Although filtered through Ely's pen, the words of these anonymous early nineteenth-century New Yorkers nevertheless give a taste of the indifference toward and even mockery of hell that some laypeople felt but did not record. Ely also encountered Catholic opposition to his evangelistic warnings. "When I want a priest I will send for one," a sick Catholic retorted, "We are of different religions." Ely "assured him, that I claimed no right to teach him...but I desired him to remember, that there is but one religion in heaven, and but one religion that leads to heaven.... With these words I left him; but he could not help railing at me."[36] What was at issue for this Catholic layman was Ely's claim that "all the men on earth could not forgive a single sin," implying that the confessions of priests were worthless.

Charles Finney noted a similar rebuff from the Germans of Reading, Pennsylvania, whom he tried to evangelize in 1829. He did not specify their religious background, but they may have been Lutherans or Catholics. "I cant begin to describe the state in which this region is, and has been for many years," he wrote to friend Theodore Dwight Weld:

> They think they are a very religious people. Whenever they are going to the communion they abstain for several days from sottish drunkenness, fighting, publick gambling generally, brothel hunting, etc., etc., and when it has gone by, they to their abominations again with most voracious appetite. This is the way they say that their Fathers went to heaven and they choose to go to heaven in the good old way.[37]

Although evangelicals tried to create communities of the "saved," the commonness of this type of rebuff again highlights the competing communities that some laypeople preferred.

Opposition to the evangelical hell also came from those who dismissed its deployment as a thinly veiled ploy to get money. An anonymous "Brother" wrote a pamphlet sometime in the 1820s warning his "Fellow-citizens" against "Modern Religious 'Travelling Ministers'" who claimed to be "sent by [God] to preach the Gospel and endeavor to rescue souls from a dreadful Hell, in which all those who do not believe as they say, must inevitably perish!" These "pretended" ministers, rather than build community, sowed division by creating rifts between those who followed them and those who did not. As the community splintered, the "Minister," if successful, would be laughing his way to the bank, "fully satisfied that his future expenses for 'bread and cheese,' lodging, &c. will be nothing."[38] This characterization of ministers as unscrupulous and greedy dovetailed with sensationalistic stories of ministers gone even further awry, seducing innocent women and acting like the devil in disguise instead of the shepherds of saved flocks.[39]

John Russell Kelso, born in a log cabin in Franklin County, Ohio, in 1831, was another mid-century anti-authoritarian skeptic. According to his unpublished Autobiography, which he recorded in a remarkable calf-skin ledger more than a foot in length (fig. 4.2), his male forebears, dating back to his great-grandfather, had all been skeptics. "During his later years," Kelso wrote, "my great-grandfather was the intimate friend of Thomas Jefferson, Thomas Paine, and Benjamin Franklin. Like these great and good men, he was an unbeliever in the Christian religion." His father was also a skeptic, but Kelso himself was deeply influenced by his mother's Methodism as a child. "She was intensely religious," he noted, "a sincere shouting Methodist." She was accustomed to punishing his childhood follies by thrashing him with a beech limb, to "infuse wisdom into a part of my body which was very capable of feeling, but which was utterly incapable of thinking or of becoming wise." This comment could be taken to foreshadow his later rejection of hell as eternal physical punishment.[40]

At the tender age of 5, the boy "concluded to try [his] hand at preaching." Rules and threats seemed to be what most struck Kelso about the religion in which his mother raised him. "At length the idea of being a preacher of the Mosaical type took so full possession of my mind," he explained, "that I concluded to invent me a god and invent conversations with him. This I did, calling my god, Dadle. The substance of all of Dadle's

FIGURE 4.2 Title Page, *John R. Kelso's complete works in manuscript written for his beloved son John R. Kelso, Junior and his posterity, 1873–1882*, The Huntington Library, mss HM 58109.

communications to me was that Annie and my other little playmates should obey me in all things, and give me most of their apples, cakes and other good things." Whenever his "little flock became rebellious and set my authority at defiance," Kelso went on, "I had simply to begin calling, in a solemn tone, Dadle! Dadle! Dadle! This never failed to bring them into more complete subjection than ever. In all I did, I did not mean to be wicked.... Indeed, without knowing it, I was simply doing what is done by nearly all intelligent persons of the priestly profession."[41] Like the anonymous "Brother," Kelso implied that ministers used threats to keep their flocks in line and simultaneously enrich their own pockets.

Kelso claimed that his own conversion experience was a travesty produced by the influence of "magnetism" upon an overwrought mind. He did not deny the "indescribably rapturous" "phenomenon" of the "change of heart" but suggested that it was human in origin. "The priests...of nearly all religions," he wrote, "being usually the most cunning of impostors, have generally understood how best to produce this phenomenon.... They have used it, with great effect, in holding the people in subjection to themselves." Although the teenaged Kelso was afflicted by religious anxiety, his responsibilities to his impoverished family often prevented him from attending church. Exhaustion and despair soon undermined his health:

> Even my sleep was disturbed by horrible visions of hell.... Only a powerful physical constitution kept me from death or insanity. For having made me suffer thus, let the hell-fire preaching priests who now fear and hate me congratulate themselves. They would gladly doom me to an eternity of such horrors if they could.

Finally, the summer after a serious bout with typhoid pneumonia brought the strapping youth down to a skeletal 100 pounds, he sought his minister's advice. The minister "decided that I was called to preach.... My mental sufferings became so great that, at one time, I left my work to take my own life. An accidental meeting with a neighbor prevented me from executing this design. The next day I became an exhorter, and, still in despair, I labored faithfully and successfully as such."[42]

Despite his misgivings, Kelso thrived in his new profession, marrying a Methodist preacher's daughter, teaching school on weekdays, and becoming a "first_class revivalist" on Sundays. Marital woes were the cause of his ultimate break with the church. Kelso's wife was in love with another man, but since he could not divorce her except on grounds of adultery, his attempt to do so besmirched both their names and called down the wrath of her father. Since public opinion was gathering around him anyway, Kelso took advantage of the controversy to "burst a bomb in the camp of the Lord and to leave all in consternation." He "had come to be an unbeliever in an endless hell of fire and brimstone, and in many other things which my church required me to preach. Indeed," he explained, "I was just in process of bursting the bonds of superstition's slavery and of becoming free." He created havoc by announcing his views in the midst of the Methodist regional conference in the mid-1850s. The presiding elder proclaimed him a "very powerful and dangerous enemy, and warned his hearers that, if my heresies were not nipped in the bud and my influence with the people destroyed, I would, within ten years, ruin the church and demoralize society." The elder's warning recalls the Calvinist clergy's reaction to "Salvation" Murray's universalism in the early republic.[43]

Kelso represented one extreme. Just as Native American revitalization prophets made the concept of hell their own, so other Euro-Americans rejected evangelical formulations of hell but not the entire prospect of future punishment. Doctor-adventurer Rowland Willard (husband of the pre-millennialist Elizabeth) also left an exceptionally detailed manuscript autobiography for his future posterity. Like Kelso, he was born to a "humble life almost verging on indigence."[44] In 1803, when he was 9, his father moved the family to a small mountain farm in Vermont because the region was then experiencing a season of Presbyterian revivals. The move forced the young boy to help support the family by toiling in the hardscrabble mountains.

Rowland left Vermont as an adolescent to journey on the Ohio River system. He spent his young adulthood learning carpentry, Freemasonry, music, and medicine in St. Charles, Missouri, between 1817 and 1825. He then left for Taos and Chihuahua, practicing medicine along the way. His father's attempt to evangelize the family had not been entirely successful, but Rowland did identify rather generically as a Protestant in Mexico, where he "was frequently importuned to be baptised a Roman Catholick." He never criticized the Church outright (as a popular doctor, his practice was at stake), but noted that "to trammel myself with such a fantastic religion, would not only be [word obscured], but in my own view sacriligious."[45] Rowland came back to the States in 1828. After still more travel, from Philadelphia to Cincinnati and down the Mississippi into Alabama, he married Elizabeth in 1832. She was then a Presbyterian, and Rowland thought he would join her church. The local Presbyterian minister went back East before admitting him, though, so the couple instead joined with the much-smaller Baptists, who had left them a pamphlet in hopes of wooing them away.

Subsequently, as we saw in chapter 3, the Willards became Millerites. In his Autobiography, written years after the Great Disappointment, Rowland admitted his error. Still, he believed that their adoption of Millerism had forced "the revolutionizing of our religious sentiments" and led to "a more thorough investigation of the Bible, & understanding in a more litteral sense than formerly."[46] Rowland began to question the very basis of his beliefs about the afterlife. His claim that he sought to understand the Bible more literally was a direct challenge to evangelicals, who purported to hold the only correct literal reading of the Bible. His examination of the

Scriptures led Willard to deny that the Bible affirmed an eternal hell of torture. But he also denied that all would be saved. Instead, he characterized the evangelical and Universalist perspectives as extremes and argued for a middle ground.[47] His position, known as annihilationism, held that those who died impenitent faced extinction in the lake of fire rather than a dubious immortality of eternal punishment. What he took issue with was the idea that temporal sins committed on earth could merit suffering forever. As a doctor who was not always able to save his patients, most starkly during the cholera epidemic that swept Cincinnati in 1832, Willard saw his fair share of earthly suffering; for that suffering to continue without end struck him as patently unjust.

"When God says that the impenitent sinner shall die the second death," he wrote, mocking the standard interpretation of what happened to the damned, "it means with them, that they shall live eternally in <u>torment</u>":

> The preaching of such horrors has perhape proved the greatest incentive of all others, to drive the ignorant into churchfolds, and not the love of God which should constrain us.... Human scaring by frightful imagery, & daring assumptions, are illy calculated to make genuine christians, but rather confident impostors.[48]

Ministers who used the threat of hell preyed on laypeople's fears. The result, Willard contended, was not always what evangelicals desired. While the majority "in all communities where orthodox religion is preached" "grow up with a full conviction of its truth," "The more considerate...when revolving the dreadful ordeal awaits the sinner, become skeptical, & not unfrequently infidel, rather than attribute to our Heavenly Father, a character so at variance with judgment & justice,—his divine attributes."[49] This sounds not dissimilar to the arguments made by John and Judith Murray about the nature of God. But Willard also had choice words for those who thought that God might grant everyone mercy and a blessed immortality. Based on the Bible, he asked, "Can we rationally come to the conclusion, that God will ever have compassion on the wicked & restore him to favour? I think it hardly probable to say the least."[50]

Willard never published his Autobiography though he likely hoped to, in order to convince more than his own immediate posterity of annihilationism. "Now dear reader," he wrote, in one example of the didactic and polemical tone he occasionally adopted, "where will you take your stand while viewing this awfully solemn subject. Will you shut your eyes to

divine testimony, & believe [^the] parrot twaddle of presumptious dogma-
tists, who catch with eager grasp the fulminations of the pulpit & the press
& in tones of authority awe the world with solemn vagueries?"[51] Like the
anonymous "Brother" and Kelso, Willard adopted the posture of the lone
commonsense gadfly sticking it to tradition-bound, hell-disseminating
evangelicals.

Willard did not invent the doctrine of annihilation, though. Adventists
Charles F. Hudson and George Storrs taught that the wicked would suffer
extinction rather than eternal punishment and spearheaded the creation
of the Advent Christian Church in 1860 from other disaffected former
followers of William Miller.[52] This church never gained many adherents.[53]
Annihilation still spelled eternal separation between the immortal saved
and the perishing damned, so for people who were primarily concerned
about the continuation of relationships after death, it was not much more
attractive than the binary of eternal heaven and hell.

Hierarchical Afterlives: Mormonism

Another antebellum religious innovator, born a decade after Willard,
attracted many more followers. Joseph Smith, Jr. (1805–1844) and the
Mormon Church he founded represent perhaps the best-known example
of antebellum religious creativity. Much has been written about Smith's
early life, and debates continue between those who treat him as an inspired prophet and others who seek to discover the human, historical roots
of the religion he founded. Whatever its provenance, Smith reimagined
the traditional afterlife to which Christians had adhered for centuries. His
revisions may have stemmed in part from his upbringing in a religiously
divided family like Kelso's, with a Universalist grandfather, a father who
"lost confidence in the integrity of churches altogether," and a deeply religious mother who brought three of Joseph's siblings into the Presbyterian
fold.[54] Smith's upbringing in western New York, where Finney raised revival fervor to a fever pitch, also shaped his religious imagination. And
one scholar has recently argued that Smith was profoundly influenced by
the omnipresence of death in the antebellum era. Seven of his mother's
eleven children perished; Joseph would have been the eighth had he not
survived a nasty case of typhoid fever as a child. According to this scholar,
early Mormonism grappled with the central problem of death: the ab-
rogation of earthly identities and relationships. Smith was right in line
with the other doubters we have seen when he "famously commented on

multiple occasions that he would be happy in hell if only he could be there with his friends."[55]

Smith turned eternal hell into a punishment designed only for the lowest of the low. On the sixteenth of February 1832, he and an associate, Sidney Rigdon, "were puzzling over a biblical passage that raised questions about rewards and punishments."[56] In the midst of their scrutiny, they received a revelation that revised the heaven/hell binary of the evangelical afterlife and instead described a hierarchical hereafter beginning with the "sons of perdition," men who had no excuse for their downfall since they "kn[e]w my [the Lord's] power, and have been made partakers thereof, and suffered themselves, through the power of the devil, to be overcome, and to deny the truth, and defy my power." The revelation continued, "It had been better for them never to have been born; for they are vessels of wrath doomed to suffer the wrath of God. ... These are they who shall go away into the lake of fire and brimstone," and to "eternal punishment, to reign with the devil and his angels in eternity, where their worm dieth not and the fire is not quenched."[57]

But the "sons of perdition" were the only ones who would never "be redeemed in the due time of the Lord, after the sufferings of his wrath; for all the rest shall be brought forth by the resurrection of the dead, through the triumph and the glory of the Lamb, who was slain, who was in the bosom of the Father before the worlds were made." The "celestial," or highest heaven, was reserved for the righteous and the just, who accepted the revelations of Christ: "these are they whose bodies are celestial, whose glory is that of the sun, even the glory of God the highest of all." The second group of the redeemed would be taken to a lower "terrestrial world": "Behold, these are they who died without law; and also they who are the spirits of men kept in prison, whom the Son visited, and preached the gospel unto them." The terrestrial sphere was a grey zone for those who fell between the clearly blessed and the clearly sinful, including the Old Testament faithful who died before Christ's coming and those more modern-day innocents who lived outside the reach of the revelations. Although not as high as the celestial world, the terrestrial was not hell. It simply "differ[ed] in glory as the moon differs from the sun."[58]

And finally, there was the "telestial" sphere, the lowest afterlife option for those who would eventually be redeemed, different from the terrestrial world as the stars from the moon. This sphere housed those who received not the gospel of Christ, neither the testimony of Jesus: these are they who deny not the Holy Spirit: these are they who are thrust down to hell: these are they who shall not be redeemed from the devil, until the last resurrection, until the Lord, even Christ the Lamb, shall have finished his work.

The occupants of the telestial sphere included those who, in the evangelical schema, would have quickly received a one-way ticket straight to eternal hell: "liars, and sorcerers, and adulterers, and whoremongers, and who-soever loves and makes a lie: these are they who suffer the wrath of God on the earth: these are they who suffer the vengeance of eternal fire: these are they who are cast down to hell and suffer the wrath of Almighty God until the fulness of times." The difference between the telestial sphere and eternal hell was that the occupants of the latter (the "sons of perdition") would never repent, while the former would ultimately be redeemed. As bad as telestial sinners might be, one had to be beyond bad to be a "son of perdition," on par with Judas Iscariot.[59]

The hierarchical afterlife that Smith offered his followers allowed for finer moral gradations than the binary option presented by evangelical Protestants and even by Rowland Willard, and the single option presented by Universalists. Smith still balanced God's mercifulness with a stern view of God's justice toward enemies of the Latter-Day Saints. "[I]f God were not to come out in swift judgment against the workers of iniquity and the powers of darkness," he wrote in the 1835 first complete edition of his *Doctrines and Covenants*, "his saints could not be saved; for it is by judg-ment that the Lord delivers his saints out of the hands of all their enemies, and those who reject the gospel of our Lord Jesus Christ." Mercy to the saints, in other words, necessitated judgment against their enemies.[60] The "us" vs. "them" in statements like these allowed Smith and his followers to condemn the persecutory non-Mormon "other" to a hell of suffering after death, while reassuring Mormons whose loved ones remained outside the fold that this hell would only be temporary unless their loved ones were as evil as Judas. Further revelations offered still more comfort, including the prospect that husbands and wives would be "sealed" to each other for eternity, that children who died before the age of 8 would be taken to the highest, celestial kingdom, and that the dead could be baptized. Polygamy can also be viewed in light of Smith's afterlife revisions, since it allowed families broken apart by death to remain together even as spouses remar-ried in this life.[61]

Smith's revelations about the afterlife struck a responsive chord. New York newspaper editor William W. Phelps "called the revelation on the three degrees of glory 'the greatest news that was ever published to man.'"[62] Apostle Parley Pratt said that part of his reason for becoming a Mormon had to do with Smith's teachings on the life to come. In their conversations together Pratt was assured that "the wife of my bosom might be secured to me for time and for all eternity," in contrast to still-common Protestant teachings that relationships begun on earth do not continue in the same way in heaven.[63] Louise Graehl, a Swiss convert who crossed the plains in 1854, also remembered that her dissatisfaction with Protestant teachings drove her to Mormonism. Her former church "could not tell me if my sweet [deceased] baby was saved, for they said there was no provision in the Bible for the salvation of children, but that we may hope that the Lord would take care of them."[64] Mormons faced ostracism from their unbelieving friends and family and were separated from them not only spiritually but also geographically, as many joined the arduous trek west that eventually ended in the Salt Lake Valley. They were profoundly reassured that their decision to adopt the newfound faith did not require them to believe that the loved ones they left behind were eternally damned.

Progress from this Life to the Next

Evangelicals considered the biblical canon closed; Mormons saw it as a work-in-progress.[65] Swedenborgians too did not view the Bible as the only and final word on matters religious, but read it in light of the metaphysical revelations of Emanuel Swedenborg (1688–1772), a scientist and erstwhile Swedish Lutheran. Swedenborg claimed that his revelations represented the Second Coming of the Lord and that they unraveled the mysteries of the universe into an orderly, organic system incorporating "three distinct orders of being: the natural world of mineral, vegetable, or animal 'ultimates,' the spiritual, and the celestial." According to Swedenborg, these orders were linked by a system of correspondences, wherein a symbol in one sphere represented reality in another. The human mind could ascertain these correspondences and aim for the higher realities that earthly forms represented.[66]

The orders of being also corresponded to a progressive and hierarchical afterlife. According to southern homeopathic doctor and Swedenborgian William Henry Holcombe, infants and children who died prematurely would attain the highest of heavens: the celestial sphere. The place of children in this highest heaven worked for the good of parents left behind, as it would make them "likely to be better men and better citizens when some society of angels in heaven holds our children as hostages for our good behavior on earth."[67] Holcombe sought to inculcate morality by appealing to the desire for future reunion rather than the fear of hell. In the Swedenborgian view of the afterlife, hell was an avoidable choice from which humans could escape even after death. The hellish realms corresponded to the lowest order of being, where the natural world was only a smokescreen for the higher celestial planes. Those who regressed in the afterlife chose to enjoy delusional fantasies that were but cheap imitations of higher realities. God did not create the hells for punishment, but permitted their existence for evil spirits and evil men who would rather stultify themselves with false and selfish delights than progress through the heavens to associate with God, the angels, and regenerate humanity.[68]

Swedenborgianism boasted no more than 3,000 members in America on the eve of the Civil War, but it exercised an important influence on groups as diverse as the Transcendentalists, utopian communalists, and mesmerists. Scholars debate whether Joseph Smith was also influenced by Swedenborgianism; the similarities between his hierarchical view of the afterlife and the Swedenborgian version are striking.[69] Unitarian William Ellery Channing's ideas of heaven and hell, as recorded in his *Memoir*, also shared affinities with Swedenborg's progressive afterlife. Channing rejected original sin and spoke of the human "capacity for transcendence, its ability to yield the new, to push in thought, imagination, and moral harmony beyond its current limits."[70] For Channing, voluntary virtue was the substance of salvation and people could continue to work toward it after death. "In this life progression is the universal law," he wrote. "Nothing is brought into being in its most perfect state.... Is it not natural to expect that in a future life our nature will be progressive, that the knowledge with which the Christian will commence his future being will be a point from which he will start, a foundation on which he will build, rather than a state in which he will eternally rest?"[71] Some evangelical revivalists also preached the possibility of progress in heaven. Lyman Beecher memorialized a congregant with the assurance that "in heaven his knowledge is growing, his mind is expanding, and his holiness and joy will increase forever."[72] But for evangelicals heaven was distinctly different from earth, and knowledge in the hereafter contrasted sharply with the confusing obscurity of the here-and-now, where humans could only see through a glass darkly. For Channing, by contrast, progress in heaven was but a continuation of the mind's development on earth.

Channing did not dismiss the possibility of future punishment. One did not have to be perfect or perfectly regenerated to enter heaven, but one could not remain impenitent. Channing adamantly refused a Universalist position as both unscriptural and socially dangerous: "It directly, palpably, and without disguise diminishes the restraints on vice. It is at war with society. It is a blow at the root of social order." He might as well have been "Damnation" Murray here. But he argued from nature and correspondences between the human and divine to make his case: "Conscience in man is an echo, if I may so speak, to the will and moral sentiments of God.... Let God be viewed as so unconcerned about character as not to punish the guiltiest life, as to fall short in his administration of the plainest requisitions of justice, and a deadly torpor would spread over the human conscience. Moral sensibility would be paralyzed." Channing anticipated and reversed Gerrit Smith's idea that belief in future punishment could do nothing but paralyze people with fear. Yet he took a less definitive position than most evangelicals on the nature of eternal punishment: "In what way we shall suffer, or to what duration and extent, the Scriptures, it seems to me, have not precisely defined, and we need not to know."[73] He encouraged people not to become overwhelmed by feelings of guilt and sin to the point where they neglected benevolent action for their society: "Men have sometime been addressed as if they had nothing to do but to remember and lament their sins.... Do not imagine for a moment that Christianity encourages an unnatural, morbid, extravagant mode of thought. It calls you to other duties and services besides the recollection of your sins; and it teaches you, even when engaged in these recollections, still to be just to yourselves...to charge on yourselves no imaginary or exaggerated guilt."[74] Channing would likely have shaken his head over lay converts who ritualistically bemoaned their guilt in their diaries and letters.

Also influenced by the Swedenborgian view of the afterlife, Spiritualists took the idea of correspondences between spheres to the next level: if such correspondences could be ascertained by humans, then "relations of the visible and invisible worlds" must also be discoverable.[75] Spiritualism is most famous for its séances and spirit-rappings, which appealed both to bereaved laypeople of various mainstream denominations, and to those who sought less conventional and formalistic religious practice. Its antebellum apologists portrayed it as a sophisticated system premised on the idea of the eternal progress of spirit and the ability of spirits to communicate with each other along the path to the highest heavens.

S. B. Brittan, editor of the Spiritualist journal *The Shekinah*, criticized the dominant Protestant theology for creating "an impassable gulf" between "the spheres of visible and invisible life." This gulf "leaves Man to grovel among the dead elements of earth. True, it gives the vague promise of immortality hereafter, but it affords no definite conception of the relations of that state and the present.... Its heaven is afar off, or is peopled with inert spirits who seem to love their ease and forget their friends." Brittan rejected such an amorphous and impersonal heaven, but he also rejected a materialist heaven meant simply to satisfy the senses. Since humans were ultimately spiritual beings, he argued, heaven should also primarily be a place of spiritual communion between the living and the spirits of their departed loved ones, and of spirits with each other, God, and the angels. "Modern theology," Brittan concluded, "suggests the idea of a huge *petrifaction*.... [But] Spiritualism brings Heaven and our departed friends back to us."[76]

Expanding upon what he called "The Celestial Life on Earth," another contributor to *The Shekinah*, W. S. Courtney, took a proto-evolutionary view of humanity's spiritual development over time and from here to hereafter. He suggested that the evangelical heaven and hell were reflections of the early stages of human development from the natural, to the moral, to the spiritual and celestial. Revealing his intellectual debt to Swedenborgianism (to which he had once subscribed), Courtney argued that the basest stage of development, the "natural life," was ruled by love of self. "This state of life dominates and tyrannizes the love of the neighbor and the love of God," he wrote, "which have to be *compelled*, the former by criminal codes, jails, and penitentiaries, and the latter by the omnipotent vengeance, fire and brimstone, and eternal hell of a selfish God." The self-absorbed would not be swayed by any motivations (like sympathy or compassion) that did not directly affect their personal well-being. "Self-love," he summarized, "is the only original sin."[77] In so saying, he might have been the eminent Samuel Hopkins himself.

But Courtney was no New Divinity man. After criticizing the "natural life," he proceeded to deconstruct the next stage of human development, the "moral life." In this still flawed stage of awareness, people knew the difference between good and evil. In contrast to evangelicals, for whom the responsibility to choose the good was the challenge of the Christian life, Courtney believed that the dependency of good on its opposition, evil, was unenlightened. In this stage of development, "every moral being must have *done* the evil," he explained, "must have partaken of the forbidden fruit—in order to *know* the good and the true." He deplored the "undeniable necessity of evil in the moral life and constitution," which he believed was "the secret cause of all the religious enormities and theological monstrosities in repute among Christians at this day": "They *fear* and worship God only as a Moral Being, ascribing to Him all the moral virtues which are inseparable from their antagonist vices: hence, without seeming to be aware of it, they, of necessity, ascribe to him the attributes of another famous character found in their theology. He is wrathful, vindictive and exemplary, condemning and approving, 'electing and reprobating.'"[78] Courtney's conflation of the Christian God with the devil was deliberately provocative: he hoped to goad non-Spiritualist readers into a reconsideration of their beliefs.

In contrast to the evangelical heaven, hell, God, and devil, products of soon-to-be obsolete stages of human development, Courtney offered the "celestial life on earth." The connections between this life and the next enabled the living to begin their progress into the celestial realms. Heaven was not a place to which the good went after death, doing nothing but worshiping God and singing songs of praise. Heaven was about the opening of the mind and its progression beyond the lower, selfish states of existence into higher realms of knowledge and understanding. Humans could begin the process of upward spiritual momentum in the here-and-now if they shook off the bonds of tradition and opened themselves to the possibility of spiritual communication.[79]

Courtney and Brittan offered an erudite and esoteric version of Spiritualism. The visions of the Honorable John Worth Edmonds were less so. A Democrat who served in both chambers of the New York State Legislature, worked as an Indian Agent, was appointed an Inspector of State Prisons in 1837, and elected as a Circuit Judge in the First Judicial District in 1845, the prominent Edmonds lent Spiritualism some prestige.[80] Soon after his wife's death in 1850 the grieving judge thought he heard her voice. A female friend introduced him to the wonders of "Spiritual Intercourse," and he soon came to believe that he was vested with the power of mediumship and could himself see into the spirit world.[81]

In a vision recorded under the title of "Personal Experience," Edmonds described seeing happy and unhappy spirits in realms seemingly akin to heaven and hell. Unlike the metaphysical speculations of Brittan and Courtney, his vision was materially detailed. The spirits were embodied to the extent that he could recognize them. The happy ones included not only his dear departed wife, but also William Penn, apparently a guardian spirit since Edmonds's childhood, Sir Isaac Newton, Emanuel Swedenborg, and Benjamin Franklin.[82] Edmonds saw these happy spirits pointing in one accord toward another realm, where "oh! what a sight I beheld! Innumerable spirits were there, engaged in perpetual pursuit of each other. They were dark and somber in appearance and the vilest passions were most apparent." Among these somber spirits was "the murderer, with his drawn dagger, with fiendish hate pursuing his victim until he struck him to the heart." The murdering spirit could never receive the satisfaction of actually striking his victim, for "lo! his blow had alighted upon impalpable air, and he had missed the darling object of his pursuit. Rage and despair devoured him at his failure and he fled howling, his intended victim pursuing him in turn with revenge and hatred rankling in him." Other evil spirits similarly found themselves thwarted by their unfulfilled desires: the adulterer grasped at "empty air"; the miser "gather[ed] up sparkling atoms" only to find his pile "turned to dust"; the hypocrite learned "that his every thought was revealed"; and the seducer, warrior, suicide, assassin, and "man of the world" were equally foiled in their nefarious schemes.[83]

This image of the thwarted spirits of sinners could have been taken from any evangelical's depiction of the terrors of hell, but Edmonds's vision continued. For according to the Spiritualist notion of progressive spiritual development, good and happy spirits could travel back and forth from higher to lower realms, bringing their wisdom to those lost in the ether of unfulfilled and evil desires. Edmonds related how he next "saw a good spirit approach. He was one, I thought, whose enthusiasm was stronger than his judgment, and he approached that awful society in the vain hope that he might be able to wean them from their evil ways." Although met with derision from the evil spirits, who mocked him even as they fled from his presence, one remained "prostrate in the dust.... It was one who had begun to progress in goodness—whose eyes were beginning to open to the evil of his ways. It was one who had begun to repent." At the sight of this prostrate spirit, "the announcement sped through Heaven, with the celerity of thought, that a fallen man might be saved, and in crowds the good spirits flocked to the scene and welcomed the rising hope that was in him. They took him in their arms and bore him in triumph from that evil place, to their own happy mansions." In referring to the abode of good spirits as "Heaven" and "happy mansions," Edmonds revealed his familiarity with biblical texts (as in John 14:2, "In my father's house are many mansions") but also his distance from the Protestant orthodoxy in his bold suggestion that "a fallen man might be saved" not by Christ, but by the ministrations of good spirits benevolent enough to travel down to the unhappy realms.[84]

Edmonds initially saw his vision as a glimpse into hell and heaven. But when he presented it at a circle, a communication from the "Spirit-world" told him that "you do not exactly understand the lesson it was intended to teach":

> The crime and misery in it, are intended to represent *your sphere,* and the sin and suffering which flow from the condition in which the greater part of mankind are placed. The bright features of purity and happiness in it, the higher spheres in the spiritual world; and the prostrate spirit who was lifted up and redeemed, those who have begun spiritually to progress.[85]

This communication revised Edmonds's materially detailed mishmash of biblical and Spiritualist ideas into a more S. B. Brittan or W. S. Courtney-esque notion of mental and spiritual stagnation (hell-like) and development (heaven-like) beginning in the here-and-now and extending into the hereafter.

Spiritualist views of the afterlife differed, as might be expected of a movement that allowed for direct revelations and communications through any number of mediums. But the Spiritualist belief in eternal dynamism and in human agency as the motor propelling an eternal spirit from unhappy stagnation to progression through realms of knowledge and light required something resembling hell. Just as Mormonism preserved a hell with which to threaten enemies to the faith, so Spiritualists used the idea of a stagnated base-level state of existence to condemn both the lack of progress and spiritual creativity that they diagnosed among the Protestant orthodoxy, and the selfish materialism of their less-esoteric peers. Those bereaved lay Americans who turned to Spiritualism while retaining their denominational allegiances cherry-picked from its promises, hoping that their loved ones were happily roaming the heavens, rather than selfishly grasping at thin air in the unhappy realms below.

Sentimentalism and Nurture

Spiritualists were hardly alone in desiring connectedness with and re-assurance about the dearly departed. Not every layperson who was dis-turbed by the prospect of future separation turned to communication with the dead. The longing for future reunion also manifested itself in denial of the possibility of hell, when push came to shove, for one's own kith and kin.

The idea that those closest to oneself could not possibly be bad enough for God to eternally condemn—for if anyone could be loved by an ordinary human being, then why not by God also?—found florid expression in the mid-century sentimentalization of death, which blunted the implications of damnation for those who took refuge in its writings and rituals. The possibility that death might come at any time for anyone had once been accepted as an unavoidable and common fact of life. But in antebellum America, death became increasingly perceived as a major event calling for elaborate rituals of preparation, mourning, and commemoration.[86] Evangelicals, as we have seen, played a role in bringing about this shift, painting death as a momentous occasion requiring serious preparation rather than as a normal and inevitable part of human existence. Epidemic diseases like yellow fever and cholera also influenced attitudes toward death. Fear of malodorous fumes from dead bodies led to the exclusion of burial grounds from urban areas and the creation on cities' outskirts of "garden" cemeteries designed to resemble peaceful parks. Meanwhile, scientific experimentation began to denaturalize death by suggesting that it might sometimes be preventable rather than inescapably ordained by an inscrutable Providence.[87]

As death became less of a familiar and natural event, the bereaved consoled themselves with detailed visions of an afterlife just like this one where their loved ones awaited them in bliss. Antebellum sentimentalists gave a resounding "yes" to a question the Bible and some earlier revival-ists had only skirted, namely, "Will We Know Our Friends in Heaven?"[88] While some laypeople, like Martha Laurens Ramsay, reposed in feelings of guilt and anxiety, others embraced comforting domestic visions of the life to come that all but excluded the possibility of hell for themselves and their loved ones. Some ministers did the same. By mid-century, retired minister David Ogden was complaining to his diary that a "common man" had asked one of his colleagues "if the Congregational ministers had not agreed together to banish the word <u>hell</u> from their sermons."[89]

The trio of mother, home, and heaven was a favorite subject of ante-bellum sentimentalists. *Mother* was supposed to create a nurturing *home* in which she taught the appropriate beliefs and behaviors that would usher her family members into a *heaven* that looked much like the home she had created on earth. We have already seen that evangelicals urged mothers to bear responsibility for the eternal welfare of their children and husbands. But the idea that a mother could gradually train her children for heaven marked a subtle but significant reaction against evangelical reviv-alism, toward the idea that continual, loving nurture was more important than inducing an immediate change of heart.

Horace Bushnell's 1847 *Discourses on Christian Nurture* epitomized this trend. Bushnell urged that "the aim, effort and expectation should be, not, as is commonly assumed, that the child is to grow up in sin, to be con-verted after he comes to a mature age, but that he is to open on the world as one that is spiritually renewed."[90] Bushnell criticized the evangelical approach to the instruction of children:

> Simply to tell a child, as he just begins to make acquaintance with words, that he "must have a new heart, before he can be good," is to inflict a double discouragement. First, he cannot guess what this technical phraseology means.... Secondly, he is told that he must have a new heart *before* he can be good.... Discouraged thus on every side, his tender soul turns hither and thither, in hopeless de-spair, and finally he consents to be what he must—a sinner against God and that only.[91]

The evangelical push for immediate conversion might backfire by creating reprobates instead of redeeming them, said Bushnell—much as Amariah Brigham had suggested that fire and brimstone preaching might produce insanity instead of saved souls.

Catharine Beecher shared Bushnell's rejection of immediate conver-sionism. Even as she used the threat of final judgment to urge produc-tivity in her *Treatise on Domestic Economy*, she herself had never actually experienced the evangelical change of heart. She had been on the verge as a young woman, but the "agonizing pain" brought about by her father Lyman's attempts at "addressing her conscience" was followed by devas-tating grief when her also-unconverted fiancé, Alexander Fisher, died in a shipwreck off the coast of Ireland. Lyman declared that Alexander was almost certainly damned. "And now, my dear child, what will you do?" he asked. "Will you turn at length to God, and set your affections on things above, or cling to the ship-wrecked hopes of earthly good?"[92]

Catharine responded with resistance and her experience profoundly influenced her little sister, Harriet Beecher Stowe. Sudden death continued to strike among the Beechers as it did many other families: their brother George committed suicide in 1843, and in the span of a decade, Harriet lost two sons, 18-month-old Samuel Charles to cholera in 1849 and unconverted teenager Henry Ellis to drowning in 1857. Harriet wrestled with the meaning of death for the unregenerate in the form that came most easily to her: fiction writing. In her 1859 *The Minister's Wooing*, set in the early years of the republic, she wove together the experiences of the pure and selfless Mary, who loses her beloved but unconverted cousin James Marvyn to the sea, and a fictionalized account of the life of Samuel Hopkins.

In the painful scenes that follow news of James's shipwreck, his mother, Mrs. Marvyn, gives voice to the grief of many. "Mary, I cannot, will not, be resigned!—it is all hard, unjust, cruel!" In the depths of her despair and anger at God for taking her unconverted son, Mrs. Marvyn, portrayed as a parishioner of Hopkins once renowned for her piety, questions her own salvation: "I can never love God! I can never praise Him!—I am lost! lost! lost! And what is worse, I cannot redeem my friends! Oh, I could suffer forever,—how willingly!—if I could save him!—But oh, eternity, eternity! Frightful, unspeakable woe! No end!— no bottom!—no shore!—no hope!—O God! O God!"[93] Mrs. Marvyn's distress over her inability to "redeem my friends" suggests the profound weight of the notion that converts bore responsibility for the eternal welfare of each other's souls.

Stowe voiced her own dissent against the preaching of eternal separation in the reassuring words of the Marvyns' loyal black servant, Candace: "I'm clar Mass'r James is one o' de 'lect; and I'm clar dar's consid'able more o' de 'lect than people tink. Why, Jesus didn't die for nothin',—all dat love a'n't gwine to be wasted. De 'lect is more'n you or I knows, honey!"[94] That Stowe put these words in the mouth of a stock black figure speaking in dialect reflects both her propensity to depict African Americans as noble, wise, and comforting, and her attribution of folksy acumen to the theologically uneducated. That Mrs. Marvyn mourns more than her husband and that Mary lapses into an equally profound sorrow also speaks to Stowe's association of mothers and female lovers with the deepest resistance to eternal separation. Hopkins, by contrast,

represents an old guard of unfeelingly and unflinchingly logical theologians who put consistency above compassion.

Stowe used fiction to explore the possibility that more were saved than
ministers might proclaim; Catharine Beecher entered the theological
arena more directly. In her 1857 *Common sense applied to religion: or, The
Bible and the people,* she suggested that the doctrines generated by the likes
of Edwards and his successors "are to be examined and tested by *the laity*
as much as by theologians, and especially are they to be examined and
decided on by *woman,* as the heaven-appointed educator of infancy and
childhood."[95] Beecher's hell was not a place to which God sent the unconverted: instead, like heaven, it was an extension of habits formed in this
life. Showing her continued indebtedness to Hopkins despite her and her
sister's qualms about the coldness of his teaching, Beecher divided the
world into "two classes of minds": the benevolent and the selfish. These
two classes started on earth and continued after death, "for we must suppose that the habits of mind which are existing in this life will continue
to increase, and if the mind is immortal, a time must come when one
class will become perfectly benevolent and the other perfectly selfish."[96]
Beecher described the sufferings of the "malignant mind" as a product
of shame, "ungratified desire," "*loss of enjoyment,*" persecution and hatred of "every other malignant mind," fear, "inactivity of body and mind,"
"consciousness of guilt," and despair. Perfectly selfish people could not
help but torment each other. "If such objects as the 'lake which burneth
with fire and brimstone, and the worm that never dies,' could be found,
no Almighty hand would need to interfere," she concluded, "while the
'smoke of their torment' would arise from flames of their own kindling."[97]

Beecher's revisions to the concept of damnation were, on the one
hand, subtle. She still divided humanity into two classes. Neither would
want to associate with the other, so the selfish would not enjoy heaven any
more than the benevolent would enjoy hell.[98] On the other hand, her hell
also shared some commonalities with that of Spiritualists W. S. Courtney
and John Worth Edmonds. The torments of hell were neither created nor
assigned by God for failure to convert, but enacted by humans on themselves and each other through "wrong action of mind": God was hardly
even necessary. As much as human agency served to create eternal suffering, however, Beecher also read a new kind of determinism into her
view of human nature. She rejected the "dogma of a depraved constitution," but asked, "Are not habits increased by perpetual repetition?"[99]
Rejecting evangelical conversionism meant rejecting the possibility of an

immediate change of heart that could undo all of the mind's malignant tendencies. Bad habits could become ingrained to the point of no return. Like Bushnell, Beecher saw "the *right* training of the human mind in infancy and childhood" as the proper way to salvation.[100]

Since mothers bore responsibility for nurturing their children, some began to assert that they—and not evangelical ministers—could say where their babes had gone after death. Little wonder that they often wrote their dead children into heaven, however disobedient they might have been on earth. Ministers who followed this liberalizing trend, like Henry Harbaugh and George Cheever, agreed that infants and even older children could not possibly be damned.[101] In contrast to the either/or nature of conversion, nurture was a gradual process, making it easier to rationalize that a loved one was on the right path to a heaven where they could continue to grow in grace, even if they were occasionally (or even frequently) imperfect.

Of course, men could also grieve the loss of their children deeply. The skeptic John Russell Kelso memorialized the death of his son, Ianthus, in verse:

> And thou art gone, Ianthus, beyond the bright blue sky,
> I'll find thee 'mong the angel bands, when I like thee should die;
> There in that high, that happy land, our sorrows all beguiled,
> I'll spend eternity with thee, my lost, my darling child.[102]

Despite (or perhaps because of) his unbelief in hell and concomitant rejection of evangelicalism, Kelso tapped into the major themes surrounding the sentimental culture of death: the expectation that the deceased was already in heaven; the understanding of heaven as a "happy land" where people would sorrow no more (rather than a theocentric and impersonal place primarily characterized by the worship of God); and the assumption that death would reunite people with loved ones who had gone before.[103]

No Time for Hell on the Overland Trail

Others simply had too much to worry about in the here-and-now to devote much attention to avoiding suffering in the hereafter and memorializing the dead. Not all travelers west were like Frederick Niles, keeping track of their own and others' religious conditions. The women and men who took to the overland trails had to cope with temporal separation from those who stayed behind, along with illness, accident, and death on the journey. Sensing that they were part of an expansion (and dispossession) of historic proportion, and that records of their travels might interest not only loved ones back East but also future generations, they kept diaries and wrote letters by the score. Emigrants frequently noted not only major natural markers along the way like Chimney Rock and Scott's Bluffs but also the deaths that occurred and the graves that they passed on their journey. One scholar has estimated an overall mortality rate of 4 percent on the trail, but to emigrants themselves the numbers often seemed higher, approaching one out of ten.[104]

Overlanders improvised coffins and grave markers from traveling trunks, crates, and the sideboards of wagons, and held makeshift funeral services. The need to make it to the final destination before winter set in meant that people could not linger along the trail and deaths could not be mourned in the same way as in a settled community. Emigrants' diaries record sorrow, stoicism, and anxiety over their own temporal well-being in the face of death, more than fears that the dead might be in a place even worse than the lonely, howling prairies where their corpses were left behind. Child mortality in particular could call forth emotions so strong as to be all but indescribable. After her 10-year-old son was accidentally thrown out of a wagon to his death, Lucia Lorraine Williams wrote to her parents that "to find him breathless so soon was awful. I cannot describe to you our feelings."[105] Williams's husband was so distraught that he "was beside himself with grief and anger" and "was about to shoot the unfortunate driver" when restrained by other members of the company.[106] Some diarists speculated that they might be the next to go. In a letter to the family of the deceased Benjamin ("Frank") Adams, S. Mathews candidly described the feelings of his company:

> One of sixteen gone from us almost at the commencement of our long journey,—how many more might there be before the termination of it, and who might not be the next victim? Frank's death very much depressed the spirits of the Company.... There was not a dry eye at his funeral.[107]

Leaving the graves of loved ones behind was painful; admitting the possibility that the loved one might be in hell was, not surprisingly, beyond the emotional capacity of most emigrants. Rather than agonize over the eternal fate of the departed, diarists instead worried whether wolves might

FIGURE 4.3 William Ranney (1813–1857), *Prairie Burial.* 1848. Oil on canvas, 28 1/2 × 41 in.

Courtesy of the Buffalo Bill Historical Center, Cody, Wyoming, U.S.A.: Gift of Mrs. J. Maxwell Moran, 3.97.

ravage their corpses and took comfort in the thought that they might meet again, intact, in the life to come.[108]

An 1848 image of a burial on the prairie by artist William Ranney illustrates the many emotions called forth by death on the plains (fig. 4.3). An emigrant family stands over a small plot that the father has dug; a child has passed away. The weeping mother, fretful sibling, and stoic father all look down toward the grave; the grandfather or perhaps minister, member of an earlier generation, looks heavenward for guidance. As one scholar has noted, "the bower of leaves above the father's head and the child's grave suggests the 'wooded vales' and 'alleys green' that were prototypes of heaven in many views of American cemeteries of the period."[109] The clouds are fleecy and non-menacing, the sky blue. In Ranney's depiction of this archetypal family's grief, we can see a quiet turn away from hell among a wider population than just self-identified Universalists or other freethinkers. The family's sorrow is counterbalanced by the salvific promise symbolized by the idyllic background that surrounds them.

Hell for the "Other"?

The assumption of heaven for loved ones did not necessarily extend to others. Just as Native American prophets, Mormons, and Spiritualists preserved some form of hell for their antagonists, so some Euro-American overlanders preserved a concept of ultimate punishment or at least ultimate separation for certain "others" while denying its terrors for themselves.

The rationalization of disappointed missionaries, that peoples were unequally favored and some could actively resist the offer of salvation, had a counterpart on the overland trails. Euro-Americans excused themselves from blame for the destruction and dispossession they wrought on the lands and lives of Native peoples who (so they told themselves) refused to accommodate to the inexorable forward march of "civilization" and hence spelled their own "inevitable" doom. Just as frustrated evangelicals spoke of the eventual damnation of the incorrigible "heathen," so overland emigrants spoke of the eventual disappearance of the Native peoples over whose lands they were traveling, while rendering the Indians who stood in their way as murderous savages deserving of death.

Many more emigrants died of cholera than at the hands of Indians, but the fear of attack colored their often-complacent attitudes toward Native deaths. Some wagon companies even explicitly organized along military lines,[110] implying a willingness to kill when emigrants believed themselves or their livestock endangered. In a letter to his friends soon after he arrived in San José, California, Wesley Tonner wrote: "We killed these two [Indians] and the one that was wounded, afterwards died. So we heard.... I do not think there was any wrong about it. I fought for my rights, and tried to kill them lest they might attack our camp we knew not when."[111] He justified the killings as a preemptive strike and the just dues of the Indian "other" who might be contemplating an "attack" on himself and his own. Tonner did not reference where he thought the dead might go, but we can be fairly certain he did not believe he was giving them a one-way ticket to heaven by killing them unprovoked.

By contrast, any emigrant who perished on the trail became a virtual martyr to the cause of westward expansion, guaranteed an impressive afterlife not only in the life beyond but also in the memory of survivors. Emigrants actively tried to ensure that future generations would not forget their struggles.[112] In *Personal Experiences of the Oregon Trail Sixty Years Ago*, for instance, Ezra Meeker referred to the overland wagons as a "mighty army" that endured the "Great American Desert, and braved the dangers of Indian warfare, of starvation, of sickness." He estimated "five thousand sacrifices of lives laid down even in one year to aid in the effort to recover the great empire, the Oregon country." "Mighty army," "sacrifices," and "empire" are all nation-building words, suggesting that the deaths of the emigrants were not in vain.[113]

Even as they mourned, respected, and assumed the best afterlife scenarios for their own deceased, emigrants trampled on the graves of Native people, opening them, examining skulls, and plundering artifacts.[114] In 1851, teenager Harriet Talcott Buckingham noted the discovery of skeletons near Council Bluffs: "The fact was elucidated," she wrote in her diary, "that, large tribes of Indians from the middle states had been pushed off by our government to this frontier region to make room for white settlers, and had here perished in large numbers by starvation." Hardly fazed, she continued: "Skulls were thick: of peculiar shape differeing from the Anglo Saxon type."[115] Similarly, while Frederick Niles tried to save himself and fellow whites from the "vortex of ruin" out West, he dismissed the eternal welfare of the nonwhite people he encountered. "Saw more Indians to day," he wrote on arriving in "South Plat" on May 23, 1860: "They were principally the squaws with their little ones. _...most of their children were in a nude state & looked more like a specie of young monkies than human beings with souls as precious as my owne."[116]

Buckingham's and Niles's dry descriptions reflect the rise of racial Anglo-Saxonism in the nineteenth century. Scholars have suggested that a growing interest in categorizing peoples paralleled contemporaneous attempts at empirically classifying the world's flora and fauna, beginning with Enlightenment scientists and percolating down to ordinary people like Buckingham and Niles. Apparent physical differences came to be seen as inherent markers of character differences, with Anglo-Saxons supposedly at the top of a racial hierarchy both in terms of appearance and temperament.[117]

But even as racial thinking became more closely tied to phenotype, religious categories of difference did not disappear.[118] Niles recognized that the Native children he saw were not a "specie of young monkies," but their "nude state" nevertheless suggested to him a soulless interior state. Just as they lacked the trappings of civilization, so they also seemed to lack the capacity for salvation. The notion that some people were closer to soulless "monkies" than to humans with "precious" (and redeemable) souls paralleled the increasingly influential idea that nonwhite peoples were somehow biologically different, that this difference spelled inferiority, and that inferiority spelled eventual but inevitable extinction. "Science" and "religion" were hardly separate spheres in the antebellum era. An older theological determinism—rejected by many white Americans for themselves but not necessarily for others—reinforced a newer biological determinism, and vice versa. Rigidifying racial classifications provided Euro-Americans with additional vocabulary for explaining their inability to convert the world. Rather than attribute it to a failure of their own religious practice, they could believe that it was a failure of the other's biology. The pseudo-science of nineteenth-century ethnology coordinated well with missionary stalemates. If people did not get saved from the fires of hell, they were showing to be true to their species. And it was easier to dispossess or even kill those who seemed to have no possibility of redemption.[119]

Where the stasis of supposedly scientific racial hierarchies did not readily permit the possibility that the favored might fall from grace or that the "unfavored" might take their place, though, the concept of damnation was malleable and deployable in multiple ways. Even as race "experts" sought to encode racial hierarchies as scientific "fact," others pointed to white Americans' maltreatment of the nonwhite "other" as evidence that the favored were indeed falling from grace: that they might be damned instead of saved, in need of their own redemption rather than the redeemers of others. While Euro-Americans' treatment of Native Americans met with some condemnation, this was even more striking in the controversy surrounding slavery. It is to the deployment of damnation in the abolitionist crusade and the proslavery backlash that we now turn.

PART THREE

Deployment and Denouement

5

"*Slavery Destroys Immortal Souls*"

DEPLOYMENT OF DAMNATION IN THE SLAVERY CONTROVERSY

"SLAVERY DESTROYS IMMORTAL SOULS," declared an article in the December 20, 1839, issue of the *Liberator*. It destroyed not only the "souls of the oppressor" but also "the souls of the oppressed" and of those too "timid and time serving" to oppose it.[1]

Real anxiety about slavery's eternal repercussions underlay the deployment of damnation rhetoric in the slavery controversy. Many abolitionists looked forward to a millennium purged of the sin of slavery but predicted divine punishment should the call for emancipation go unheeded. They did not merely condemn slaveholding as wrong: they damned its unrepentant practitioners and all who stood idly by for imperiling the souls of slaves. Slavery's apologists did not take this sitting down. Instead, they turned the rhetoric of eternal condemnation against the "infidel" radicals of the North, who failed to see that the Bible sanctioned slavery. These apologists also spoke of saving slaves from hell, but depicted slavery as a ripe missionary field and the means through which benighted Africans could be rescued from the "darkness" of heathendom.

While the political needs of forming a virtuous republic and the evangelical imperative to gain converts helped hell survive in the new nation, the persistence of slavery secured hell's continued deployment in antebellum civil and political discourse, despite the growing discomfort of some Americans with the concept.[2] The institution called for the harshest condemnations its opponents and defenders could conjure. At a time when the threat of eternal punishment for the unrepentant still resounded from pulpits and leapt from the pages of newspapers, it is hardly surprising that each side seized it as a weapon against those with whom they disagreed and as an argument to sway the noncommittal. Damnation even survived as a rhetorical weapon for those abolitionists who rejected belief in eternal fire and brimstone, like the doubters in the previous chapter. Hell's familiarity to antebellum Americans and its applicability to the nation as a whole made it a potent and provocative warning even as slavery's apologists responded with similar language.[3] Like the Murrays in the Revolutionary era, slavery's opponents and defenders tied the behavior of individuals to the welfare of the nation, extending the threat of hell from the personal to the political. The idea that the "living in the pit" could be discerned in this life brought the threat of eternal separation to the here-and-now; when applied to the nation along antislavery and proslavery lines, the binaries of "saved" and "damned" presaged national disunion. Americans' failure to resolve the question of slavery imperiled their self-proclaimed identity as a "Redeemer Nation." As much as they hoped to usher in the millennium by saving the world from the fires of hell, they realized that the redemption of their own nation might have to come first.[4]

The "Perishing Soul" Motif

In the first decades of the nineteenth century, white antislavery sentiment still centered on the hope of gradual emancipation eased by colonizing blacks out of the country. The American Colonization Society was founded in 1816, just six years after the American Board of Commissioners for Foreign Missions, and shared its view of the world as in need of American intervention. Colonizationists vested African Americans—especially men—with the responsibility to uplift Africa and save the African "heathen." Colonizationism was also rooted in the profoundly racist notion that blacks and whites could not coexist peacefully.[5]

The deployment of the threat of hell against the institution of slavery and its practitioners became a familiar refrain when some opponents of slavery shifted from gradual emancipation to immediatism in the 1820s and 1830s. Gradualism drew from Calvinistic notions of human depravity and inability, whereas immediatism grew out of changing evangelical ideas about human ability and perfectibility. Slaves and free blacks, of course, had always agitated for immediate emancipation; many opposed colonization as a racist ploy to remove them from the only country they knew and had helped to build. Immediatism as a wider interracial strategy called on Americans to stop delaying emancipation, paralleling the revivals that called for immediate and voluntary conversion.[6] Because not every anti-slavery advocate shifted to this strategy, immediatists had to convince not only slavery's supporters, but also gradualists, of their position.

Reflecting on the sinfulness of slavery, Theodore Dwight Weld used the same language of moral ability and threats to the soul with which revivalists encouraged voluntary conversion by free agents and temperance reformers denounced the ills of alcohol. In an 1833 letter to abolitionist friends, Weld wrote:

> I say then: God has committed to every moral agent the privilege, the right and the responsibility of personal ownership. This is God's plan. Slavery annihilates it, and surrenders to avarice, passion and lust, all that makes life a blessing. It crushes the body, tramples into the dust the upward tendencies of intellect, breaks the heart and kills the soul.[7]

After his conversion by Finney, Weld had worked as a temperance man. This background led him to see slavery as an institution that "killed the soul," much as liquor impaired the moral faculties, by denying slaves the moral agency and "upward tendencies of intellect" that would allow them the Christian freedom to choose repentance and the way of salvation.

The argument that slavery imperiled the eternal welfare of slaves—what we might term the "perishing soul" motif—echoes the quotation that opened this chapter: "Slavery Destroys Immortal Souls." Other abolitionists drew on the motif too, though at times awkwardly. Like Weld, the young William Lloyd Garrison was influenced by the piety of a parent figure, in his case, his Baptist mother.[8] In 1830, while jailed for libel, Garrison pondered how his own temporary imprisonment compared to the permanent captivity of a slave. He wrote to his friend Ebenezer Dole:

> Now, how is it with the slave?...A thick darkness broods over his soul. Even the "glorious gospel of the blessed God," which brings life and immortality to perishing man, is a sealed book to his understanding.... He is made an abject slave, simply because God has given him a skin not colored like his master's; and Death, the great Liberator, alone can break his fetters.[9]

Garrison's analysis here awkwardly joined the "perishing soul" motif with the idea that death meant liberation. If slaves' souls were in "thick darkness" and the gospel of immortality a "sealed book" to them, then death should be less the "great Liberator" than the transition to an even worse condition. Of course, Garrison did not draw this conclusion, perhaps signaling his later unorthodox turn.

The "perishing soul" motif drew from the revivalist idea that the ability to hear and understand the unvarnished gospel was prerequisite to making a clear and voluntary choice for salvation. The motif emphasized the need not only to free but also to missionize the slaves and liberate their minds from "darkness" by teaching them to read the Bible for themselves. The Rev. Amos Phelps's 1834 *Lectures on Slavery and Its Remedy* pointed to the hypocrisy of sending missionaries overseas while ignoring the eternal welfare of slaves at home. Phelps lamented: "There are more than two and a half millions of human beings—of immortal minds, almost in the darkness of Paganism itself, and rushing on, in all that darkness, to the realities of eternity, and we are christians, and are sending the light of the gospel over all the earth, and yet we may not touch a system of oppression, which is shutting out this light of life from these millions at our very door, because forsooth it is no concern of ours!"[10] For the Christian abolitionist, the hell of slavery in the here-and-now was ever close to hell in the hereafter, and the benefits of ending the "system of oppression" accrued to both the earthly and eternal well-being of slaves.

Virginia-born Thomas Lafon gave voice to an even more vehement critique of the neglect of slaves in American missionary efforts. Following his evangelical conversion, Lafon, a former slaveowner, became persuaded of the sinfulness of slavery. He joined the Sandwich Islands mission in 1836 but quit after five and a half years, disillusioned by the ABCFM's acceptance of the profits of slave labor. In 1843 he issued a pamphlet, "The Great Obstruction to the Conversion of Souls at Home and Abroad," published by the Union Missionary Society (the predominantly black predecessor to the antislavery American Missionary Association[11]). Lafon began by analyzing the character of the "heathen," a favorite avocation of foreign missionaries, as we saw in chapter 2. He explained that "heathens" fell into three categories: idolaters, the oppressed, and those who were both. "In idolatry," Lafon wrote, "there is ignorance of the true God," and hence worship of many false gods. By contrast, "under oppression there is ignorance of almost every thing." He explained, "Most heathen nations are under one or both of these," but pure oppression was "far the most destructive in its effects." Where idolatry led to "delusion and darkness," in "oppression there is mental paralysis and death."[12]

Idolatrous "heathens" were largely to blame for their own condition, Lafon claimed, but the oppressed were victims of circumstances outside their control. African American slaves fit the latter bill exactly. They were perishing in a "soul-destroying system" because "the crushing of the intellectual faculties is a more hopeless and remediless injury than all the superstitious practises of idolatry."[13] Evangelical conversion was impossible because slavery shackled the mind and prevented the exercise of real moral agency. To Lafon, it was the very height of absurdity and hypocrisy to take money from slave labor to minister to "heathens" in other parts of the world. "In a mere mercantile point of view," he queried, "what could possibly be gained by oppressing, degrading and heathenizing a part of our race at home, to obtain the means to send the gospel to reclaim others from that condition abroad?"[14] Just as home and foreign missionaries cited numbers to dramatize their need for men and money, so Lafon did the same to dramatize the need to emancipate and missionize the oppressed slaves. He estimated that in the thirty years of their existence, the three major American missionary boards had saved fewer than 40,000 souls. During that time, the population of slaves had increased "a million and a half!" Lafon scoffed at the claim that many slaves were Christian: "Without undertaking to say that these supposed conversions are spurious, we do say, on the testimony of those well qualified to form a correct opinion in the premises, that the religion of a large portion of the degraded slaves consists chiefly in superstition, fanatical practices, and an obsequious servility to the tyrant that rules them." For Lafon and other white abolitionists, the "perishing soul" motif also explained why colonization could never work: the slaves were imperfectly Christian themselves, so how could they be expected to Christianize Africa?[15]

Lafon, Phelps, and other white abolitionists used the "perishing soul" motif to arouse the consciences of white Americans. But the deep paternalism in their portrayal of slaves' souls as shrouded in "darkness" and endangered without their intervention made the motif amenable to southern defenders of slavery, too. In the face of abolitionist challenges, slavery's apologists seized on it to urge slaveholders to put more effort into Christianizing their slaves so as to be able to present the system to the world as a divinely sanctioned missionary institution.

In his 1842 *Suggestions on the Religious Instruction of the Negroes in the Southern States*, Charles Colcock Jones, a Presbyterian minister from Liberty County on the coast of Georgia, echoed Lafon and Phelps in identifying the slave population as a special missionary field. "Were the negroes

but an inconsiderable handful of people, they might be left to fall in with
the mass, and be benefited by the means of grace enjoyed by all, without
any special efforts being made for them. But," he continued, "they make
up one sixth of our entire population, and are steadily increasing, and
seem destined to become an immense multitude! Will you let them alone?
Shall we do nothing for them? Surely they do demand the attention of all
men who love their country, and who seek the improvement and salvation
of their species."[16] It is hardly surprising that Jones, who was educated at
eminent institutions in the Northeast, including Phillips, Andover, and
Princeton, had recourse to the same argument espoused by similarly educated antislavery activists. But Jones, who as a young man had struggled
over the morality of slavery, assuaged his conscience with efforts to evangelize the slaves and paint slavery as a missionizing institution whose
benefits outweighed its negatives.[17]

In his *Suggestions*, Jones reminded slaveholders of their responsibility
for the souls of their slaves. "Owners are remiss in the discharge of their
duties to their people, in respect to their better and higher interests," he
lamented. "Plantations that now lie all abroad over the face of the country, wildernesses and moral wastes, through the judicious, Christian, and
persevering efforts of owners, might be converted into fruitful fields and
vineyards of the Lord; but the work is not done, neither indeed is it in
progress." Without Sabbath schools, slaves would grow up to walk the
path to hell: "What a multitude of children and youth growing up in ignorance and sin, and thronging the road to eternal destruction!" Those
who failed to perform their Christian duty would be held responsible: "If
nothing more is done, than is now doing; if we do not multiply men and
means more rapidly than in years past," Jones warned, "what multitudes
of these poor people are destined to go down, annually, from the very
bosom of a land denominated enlightened, and Christian, and benevolent, into everlasting ruin! What shall we say in that day when God shall
make inquisition for the blood of these souls, slain in our hearing, and in
the sight of our own eyes, and neither did we send, nor did we go to their
deliverance?" Such warnings echoed those that revivalists and foreign
missionaries directed both at themselves and at their converts: all must
spread the gospel or risk their own souls.[18]

Not surprisingly, proslavery invocations of the "perishing soul" motif
diverged from white abolitionists' in their recommendations for how to
evangelize the slaves. After Nat Turner's rebellion in 1831, southern laws
prohibiting the teaching of literacy to slaves became more stringent, while

"encouragement of oral instruction of slaves in the Christian faith" ramped up.[19] Jones told "the friends of religious instruction" not to get involved in "questions touching the civil condition of the negroes: 1 Tim. vi. 1–8; nor turn aside from the main work to combat incidental evils. Time is wasted, the great cause is retarded and prejudiced."[20] For Jones, the lived realities of slavery were not incompatible with Christianity. All slaves needed to know were "the main facts of Scripture history" and "the doctrines and duties": "depravity, regeneration, repentance, faith, the Christian graces, and relative duties, &c." Teaching them these basics would not only save their immortal souls, but would also set slaveowners right with God. To Jones, slavery did not have to keep slaves' moral agency fettered or their minds shrouded in "ignorance," as the white abolitionists claimed. Rather, it could raise them from "ignorance" just enough to bring them to "life eternal." "This," he concluded, "is the will of God—this is our duty—the great duty of the Southern Church."[21]

This proslavery religious logic and the important role hell played in it comes out clearly in a collection of sermons by Alexander Glennie, Rector of All-Saints Parish in the Waccamaw region of southern Georgia. Published in 1844, two years after Jones's text, and entitled *Sermons Preached on Plantations to Congregations of Negroes*, Glennie's sermons were meant to be read to slaves by slaveowners in regions where ministers and missionaries were few and far between. Glennie included texts for occasions such as Christmas, Good Friday, and Easter, as well as untitled sermons dealing with subjects ranging from lying and adultery to salvation in Christ and the last judgment. Many of the sermons warn of the hell that awaits not only those who do not believe but also those who misbehave in ways defined by masters claiming to speak for God.[22]

In a sermon on Ananias and Sapphira, for instance, Glennie warned slaves against lying, since God would find out their falsehoods even if their masters did not. Ananias and Sapphira, two wealthy patrons of the early church, were struck dead after claiming to have donated the full proceeds from the sale of a field but actually withholding a percentage for themselves.[23] Although slaves hardly had to worry about failing to tithe appropriately, they nevertheless had to worry about the consequences of deceiving their masters. "Does it not shew you how God hates a lie?" Glennie asked. "Does it not tell you that lying lips are an abomination unto him? Does it not convince you, that those how [sic] continue to live guilty of this sin, shall be punished forever? What says the Bible about it? It is written, 'all liars shall have their part in the lake which burneth with fire and brimstone.'" He continued: "Do not be tempted to say, as too many wicked people do, oh nobody will know it: nobody will see it: remember that God is always looking at you. He sees all that you do; he hears every word that you say; he knows all that you think about; and he can in a moment strike you dead: he is able to destroy both body and soul in hell."[24]

In another sermon on servitude, Glennie told slaves that their condition in life mattered little with regard to their eternal salvation. Rather than grumble about their situation, they should be content, in the words of Ephesians 6:7: "With good will doing service, as to the Lord, and not to men." Conflating good service to their masters with good service to God, Glennie warned:

> With regard to you; the disobedient servants amongst you ... unless they repent and turn from the service of the devil to the service of God, shall surely "be punished with everlasting destruction from the presence of the Lord, and from the glory of his power." Whilst the obedient servants amongst you, the faithful, the true, the godly servants, who are living "as the servants of Christ," "doing service as to the Lord and not to men," shall, if they continue steadfast unto the end, be blessed forever.[25]

It is impossible to know the extent to which the threat of hell in these sermons was deployed for social control or meant altruistically, though paternalistically, to save the souls of slaves. Social control and evangelization were inseparable in the minds of Christian slaveowners like Jones and Glennie. Slaveowners who preached the gospel to their slaves not only rescued their own and possibly their slaves' "perishing souls" from perdition, they argued, but also created better and more obedient servants.

The paternalism in the "perishing soul" motif, and the way southern slaveholders used it to justify the system of slavery, did not escape the notice of black abolitionists like David Walker, a used clothing dealer living in Boston. In 1829 Walker circulated his ideas in an incendiary pamphlet, the *Appeal in Four Articles; Together with a Preamble, to the Coloured Citizens of the World*. He hoped the *Appeal* would reach African Americans both North and South; the literate could pass the message orally to illiterate slaves.[26] Slaveholders "keep us sunk in ignorance, and will not let us learn to read the word of God, nor write," Walker wrote. Yet unlike white abolitionists and slaveholders, Walker never once suggested that this "most death-like ignorance" would damn the very souls of his enslaved peers if left uncorrected.[27] Instead, he called his people "next to the Angels of God" and "candidates for the eternal worlds," and urged them to fight against their enslavement.[28] He also argued that religion as practiced by "Europeans and their descendants" might lead one to "believe it was a plan fabricated by themselves and the *devils* to oppress us."[29] His descriptions of the hypocrisy of Christian slaveholders, who prevented slaves from worshiping together or reading the Bible, gave the lie to the apologists' claim that slavery could be a staging ground for the salvation of souls. At the same time, his assertion that God was on the side of the slaves, whether or not they were "sunk in ignorance," challenged the paternalism in the white abolitionists' argument that slaves would remain shrouded in eternal "darkness" without their intervention.

For his part, Frederick Douglass sounded much like Thomas Lafon when he used the "perishing soul" motif to criticize white Christian hypocrisy in the Appendix to his *Narrative*. "They love the heathen on the other side of the globe. They can pray for him, pay money to have the Bible put into his hand, and missionaries to instruct him; while they despise and totally neglect the heathen at their own doors."[30] A couple paragraphs later Douglass included "A Parody" that mocked white Americans' fixation on "heavenly union" and the disconnect between their preachers warning of hell while buying and selling slaves:

> Come, saints and sinners, hear me tell
> How pious priests whip Jack and Nell,
> And women buy and children sell,
> And preach all sinners down to hell,
> And sing of heavenly union.
>
> . . .
>
> They'll church you if you sip a dram,
> And damn you if you steal a lamb;
> Yet rob old Tony, Doll, and Sam,
> Of human rights, and bread and ham;
> Kidnapper's heavenly union. [31]

Douglass used "heavenly union" as a repeating and sarcastic refrain throughout the poem.

Maria Stewart also alluded to the "perishing soul" motif in her 1835 *Productions of Mrs. Maria W. Stewart, Presented to the First African Baptist Church & Society, of the City of Boston*. Stewart, born in Connecticut in

1803, orphaned five years later, and bound to a clergyman's family, noted that she had "had the seeds of piety and virtue early sown in [her] mind; but was deprived of the advantages of education, though my soul thirsted for knowledge." She made a "public profession" for Christ in 1831 and connected her conversion to her activism against racial prejudice. She applauded "the most noble, fearless, and undaunted David Walker" and sought to emulate his example.[32]

In her Boston speeches Stewart compared the "condition" of free blacks in the North to that of the slaves. "Tell us no more of southern slavery," she blazed, "for with few exceptions, although I may be very erroneous in my opinion, yet I consider our condition but little better than that." Stewart focused on "the chains of ignorance" that oppressed even the free, declaring that there were "no fetters so binding as those that bind the soul, and exclude it from the vast field of useful and scientific knowledge."[33] Part of the fault lay with their circumstances: "I am sensible, my brethren and friends, that many of you have been deprived of advantages, kept in utter ignorance, and that your minds are now darkened."[34] But part of the fault lay with her people themselves: "It was our gross sins and abominations that provoked the Almighty to frown thus heavily upon us, and give our glory unto others." Although Africa was once great, she argued, "it is of no use for us to boast that we sprung from this learned and enlightened nation, for this day a thick mist of moral gloom hangs over millions of our race." Unlike white abolitionists and slaveowners who suggested that blacks could not be "uplifted" without their aid, Stewart told her people that they needed to take matters into their own hands and pull themselves out of "moral gloom."[35]

Stewart privileged education as the primary way to curb white prejudice and end the system of slavery: "methinks were the American free people of color to turn their attention more assiduously to moral worth and intellectual improvement, this would be the result: prejudice would gradually diminish, and the whites would be compelled to say, unloose those fetters!" She tapped the "perishing soul" motif's paternalism when she suggested that "continual hard labor deadens the energies of the soul, and benumbs the faculties of the mind."[36] Echoing the white evangelical guidebooks that instructed lay readers to make good use of their time, Stewart critiqued "the greater part of our community" for wasting their energies "following the vain bubbles of life with so much eagerness," urging them instead to improve themselves.[37]

She also offered specific instructions tailored to women and men. "O, woman, woman," she entreated, "would thou only strive to excel in merit and virtue; would thou only store thy mind with useful knowledge, great would be thine influence." Like the ATS "To Mothers" tract, Stewart told the "daughters of Africa" to "instill these principles into the minds of your tender infants": "So shall your skirts become clear of their blood."[38] To the "sons of Africa," she urged courage and action: "Talk, without effort, is nothing; you are abundantly capable, gentlemen, of making yourselves men of distinction; and this gross neglect, on your part, causes my blood to boil within me." Stewart implored her male audiences "to flee from the gambling board and the dance-hall."[39] She sought to shame them into defiance by highlighting how she—a woman—repeatedly exposed herself to danger: "Shall I, for fear of feeble man who shall die, hold my peace?...Ah, no! I speak as one that must give an account at the awful bar of God; I speak as a dying mortal, to dying mortals."[40] Follow my example, she urged repeatedly, or the blood of the damned will also be on your hands.

It was the evangelical peer pressure argument again: it did not matter if you were man or woman, black or white: all were culpable who knew their duty but failed to do it: "O, how will they feel in that day to see their skirts filled with the blood of souls? Will not their eye-balls start from their sockets, to see sinners who have stumbled into hell over them?...O, the value of time! O, the worth of immortal souls!"[41] Stewart's injunctions to free blacks had urgent implications for emancipation. Proslavery whites and colonizationists were watching them for evidence that African Americans could not thrive outside the institution of slavery or as equal citizens within the country of their birth. But "it appears to me that there are no people under the heavens so unkind and so unfeeling towards their own, as are the descendants of fallen Africa," Stewart bemoaned. "It is useless for us any longer to sit with our hands folded, reproaching the whites; for that will never elevate us."[42]

Like Walker and Stewart, Henry Highland Garnet was not interested in persuading white audiences to take pity on the souls of slaves. In his 1843 "Address to the Slaves of the United States of America," he sought to incite the slaves themselves to action, urging outright defiance:

The forlorn condition in which you are placed does not destroy your moral obligation to God. You are not certain of Heaven, because you suffer yourselves to remain in a state of slavery, where you cannot obey the commandments of the Sovereign of the universe. If the ignorance of slavery is a passport to heaven, then it is a blessing, and no curse.... The diabolical injustice by which your liberties are cloven down, NEITHER GOD, NOR ANGELS, OR JUST MEN, COMMAND YOU TO SUFFER FOR A SINGLE MOMENT. THEREFORE IT IS YOUR SOLEMN AND IMPERATIVE DUTY TO USE EVERY MEANS, BOTH MORAL, INTELLECTUAL, AND PHYSICAL, THAT PROMISE SUCCESS.[43]

Like the white abolitionists, Garnet argued that slavery was hardly a boon to souls. But he argued that it was incumbent on the slaves to change their own situation, for God would not excuse them from hell and usher them into heaven simply because they were slaves.

Slavery as Hell; Slaveholders as the Damned

As a child, Garnet had escaped from slavery with his family; slaves for whom escape was virtually impossible were unlikely to appreciate his warning that their souls were endangered the longer they stayed in slavery, or Stewart's claim that continual hard labor "benumbs" the mind, any more than they appreciated being told by white abolitionists that they were shrouded in "heathen darkness." Even less welcome was the slaveholders' argument that slavery was a way station for saving their souls. Rather than worry that their souls were in danger of hell if they remained enslaved, they argued that slavery itself was hell. As far as they were concerned, slaveholders, not slaves, deserved eternal punishment for the injustice of inflicting living hell on human beings.[44] As one former slave put it, "In dem days it was hell without fires. This is one reason why I believe in a hell. I don't believe a just God is going to take no such man as that [her former master] into his kingdom."[45]

Another ex-slave turned the belief that hell was a place for cruel masters into a satirical poem. In his 1887 autobiography, Thomas James, born a slave in 1804, titled his undated poem "A Vision," and characterized it as a "Scene in the nether world—purporting to be a conversation between the ghost of a Southern slaveholding clergyman and the devil!" In the poem, a "Southern Preacher / In tasseled pulpit, gay and fine," who "strove to please the tyrants, / To prove that slavery is divine" finds himself in the fires of Hell as "a slave, [who] can't get free / Through everlasting ages." In an ironic twist, the devil tells the clergyman that "you shall have a Negro sent / To attend and punch the fire."[46] The poem presents a fine example of the role reversal that many present and former slaves looked forward to in the afterlife. As in folk traditions, where the weak triumph over the strong and the poor over the rich, ironic reversal offered slaves a hope for ultimate justice and the possibility of having the last laugh.[47]

The Life of Omar Ibn Said, a narrative handwritten in Arabic by a Muslim slave captured in West Africa, also drew on the threat of hell to forward an implicit critique of slavery. Written in the wake of Nat Turner's rebellion, the text was not overtly insurrectionist; Omar even expressed satisfaction with his current masters. The memoir may have worked to ease the fears of white Southerners who wanted evidence that not all slaves were Nat Turners in waiting. As an educated and literate slave whom they believed had converted to Christianity, Omar provided hope for the evangelization of other African Muslims. But as one scholar has recently argued, Omar's *Life* can also be read as a protest produced under "conditions of persecution."[48]

Especially significant is Omar's decision to open his *Life* with a chapter (*sura*) of the Qur'an, the *Surat al-Mulk*. The chapter "contends that it is God who is the owner of all and everything; through his choice of *Surat al-Mulk*, Omar seems to refute the right of his owners over him."[49] The *sura*, which Omar apparently reproduced from memory, is replete with warnings for those who reject the Prophet Muhammad's message:

> We have prepared the scourge of Fire for these, and the scourge of Hell for those who deny their Lord: an evil fate!
>
> When they are flung into its flames, they shall hear it roaring and seething, as though bursting with rage. And every time a multitude is thrown therein, its keepers will say to them: "Did no one come to warn you?"

Omar may have seen himself as a messenger sent to "warn" those who ignored God's ownership of all at risk of being flung into hell (*juhanam*). The *sura* continued:

> Whether you speak in secret or aloud, He knows your innermost thoughts . . . .
>
> Are you confident that He who is in heaven will not cause the earth to cave in beneath you, so that it will shake to pieces and overwhelm you?

Masters might have read the idea that the Lord "knows your innermost thoughts" as a parroting back of their injunctions not to lie or steal (as in Glennie's sermons). But it could also be taken as a warning of ironic reversal that the "confident" might yet see the earth "cave in beneath" them.[50]

Where the "perishing soul" motif focused on the slaves' eternal welfare, the critique of "slavery as hell" focused on the horrors committed against slaves' bodies in the here-and-now, for which slaveholders would pay in the eternal hell hereafter. In his *Narrative*, Frederick Douglass wrote of seeing his aunt beaten: "It was the first of a long series of outrages, of which I was doomed to be a witness and a participant. It struck me with awful force. It was the blood-stained gate, the entrance to the hell of slavery, through which I was about to pass. It was a most terrible spectacle."[51] The hell of slavery also included human demons. Douglass described his mistress's angelic face as giving way to "that of a demon" the more she fell "under the influence of slavery." Covey, the slave-breaker, was even more devilish. Douglass testified to his "power to deceive" and used words like "the snake" to label him. "Will not a righteous God visit for these things?" Douglass queried.[52]

For black abolitionists, political acts supporting slavery were also demonic. The Committee on Slavery of the New England Conference of the African Methodist Episcopal Church resolved in a January 26, 1854, report,

> That in the enactment and passage of the Fugitive Slave Law, and the more recent act, namely, the repealing of the Compromise of 1820, in the passage of the Nebraska Bill—in these wicked and cruel acts are burning coals of fire, which will burn to the lowest hell. Over them all hovers the dark angel of night, covering them with the dark mantle of wickedness.[53]

The resolution uses the language of hell rhetorically to condemn these acts in the worst possible terms, but this hardly negates the possibility that its drafters looked to an actual hell after death for those guilty of such crimes on earth as the passage of the Fugitive Slave Act.

The depiction of slavery as hell was a theme white abolitionists picked up on as well. In 1839 Weld and his new bride, Angelina Grimké, the abolitionist daughter of slaveholders, compiled a searing collection of eyewitness accounts of the physical horrors of slavery, *American Slavery As It Is*. They quoted the Editor of the *Maryville Intelligencer*, "in speaking of the sufferings of the slaves which are taken by the internal trade to the South

West," as urging readers to "Place yourself in imagination, for a moment, in their condition. With *heavy galling chains,* riveted upon your person; *half-naked, half-starved;* your back *lacerated* with the 'knotted Whip;' traveling to a region where your *condition through time will be second only to the wretched creatures in Hell.*"[54] Meanwhile, the *Child's Antislavery Book,* published by the Sunday School Union, told the story of a slave boy, "Little Lewis," and his mother, who went insane and tried to commit suicide following the sale and separation of her family. Rather than condemn her, as the "perishing soul" motif might have done, the story instead sought to arouse the compassion of its young readers, telling them that "during these dreadful fits of insanity she would bewail the living as worse than dead, and pray God to take them away. Then she would curse herself for being the mother of slave children, declaring that it would be far better to see them die in their childhood, than to see them grow up to suffer as she had suffered."[55] She recovered and tasted freedom before she died; at last she "went to her home above to be comforted after all her sufferings, while," the story tells us, "her cruel masters who enjoyed their ease here shall be tormented."[56]

Ironic reversal also underlay some white abolitionists' combination of the "perishing soul motif" with the "slavery as hell" metaphor. While slaves' souls might be endangered from lack of the gospel, they contended, slaveholders' souls were more endangered because they had access to the gospel but flouted its precepts by perpetuating the hellish system of slavery. The notion that the more "enlightened" were more endangered for their failures is reminiscent of the argument put forward by city missionary Ezra Stiles Ely, that Christians would suffer more than the "heathen" at the final judgment if they failed to do their duty and spread the gospel to their peers. In his *Lectures on Slavery and Its Remedy,* for instance, Amos Phelps quoted a Rev. Mr. Paxton, who spent forty years in the slaveholding states as a teacher, pastor, missionary, and even a slaveholder. Paxton observed that very few slaves were taught to read the Bible or allowed to attend services:

> The slave is blamed for not attending preaching. He may deserve blame; but taking the whole case into view, the fault does not altogether lie on the slave. The master who holds him in slavery, who requires his constant labors, is often justly chargeable in the sight of God with the irreligion of his slaves; and that many a professor of religion will at last have a fearful reckoning on this matter, I have

no more doubt than I have that we have a Master in Heaven, "who is no respecter of persons."[57]

This language is similar to that used by Charles Colcock Jones to shame slaveowners into evangelizing their slaves. But where Jones believed that the remedy lay in masters providing religious instruction for their slaves, Phelps believed that the answer was emancipation.

Lydia Maria Child, in her 1833 *An Appeal in Favor of that Class of Americans Called Africans*, also devoted considerable attention to the influences of slavery on slaveholders. To lend the weight of firsthand authority to her discussion, she quoted "the testimony of Jefferson, who had good opportunities for observation, and who certainly had no New-England prejudices": "There must, doubtless, be an unhappy influence on the manners of the people, produced by the existence of slavery among us.... The man must be a prodigy, who can retain his morals and manners undepraved in such circumstances."[58] Although condemning the system of slavery in terms as harsh as any male abolitionist, however, Child, whose Unitarian brother introduced her to Ralph Waldo Emerson and Margaret Fuller, refrained from taking her condemnation of individual slaveholders so far as to sentence them to eternal damnation. Instead, she anticipated the more measured and morally ambiguous language of Abraham Lincoln in the Second Inaugural, when she wrote that "human nature is every where the same; but developed differently, by different incitements and temptations.... It is the system, not the men, on which we ought to bestow the full measure of abhorrence."[59]

Emerson applied his own philosophy of self-reliance to slaveholders and also found them lacking. "A man who steals another man's labor," he argued, "steals away his own faculties.... The habit of oppression cuts out the moral eyes, and though the intellect goes on simulating the moral as before, its sanity is invaded, and gradually destroyed."[60] Emerson's language of compromised moral agency echoed the Christian abolitionists' argument that slavery damned the souls of slaves because it prevented them from making free moral choices. Although he did not use eternal damnation as the ultimate threat, Emerson suggested that because the slaveholder became reliant on the slave's labor, he also could not be self-reliant.

While Child and Emerson did not damn slaveowners to hell, William Lloyd Garrison was a master of denunciatory, "us" vs. "them" attacks on those who committed the crime of slaveowning. Seeking support for his immediatist cause in the early 1830s, he bemoaned the weakness of the English language in proportion to the evil of slavery. To Garrison, moral suasion and harsh language were integrally related: much as Finney and other evangelical revivalists saw the threat of hell as essential to producing conversions, so Garrison saw the threat of personal and national punishment as essential to changing peoples' attitudes toward slavery. In his April 1833 "Address before the Free People of Color," Garrison not only used the rhetoric of damnation but also told listeners and readers why: because "The English language is lamentably weak and deficient in regard to this matter. I wish its epithets were heavier—I wish it would not break so easily—I wish I could denounce slavery, and all its abettors, in terms equal to their infamy." "How ought I to feel and speak?" he asked:

> As a man! as a patriot! as a philanthropist! as a Christian! My soul should be, as it is, on fire. I should thunder—I should lighten. I should blow the trumpet of alarm, long and loud. I should use just such language as is most descriptive of the crime. I should imitate the example of Christ, who, when he had to do with people of like manners, called them sharply by their proper names—such as, an adulterous and perverse generation, a brood of vipers, hypocrites, children of the devil who could not escape the damnation of hell.[61]

For Garrison in the early 1830s, there could be no harsher or more insulting accusation than that slavery damned to hell those who perpetuated it.[62] That the accusation provoked a strong reaction can be seen in an 1833 Boston handbill urging Garrison's tar and feathering. The handbill explicitly took offense that, while in London, he stood by as another abolitionist trumpeted that "the blackest corner in Hell's bottomless pit ought to be, and would be, the future destination of the Americans!"[63] The insult was especially galling in an era when many Americans were defensive about the young nation's reputation abroad.

Imagine also the sentiments of the Honorable Harrison Gray Otis, when in 1835 Garrison reminded him that he was nearly 70 years old and would "be soon called to stand at the tribunal of Him who died to redeem as well the blackest as the whitest of our race!" Otis, an "eminent lawyer" who had served as Senator from Massachusetts and Mayor of Boston, and the Honorable Peleg Sprague, Senator from Maine, had given heated speeches against immediate abolitionism at Faneuil Hall. In denouncing

Otis, Garrison went so far as to envision the epitaph to be carved on his tombstone:

Here lies the body of

H--------G--------O-------

*   *   *   *

Reader, weep at human inconsistency and frailty!
The last public act of his life,
A life conspicuous for many honorable traits,
Was an earnest defense of
THE RIGHTS OF TYRANTS AND SLAVE-MONGERS
To hold in bondage, as their property,
The bodies and souls of millions of his own countrymen!
. . .
Pause, terrible Truth!
He has gone to the judgment-seat of Christ!
"Inasmuch as ye did it not unto one of the least of these
my brethren, ye did it not to me."[64]

To Sprague, Garrison was no less direct: "As far as one man can be answerable for all the horrors and blasphemies of American slavery, I believe you will be held responsible at the tribunal of the judgment day. I weep, I shudder, at your degradation. There seems to be no flesh in your heart.... May God grant you speedy repentance unto eternal life!"[65]

Garrison printed these denunciations in *The Liberator*. His children reprinted the texts in their biography of him; they noted that his language "scandalize[d]" Otis and other members of the old guard, "who assuredly had never been publicly impeached before in such a manner."[66] Garrison was barely 30 at the time, lacked a college education, and had no social background to speak of. That such an "obscure young man" got under their skin with the rhetoric of a final judgment awaiting "tyrants" and their defenders speaks to the provocative potential of such language in the antebellum era, when many Americans still feared hell, and those who did not were at least exposed to the doctrine in sermons that rained from pulpits and warnings that proliferated in newspapers and tracts. Garrison's "inflammatory articles in the Liberator, highly insulting to the feelings of a great majority of our fellow-citizens, attacking with a frantic maliciousness their character and motives, manifesting an insolent defiance of public opinion, and a determination to persist in braving it," as an anti-Garrisonian Boston newspaper put it, spurred the formation of an angry crowd who attacked men who looked like Garrison and tore the "tracts and papers of the society" to shreds.[67]

Damned Nation

In targeting men like Peleg Sprague and Harrison Gray Otis, nephew of the Revolutionary War hero James Otis and famed writer Mercy Otis Warren, Garrison and other immediate abolitionists showed that they would not stop at attacking southern slaveholders alone. They condemned all who failed to support their immediatist agenda, and ultimately, the nation as a whole. The guilty nation deserved God's wrath not because the Puritan covenant still held mystical sway for most Americans, but because those citizens who should have known better were complicit through their complacency. Northern politicians like Sprague and Otis did not do enough to save themselves by saving others, whether slaves, slaveholders, or apathetic Northerners. If communities were chains of individuals influencing each other to weal or woe, the nation was just one such community writ large.

Garrison was particularly incensed that Sprague and Otis attacked the abolitionists at Faneuil Hall, where revolutionaries like Otis's own uncle had famously championed American liberty. "I mean to make your harangue, and the speeches of your associates, of signal use in the anti-slavery struggle," Garrison wrote. "They are crowded with evidence of our national guilt.... Upon your authority I will prove that there is not a drop of blood extracted from the bodies, nor a tear which falls from the eyes, nor a groan which bursts from the bosoms of the heart-broken slaves, for which the North is not directly responsible."[68] Sprague and Otis were especially despicable because they had used their positions of respect and influence to sway Northern public sentiment against the abolitionists, thus perpetuating the system of slavery in Garrison's eyes.

If non-slaveholding individuals could be as blameworthy as slaveowners and the North as guilty as the South, then the whole nation had to fear God's punishment. The language of violence, judgment, and individual and national guilt permeated abolitionists' writings. "Slaveholding, then, is in all cases a sin," wrote Amos Phelps in his *Lectures on Slavery*. "In all the circumstances of its existence, the mark of guilt is upon it—deep, crimson, blood-stained guilt. That individual who practices it is a guilty individual. That nation which does so is a guilty nation. And sooner or later, if they repent not, the God, to whom vengeance belongeth and who claims it as his prerogative to repay, will repay. He will visit for this thing—yea his soul will be avenged on such a nation."[69]

Similarly, David Walker couched his "Appeal" not only as a call for slaves to fight back against their enslavement but also as a notice to white America. In just one of many examples Walker warned: "Perhaps they will laugh at or make light of this; but I tell you Americans! that unless you speedily alter your course, *you and your Country are gone!!!!!!* For God Almighty will tear up the very face of the earth!!!"[70] At times Walker suggested that he hoped national destruction would be averted by repentance, but at other times he sounded less than hopeful about that possibility, and less than perturbed about God's impending intervention to bring about justice for the slaves. Walker suspected that individuals would refuse to repent, ensuring their eternal damnation at the bar of God after death and devastation in the here-and-now.

Maria Stewart likewise warned white Americans that God would soon restore her people. He had promised to raise Ethiopia; once African Americans set their minds on the pursuit of knowledge rather than material pleasures, His wrath would fall on America. "Oh America, America, foul and indelible is thy stain!" she wrote. "Dark and dismal is the cloud that hangs over thee, for thy cruel wrongs and injuries to the fallen sons of Africa.... Thou art almost become drunken with the blood of her slain." She continued with a vision of what was to come:

> O, ye great and mighty men of America, ye rich and powerful ones, many of you will call for the rocks and mountains to fall upon you, and to hide you from the wrath of the Lamb, and from him that sitteth upon the throne; whilst many of the sable-skinned Africans you now despise, will shine in the kingdom of heaven as the stars forever and ever.[71]

Stewart combined ironic reversal drawn from the Book of Revelation with the "damned nation" warning to highlight the salvation of her people and judgment of America.

The Decline of Hell?

The abolitionists' warnings and hopes for ultimate justice on individuals and the nation were part of an American jeremiad tradition. As the

1830s wore on, many became less and less hopeful that other Americans would repent or that God would excuse the nation from its guilt. It became abundantly clear that emancipation would not occur quickly or easily. The proslavery defense that slavery was a positive good was picking up steam. Proslavery theologians found that abolitionists had difficulty rebutting their literal reading of the Bible's support of, or at least indifference to, slavery. Meanwhile, the question of women's rights roiled the antislavery movement in response to public lectures by activists like the Grimké sisters and Lydia Maria Child. Some abolitionists became disillusioned with what they saw as the churches' failure to embrace their reforming agenda.

By the 1840s antislavery activists no longer just divided along immediatist and gradualist lines. Many moderates continued to try to work within the churches. Some acknowledged that a literal reading of the Bible did not support the claim that slavery was a sin. They moved instead toward "a progressive and experiential understanding of biblical truth" according to which, as humans advanced in moral knowledge, they came to realize that certain behaviors sanctioned in biblical times (e.g., slavery and polygamy) were no longer acceptable. Individual slaveowners could only be held guilty so far as the surrounding society progressed as a whole and they did not. The moderates held that individual slaveowners could be good people caught in a bad situation and tried to work across the growing sectional divide and increasingly deadlocked slavery debates.[72]

Other abolitionists departed even further from standard evangelical doctrine, calling forth southern proslavery criticisms of the North as damned because of its abolitionist heretics. Garrisonian "come-outers" preferred to leave the compromised and compromising churches and urged separation from the South with the slogan "No Union with Slaveholders." They also advocated tactics of nonresistance to forward their agenda, which included women's rights. By contrast, radicals like John Brown saw God's justice as something to look forward to and speed along—even by means of violent acts.[73] The hypocrisy of supposed Christians was a constant refrain in abolitionist rhetoric, from the "Appeal" of David Walker to Garrison's editorials in the *Liberator*. These attacks grew more pronounced among Garrisonians and radicals in the late 1830s and beyond. It was perhaps to be expected that, to the extent these abolitionists attacked Christianity as practiced in America, they would come to question its very foundations.

This was certainly the case for Garrison himself. In the early to mid-1830s, he was still a "pillar of rectitude in religious matters," targeting "irreligion" and atheism alongside slavery.[74] But the mainstream churches' rejection of his agenda and complacent support of gradual emancipation frustrated him. That some of his earliest supporters were freethinkers like Abner Kneeland and Bronson Alcott, and Unitarians Samuel Joseph May and Samuel E. Sewall, led him to realize that "if the religious portion of the community are indifferent to the cries of suffering humanity, it is no reason why I should reject the cooperation of those who are more deeply interested, though they make no pretension to evangelical piety."[75] Garrison's interest in the perfectionism of John Humphrey Noyes, the Quakerism of James and Lucretia Mott, and the Unitarianism of Theodore Parker also influenced his departure from his Baptist upbringing and his support of nonresistance. By 1846 Garrison anticipated Spiritualist James Richardson, Jr.'s conviction that "ideas, opinions can not damn the soul" when he asked in the *Liberator*, "who shall dogmatically assume to decide what is heresy, or inflict vengeance upon the heretic?"[76]

By 1849 we can see a definitive break in Garrison's personal attitude to the doctrine of damnation if we look at his private response to the passing of his young son, Charles Follen. Charles was scalded to death in a hot tub in an attempt to cure brain fever. In a letter to his friend Elizabeth Pease, Garrison wrote:

> Discarding, as I do, as equally absurd and monstrous, the theological dogma, that death settles forever the condition of those who die, whether for an eternity of bliss or misery for the deeds done here in the body—and believing, as I do, without doubt or wavering, in the everlasting progression of the human race. . .—I see nothing strange, appalling, or even sad in death.

Garrison trusted that his son was now developing in a heaven of eternal progress. What saddened him was "the conviction that his death was premature; that he was actually defrauded of his life through unskilful treatment; that he might have been saved, if we had not been most unfortunately situated at that time." Garrison did not represent his son's death as part of God's providence, but as a result of faulty medical practices.[77]

What did this shift in underlying convictions mean for Garrison's rhetoric? He rejected the "perishing soul" motif in the Hartford Bible Convention of 1853. The Convention had been called in early June "for the purpose of freely and fully canvassing the origin, authority, and influence of the Jewish and Christian Scriptures." Among its conveners was the famous Spiritualist Andrew Jackson Davis. At the Convention, Garrison resolved "that it is the climax of audacity and impiety for this nation to pretend to receive the Bible as the inspired Word of God, and then to make it a penal offence to give it to any of the millions who are held as chattel slaves on its soil, thus conspiring to make them miserable here and hereafter." While Garrison might seem to have been using the "perishing soul" motif here, he also resolved, earlier in the speech, that it "is self-evidently absurd" to take the Bible as the "Word of God" and "the only rule of faith and practice."[78] Thus he was actually criticizing the hypocrisy and paternalism of so-called Christians who would deny what *they* saw as the only means of salvation to the slaves, rather than implying that any slaves would actually be miserable hereafter as a result. Garrison could also, at times, sound almost moderate, as in the following transcript from the annual meeting of the New England Antislavery Convention in 1858:

> Much as I detest the oppression exercised by the Southern slave-holder, he is a man, sacred before me.... He is a sinner before God—a great sinner; yet, while I will not cease reprobating his horrible injustice, I will let him see that in my heart there is no desire to do him harm,—that I wish to bless him here, and bless him everlastingly.[79]

Elsewhere, though, Garrison continued to use damnation rhetoric to justify his come-outer position. His response to the death of James K. Polk in 1849, the same year his son died, contains language that he might well have used in the early 1830s: "The transition from the Presidential chair to the grave has been swift and startling.... He probably died an unrepentant man-stealer."[80] In 1854 Garrison famously burned copies of the Fugitive Slave Act and the U.S. Constitution, denouncing the latter as "a covenant with death and an agreement with hell" (an accusation he repeated on more than one occasion).[81] And in the same 1858 Convention in which he blessed the Southern slaveholder, he denounced the American Tract Society for declaring "its purpose never to issue a single tract in condemnation of slavery as a system, or of slaveholding as an act... thus leaving them [the slaves] without God and without hope in their chains, and remorselessly consigning them, as far as in their power, to the doom of the damned in the life to come"—as clear an invocation of the perishing soul motif as any. He resolved that since the Society "exhibits a spirit so satanic, and retains a position so impious, it must be sorely displeasing to a just God, and an act of exceeding criminality, to contribute to its treasury."[82]

Then, two years later, in his *Liberator* column on Lincoln's election in 1860, Garrison painted slaveowners as both damned and demoniacal:

> The election of...Lincoln...has operated upon the whole slave-holding South in a manner indicative of the torments of the damned. The brutal dastards and bloody-minded tyrants, who have so long ruled the country with impunity, are now furiously foaming at the mouth, gnawing their tongues for pain, indulging the most horrid blasphemies, uttering the wildest threats, and avowing the most treasonable designs. Their passions "set on fire of hell," are leading them into every kind of excess, and they are inspired by a demoniacal phrenzy.

Garrison went on to apply the doomsday language of Revelation to the South: "Therefore shall her plagues come in one day, death, and mourning, and famine; and she shall be utterly burned with fire; for strong is the Lord God who judgeth her."[83]

As someone who had grown up in the evangelical fold, Garrison knew the effects of hellfire threats on people firsthand. And he undoubtedly remembered the angry reactions to his damnation rhetoric in the early 1830s. Telling people or an entire region that they were damned for sins they refused to acknowledge could be a significant insult. The threat of hell could be a "weapon of honor," to borrow from an historian of an earlier period, and Garrison's tirades in the 1840s and beyond continued to provoke censure from proslavery defenders and gradual emancipationists affronted by the accusation that they and their nation were damned or in league with the devil.[84] In response to his claim that the Constitution was a "covenant with death and an agreement with hell," for instance, a Boston correspondent called Garrison a "black-hearted traitor" and alleged that his "infamous sentiments" were "spurned by the community at large, with appropriate contempt."[85]

Garrison's public warnings and accusations got under people's skin. He was an effective tactician, but we cannot dismiss him as an insincere opportunist who used the language of hell when convenient and rejected it when not. Even though, by the 1840s, he no longer believed that individuals could be eternally damned for rejecting the divine inspiration of the Bible, the possibility that God would rain judgments and temporal destruction on the nation because of its transgressions against the slaves still held meaning. Antebellum Americans knew about the historical rise and fall of nations and feared the worst for a sinful America. Hence Garrison and his followers chose separatism when they felt that the nation was too far gone in its sins to be redeemed. Although Garrison rejected hell for his own loved ones, his idea of "'disunion,' which separated the sacred from the profane portions of the country,"[86] divided the nation into an us vs. them as much as any evangelical might divide people into the "saved" and the "damned."

Philanthropist Gerrit Smith provides another example of the simultaneous "decline" and persistence of hell in the worldview of a radical abolitionist. Smith never joined a particular denomination, but "gave generously to the American Bible Society, the American Tract Society, and the American Sunday School Union."[87] He also supported reform movements ranging from temperance and prison reform to women's rights and antislavery. By the 1850s, abolitionism had become his raison d'être. Disillusioned by nonresistant moral suasion's apparent inability to bring about immediate emancipation, he lent his support to the more radical, non-Garrisonian wing of abolitionism, which did not distance itself from the nation but sought to reform it through violence if necessary. Specifically, Smith supported the militant John Brown in his plan to attack the arsenal at Harper's Ferry and arm the slaves to fight for their emancipation throughout the South.[88]

In late 1858 and early 1859, as the resolve to raid Harper's Ferry reached a fever pitch for Smith, Brown, and collaborators Frederick Douglass and James McCune Smith, Gerrit gave a series of lectures at the abolitionist Church of Peterboro, advocating what he called "The Religion of Reason." These lectures showed just how far he had come from the evangelical worldview he had shared in the 1830s. The gist of Smith's increasingly radical view was that "the religion of all holy hearts would be substantially the same" and that "true" Christianity and salvation in the hereafter hinged on reason and not on traditional interpretations of biblical doctrine.[89] "I am not blaming them [evangelical ministers] for teaching the divinity of Christ, the atonement, an eternal hell, and the plenary inspiration of the Bible," he noted in his first lecture. "What I blame them for, is their teaching that they who do not understand and receive these doctrines must perish. I might admit that Jesus taught all these doctrines. But where did He teach that if a man does not understand and receive them, he shall perish?"[90] As we saw in the Introduction, Smith mocked belief in "eternal hell," alleging that if people truly believed in it, it would create national paralysis. "Let the American people wake up with [the belief] to-morrow, and none of them would go to their fields, and none to their shops, and none would care for their homes," he alleged. "Even the beginnings of such a belief are too much for the safety of the brain."[91] Smith himself "confess[ed]—perhaps to my shame and condemnation—that I do not feel a deep and abiding interest in the next stage of our being. Far less concerned am I to know what is the future state than to know and do the duties of the present."[92] He instead prioritized the "One Test of Character," which demanded right actions toward others over correct beliefs.[93] His emphasis on action came on the eve of what he and his fellow radicals saw as holy violence against the sin of slavery.

Despite his rejection of an eternal hell to which one would be condemned based on beliefs, Smith could still affirm a "philosophically and necessarily true" future punishment based on actions. "Enough knowledge for me and for all men on this point is that in the life to come 'it shall be well' with the righteous and 'ill' with the wicked," he maintained, "and that the 'Judge of all the earth will do right,' as well there as here."[94] In deeming God a "Judge" who decides the fate of the righteous and wicked, Smith showed that he was far from a religious relativist. Although some Christians might accuse him of preaching a "false" religion, Smith hurled the same language back at them, accusing them of preaching "a spurious and Satanic religion" because of their "murderous prejudice against the colored races." In response to those who called him and his supporters "infidels," he retorted:

> When they charge us with being infidels because of our defective creeds, let us charge them with being infidels because of their wicked deeds.... All persons are atheists who do not honor God by honoring his children. Hence, all are atheists who refuse to eat with their colored brethren, or to sit by their side in the carriage or the pew. And if there are Christians that vote for men who recognize the legality of Slavery, and wield the power of their office to perpetuate the bondage of the slave, none the less atheistic is such voting.[95]

Like Garrison, Smith could give as well as he could take. His portrayal of slaveholders and bigots as "atheists" and "infidels" echoed the missionized peoples and slaves who depicted their oppressors as much more depraved than themselves.

Smith saw violence in the cause of emancipation as sanctioned by the "Religion of Reason," but he did not anticipate the amount of bloodshed that would attend the raid on Harper's Ferry: seventeen dead, John Brown and four others captured, and not a single slave freed.[96] Smith's profound guilt over the lives lost caused a nervous breakdown that revived the fear of hell in him. He was committed to an insane asylum in November 1859; prescribed marijuana, brandy, and occasionally morphine, he raved about going to hell.[97] By the summer of 1860, he had disavowed his support of violence and his participation in the raid, distanced himself from his African American friends, and given up his hopes of creating a perfected, interracial society. But he still used "damned nation" imagery in an April 1861 speech in Peterboro, soon after Confederates fired on Fort Sumter. "The end of American Slavery is at hand," he predicted. "That it is to be in blood does not surprise me. For fifteen years I have been constantly predicting that it would be. From my desk in Congress I repeated the pre-diction, and said that this bloody end 'would be such a reckoning for deep and damning wrongs—such an outbursting of smothered and pent-up revenge as living man has never seen.'"[98] The concept of a future reck-oning for the damnable sins of the nation's citizens remained in Smith's religious imagination despite his vacillating belief in the evangelical hell.

Even Theodore Parker at times linked his condemnation of slavery to the language of eternal punishment. Parker was a Unitarian min-ister attuned to transnational developments in biblical criticism, and of all the abolitionists considered here was the most overtly hostile to the concept of damnation. He remembered his mother as being deeply religious, although "the dark theology of the times seems not to have blackened her soul at all," as he wrote in his *Autobiography*. Nor did this "dark theology," to which he would have been exposed as a child of New England growing up in the heady revival atmosphere of the 1810s and 1820s, "blacken" his own soul for long. Indeed, damnation was the first mainstream Protestant doctrine he dispensed with in his career as a religious liberal. "In my early childhood," he wrote, "after a severe but silent struggle, I made way with the ghastly doctrine of eternal damna-tion and a wrathful God; this is the Goliath of that theology. From my seventh year I have had no fear of God, only an ever-greatening love and trust."[99] Parker's rejection of hell opened him to other unorthodox ideas, which he picked up through his studies of German biblical criticism and exposure to Unitarianism and Transcendentalism at Harvard in the 1830s.[100] The Protestant minister used the Bible as a "fetish," he claimed, to which he "prostitutes his mind and conscience, heart and soul...on [the authority] of an anonymous Greek book, he will believe, or at least command others to believe, that man is born totally depraved, and God will perpetually slaughter men in hell by the million though they had committed no fault, except that of not believing an absurd doctrine they had never heard of."[101] In a long letter to his congregation upon leaving the ministry due to consumption, he similarly mocked the "imperfect, wrathful Deity" worshiped by both Protestants and Catholics "who creates men to torment them in an endless hell, 'paved with skulls of infants not a span long.' "[102] That many of his contemporaries saw Parker as an extreme liberal and heretic suggests that these views remained on the fringe in the dominant culture.

Like the others, Parker still dealt with the need for and enforcement of justice. His theodicy, the way in which he explained suffering and evil, is telling. According to Parker, suffering in this world was a means of testing and refining human character, a process that began in the here-and-now but continued into eternity:

> Suffering for error and sin is a fact in this world. I make no doubt it will be a fact in all stages of development in the next world. But mark this: it is not from the anger or weakness of God that we suffer; it is for purposes worthy of His perfection and His love. Suffering is not a devil's malice, but God's medicine. I can never believe that evil is a finality with God.[103]

In other words, Parker taught that suffering and punishment were corrective rather than vindictive, progressive rather than final.

In applying this idea to slavery, Parker asked God to rain chastisements on the nation, not to repay it for its unrepentance as other abolitionists suggested, but to teach it to leave the sin behind. In a Thanksgiving Day prayer, he thanked God for His many blessings on the nation, but also declared:

> And still more in our prayer we remember the millions of our brothers whom our fathers chained, and whose fetters our wicked hands have riveted upon their limbs. O Lord, we pray thee that we may suffer from these our transgressions, till we learn to eschew evil, to break the rod of the oppressor, and to let the oppressed go free; yea, till we make our rulers righteousness, and those chief amongst us whose glory it is to serve mankind by justice, by fidelity, and by truth.[104]

For Parker, slavery was an example of a backwards institution that people must overcome in order to progress to a more perfect realization of their nature as created by a perfect God. Teaching humans to live up to their nature was, to Parker, the purpose of religion, and an essential part of that nature was to care for one's neighbors. Inequalities were not to be righted by God by means of judgments after death or vengeance on the nation (though divine punishment could help people wake up to their responsibilities), but by human action in the here-and-now.

Parker's liberal congregation appreciated his unorthodox views. Garrison himself "virtually became a member" after the 1830s, appreciating Parker's "bold and unfaltering testimony against slavery."[105] But, like Garrison and Smith, Parker did not hesitate to invoke the concept of damnation to condemn slavery and its attendant ills when he tried to reach a wider audience. In a published 1851 sermon on the "Chief Sins of the People," for instance, he decried the Fugitive Slave Act by telling a host of historical tyrants and evildoers to teach a lesson to modern-day slaveholders and kidnappers. "Go tell them that the memory of the wicked shall rot,—" he urged the long-dead despots, "that there is a God, an Eternity, ay! and a Judgment too! where the slave may appeal against him that made him a slave, to Him that made him a man!"[106]

Although the fear of personal damnation faded from their worldviews, then, Garrison, Smith, and Parker still occasionally tied their condemnations of slavery to the threat of future punishment. They were savvy tacticians, and they sometimes submerged their own religious views for strategic purposes. This does not mean that they were hypocrites: they were pragmatists who recognized the power of the threat of personal and national damnation to provoke those for whom the threat still held meaning. If the cultural climate had been such that the threat of hell would fall on deaf ears, after all, why would abolitionists who rejected the threat for themselves bother to use it at a national level?

Their provocations certainly inflamed slavery's defenders. But since their rejection of basic evangelical doctrines was also publicized, they were easy targets of proslavery southerners who accused them of infidelity and fanaticism and turned the language of damnation back on the North.[107] In 1850, an author who went by the penname AMOR PATRIAE declared that slavery was expressly commanded in the Bible and that those who denied the command were infidels in danger of hell. "It will be well to remember, it was for the breach, not the observance of his laws, for which the Jews were so severely punished!" the author wrote. "And so it will be with all who refuse to go and buy, setting up their own righteousness superior to the God that made them! It is a trick of the evil one; and must be eschewed as a most deadly poison to the soul, or it will weigh it down to the Bottomless Pit."[108] The author continued by invoking the "damned nation" argument, but flipped it to suggest that it was the radical abolitionists of the North, and not the slaveholders of the South, who imperiled the nation by their nonliteral and unorthodox uses (and misuses) of the Bible: "After the atmosphere of this happy country has been made foul by the pestiferous, pestilential breath of crazy-headed, or knavish abolition fanatics, 'with tongues set on fire of hell!' not a spark of truth has been found, or can be found, authorizing their nefarious proceedings, in the Bible!"[109]

In 1859 Fred Ross, minister of a Presbyterian church in Alabama, similarly argued that Southerners were growing more pious and reading the Bible more frequently, while "some anti-slavery men have left the Bible, and wandered into the darkness until they have reached the blackness of the darkness of infidelity."[110] And that same year, in an angry letter to Lydia Maria Child, Eliza Margaretta Chew Mason, wife of Senator James Mason, a Southern Democrat, asked, "Do you read your Bible, Mrs. Child? If you do, read there, 'Woe unto you, hypocrites,' and take to yourself with twofold damnation that terrible sentence; for, rest assured, in the day of judgment it shall be more tolerable for those thus scathed by the awful denunciation of the Son of God, than for you. *You* would soothe with sisterly and motherly care the hoary-headed murderer of Harper's Ferry!" Mason told Child that the care southern women provided their slaves put to shame Northerners' neglect of their own poor, and warned her to "take first the beam out of thine own eye" before criticizing the South.[111]

Mason's reference to the suffering northern poor tapped a familiar refrain in southern defenses of slavery as an institution. Moving beyond the argument that the North harbored fanatics, George Fitzhugh claimed that the entire basis of its society was antithetical to "Christian morality" in his 1857 *Cannibals All! Or, Slaves without Masters*. Fitzhugh depicted northern free labor as a brutally individualistic and selfish system where each person looked out for himself or herself alone. "Man is not naturally selfish or bad, for he is naturally social," he claimed. "Free society dissociates him, and makes him bad and selfish from necessity" as men scrambled for wealth. But "it is said in Scripture, that it is harder for a rich man to enter the kingdom of heaven than for a camel to pass through the eye of a needle." In Fitzhugh's view of northern capitalism, the responsibility for the souls of others that evangelicals sought to inculcate in order to create a virtuous and "saved" community was simply "impracticable." In the dog-eat-dog scramble to strike it rich, people could not care enough about others to ameliorate their earthly conditions, much less the state of their souls. By contrast, Fitzhugh claimed that "slave society" was characterized by the "natural morality" derived from paternalistic relationships of careful oversight.[112]

Most Northerners, of course, did not agree with Fitzhugh, but northern opponents of immediatism nevertheless also worried about the consequences on their society of abolitionists' unorthodox turn. In language echoing that of the Northeast's Calvinist ministers against "Salvation" Murray, the *New Hampshire Patriot* worried that the Garrisonians' opposition to the Constitution was founded on the breakdown of religious "sanctions":

All the restraints of religion, all the restraints of morality, and every principle which constrains men to be true to their promises, to respect faith and to be honorable, must be banished from the hearts of the American people, before they can be brought to commit the great crime of strangling freedom in the overturn of their constitution.

"Will [the people of this State] remain silent spectators," the article asked, "and see the progress of ideas which threaten the overthrow of order, regulated freedom, and every cherished institution in the land?"[113] Similarly, the moderately antislavery *Lowell Journal* took issue with the abolitionists' denunciations of the northern clergy and churches:

Whatever might be the object of those who attacked the church and the ministry in this wholesale denunciatory manner, styling them the children of hell, and the oracles of the devil, the effect was to increase infidelity, immorality and crime.... We could not help observing...when we saw ministers of the gospel arraigned in a public assembly as "scoundrels, in league with Satan," what all this amounted to. How was good to come out of so much evil?[114]

And an article in the *Exeter News-Letter*, reprinted in the *Liberator* so abolitionists could see what they were up against, flipped the "slavery as hell" metaphor to indict abolitionists for inciting hellish social havoc through their radical iconoclasm:

> The Clergy, the Church, religion in every form it has appeared on earth or in heaven, has come under their polluted attacks.... The inmates of the lowest rum-shops and brothels in the city, would be ashamed, and hold down their heads in disgust at their wretched slang and low abuse. What do these people mean? What would they do? Carry out their principles—reduce society to the condition they would have it—and there would be a hell on earth.[115]

These anxious warnings might well have been written by "Damnation" Murray against the spread of Universalism in the early republic.

Hell's Effectiveness for Reform

The heterodoxy of some abolitionists, and the threats of damnation hurled back at them by slavery's apologists and northern sympathizers, brings us back to the popular but too simple idea that hell declined with the dawn of the Enlightenment. The fear of hell certainly waned for some laypeople and religious groups and in some abolitionists' personal beliefs. But this was not reflected in their most vitriolic political rhetoric.

How effective were the abolitionists' various strategies of condemnation? When used by white abolitionists and proslavery defenders, the "perishing soul" motif cast slaves as "heathens" lacking the agency to save themselves. It also required audiences to rank the relative worth of various unchristianized peoples. At a time when compromise ruled the day, funding home and foreign missions was less controversial than freeing the slave population immediately, especially when white Southerners claimed that they were already taking steps for their evangelization. The "slavery as hell" analogy, with its attendant depiction of slaveholders as the damned, was certainly effective in reinforcing for abolitionists the righteousness of their cause.[116] But it was also effective in riling up slaveholders who felt that their honor had been attacked and argued that the "infidel" North was damned instead.

Proslavery defenders and gradual emancipationists could also use the "damned nation" argument to critique the radicals of the North. But, more than the other strategies, this one had a chance of persuading the apathetic that slavery was a national sin in which they too were implicated and for which they too would pay.[117] After his lengthy exposition of anni-hilationism, and toward the end of the Civil War, for instance, western doctor-adventurer Rowland Willard wrote:

> The nation has been sorely chastised for their iniquity.... The cries of humanity have assended unto God, & He has come down to avenge them.... The cruelty of the slave lash practiced on the dumb beast, would greatly peril the innocense of the executioner, & how much more when the victim is human like himself. Neither God nor humanity can tollerate, but condemn the evil.... Hense the flow of blood, & the sacrifice of those has been without stint & cannot be staid until vengeance is satisfied. Evil will only result in evil fruits of expiation. Its cause is downwards & damning, & only salutary in results expiatory & reformatory.[118]

Willard's argument, incorporating the concepts of sin, justice, and venge-ance, suggests his exposure to abolitionist interpretations of slavery and of the war as resulting from the nation's sins and God's just judgments.

The "damned nation" argument drew its power from the evangelical appeal to peer pressure and the responsibility of the saved to redeem the damned at peril to their own souls. It linked personal guilt with national judgment and put the fate of the whole country in the hands of individual sinners judged by a righteous God. For audiences disposed to think of America as a chosen nation, the allegation that it might be damned in-stead struck a sensitive nerve.

Uses of the concept of damnation in the controversy over slavery show that it was not simply a conservative, premodern doctrine deployed by churches as an "attack on the soul"[119] or to keep the masses in line, though that could certainly be said of the sermons preached to slaves by ministers like Alexander Glennie. The uses of hell rhetoric by black and white abolitionists, including the slaves themselves, turned Glennie's and other southern ministers' dreams of creating a docile, God- and master-fearing workforce upside-down, as the oppressed invoked hell to affirm the possibility of absolute justice and the ultimate righting of wrongs. These radical uses of hell complicate the scholarly view of the concept as "arcane," "bizarre," and fundamentally conservative.[120] When scholars dub abolitionists radical, they focus on opposition to slavery, but if they extracted and only looked at abolitionists' uses of damnation rhetoric, they might find it the epitome of conservative religiosity. But that reflects contemporary, not antebellum, proclivities. The abolitionists' opposition to slavery was intimately linked to their belief in ultimate justice. The argument that hell awaited oppressors posited a higher tribunal than a nation's highest courts, a powerful idea in an age that saw the passage of the Fugitive Slave Act and the Dred Scott decision. Even for those abolitionists who rejected belief in personal damnation, its usefulness as a concept with which to condemn the nation made it a powerful rhetorical weapon in the fight against slavery. Damnation presented the ultimate consequence of, and the ultimate language with which to condemn, the slavery to sin and the sin of slavery, even as it offered slavery's apologists a language with which to deflect the blows.

6

"Our Men Die Well"

DAMNATION, DEATH, AND THE CIVIL WAR

A man may fight and die for his country and lose his soul!
ALEXANDER DAVIS BETTS, Confederate Chaplain

He was, on principle, devoted to the cause of his country, for which he has so heroically died. Wherefore we may trust, that through the mercy of our God in Jesus Christ, he has received the crown of life.
BENJAMIN B. BABBITT, Rector of Christ
Church, Andover

ILLINOIS NATIVE AND Union soldier Lewis N. T. Allen was no stranger to the sight of death when he returned to Vicksburg with his company in October 1863. Allen had participated in the siege of Vicksburg earlier that year and had seen scores of men fall in battle. A practicing evangelical and antislavery man, he had entrusted his own life to God's providence in the heat of combat and explained the deaths of others as necessary sacrifices to eradicate the sin of slavery. But despite his familiarity with death and his confidence that the war was just, the sight of the "bleach[ed]" bones and "moulder[ing]" bodies of "our poor soldiers" lying unburied on the battlefield at Vicksburg months after the siege disturbed him greatly. The bodies of these "poor fellows" might rot, Allen noted, but "the soul must live not with the body, but in an eternal world, eather in happiness and bliss, or in torment forever." He continued, "It is enough to make ones heart sucken to walk over the ground when a battle has been fought, and think of the many poor souls, that have departed there, and many that have not been prepaired for that separation."[1]

Allen was hardly alone in thinking that death in the service of the nation might not open a portal to heavenly bliss for those not properly "prepaired."[2] Chaplains and evangelical agencies North and South saw the conflict not only as a "just war" between the holy and unholy but also as a grand missionary opportunity. Even as they invoked apocalyptic imagery and hurled the rhetoric of damnation against each other in the lead-up to war and in interpreting the outcome of major battles, religious leaders on both sides also focused on the souls of their own soldiers.[3] The fear that the slain might not be heaven-bound spurred last-minute attempts to bring about deathbed conversions and contrasted sharply with later hagiographic literature that firmly placed the valiant dead in a heaven much like home. The harsh realities of war—violence, illness, injury, and the mounting scale of death—contributed to this shift. Some people became more skeptical in the face of such widespread carnage, but many instead preferred to believe that their loved ones had died to save the country and in so doing had saved their own souls.

For the concept of damnation in America, the Civil War was both a culmination and a crossroads. Neither warnings of damnation nor virtual canonization of the dead was a new phenomenon by the 1860s, though amplified by the tumult of battle. But by the end of the war, the sheer scale of death accelerated the trend toward assuming heaven for loved ones and muted the rhetoric of fire and brimstone in the mainstream evangelical denominations. Still, hell never disappeared: other groups, from disappointed ex-slaves to conservative white Christians, continued to deploy the threat of damnation to solidify group identity and condemn what they saw as adverse behaviors long after the war had ended.[4]

The "Multitudinous Vices of the Camp"

Stationed with his fellow Union soldiers at Fort Marrow, West Virginia, Corporal Henry Breidenthal of the Ohio Volunteer Infantry's 3rd Regiment was displeased with the moral atmosphere of camp. Breidenthal had enlisted as an ardent antislavery man; he believed that other social ills also contributed to the nation's peril. He wrote in his diary,

> our National sins I have no doubt has brought down upon us the
> Divine displeasure—our sabath breaking, our Intemperance and

our complicity with African Slavery __ a crime of sufficient ennor-
mity to sink this great nation to the lowest depths of perdition_
[^and] if not speedily banished from us will be the death knell of or
republic.[5]

Breidenthal took to heart the link evangelical reformers made between
individual and national sins. He believed that "God will no more hold a
nation guiltless than individuals" and worried about his fellow soldiers'
fondness for gambling, swearing, drinking, and dancing (and worse still,
occasionally on the Sabbath).[6] Even as they were supposed to be fighting
to eradicate the sin of slavery, they were simultaneously indulging in vices
that showed their lack of understanding of the stakes involved.

"The society here is not congenial to my tastes," he complained on
October 10, 1861. "I formed a resolution 7 years ago to this affect—that
unless I could move in respectable society as an equal, I would not associate with any." Breidenthal described "the character—the general character
I mean__ of our soldiery" as

> lowbred, their aspirations rising but little above the instinct of the
> animal creation—sacrificing their finer feelings to their evil pro-
> pensities, and forgetting that they are rational beings endowed
> by an allwise Creator with immortal natures _ powers _ physical
> mortal & moral [^that] were not designed by God when he created
> them in his own image and likness to be wasted at the card table or
> grog shop or in using the scathing oaths or multitudinous vices of
> the camp.[7]

Breidenthal admitted that he had personal experience with similar "vices."
At a young age he had been "thrown upon an unkind world" and had
fallen prey to numerous temptations. "And now my friend," he asked his
diary, "will you censure me ~~until~~ [?] after having striven 7 long years to
regain what the vices of the times caused me to lose [?] _ character_ if
I condemn those sins that like a millstone almost sunk me to perdition?"[8]

Not unexpectedly, his campmates were hardly taken with his attitude.
"Some one of two individuals," he mourned a month after his initial entry,
"have write home an infamous lie, that I was above speaking to common
soldiers."[9] Two days later his "Spirits" were still "poor," but he determined
to neither "weep nor groan though I am chained to the rock (Prometheus
like) of public opinion while the vulture Slander [^is] tearing my vitals with

its <u>mouth of</u> Gossip and its <u>talons</u> of <u>defamation</u> <u>and</u> <u>lies</u>." Breidenthal's unwillingness to "play cards morris checkers and dance" with his compatriots stemmed from his fear of once again falling down the slippery slope to the very borders of hell.[10]

Breidenthal would not have approved of a camp incident involving John Russell Kelso, the skeptic from Missouri who, after serving as a child preacher (of his own religion) and Methodist exhorter, had shocked the Methodist connection with his renunciation of hell. Kelso took the Union side in the war, believing that slavery enervated the "wealthy classes of the South," who "came to regard <u>honest</u> <u>labor</u> <u>as</u> <u>disgraceful,</u> <u>wealth</u> <u>as</u> <u>the</u> <u>only</u> <u>necessary</u> <u>virtue, and</u> <u>their</u> <u>own</u> <u>selfish</u> <u>interests</u> <u>as</u> <u>the</u> <u>principal</u> <u>object</u> <u>a</u> <u>government</u> <u>should</u> <u>exist</u>."[11] On one memorable occasion in early 1862 Kelso regaled his fellow soldiers with a mock funeral sermon for an "ancient bovine" that they had been served for dinner as "a mess of execrable unmasticatable cartilage mis-called beef."[12]

"At an early age," Kelso told a crowd he estimated to be in the "thousands," the "lamented Old-buck experienced a change of <u>heart_</u> a change of <u>something</u>, any way, that tended greatly to preserve his virtue. Indeed his strict chastity_ the result of this change_ was a model for the imitation of all young bulls and all young men." Nor did Kelso stop at mocking the conversion experience. He continued, "So of his temperance. He never befouled his mouth, his breath, or his morals, with intoxicating drinks or with tobacco. His piety, too, was never questioned. Though he was never heard praying aloud,_ as men often pray to be heard of their fellows_, he was often heard to groan_ to say '<u>um-m-m</u>,' as the most godly men often do in the amencorner of the church." Kelso continued by describing the "murder" of the cow for their dinner, assuring his audience that while "Old-buck" was probably now "gamboling upon the green pastures that surround the gates of the New Jerusalem," his butcher, the "wretched cow-killer," would pay, in a classic scenario of ironic reversal:

> The gaunt form of the murdered Old-buck, stands before his affrighted eyes, and bellows "<u>um-m-m-m</u>," in his agonized ears. Whole regiments of gaunt soldiers, made miserable dyspeptics by eating his beef...bellow, "<u>um-m-m-m</u>," in his ear. He tries to scream, but can only bellow, "<u>um-m-m-m</u>." He is changed into an emaciated old ox, toothless, deaf and blind. He chews his cud but imagines that he is trying to chew some of his own beef.

No doubt Kelso's early experiences as a Methodist preacher informed his ability to deliver this "sermon" with such satirical flourish. He concluded with that most familiar of evangelical cautions: "What a terrible warning this ought to be."[13]

The mock sermon "called forth enthusiastic applause from the audience" and, Kelso gloated, "we were never afterwards furnished with beef quite so bad."[14] An ability to laugh at the serious (conversion, death, punishment) did not necessitate doubt or mockery under different circumstances: it might have simply been a way to release tension in the moment. These Missouri men were used to violence, as bloodshed ran rampant in the border states even before official hostilities commenced. Kelso's soldier and officer audience enjoyed the humorous break but did not necessarily reject the principles Kelso mocked when ill, injured, and/ or near death themselves.

"I Know I Never Occupied a Field of Greater Usefulness": The Civil War as Missions Opportunity

It was the job of evangelical chaplains and tract societies to make sure these principles were not forgotten. Evangelicals on both sides viewed camp life as dangerous to the spiritual welfare of fighting men. Like Breidenthal, they worried that the itching anticipation of combat, coupled with the intervening tedium (and overwhelming maleness) of camp life, conduced to immorality. Confederate J. C. Granbery of the Methodist Episcopal Church South understood that soldiers "have given up the care of their pastors, the fellowship of their christian brethren, the stated services of the sanctuary, the hallowed influences of home and of female society.... It is not strange that they should cast off the fear of God, and seek pleasures in vices which once they abhorred."[15] Similarly, the Protestant Episcopal Church of Charlotte, North Carolina, told its Confederate readership that "it is hardly to be wondered that the majority of private soldiers, who are mostly unlearned men and without the benefit of instruction, either mental or spiritual, with no chaplain to care for their souls, should ignorantly deride what they do not understand, and have not given a serious thought to."[16] With such a view of the soldier's life as a swirl of temptation and ignorance that could send them to everlasting hell, it is hardly surprising that evangelicals on both sides saw the war not only as a battle for or against slavery but also as an evangelistic opportunity for the souls of their own.

Methodist George Shane Phillips was an indefatigable laborer for the Lord. He had served as a Deacon and Elder in the North Ohio Conference in the 1840s and had spent the 1850s as a missionary in California. Like his evangelical peers, he was driven by the desire to save his fellow humans by leading them to salvation in Christ. His sermon notes from his prewar career reveal as typical his views on the afterlife and future punishment. He luxuriated in the hope of heavenly reunion but railed against the likes of "Universalists," "Infidels," and "Backsliders," warning of the "lashes of a gilty concience" and the "eternal punishment" that would follow failure to repent.[17]

As much as Phillips had labored in the cause of Christ for the twenty years preceding the Civil War (and he was nothing if not a workaholic), though, nothing prepared him for the "field for usefulness" that he encountered when he joined the 49th Regiment, Ohio Volunteer Infantry, then stationed in Tennessee, as a chaplain in May 1863. Where Henry Breidenthal had seen his fellows as a rowdy lot uninterested in spiritual matters early on in the war, Phillips found the situation to be quite the opposite. Lincoln's proclamation of emancipation just a few months earlier had energized both sides, but a war that most had hoped would be short was dragging on and escalating into total combat as massive casualties on the battlegrounds of Shiloh, Antietam, and Fredericksburg dashed hopes for a "civil" civil war. The scale of violence, disease, and death changed the atmosphere in soldiers' encampments on both sides. Phillips's regiment, which had participated in the Battle of Shiloh in April 1862 and had lost its commanding General, senior captains, and many other men in a series of battles in early 1863,[18] clamored for the advice and assistance of chaplains like himself to make sense of their suffering and losses. "Poor fellows how very very much they needed a chaplain," Phillips wrote to his wife on June 1. "Never in all my life have I preached to men who were seemingly so anxious for the word of life." Noting that an "extensive revival" was spreading through Murfreesboro, he continued, "If we remain here for any considerable time there will be such a work as the world has never seen." For Phillips, who had not yet seen or participated in battle himself, the soldiers' interest in the gospel of salvation made the "terable war for the right" doubly worth it, as it might not only save the country from impending doom but also soldiers' souls from hell.[19]

Another Union chaplain, David Weston, similarly saw his work as a "great missionary enterprise."[20] Laboring among the wounded in Fredericksburg, he noted that "There was no difficulty in approaching them, learning the feelings of their hearts, and impressing them with the importance of eternal things. They were ready and ever eager to hear. The fearful scenes they had witnessed, the dangers they had met, the sufferings they had endured, had softened and subdued them, and already directed the thoughts of many to the interests of their souls. Many were near to death, and felt the need of salvation."[21] One soldier "who had recently suffered amputation of the right arm" not only prayed for his own salvation, but "knelt upon an empty cot and poured out his soul in supplication for the eternal welfare of his suffering and dying comrades," Weston wrote. "There was many a tear shed before he closed, and then, when we asked those who desired to be Christians to raise their hands, many a hand was raised showing that many a heart had been touched."[22] As painful as was the sight of wounded and dying soldiers, Weston believed that the constant exposure to injury, disease, and death could have the beneficial effect of forcing men to pay attention to the state of their souls.

The 1872 memoirs of A. S. Billingsley, who served in the United States General Hospital at Fortress Monroe, Virginia, offer a glimpse of how a chaplain might converse with a dying soldier. Billingsley based many of his sketches on his wartime diary, where he recorded "spiritual diagnos[e]s" of the many patients he visited.[23] In keeping with postwar imagery of soldiers' deaths as happy and their final resting place as heaven, the majority of Billingsley's sketches ended with deathbed conversions and uplifting testimonies. Still, in order to achieve these apparent conversions Billingsley frequently fell back on the threat of hell and well-developed warnings about the need for immediate repentance.

Attending a surgical amputation performed on one Captain John A. Fee, for instance, Billingsley "spoke to him about his future prospects and asked him, 'If you should die in the operation, captain, do you feel prepared to go?'" The captain "made no pretensions to piety" and fearlessly responded, "'No, . . . *I don't know as I do.*" Like other laypeople who thumbed their noses at the fear-mongering of priests, Fee initially scorned the chaplain's advances. Soon after taking chloroform, "he began to say bad words." Fearful for the patient's eternal welfare should he die on the operating table with impious words on his lips, the surgeons themselves hesitated to begin the procedure. Instead, they waited for the "stupefaction" to pass, after which Billingsley "began to persuade [the captain] to repent and come to Jesus." Telling him the story of the crucified thief whom Jesus pardoned at the final moment, Billingsley warned,

Doubtless it will soon be with you, as it was with that dying thief, your *very last* chance. Now is the crisis of *your* soul. It is salvation *now*, or never; it is believe and be saved *now*, or refuse and be lost forever; it will soon be salvation or damnation!...Just think, captain, of the Saviour's love in suffering and dying to save us, and of his ability and willingness to save you; think, too, how lamentable it will be to die for your country and lose your own soul! Think of the torments of hell; of the lashings of a guilty conscience; of the gnawings of the undying worm; of the "everlasting fire;" of the weeping, wailing, and gnashing of teeth, you will soon bring upon yourself, unless you soon repent!

Billingsley's impassioned words led the awakening captain to request a prayer before the operation commenced. Fee survived the amputation (barely), and in the ensuing days apparently reconsidered his former unbelief and apathy. On a post-operative visit, Billingsley found the captain greatly weakened by the surgery and on the verge of death. He reiterated the warning just to make sure: "Delay is dangerous. It is glorious to die for your country; but it is lamentable to die, and be lost." The dying Fee responded that "he loved the Saviour, and that he was precious to him." Taking this as a sign that he was finally saved, Billingsley concluded, "We trust he went happy."[24]

Confederate chaplains were equally convinced of the need to save their own soldiers. Chaplain A. D. Betts of the 30th North Carolina echoed Billingsley in his December 31, 1864, diary entry: "A man may fight and die for his country and lose his soul! Mohammed taught that all who died for his cause would be saved and some men in this day seem to think that all who are killed in defense of their country are saved; but the Bible assures us 'the pure in heart' shall 'see God.'"[25] The belief that soldiers' souls were endangered even though they risked their lives for the country drove chaplains to volunteer despite the paltry salary they generally received and the often-harsh conditions under which they ministered.[26]

Still, there were never enough volunteers to tend to soldiers in either army. So chaplains also distributed reading materials, just as they had done before the war to reach populations wider than regular church attendees. Not long after he joined the 49th Ohio, George Phillips told his wife that he had passed out over two thousand pages of tracts, including Methodist reading materials, a hundred hymnbooks, and some testaments.[27] Printed materials were more readily available in the North, which had more presses and established tract distribution societies. In 1861, the American Tract Society began mustering donations to make its publications available to Union soldiers free of charge.[28] Other, smaller denominational organizations also printed and distributed their own pamphlets and newspapers.

Having split from the formerly national (though heavily northern) evangelical organizations like the ATS, the Confederacy had to turn to fewer southern presses to produce its own reading material for soldiers.[29] While the North could boast of its Jonathan Edwards, Samuel Hopkins, and Charles Finney, some southern theologians thought that northern piety had disintegrated into laxity by the time of the Civil War and sought to display their superior righteousness and theological rigor.[30] If the South had had no Jonathan Edwards back in the day, by the time of the Civil War it did have its own Rev. John E. Edwards, who disseminated equally frightening warnings in tracts with titles like "A Word of Warning to an Impenitent Sinner" and "The Wounded Soldier," both published by the Evangelical Tract Society of Petersburg, Virginia. "When you walk and work by day, and when you seek your pleasures or sleep by night," Edwards cautioned in the former title, "you are suspended by the gossamer thread of life over the bottomless pit of hell! O! how awful, perilous, and alarming is your condition. And yet you will not believe it. You imagine yourself secure, when there is nothing but the mercy of an offended and insulted God that keeps you from sinking down to the regions of eternal death." Had this Edwards not gone on to recount the 1835 case of a young man who, after mocking the church, was killed in a fall from a horse, we might surmise that this passage came from the original Edwards himself.[31]

In "The Wounded Soldier," the southern Edwards made his words of warning even more specific to an audience of injured Confederates. Do not think, he admonished readers who were likely hospitalized, awaiting painful operations, or suffering from the after-effects of the same, that God did not protect you: "The shot or shell that bereft you of a limb, or disfigured your face, or inflicted a painful and serious wound upon your body, might have entered a vital part, and hurried you instantly into eternity. What a God's mercy that your life was spared." Edwards urged the wounded to take advantage of their second chance to repent and be saved, because

> the wound in your body may not heal. It may grow worse, day by day, until death steps in to do his office, and summon you to the

judgment. Or, should you recover, it may be only to go to into battle again, to fall *suddenly*, without a lingering wound—to go from the gory bed of death, amid the roar of artillery and the dying groans of the slaughtered around you, into the presence of a neglected Saviour and an insulted God, to hear the fearful and appalling sentence, "Depart, *depart*—into the blackness of darkness forever."

Edwards told soldiers that weeping in the face of "the most excruciating pain" as well as "under the pressure of bereavment or mental distress" was neither "unmanly" nor "childish," since it could signal the breaking down of pride and prime the soul for accepting salvation. "Too many have made up their minds," he lamented, "that a profession of religion is incompatible with the profession of arms. This is all a mistake." Edwards thus tried to make the "profession of religion" a feature of manliness and its rejection the sign of a fool.[32]

Another Confederate tract, by "A Young Lady of Virginia," urged soldiers to convert even if they were far from the safety and comforts of home.[33] Instead of positioning white Confederate women as in need of manly protection against the Union foe, the author positioned soldiers as endangered without the intervention of their female kin: "There are hearts at home ready to break for you, but they cannot protect you. Your mother would willingly interpose her own loving breast between your own and the fatal ball, but her love, her tender, unselfish love, *cannot* afford you a shield." Nor could the prayers of sisters or wives:

Their yearning hearts will follow you, and if you fall they will weep in agony; but their earnest, beautiful love, cannot turn from its course, the messenger of death, nor save your soul from the fiends, who would exultingly hail its entrance into hell. While our country is reaping its fruits, whose seed you have sowed in pain and watered with your blood, while history perpetuates the memory of your valor and your patriotism, must you in hell lament that you were ever born? Oh no! no! no! There is One "mighty to save," One who loves you far more than your tender mother.

Turn to Jesus, the "Young Lady of Virginia" advised, and spare your loved ones from the bitter misery of mourning not only your death but also the eternal loss of your soul.[34]

Even as they warned soldiers that death in the line of battle did not ensure eternal victory, chaplains and tract writers did not want to be accused of bringing down morale. They tried to walk a fine line between threatening and lauding soldiers for their service to the country. J. C. Granbery, in his "Address to the Soldiers of the Southern Armies," praised Confederates for fighting not only for the South but also for the survival of "true" Christianity against "the insolent enemy who would thrust false doctrines and traitorous prayers into the throats of our preachers and the ears of their congregations." As defenders of the cross and the Confederacy, Granbery promised that the "gallant soldier"'s "name shall be written in immortal story, and sung in immortal song." But he also made clear that soldiers were not guaranteed actual immortality unless they converted, because of the "immorality and utter irreligion to which temptations abound in the camps" and the "imminent peril of sudden death." While eulogizing soldiers as "the very flower of our population, our hope and pride, the youth and manhood of the land," Granbery also quizzed them in no uncertain terms: "Are you willing to rush into eternity with your many crimson sins—with the grievous sin of forgetting your Creator and neglecting the great salvation, unconfessed, unrepented, unforgiven?" He closed by melding the twin virtues of army service and Christianity in a martial metaphor: "Comrade, I wish to enlist you as my fellow soldier in a nobler cause than even that of Southern independence. 'Fight the good fight of faith.' There is no leader comparable to the Captain of our salvation.... To-day join this army, and never desert your colors. Though you die, you will live forever."[35]

Heavenly Consolation in Dying for the Nation

Martial metaphors and attempts to balance consolation with conversion also traversed the pages of hymnbooks soldiers received. The messages in hymns were subtler than the exhortations in tracts. Rather than underlining the threat of hell, the hymns by and large emphasized the promise of heaven. Whereas tracts could work as mini-sermons that built through metaphor, Bible verse, and present-day example to climactic altar calls, hymns tugged at the heartstrings through a combination of familiar melodies with simple and sometimes sentimental lyrics. Hymns also drew their power from repetition and warm associations of singing around the family hearth, at the local neighborhood church, or at outdoor meetings.

Typical of the volumes handed out to Union soldiers was the American Tract Society's *The Soldiers' Hymn-Book, with Tunes*. Many of the hymns would have been familiar to anyone who had visited an antebellum evangelical church, but in a brief preface this pocket-sized compendium emphasized the changed circumstances in which soldiers found themselves. They would not be singing these hymns in the safety of a sleepy Sunday morning church service. No, "your peril is much greater," the Society's agents warned, and "you need therefore a greater friend. Other friends are now away; you need one always near. Other friends are weak; you need a strong friend. Such a friend is JESUS."[36] The songs in the hymnal sought to impress upon the soldier the need to follow Christ, the comfort that faith could offer amidst the dangers of battle and disease, and the joys of heaven should he die a believer. "We're travelling home to heaven above: / Will you go?" asked one hymn:

> Oh, could I hear some sinner say,
> "I will go."
> Oh, could I hear him humbly pray,
> "Make me go;"
> And all his old companions tell,
> "I will not go with you to hell;
> I long with Jesus Christ to dwell:
> Let me go."

Other hymns similarly entreated soldiers to make sure that heaven would be their inheritance with a gentle questioning format. "Oh say, will you be there?" went the chorus of a hymn by the same title, which waxed poetic on the glories of the "region fair," which lay "upon that bright eternal shore." Another asked, "Shall I among them [the saints] stand?" and, more ominously, "What if my name should be left out, / When thou for them shalt call?"[37]

Hymns with military overtones had double meanings for soldiers involved in actual war. "When the battle is fought and the victory won," went one hymn, "Life's trials are ended, and life's duties done, / Then Jesus our Saviour will welcome us home; / No more in this desert of sin we shall roam." Written by William Bradbury (known for composing the tunes to "Jesus Loves Me" and "Just As I Am, Without One Plea"), and published in his bestselling 1861 *The Golden Chain*, the hymn was not originally intended for soldiers but "written expressly for the Sabbath school."[38] Yet it is easy to imagine that soldiers may have interpreted these lines to mean that fighting and dying in literal battle (rather than spiritual battle) would usher them to heaven. The next stanza did nothing to dispel the notion: "The most youthful soldier will then have a share, / In heavenly mansions prepared for us there." The refrain spoke not only to the prospect of heaven but also to soldiers' longing for home: "Safe, safe at home, safe, safe at home / No more to roam, no more to roam...[x2]."[39]

Confederate soldiers sang similar hymns from their own pocket-sized hymnbooks. "SINNERS, turn, why will ye die?" asked one tune (originally written by Charles Wesley) in *The Soldier's Hymn-Book: for Camp Worship*, published by the Soldiers' Tract Society of the Virginia Conference of the Methodist Episcopal Church South.[40] Like those in the Union volume, these hymns celebrated the joys of heaven and used martial terminology to describe the process of getting there. "Fearless of hell and ghastly death, / I'd break through every foe: / The wings of love and arms of faith / Would bear me conqu'ror through," promised another familiar hymn, this by Isaac Watts.[41] A hymn titled "The Christian Soldier" was even more explicit. "OH! when shall I see Jesus, / And dwell with him above. . .?" it began. The answer was not yet, though soon:

> But now I am soldier,
> My Captain's gone before,
> He's given me my orders,
> And tells me not to fear;
> And if I hold out faithful,
> A crown of life he'll give,
> And all his valiant soldiers
> Eternal life shall have....[42]

Holding out "faithful" could be interpreted in more than one way; if a soldier was faithful to the cause and to his earthly captain but less clearly so to Christ, would he still go to heaven? The hymn did not say, allowing soldiers to understand it as they would.

One way to bridge the gap between the notion that soldiers' eternal welfare was imperiled by the temptations of camp and the hazards of battle, and the seemingly opposite idea that dying for one's country guaranteed a passport to heaven, was to focus on the deathbed and the possibility of a last-minute conversion. As we saw in chapter 2, evangelical ministers in the antebellum era had suggested that deathbed repentance was possible but still stressed the importance of advance preparation should death be instantaneous or one's wits flee in the final moments. The tracts soldiers received and discourses they heard also warned them to make their salvation secure well before death might strike. But after major battles, as soldiers lay dying en masse with ministers few and far between, chaplains and survivors who were left with the unhappy task of informing relatives back home relaxed their views and offered the purported confessions of mortally wounded soldiers as proof they had been translated to heaven. Hence A. S. Billingsley's semi-confident pronouncement that the once-apathetic Captain John A. Fee "went happy" ("we trust"). Similar diagnoses of the dead and dying, optimistic yet with a hint of uncertainty, proliferated as chaplains and surviving friends wrote home with assurances that loved ones were in heaven (we hope, we trust, we assume). Women and men on the home front welcomed such assurances and perpetuated the notion that the dead could be sanctified by their sacrifice. "And when you come to pass from earth away," vowed one Mollie Thompson from Clopton, Tennessee, to a company of Confederate soldiers, "whether amid the din of battle strife or in your own peaceful homes, may you, when you stand in the twilight of two worlds, be enabled to look back on this as the greatest act of your life, and may it suffice to obliterate from God's book of justice all your past offenses."[43]

Better yet, sometimes the dying left their own letters behind, reassuring loved ones that they would meet again. Such was an iconic deathbed communication written by "Thornton" and originally printed in the *Detroit Free Press*. "Two bullets have gone through my chest," the dying man wrote,

> and directly through the lungs…. I have won the soldier's name, and am ready to meet now, as I must, the soldier's fate. I hope from heaven I may see the glorious old flag wave again over the undivided Union I have loved so well.
>
> Farewell, wife and babes, and friends! We shall meet again.
> Your loving
> THORNTON.[44]

The anxiety with which soldiers sought to communicate how they had died and families awaited the news—whether in the faith or without any clear indication of how they stood with Christ—bespoke not only a longing for heavenly reunion but also a fear that eternal separation might loom instead.[45] The carefully worded comfort offered by chaplains and others who claimed to have witnessed the last breaths of dying soldiers reflected their awareness that anything less than heavenly consolation would be a double blow to the memory of soldiers and to their families and friends. The softening of fire and brimstone for those killed during the Civil War drew from the continuing fear of hell, even if it only lurked in the back of people's minds.

The hardships of war and the sight of suffering and death took a toll not only on soldiers but also on the chaplains and ministers who were charged with helping them to interpret their ordeal. George Phillips, who had been so excited about the missionary opportunity the war presented when he joined in May 1863, became much less enthusiastic about war and more understanding of his men's foibles after witnessing battle himself and participating in endless "forced marches through the hot sun and dust." By September 1863, while his regiment was in hot pursuit of Braxton Bragg's army, Phillips was writing to his wife, "Our men are growing wild, but little can be done for them [^morally] when thus kept going, and they get weary, and im patient, and perfectly indifferent." Phillips admitted that he no longer even had enough reading material "to circulate among them."[46] By June 1864 he was writing to his daughter Sally, "You can form no idea of the conditi of things during a heavy battle. Men come in with all kinds of wounds, some in a dying condition some shot all to pieces and living despite of all their wounds. No one is more in demand than the chaplains at such times. Here is a man wanting you to pray for him, another wishes baptism, another wishes to send his dying words through you to some friend, a parent brother or sister, or betrothed one." Where Phillips once welcomed the opportunity to evangelize, he now concluded: "I long to see the end of this 'crul war', when this vast body of men shall return home and engage in the pursuits of civil life."[47]

Phillips's acknowledgement that morality could hardly be inculcated on the march, and that the supply of chaplains could hardly meet the demand after a major battle, moderated his perspective on what happened to soldiers if they died before making a confession of faith. He had earlier seen unconverted soldiers as in danger of hell without intervention, but by 1864 the battle-weary chaplain began to suggest that the Union dead were hallowed by their sacrifices and in turn hallowed the ground where they died and were buried. As he passed the graves of Union men in Georgia about a week after his letter to Sally, he wrote to another daughter, Fanny, that "the whole area" thus far covered by

Sherman's march "has been made doubly sacred to the Union as the resting place of our noble sons and fathers. Our men die well. Never have have [*sic*] I seen under any condition in life the power and excellency of the Gospel as I have seen it here. I might volumes without exhausting the subject."[48] Phillips did not explicitly state that the dead soldiers had been saved, but "Our men die well" implied as much in the language of evangelicalism. His earlier remark that not enough chaplains serviced the ranks meant that he assumed rather than witnessed the vast majority of these "good deaths." Underneath this assumption lurked significant questions about a soldier's sacrifices for his country and whether those sacrifices might save him from hell.[49] If not enough chaplains were available to minister to the diseased and wounded, then might not God excuse a dying, unconverted man if he *wanted* a chaplain's guidance but none was there to help? And might not a dying man have been quietly Christian even if no one heard his last words or saw him express outwardly religious sentiments in the camps (and even if he enjoyed the occasional card game, booze, or dance, and possibly even on the Sabbath)? The exhausted 47-year-old Phillips himself succumbed to disease and fatigue before he could fully work out his own views on these questions, dying at his Wooster home on March 30, 1865, just days before Lee's surrender at Appomattox. He was hardly the only religious leader grappling with these issues.

Consider Benjamin Babbitt's "A Sermon on the Death of Walter L. Raymond, a Union Soldier," a fairly typical (and telling) memorial discourse preached on Sunday, the third of April 1865. The Rector of Christ Church at Andover, Massachusetts, Babbitt had not witnessed the horrors of war or the deaths of soldiers firsthand. Military chaplains had the burden of imparting to family members news of loved ones' deaths; the clergy who stayed behind were charged with further memorializing the departed and giving more meaning to their deaths than a brief letter could provide. Walter L. Raymond's case was particularly painful for his family; he had died of severe pneumonia on Christmas day 1864 in Salisbury, a Confederate prison in North Carolina, and had been unceremoniously buried, probably in an unmarked grave. His parents did not hear the news until mid-March 1865.

Babbitt's choice of text set the tone for his discourse: "BE THOU FAITHFUL UNTO DEATH, AND I WILL GIVE THEE A CROWN OF LIFE.—Rev. ii. 10." Babbitt subtly refigured the meaning of "faithfulness" here to include more than devotion to God. "Our young friend," he reassured his audience,

...obeyed this injunction, suffering the tortures of a rebel prison, faithful even unto death. We may cherish the hope that his faithfulness to his flag was more than merely natural stubbornness; that it grew out of Christian firmness. He was, on principle, devoted to the cause of his country, for which he has so heroically died. Wherefore we may trust, that through the mercy of our God in Jesus Christ, he has received the crown of life.[50]

In suggesting that Raymond was in heaven ("we may trust") because of his "faithfulness to his flag," which in turn connected (we may "hope") to his "Christian firmness," Babbitt conflated devotion to the nation with devotion to the Lord. Still, as his discourse continued, Babbitt tried to make clear that he was not substituting a civil religion of nation-worship for Christianity, and that dying for the country was not sufficient to ensure salvation.[51] He offered example after example to prove that Raymond was truly a Christian, painting him as a virtual paragon of the pious soldier. He enjoyed reading devout literature, Babbitt reported, and even in the camp, "the lessons of home and of the Sunday-school were not forgotten; he carried his religion into his tent, and forgot it not on the battle-field."[52]

The ultimate test of Raymond's faith, according to Babbitt, came when he was forced to face the "hardships of a southern prison." Despite his "keener relish than most men for the good things of the table," which made the meager food he was given at the prison difficult to bear, Raymond did not give up his "loyalty to his God, or his country," or "forget the lessons which he had learned in his childhood at home or in the Sunday-school." According to a fellow prisoner who had witnessed his death, his final words were exemplary in piety. Just before he gave up the ghost, Raymond said, "in a strong, clear voice, 'I am going to die. Go tell my father I am ready to die; for I die for God and my country'; and then looking up with a fond and heavenly smile, he died." Babbitt hammered home the point: "Think you not that such a man as this was,—whose integrity was so constant, whose trust in God was so firm, who suffered such a terrible trial of imprisonment, without yielding in the least, and who stood firm to the end, and died, in the confidence of his God, for the cause of his country,—think you not that such a man reaped the promised reward of the just? Most surely he did! He was faithful unto death; and so we doubt not God has given to him a crown of life."[53]

Just as letters about the last words of dying soldiers addressed an underlying fear that they might not actually have repented in time to be saved, so Babbitt's hagiographic testimony about Raymond's piety suggested an anxious subtext: was he *really* saved? About two-thirds of the way through the discourse, a troubling detail emerged: Raymond had not yet united with a church at the time of his death. By offering so many proofs of Raymond's religious nature, Babbitt tried to convince himself and his hearers that this was only a minor detail, that Raymond had intended "to stand forth in the church a Christian man," and that there should be no question that he was residing happily in heaven at the very moment they were memorializing him on earth.[54]

Further shades of doubt emerged in Babbitt's acknowledgment that Raymond had never been very vocal about his faith. "He was eminently a man of deeds, rather than words; of facts, not of sentiments," Babbitt described. "Like the lightning's flash, such men do their work before they tell their story in noisy words. He made himself felt as a religious man, without talking about religion. He was prepared for death, without making much ado about preparation." Reading between the lines (strikingly similar to Kelso's mock-sermon about the reticent Old-buck), we might see some hesitation about Raymond's lack of obvious preparation for death and uncertainty about whether he had really escaped hell. That Raymond had never been vocal about his faith meant that the proofs Babbitt offered about his salvation were, by and large, hearsay. Babbitt even admitted, "Now such religion as this has its defects. None of us are perfect."[55]

Still, Babbitt could hardly close out the memorial without reiterating his belief that, although Raymond had not had a discernible and dramatic conversion experience, he was saved. He had been raised in the faith (here Babbitt echoed Horace Bushnell's notion that Christian nurture might be salvific) and had apparently never abandoned it despite his reticence. "We are satisfied to accept what he has written," Babbitt concluded, "and the last word which he sent to us, as evidence—though brief and concise, yet sustained by his telling life and death—as evidence to the point, and amply sufficient too, to show that his heart was right."[56]

Although he had downplayed the civil religion angle while playing up Raymond's supposed piety, Babbitt ultimately returned to Raymond's sacrifice for the nation to buttress his claim that the soldier was saved. Raymond had "died for no common cause." Sounding much like the Confederate J. C. Granbery, who had said that his side represented the truest ideal of a godly nation, Babbitt continued, "It is sweet to die for one's country; but when the standard of that country is the symbol not only of its own liberties, but of human rights, the brotherhood of man, and Christian progress, it is then, indeed, glorious to die for that standard."[57] Raymond had not just died for any old flag, said Babbitt: he had died for a Christian country, rendering his sacrifice salvific.

In writing about the infamous Andersonville, A. S. Billingsley similarly assumed the best of the soldiers who perished there. He described the prison as a hell on earth:

> With thirty-five thousand starved, half-naked prisoners, crowded into an area of some twenty-five acres, literally covered all over with lice and vermin; breathing an atmosphere filled with poisonous, fetid odors, arising from sinks and putrid corpses, it presented a scene awfully terrible and horrible beyond description. The very thought of it is appalling. To think of it carries the mind down to the infernal regions, and makes one think of the torments of hell. And so appalling was the scene, and horrible the sight, that the brave heroes...instinctively exclaimed, "Can this be hell? can this be hell?"[58]

Billingsley mused on the suffering and deaths of the prisoners at Andersonville. "*How did they die?* Having no regular spiritual adviser generally, but little is known of their prospects, or preparation for the future." Yet how could hell be the final resting place for those who had endured hell on earth? He was not present to witness the prisoners' deaths, but Billingsley nevertheless concluded that "a number 'made perfect through suffering' gave bright evidence of repentance; for whom to die was gain. And from the patient suffering, calm submission, and humble resignation, and true patriotism they exhibited, doubtless many hundreds of them died happily, and have gone beyond the reach of rebel tyrants, 'where the wicked cease to trouble, and the weary are forever at rest.'" Billingsley resoundingly endorsed the creation of a monument "to the memory of these heroic martyrs," to the "immortal heroes lying beneath it," who had died "that we and our country might live." Just as in Babbitt's sermon, though, a shade of uncertainty crept in as Billingsley cited a key statistic: 13,065 had died at Andersonville, including 180 rebels. If 13,065 had died, then the "many hundreds" who "doubtless" died happily was not so large a percentage after all, and the "immortality" of the remainder perhaps not so blissful.[59]

Deserting to Hell

Tying national sacrifice to heavenly rewards had a negative corollary: behaving badly toward one's fellow soldiers or deserting became equivalent to the most hellworthy of sins. Among those presumably not saved at Andersonville, for instance, Billingsley included a gang of Union prisoners who had "made it their business to beat, plunder, and murder prisoners as they came into camp, and as opportunity favored." Six were found guilty, and Billingsley described how a Catholic priest "began to try to induce them to 'prepare to meet their God'" after they were sentenced to death. But rather than heed his warnings, the six "exhibited a degree of wonderful unconcern about their impending crisis. Vain, delusive hope! Blinded by sin, hardened by crime, and deceived by their false hopes, like the careless sinner, they cried peace and safety when sudden destruction was near. How awful and tragic the scene!" Interestingly, the soldiers' apparent Catholicism was not a major factor in the Protestant Billingsley's account. The priest had done what any evangelical might have done in the same situation. The soldiers' sin was not only abusing their fellows but also and more importantly, dishonoring the nation for which they presumably fought. "What a foul blot upon American soldiery," Billingsley lamented, "and what a deep disgrace to the United States army!"

> It is the crisis of Andersonville, and to the condemned the crisis of the soul. The awful form of death seems to stand out before them. "The door of the eternal world is swinging open;" the grave yawns to receive them. Crime, judgment, and stern retribution are making their terrible impressions.... The hour is up; their time is out. The drop falls, and they are launched from time into eternity. There they hang, swinging in the air, gone to reap the fruits of their own doings in their eternal reward. How sad![60]

Equally harsh was the punishment meted out to anyone who deserted his service to the nation: "He shall be *shot to death!*" Describing the execution of deserters, Billingsley wrote: "It is a dread moment.... The awful form of Death stands out alone! The door of the unseen world is swinging open! Crime, judgment, and stern retribution are working their terrible impressions. Swift, vivid thoughts are in every heart, and 'God have mercy on him!' breathes from every lip." Billingsley went on, "Such is the sad fate of the *deserter:* a grief and shame to his parents; a disgrace to his country, and a curse to the army. CAST OFF!... Oh, how lamentable! to be cast off by the world, and by all earthly friends, is terrible and severe!" But "being cast off by God" into eternal hell was far worse. And for what? "Simply because he had deserted the flag of his country and gone over to the enemy." Lest his postwar readership think themselves out of danger from this sin, Billingsley concluded with an altar call comparing desertion of country to desertion of God. The former, "it is true, is a great sin and crime; but it is nothing, sinner, to your sin in forsaking God and rejecting the Saviour," he warned. "In mercy, God now waits, delays the day of your execution. He has waited long—is waiting still! But he will not always wait.... Oh, then, my impenitent friend, let me entreat you to repent and come to Jesus, and come just now."[61]

Reunion ... Now and in the Future

Other postwar evangelicals largely curtailed their deployment of the threat of hell toward ordinary folk, reserving it for those who clearly did not fit into the genteel ideal of a reunited Christian nation. Northern prison camps were as brutal as the Confederate, and deaths no less painful or mourned on either side. As a number of scholars have pointed out, a shared sense of sacrifice and suffering brought North and South back together after the war in a reunion achieved at the expense of racial justice.[62] These scholars have largely focused on reunion in the here-and-now, but beliefs about reunion in the afterlife also contributed to this trend.

Elizabeth Stuart Phelps's bestselling *The Gates Ajar* collapsed the distance between the war's antagonists by ignoring the causes of the war and focusing on the grief of female survivors. It gave definitive material shape to the heaven where they would await their loved ones. Phelps was the daughter of prominent theologians on both sides of her family. She grew up at Andover, a mecca for apologists of Calvinism who saw themselves as the spiritual heirs of Jonathan Edwards. When Phelps was 8, her mother died. Her young brother's baptism took place at the side of their mother's coffin; her stepmother (who was also her aunt) died several years later; and her father apparently took her to numerous funerals for instructive purposes. As one historian has written, Phelps's writings gave evidence of "the nightmarish force of an imagination steeped in Calvinist hellfire and her own morbidity."[63]

Phelps came of age during the Civil War. As a young woman, she became close friends and perhaps romantically involved with Samuel Hopkins Thompson, a student at the seminary. Thompson enlisted in the army soon after graduating in 1861 and died at Antietam a year later.[64] Biographers have speculated that this crushing blow led Phelps to write *The Gates Ajar* in her early twenties. In her autobiography, *Chapters from a Life*, Phelps herself suggested that it was the communal mourning brought about by the widespread losses in the war that compelled her to write the book, particularly the mourning of women on both sides who had lost fathers, brothers, sons, and husbands.[65]

The story of *The Gates Ajar* is simple: having lost her beloved brother Roy in the Civil War, 24-year old New Englander Mary Cabot finds herself in the depths of despondency and full of anger against God for having taken her life and joy. She finds no comfort in the platitudes of the aptly named Dr. Bland or the inquiries of Deacon Quirk as to her "spiritooal condition" after her brother's passing.[66] Instead, she wallows in the "luxury of grief" and bemoans a heaven that she thinks is "dreadful," a place from which her brother "can have no thought of me, cannot remember how I loved him, how he left me all alone;" a place where "the singing and the worshipping must take up all his time. God wants it all. He is a 'Jealous God.'"[67] Mary's vision of heaven as a place of eternal worship where loved ones would not remember each other is, for her, almost akin to a hell. She compares her feelings on hearing of Roy's death to the torments of the damned: "Those two words—'Shot dead'—shut me up and walled me in, as I think people must feel shut up and walled in, in Hell. I write the words most solemnly, for I know that there has been Hell in my heart."[68] Mary's (Phelps's) equation of grief with hell—something that used to seem so ordinary with something so extraordinary—implied that suffering on earth could be hell enough, and that the evangelical hell of fire and brimstone was too horrible and ridiculous to even deserve comment.

In the midst of her despair, Mary's widowed aunt, Winifred Forecythe, arrives with her young daughter, the aptly named Faith. Having experienced the death of her husband, Winifred can sympathize more deeply than other well-wishers. She presents to Mary a vision of the afterlife that is essentially a restoration of her life before Roy's departure for the army: "he will meet you at the door in this other home, and lead you into the light and the warmth."[69] Aunt Winifred promises that those in heaven can see and comfort those below in preparation for the life to come, where there will no longer be any warfare, no more partings or separations, everyone will be beautiful, and material pleasures like pianos and gingersnaps can be enjoyed forever. Winifred's heaven is anthropocentric; humans will recognize each other, and relationships begun on earth will continue. God is present not as a sovereign demanding constant worship, but rather as the "centre of all possibilities of joy. ... Human dearness will wax, not wane, in heaven; but human friends will be loved for love of him."[70]

As for hell, it "belongs to the unutterable things." Phelps did not question the existence of hell but, through Winifred, assured readers that "God will take care of it." Even if loved ones somehow ended up on the other side of the eternal chasm, she promised that "in some way the void *must* be filled, for He shall wipe away tears. But it seems to me that the only thought in which there can be any *rest*, and in that there *can*, is this: that Christ, who loves us even as His Father loves Him, can be happy in spite of the existence of a hell. If it is possible to Him, surely He can make it possible to us."[71] With that, Phelps dismissed the question of hell as something her readers did not really need to worry about, something that God would work out to their benefit in the grand scheme of things. At the conclusion of the novel, Winifred herself dies of breast cancer, but Mary, having fully internalized her comforting view of heaven, finds the strength to live on and to care for her little niece, Faith.

The reception of *The Gates Ajar* exceeded Phelps's wildest expectations. Just weeks after its publication, her publisher sent her a check for six hundred dollars, telling her, "Your book is moving grandly. ... It has already reached a sale of four thousand copies."[72] The book would go on to sell nearly 80,000 copies in the United States, more still in Great Britain, and be translated into French, German, Dutch, and Italian. It spawned unauthorized *Gates Ajar* paraphernalia, from paper collars to cigars. It buried its unprepared author in a "New England snowstorm" of letters, some from mourners who thanked Phelps for her comforting vision of heaven, and others from critics who castigated Phelps for her "ungodly book."[73] As Phelps later remembered it, "She had outraged the church. She had blasphemed its sanctities. She had taken live coals from the altar in her impious hand. The sacrilege was too serious to be dismissed with cold contempt. Opinion battled about that poor little tale, as if it had held the power to overthrow church and state and family."[74] The problem with Phelps's vision was not that it was particularly new or radical (one contemporary reviewer wrote that "she presents no novel views—propounds no startling theories—of the heavenly state"), but that it translated the diverse, percolating lay yearning for future reunion into a simple story, presenting a heaven that gave "undue prominence to earthly affections and ties, and means and elements of happiness."[75]

The same reviewer blamed Phelps's gender for her sentimental and materialistic heaven, criticizing a "great weakness and a very unhealthy state of mind" in its young author, who was much too morbid for her age. The reviewer dubbed Phelps's speculations "a woman's way.... The argument is based, so far as there is argument, not simply upon Scripture teaching, or the philosophy of things, but mainly upon the dictates and demands of the human heart."[76] In her autobiography, Phelps made clear that she did indeed envision women as her primary audience, "the helpless, outnumbering, unconsulted women; they whom war trampled down, without a choice or protest; the patient, limited, domestic women, who thought little, but loved much, and loving, had lost all,—to them I would have spoken." "For it came to seem to me, as I pondered these things in my own heart," she further explained, echoing the posture of the biblical Mary, "that even the best and kindest forms of our prevailing beliefs had nothing to say to an afflicted woman that could help her much. Creeds and commentaries and sermons were made by men. What tenderest of men knows how to comfort his own daughter when her heart is broken? What can the doctrines do for the desolated by death? They were chains of rusty iron, eating into raw hearts" (a passage that strikingly recalls Mary Corinna Putnam's "There is a point where the doctrines shrivel").[77] Phelps offered her readers an afterlife where God was practically obliged to reward humans for their endurance of hellish suffering on earth, almost a reversal of the Calvinist heaven, where humans endlessly worshiped a sovereign God as the just due for saving them from a hell they deserved.

Phelps's imagined heaven was essentially a haven for white middle-class gentlepeople meant to comfort those left behind. Words like "slave," "slavery," and "Confederacy" make no appearance in the novel. By focusing on the consolation survivors could take from the promise of future reunion, and ignoring the question of who would go to hell and why, the novel smoothed over the angry allegations of judgment, vengeance, and the fury of a righteous God that each side had hurled against the other. It did not speak exclusively to a northern audience but implied that the nation as a whole had already paid dearly, especially the women on both sides who had played no part in politicking and warmongering. Phelps's target in the novel was not the Confederacy; it was cold and unfeeling ministers who would not provide the specific reassurance she desired.

By the time her novel was published, however, Phelps was basically attacking a straw man: chaplains and ministers who had been through the war were, as we have seen, hardly so rigid or callous toward those who had lost loved ones. Nor did they shy away from materialistic and anthropocentric speculations about heaven. Postwar evangelicals also speculated about mansions where mothers awaited their loved ones after death, rhapsodized about the "endless spring and eternal day" that lay in store, and gilded Heaven with more spectacular décor than the most ostentatious Gilded Age mansions. Like Phelps, these evangelists did not jettison hell but suggested that it was a threat only to those who were clearly outside the pale: Darwinists, infidels, and theological liberals who rejected a literal reading of the Bible.[78]

"There Is a Just God in Heaven"

As they saw themselves left out of postwar visions of reunion, and saw their hopes for meaningful equality dashed by northern concessions to the South, some African Americans continued to threaten the nation with the rhetoric of divine judgment.[79] Henry McNeal Turner was one of the most outspoken black leaders to do so. He had thrown himself into Reconstruction politics in the early postwar years. But although he won election to the Georgia legislature in 1868, he was soon expelled with twenty-three other African American members. In his outraged speech before the assembly, Turner raised rhetorical questions about his own soul in defense of his humanity: "I am here to demand my rights, and to hurl thunderbolts at the men who would dare to cross the threshold of my manhood.... The great question, sir, is this: Am I a man?... Have I a soul to save, as you have? Am I susceptible of eternal development, as you are?" He warned the assembly, "There is a just God in Heaven...who, despite the machinations of the wicked, never fails to vindicate the cause of Justice, and the sanctity of His own handiwork."[80]

As Turner became more disillusioned with white American society, his thinking about the afterlife became more political and polemical. Whereas the young Turner had listed typical things like gambling, drinking, and swearing as the sins that would cast a person into hell, his biographer explains that the later "Turner's inferno came to be populated by those persons who launched deadly assaults on the persons and rights of black Americans.... Conversely, those who spoke out on behalf of equal rights and fair treatment of people of all races would go to heaven."[81] In contrast to Phelps's whitewashed, domesticated heaven, "There are as many blacks as whites in the universe," Turner wrote in the 1880s. "There are black worlds, and, I believe, millions of black angels in heaven. In fact, there are angels of all colors there." Turner told whites that "we have as much right biblically and otherwise to believe that God is a Negro, as you buckra, or white, people have to believe that God is a fine looking, symmetrical and ornamented white man."[82]

In his 1886 "The Negro in Politics," black newspaper editor T. Thomas Fortune also drew on the language of a final judgment to condemn Reconstruction politicians too eager for reconciliation at the expense of blacks. He was livid at those who "had made the South bankrupt in purse, a squeezed lemon, and a hell for colored people." He continued, "May the God of eternal justice and righteousness mete out to the rascals, in the day of reckoning, reward commensurate with the enormity of their rascality." Four years later, he noted that "it was not the colored Christians, but the white Christians, who, to their eternal shame and damnation, drew the color line, and continue to draw it, even unto this hour." Like Turner, Fortune drew on a long tradition of rhetorical "thunderbolts," dating back to slave beliefs in ironic reversal and hell as a place for masters, and to the appeals of David Walker, Maria Stewart, and Henry Highland Garnet.[83]

Black leaders were not the only postwar Americans to criticize the shape of Reconstruction and its aftermath. One angry veteran was our old acquaintance, skeptic John Russell Kelso. When last we met him, he was regaling his camp with a mock funeral sermon over the tough remains of a gristly steer. Kelso had once believed that African Americans should be colonized out of the country. By the end of the war, though, he had become radicalized by bloody hostilities with proslavery forces in the border states. Kelso was elected as an Independent Radical to the Thirty-Ninth Congress in March 1865 and used his two-year tenure to advocate for a radical postwar agenda. Just as William Lloyd Garrison, Gerrit Smith, and Theodore Parker had sometimes masked their unorthodox views with the angry, morally charged language of judgment and collective guilt for the sin of slavery, so Kelso submerged his personal skepticism and used damnatory and demonic rhetoric in a speech after the end of hostilities. He denounced the rebels as traitors who, "Like Milton's Satan, overthrown in arms, cast down from the high positions they once occupied, maddened by disappointment, and burning with revenge...are now endeavouring to accomplish by guile, those dark designs which they long attempted to

accomplish by <u>force</u>.... With hands still reeking in the blood of our mur-
dered brothers, and still clothed in garments torn from the cold forms of
our heroic dead, they have the effrontery to claim equal rights and privileges with the patriotic defenders of our beloved country."[84] We cannot let
this happen, he thundered.

Nor—and here he revealed just how politically radical he had become—can we any longer disenfranchise the ex-slaves. "If it be true that
we should <u>do</u> <u>unto</u> <u>others</u> <u>as</u> <u>we</u> <u>would</u> <u>that</u> <u>they</u> <u>should</u> <u>do</u> <u>unto</u> <u>us</u>, and
if we would not that others should enslave us on account of our color, or
deprive us of the elective franchise, how dare we, a Christian people, do
these things unto them? Can we hope for God's blessing if we continue to
violate this His solemn commandment?" Kelso could have been any evangelical abolitionist as he continued: "Have not the judgements of the last
five years been sufficient to teach us wisdom? Have not these judgements
come upon us as the direct consequence of the crime of slavery? Shall we,
then, defiantly commit the same crime under another name, and thus
call upon ourselves still more fearful judgements? For my part, I think we
have been punished enough, and I, for one, am willing to do justice to <u>all</u>
<u>men</u>, even to the despised <u>African</u>."[85] Recognizing that most Americans
saw themselves as "a Christian people," the skeptic Kelso deployed the
"damned nation" trope to hold them accountable to their own warnings,
reminding his audience that the prediction of divine punishment had already begun to come true during the war itself and that "more fearful
judgements" might come if justice was not served.

"Religion . . . Rushed, like a Hungry Vulture, into the Conflict"

Although Kelso submerged his skepticism and disillusionment in this
postwar speech, they were vividly apparent in his Autobiography, completed in 1882. Remembering the origins of the war, Kelso attacked the
religious arguments both sides had deployed against each other, including the very rhetoric of judgment and punishment that he himself
had earlier used:

> Religion, that greatest of all fomenters of discord and of blood-
> shed, rushed, like a hungry vulture, into the conflict.... While
> the secession priest was informing his god, with these frantic and

blasphemous yells, that slavery was a divine institution, founded and fostered by this god himself, the Union priest, often not far away, was informing this same god, with equally frantic and blasphemous yells, that slavery was an institution of hell.... What this god would have done had the two parties been equal in strength, I do not know. As it was, he evidently helped the stronger party.[86]

In questioning each side's claim to be fulfilling "god's" will, Kelso echoed the earlier (and equally unusual) Abraham Lincoln's famed declaration in his Second Inaugural Address that "both read the same Bible, and pray to the same God." While Kelso sarcastically observed that "god" had favored the "stronger party," however, Lincoln had left open the possibility that there might in fact have been a providential God who was directing events. Picking up on the "damned nation" accusation, Lincoln acknowledged that the entire nation was complicit in and was now paying for the sin of slavery:

> Fondly do we hope—fervently do we pray—that this mighty scourge of war may speedily pass away. Yet, if God wills that it continue, until all the wealth piled by the bond-man's two hundred and fifty years of unrequited toil shall be sunk, and until every drop of blood drawn with the lash, shall be paid by another drawn with the sword, as was said f[our] three thousand years ago, so still it must be said "the judgments of the Lord, are true and righteous altogether."[87]

Lincoln depicted the depredation and deaths of the war—on both sides— as punitive rather than salvific.

Mocking where Lincoln was measured, Kelso was also less confident that the war had achieved anything true or righteous. If, for Kelso, "The whole matter of heaven and hell is a monstrous imposition gotten up by priest_hood as a means of keeping the people in subjection to themselves, and of making money without honest labor," then the comforting hopes of Elizabeth Stuart Phelps and her legions of readers were empty illusions. The reference to "honest labor" paralleled Kelso's wartime critique of the "wealthy classes" of Southerners who were made lazy by relying on slave labor. Kelso even used the language of slavery to describe what priests did to their flocks: "When they have made you believe in an awful hell, on one side, which, without their aid, you can not escape, and in a glorious heaven, on the other, which, without their aid, you can not obtain, they have made you their slave."[88] Kelso and other skeptics after the war found little comfort in their compatriots' wistful visions of heaven, even as they abandoned hope that a righteous God was overseeing earth's goings-on and would eventually punish wrong-doers in the life to come.

Epilogue

JAMES MARTIN PEEBLES (1822–1922) was a man of many occupations: scientist, physician, author, longtime vegetarian, one-time Universalist minister, and ardent evangelist for Spiritualism. He also loved to travel the world. Among his many books was the 1875 *Around the world: Or, Travels in Polynesia, China, India, Arabia, Egypt, Syria, and other "Heathen" Countries.*[1] Peebles used the term "heathen" ironically. Much as Herman Melville had done in *Typee*, he flipped the tables on missionaries who thought they were saving the world's peoples. Describing the "splendidly-made race" of Samoans, for instance, he wrote: "And these Samoan chiefs are called 'savages,' 'degraded heathen,' to whom tobacco-using, wine-drinking Christian missionaries must be sent to save them from hell!"[2] He might well have ended the exclamation with an incredulous question mark instead.

In addition to commenting on the people and places he encountered, Peebles also liberally sprinkled his travelogue with reflections about spirit communication and the religious atmosphere of his day. On one such tangent, he mused about the assassination of President Lincoln at the end of the Civil War. While others busily made Lincoln into a pious Christian after his death and Elizabeth Stuart Phelps placed him in heaven with other Christian soldiers in *The Gates Ajar*, Peebles claimed that Lincoln was an "infidel" because he had not been baptized or "born again." According to the "orthodox creed," said Peebles, "Lincoln, the martyred president, is in hell,—wailing this moment with the *damned in hell!*" Peebles then made a familiar move, claiming to favor hell with Lincoln and other famous "infidels" over the Christian heaven:

> I would prefer hell—whatever it may be—with Lincoln, Franklin, Jefferson, Adams, Madison, Washington, Shakspeare, Byron, Burns, Shelley, Edgar A. Poe, Dickens, Humboldt, and the whole

galaxy of political, intellectual, and moral lights of the world, to that little jasper-walled heaven of the sectarian Christian, where a few lonesome, long-visaged saints, saved through another's merits, wave palms, and serenade the Jewish Jehovah for ever!

Peebles predicted that "Orthodox Christianity, with its fanaticism, superstition, and cramping creeds, is rapidly sinking, in enlightened countries, into hopeless decrepitude and remediless decay. It has failed to save the world."[3]

Like Kelso and other skeptics we have encountered along the way, Peebles thought that damnation was on the outs by the late nineteenth century. But missionary William Speer held a very different opinion. Born the same year as Peebles, Speer was also well-traveled, having served in China, Hawaii, California, Wisconsin, and Minnesota. In 1870 he published a massive tome on *The Oldest and the Newest Empire: China and the United States*. Although Speer thought of the unevangelized Chinese as "heathens" who were perishing without missionary intervention, he also believed that they would be receptive to the gospel and the benefits of western "civilization." He applied biblical prophecy to China, interpreting Isaiah 49:12 ("these shall come from far; and lo, these from the north and the west, and these from the land of Sinim") as referring to the "final commingling of the opposite courses of civilization," when "China, the last and largest and stoutest nation among all that have resisted the truth," came in contact with the West and "worlds above and below" "rejoic[ed]."[4]

But Speer also worried about anti-Chinese violence and xenophobia on the US's western shores. He, too, referenced the late war but told readers to remember the "stern assurance" that all nations were under God's "supreme government," which oversaw the right and wrong doings of nations and men. As had "Damnation" Murray, Speer warned that God's moral government would demonstrate "divine justice and power by the terrible punishment of oppressors and wrongdoers, and the compensation of those who have suffered from them." This had already been most powerfully proven in the "history of African slavery and the judgments it brought upon us." Speer invoked the classic features of the "damned nation" argument, which linked divine punishment in this life and the next with the sins of individuals and nations. He then applied the lesson to the treatment of Chinese immigrants:

If we choose to inaugurate a similar course of wrong in the case of the Asiatic pupils whom God has sent here to be taught from the book of knowledge which he has put for the purpose in our hands, then we and our children must make up our minds to receive a similar or even a more tremendous retribution than that which has filled the land with blood, with ashes and with tears.[5]

As chauvinistic as was his view that God had uniquely favored Americans to "teach" their "Asiatic pupils," Speer was exceptional in his championship of the Chinese. Just as for many missionized people, slaves, and abolitionists, his God of retribution was absolutely necessary to ensure justice in this world and the world to come.

What Difference Did Hell Make?

Speer and Peebles could not have been further apart. Their perspectives emerged from a varied history of contestation and creative tension between hell's apologists, skeptics, innovators, the uncertain, the anxious, and the mocking. Hell mattered in America. As vivid as were the voices of people like Peebles, Gerrit Smith, and "Salvation" Murray, hell survived not just because evangelical clergymen declared it to be an "orthodox" and scriptural concept. Hell remained vital because it proved to be a useful concept in a young nation founded on the premise of republican virtue where different religious bodies competed for converts, interest groups vied for sociopolitical influence, and oppressed peoples called for ultimate justice. The more useful it remained, the more doubters and dissenters attacked it as a nefarious invention of fearmongering ministers. And the more it was attacked, the more believers cast those who denied its reality into its darkest pits, even if these believers no longer feared its horrors for themselves. The fact that condemnation of unbelievers is built into the very concept of hell put doubt and dissemination into a symbiotic, mutually reinforcing relationship that shows no signs of ending any time soon.

What were the consequences of hell's survival in the new United States? Although tangible or quantifiable evidence of influence and importance is impossible to muster definitively, we might consider the counterfactual. What if hell had declined in the young nation to the same extent as scholars argue was the case in Europe? Did hell's survival, in other words, make any difference?

To argue that the dissemination of hell and its application to seemingly immoral behaviors helped to ensure the success of the new nation (as late eighteenth- and nineteenth-century evangelicals claimed) would be a stretch and is beyond the ability of historical method to demonstrate. Still, the fact that many believed this to be the case suggests that hell's survival was important in reassuring early Americans that founding a republic on the virtue of its citizens might indeed be a feasible endeavor. The fear of hell played a role in regulating behavior and belief and in shaping antebellum Americans' attitudes toward each other and the world. If evangelicals had dropped hell from their worldviews, revivals would not have had life-or-death intensity, missions movements would likely not have taken off, and social reform crusades may not have seemed as immediately pressing.

There is perhaps no better summary of the catalytic credo linking personal and national guilt than this statement by the Sandwich Islands missionaries:

> We fear for our country, because men in the church manufacture, vend, and drink ardent spirit; because they break the Sabbath; because they are concerned in slavery; because they are impure; because they are covetous and profane; in short, because they disobey God. If they are not chargeable with personally committing the sins specified, they are more or less guilty by participation.[6]

The belief that one's own eternal safety was tied to the sins of others, and to one's success or failure to change their hearts and habits, implicated and invested Americans in the welfare of their peers at home and abroad. This impulse could lead to the attack against slavery, but it could also lead to the wholesale damning of entire regions of the nation and the world. Of course, other countries in which hell was less significant also abolished slavery—even, in some cases, without war. Still, we might postulate that in the American case, hell's prominence on both sides of the aisle contributed to the impasse that led eventually to a long and brutal war. Meanwhile, the notion that entire peoples might be endangered without American intervention continues to shade attitudes toward foreign countries, even if the idea has become largely secularized in public discourse today.

Hell Today

Hell remains a concept that Americans take both lightly and very seriously. To write about hell is to invite raised eyebrows. "What in the world drove you to that subject?" I have often been asked. Sometimes I will even hear things like, "But you look so well-adjusted! How did you get interested in hell?" The questions presuppose that hell is off-the-radar for most people. The language of fire and brimstone is less common today than in the first century of nationhood and is as likely to be deployed mockingly as seriously. The "dammit doll," for instance, sold at retailers from Amazon to Nordstrom, advertises itself as a unique stress reliever as the user whacks a brightly colored cotton ragdoll against a wall yelling "dammit! dammit! dammit!" As one Amazon purchaser notes, the doll's effectiveness is such that when missing, it elicits reactions like "Damn it! Where the hell is my Dammit Doll, damn it? Damn it! Where IS it?" The casual "where the hell" here is all the more striking considering that hell's use as profanity was once cautiously rendered as "h—ll" or "h—l."[7] And when hell is used seriously, it often catches people off guard. Recently, some of my students incredulously and somewhat mockingly pointed out a colorful van on campus plastered with such slogans as "TURN OR BURN," "PREPARE TO MEET THY GOD," and "Warning Queers Fornicators Idolators Thieves Drunks Adulterers Liars God Haters Judgement"—clearly a sight with which they were neither familiar nor comfortable (fig. E.1).

But as the van's slogans suggest, hell also remains vital to hundreds of millions of Americans and continues to appear on the doctrinal statements of many churches.[8] In addition to incredulity, my interest in hell has also been met with utter gravity and earnestness. A high school teacher bemoaned what he saw as Americans' loss of belief in damnation: it once kept people in line, he argued, and now what do we have to ensure morality? A former prison guard assured me that he had seen evil with his own two eyes and believed that there had to be a hell to house and punish evildoers after death. And the father of a friend recently discovered an "equation" he could use to determine the proportion of saved versus damned the world over.

These contemporary attitudes toward hell highlight two important points. The first—judging by the "dammit dolls," the incredulous reaction of the students looking at the van, and similar, skeptical responses to the mention of hell—is that the concept no longer exercises as firm a hold on the American imagination as it once did. According to a 2008 article from the Pew Forum, only 59 percent of Americans believe in hell while 74 percent believe in heaven. The article suggested that this disparity has resulted from "Americans' optimism and tolerance for diversity." "So hell is disappearing, absolutely," a scholar cited in the article concluded.[9]

FIGURE E.1 Image of van at Stanford University, Palm Drive (The Oval), April 4, 2013.

Photograph by author.

Still, the responses of people like the prison guard suggest that belief in hell is far from disappearing in contemporary America. A 59 percent majority is hardly insignificant and may in fact be a low estimate, since a Gallup poll showed that 70 percent of Americans believed in hell in 2004.[10] Surely Americans did not suddenly become more optimistic and tolerant of diversity between 2004 and the more recent Pew poll. In fact, the opposite might have occurred as the language of good vs. evil permeated the political arena in the years after 9/11. Whatever the figures, belief in and uses of the concept of damnation have clearly not faded in America to the extent that some scholars have suggested (or perhaps hoped). Deployments of damnation can be heard from the fringes to the center. The Westboro Baptist Church regularly makes the news with its inflammatory protests sending basically everyone but themselves to hell. Each year around Halloween, "hell houses" take visitors into horror chambers showing the gory consequences of abortion, drugs, AIDS, and the like. But it is not just the diehards who draw on the concept of hell. The death of Osama bin Laden in May 2011 spurred shouts of "O-B-L, you're in hell!" by large crowds gathered outside the White House; a sensationalistic cover for the *New York Daily News* showed a picture of bin Laden next to the words "ROT IN HELL!" In a nationwide CNN poll conducted soon after, 61 percent of respondents agreed that bin Laden is in hell, 25 percent were unsure, and only 10 percent disagreed.[11]

Debates over the eternality and justness of hell also continue to roil the realm of popular theology. In 2004 Carlton Pearson, Oral Roberts-trained pastor of a megachurch in Tulsa, was declared a heretic for preaching universal reconciliation and what he calls the "gospel of inclusion."[12] Several years later, the controversy over Rob Bell's bestselling *Love Wins* (2011), which disavows a God who could damn hundreds of thousands of well-meaning people to eternal torment, surged. Evangelicals responded quickly and angrily; Baptist John Piper dismissed him with a summary "Farewell Rob Bell."[13]

The concomitant trend away from the fear of hell for one's self and loved ones also continues to this day. Another Gallup poll, this one dating from 1988, found that "Americans who said there was a hell where people who led bad lives without being sorry are eternally damned were quite optimistic that they would not be going there themselves. Only 6% said their chances of going there were good or excellent, and 79% said their chances were poor."[14] On the one hand, we might interpret these results as a sign that, in denying ultimate consequences for their own actions, Americans have abdicated personal responsibility.

But perhaps we might also see in the lay rejection of hell for self and loved ones a creative, middle of the road response to the concept of damnation that has in fact helped to ensure its survival. As we have seen, the thought that hell could be one's eternal destination could present a profound psychological burden. Hoping that God might make exceptions for extenuating circumstances lightened the burden. It presented people with a morally complex deity in which to believe, while preserving God's ability to promise ultimate, absolute justice in a far from perfect world. In the late nineteenth-century words of the disappointed yet still faithful Henry McNeal Turner:

> The scenes that have passed under my eyes upon the public highways, the brutal treatment of helpless women which I have witnessed...is enough to move heaven to tears and raise a loud acclaim in hell over the conquest of wrong. But we will wait and pray, and look for a better day, for God still lives and the LORD OF HOSTS REIGNS.[15]

Notes

INTRODUCTION

1. Gerrit Smith, "The Religion of Reason," Peterboro, June 19, 1859, in *Sermons and Speeches of Gerrit Smith* (New York: For Sale by Ross & Tousey, No. 121 Nassau Street, 1861; repr. New York: Arno Press and *The New York Times*, 1969), 50–51.

2. "Document 36: Speech by Peter Paul Simons. Delivered before the African Clarkson Association. New York, New York. April 23, 1839," originally printed in the *Colored American* (New York), June 1, 1839; reprinted in C. Ripley, ed., *The Black Abolitionist Papers, vol. 3, The United States, 1830–1846* (Chapel Hill: University of North Carolina Press, 1991), 292.

3. For statistics, see David Sehat, *The Myth of American Religious Freedom* (New York: Oxford University Press, 2011), 51–52.

4. See D. P. Walker, *The Decline of Hell: Seventeenth-Century Discussions of Eternal Torment* (Chicago: University of Chicago Press, 1964); Paul C. Davies, "The Debate on Eternal Punishment in Late Seventeenth- and Eighteenth-Century English Literature," *Eighteenth-Century Studies* 4, no. 3 (Spring 1971): 257–76; Philip C. Almond, *Heaven and Hell in Enlightenment England* (Cambridge: Cambridge University Press, 1994); Geoffrey Rowell, *Hell and the Victorians: A Study of the Nineteenth-Century Theological Controversies Concerning Eternal Punishment and the Future Life* (Oxford: Oxford University Press, 1974); Jeffrey Burton Russell, *Mephistopheles: The Devil in the Modern World* (Ithaca, NY: Cornell University Press, 1986); Jean Delumeau, *Sin and Fear: The Emergence of a Western Guilt Culture, 13th to 18th Centuries* (1983; St. Martin's Press, 1990); Stuart Schwartz, *All Can Be Saved: Religious Tolerance and Salvation in the Iberian Atlantic World* (New Haven: Yale University Press, 2008); and Andrew Delbanco, *The Death of Satan: How Americans Have Lost the Sense of Evil* (New York: Farrar, Straus & Giroux, 1995). Most of these authors tend to focus on elites. By contrast, Schwartz, who focuses on the Catholic Iberian Atlantic, suggests that tolerance began at a grassroots level as laypeople encountered those of other faiths and rejected the notion that they might be damned. More recently, scholars of American religion have begun to question the popular narrative of decline and

have shown the persistence of the devil and evangelical horror in American religious and political life. See W. Scott Poole, *Satan in America: The Devil We Know* (Lanham, MD: Rowman & Littlefield, 2009), and Jason Bivins, *Religion of Fear: The Politics of Horror in Conservative Evangelicalism* (New York: Oxford University Press, 2008).

5. See Sacvan Bercovitch, *The American Jeremiad* (Madison: University of Wisconsin Press, 1978); Andrew Murphy, *Prodigal Nation: Moral Decline and Divine Punishment from New England to 9/11* (New York: Oxford University Press, 2009); and Harry Stout, *The New England Soul: Preaching and Religious Culture in Colonial New England* (New York: Oxford University Press, 1986).

6. Disestablishment was not implemented at the same time across the board. In New England battles over state support continued well into the nineteenth century, with Connecticut, New Hampshire, and Massachusetts disestablishing in 1818, 1819, and 1833, respectively. Roger Finke and Rodney Starke, *The Churching of America, 1776–2005*, 2nd ed. (New Brunswick, NJ: Rutgers University Press, 2005), 60–61.

7. Thomas Paine, *The Age of Reason. In Two Parts.* (New York: Published by G. N. Devries, Corner of Vesey-Street and Broadway, 1827), 6, 12–13. On Paine's skepticism, see Amanda Porterfield, *Conceived in Doubt: Religion and Politics in the New American Nation* (Chicago: University of Chicago Press, 2012), chap. 1 "Faith in Reason and the Problem of Skepticism."

8. According to Michael P. Young, some social historians held that "the direction this anxiety and guilt typically took—the imperative of spiritual rebirth through the reformation of sins like drinking, profaning the Sabbath, adultery—was at best a displacement or at worst a cover for material or domestic interests" (*Bearing Witness Against Sin: The Evangelical Birth of the American Social Movement* (Chicago: University of Chicago Press, 2006), 25). See Paul Johnson, *A Shopkeeper's Millennium: Society and Revivals in Rochester, New York* (New York: Hill and Wang, 1978); Mary Ryan, *Cradle of the Middle Class: The Family in Oneida County, New York, 1790–1865* (Cambridge: Cambridge University Press, 1981); and Charles Sellers, *The Market Revolution: Jacksonian America, 1815–1846* (New York: Oxford University Press, 1991). Tocqueville quote from *Democracy in America*, vol. 2, second book, chapter IX (New York: J. & H. G. Langley, 1840; Vintage Books Edition, 1990), 127.

9. Sehat and Porterfield both offer a narrative of increasing evangelical control in the early republic. Porterfield writes: "In a world where violence, cheating, and unrest were common, appeals to the authority of the Bible and punishments for sin proved more effective means of discipline than appeals to the rational nature of mankind" (*Conceived in Doubt*, 12). This book is in many ways complementary to these studies, but it differs in tone. Rather than regret how evangelicals coercively managed skepticism and dissent out of the picture, it gives ordinary people more agency to accept or reject the truth-claims they were

offered about both hell and skepticism alike. Some scholars are moving away from treating their characters as liberal agents who could and did make rational choices, portraying them instead as haunted by discourses both articulated and unarticulated, present and looming (see, for instance, John Lardas Modern's *Secularism in Antebellum America* (Chicago: University of Chicago Press, 2011)). I am sympathetic to this position but do not want to entirely explain antebellum responses to hell as haunted, managed, or controlled. Doing so is all too easy for a concept many have already seen as irrational and bizarre. See note 11.

10. On age and life expectancy, see Jill Lepore, *The Mansion of Happiness: A History of Life and Death* (New York: Alfred A. Knopf, 2012), p. xii. James C. Riley estimates global life expectancy at birth to have been 28.5 years in 1800. "Estimates of Regional and Global Life Expectancy, 1800–2001," *Population and Development Review* 31, no. 3 (Sept. 2005): 537–43. German physician quoted in Samuel Morris Brown, *In Heaven as It Is on Earth: Joseph Smith and the Early Mormon Conquest of Death* (New York: Oxford University Press, 2012), 18–19.

11. In *Secularism in Antebellum America*, Modern contends that a key distinction of the secular age is the "naturaliz[ation] of religion as an option rather than an obligation" (3), yet an option whose "range of available choices had been patterned and shaped by circumstance" (7). Protestants naturalized their way of seeing religion and the self—as interior, individualized, and agentive—opening space for a "secular" public realm of supposedly unmediated neutrality that shared a haunting metaphysics with Protestantism.

This book does not dispute Modern's searching exploration of the dynamics of antebellum secularism. The urgent dissemination of hell in this era was critically related to the shifting view of religion as pressing option rather than inherited obligation. For evangelicals, heaven or hell, salvific ("true") religion or damnatory ("false") religion, was the key option individuals faced for their own future welfare and that of their families and communities.

But unlike Modern's story, which is "at odds with the stories that its subjects tell about themselves and their capacities" (10), *Damned Nation* is attentive to the worries, scorn, and doubts of antebellum Americans. In explaining the voluntary shift, I take theology into account, as did many nineteenth-century Americans. Modern is less interested in matters of theological content: "Although respectful of the commitments of historical actors and their self-consciousness of religious commitment and/or denominational affiliation, I have not reduced religious conflict to matters of theology and/or doctrine" (293). But this is arguably itself a reduction of theology and doctrine to something "else"—in Modern's case, a flirting with the "possibilities of social and technological determination" despite avoiding "the metaphors of false consciousness" (289).

I remain interested in the stories people consciously told to and about themselves and their world not because these stories should necessarily be taken at face value, but because they motivated how people thought about their identities, actions, and interactions with others. And I contend that the threat of hell was a key element of antebellum stories. This is not to say that I see individuals' choices (and their sense of having a choice) as entirely free, unconstrained, and self-conscious—the choice between heaven and hell was hardly so, not least because the significant threat of excruciating and everlasting pain and suffering gave hell a coercive power that made it very difficult to reject. But many antebellum Americans believed they had the natural ability to choose between heaven and hell, even if they lacked the ability to make unmediated choices because of their entanglement in networks of their own making but never entirely of their own control. This was an Edwardsean framing. Where Edwards believed that the moral inability to freely choose salvation could be regenerated, Modern sees the haunting webs of the secular age as indelible precisely because they have been naturalized and thus largely unrecognized as created.

Within Modern's query (via Charles Taylor)—what does it feel like to live in a secular age?—I ask questions that antebellum Americans might more easily have recognized: what did it feel like to live with the fear that you, your loved ones, and the vast majority of the world could be damned? What did it feel like to live under the anxious obligation to save as many as possible? What did it feel like to reject this sense of fear and obligation? And I see theology as critical for understanding what Modern only glosses: What underlay the evangelical urge to propagate, systematize, and grow? Why did evangelicals print so many tracts? What was their motivation?

In contending that hell matters to these questions, I follow the lead of Robert Orsi, who urges that "to take religious experiences of real presences seriously means understanding imaginary beings as having historical life and agency of their own, which does not entail ignoring questions of social power but understanding how these figures are implicated within, but also cause trouble for, arrangements of power." "Competing and Complementary Approaches in American Religious History," in Philip Goff and Rebecca Vasko, eds., *Proceedings: First Biennial Conference on Religion and American Culture*, June 4–7, 2009, Omni Severin Hotel, Indianapolis, Indiana (The Center for the Study of Religion and American Culture, Indiana University-Purdue University Indianapolis, 2009), 16–17, http://raac.iupui.edu/files/9213/6724/5498/Proceedings2009.pdf.

12. Tocqueville, *Democracy in America*, vol. 2, second book, chapter IX, 126, 125.

13. See note 11.

14. On changing attitudes toward death in Europe and North America, see Philippe Ariès, *Western Attitudes Toward Death: From the Middle Ages to the Present*, trans. Patricia Ranum (Baltimore: Johns Hopkins University Press, 1974); Peter Marshall, *Beliefs and the Dead in Reformation England* (New York: Oxford University Press, 2002); John McManners, *Death and the Enlightenment: Changing*

Attitudes to Death among Christians and Unbelievers in Eighteenth-Century France (Oxford: Oxford University Press, 1981); David Stannard, *The Puritan Way of Death: A Study in Religion, Culture, and Social Change* (New York: Oxford University Press, 1977); Vincent Brown, *The Reaper's Garden: Death and Power in the World of Atlantic Slavery* (Cambridge, MA: Harvard University Press, 2008); Gary Laderman, *The Sacred Remains: American Attitudes Toward Death, 1799–1883* (New Haven: Yale University Press, 1996); Brown, *In Heaven as It Is on Earth*; Ann Douglas, "Heaven Our Home: Consolation Literature in the Northern United States, 1830–1880," *American Quarterly* 26, no. 5, Special Issue: Death in America (Dec., 1974): 496–515; and Mark Schantz, *Awaiting the Heavenly Country: The Civil War and America's Culture of Death* (Ithaca, NY: Cornell University Press, 2008), which is less about the Civil War than about the antebellum era.

15. For examples of scholarship that has (over)emphasized American optimism, see Ernest Lee Tuveson, *Redeemer Nation: The Idea of America's Millennial Role* (Chicago: University of Chicago Press, 1968), which focuses on Americans' belief in their "manifest destiny" as a nation chosen to redeem the world, and Bercovitch, *The American Jeremiad*, which downplays the darker strain of jeremiad literature and reads it primarily as a vehicle of hope. Murphy picks up on similar themes in *Prodigal Nation*. And Robert Abzug's *Cosmos Crumbling: American Reform and the Religious Imagination* (New York: Oxford University Press, 1994) follows this optimism to its "crumbling" in the years leading up to the Civil War. My work argues for a less confident America by drawing our attention to fears and anxieties throughout the first century of nationhood.

16. As a synthetic survey that highlights specific case studies from theological elites to a diversity of laypeople, this narrative inevitably leaves out some groups and figures. I hope to suggest avenues of inquiry and further research; I cannot present the last word on the subject, even if I also am not presenting the first.

17. See James Morone, *Hellfire Nation: The Politics of Sin in American History* (New Haven: Yale University Press, 2004), and Young, *Bearing Witness against Sin*. Morone contends that "Political life constantly gets entangled in two vital urges—redeeming 'us' and reforming 'them'" (3). These urges play out in two ways: (1) reformers believe that sin resides in the individual and seek to ban specific behaviors (i.e., intemperance), and (2) reformers believe that sin resides in society and needs to be eradicated at a structural level. Young argues that evangelicals harnessed their guilt through the fusion of orthodox and populist forms. The focus on the "special sins" of the community (Calvinist orthodoxy) and the focus on intense personal religious experiences (populists) together implicated the individual in the sins of the nation and made his/her own spiritual welfare dependent on the spiritual welfare of the nation as a whole.

While very clear, these schemas simplify and dichotomize what was often blurrier on-the-ground.

CHAPTER 1

1. John Murray, *The Life of Rev. John Murray, Preacher of Universal Salvation, with Notes and an Appendix*, by Thomas Whittemore (Boston: Printed at the Trumpet Office, 1833), 207, 185.

Scholars have disagreed as to whether Murray was the "founder" of the Universalist denomination in America. The German Baptist Dunkers and the Rogerenes of Connecticut had espoused universalist ideas in the early eighteenth century, and in 1741, the year Murray was born, George de Benneville brought universalistic ideas rooted in the teachings of Georg Paul Siegvolck, a seventeenth-century German mystic, to Germantown in Pennsylvania. Nevertheless, Murray was instrumental in institutionalizing the denomination. The first Universalist society was formed in 1779 in Gloucester, and Murray became minister of the first Universalist church in America in 1780, also dedicated in Gloucester. See Peter Hughes, "The Origins of New England Universalism: A Religion without a Founder," *Journal of Unitarian Universalist History* 24 (1997), 31–63; Ernest Cassara, "John Murray and the Origins of Universalism in New England: A Commentary on Peter Hughes's 'Religion without a Founder,'" *Journal of Unitarian Universalist History* 26 (1999), 72–92; Russell Miller, *The Larger Hope: The First Century of the Universalist Church in America, 1770–1870* (Boston: Unitarian Universalist Association, 1979); Ann Lee Bressler, *The Universalist Movement in America, 1770–1880* (New York: Oxford University Press, 2001); E. Brooks Holifield, *Theology in America: Christian Thought from the Age of the Puritans to the Civil War* (New Haven: Yale University Press, 2003), 220–21; and Stephen Marini, *Radical Sects of Revolutionary New England* (Cambridge, MA: Harvard University Press, 1982).

2. Murray, *Life of Rev. John Murray*, 207 (emphasis in original).

3. Some of the sources that refer to the two Murrays as "Salvation" and "Damnation" include A. G. Vermilye, "Memoir of the Rev. John Murray, First Minister of the Church in Boothbay," in *Collections of the Maine Historical Society* (Portland: Published for the Society, 1859), 166; Abel C. Thomas, *Autobiography of Rev. Abel C. Thomas: Including Recollections of Persons, Incidents, and Places* (Boston: Published by J. M. Usher, 37 Cornhill, 1852), 119; *The Gospel Advocate*, vol. 1 (Published by Simon Burton, 1824), 93; *The Historical Collections of the Topsfield Historical Society* (Published by the Society, 1921), 44; John Quincy Adams and Charles Francis Adams, *Life in a New England Town: 1787, 1788* (Boston: Little, Brown and Company, 1903), 73; Euphemia Vale Blake, *History of Newburyport: from the earliest settlement of the country to the present time: with a biographical appendix* (Newburyport: Published by s.n., 1854), 375–76; and Miller, *The Larger Hope*, 15.

4. The three Murrays were hardly the only Americans involved in the late eighteenth-century controversy over universal salvation. Timothy Dwight, John

Stancliff, Andrew Croswell, John Cleaveland, Charles Chauncy, and Ezra Stiles also opposed the Universalist Murrays; Elhanan Winchester and Chauncy espoused their own versions of universal salvation; and John Adams, Nathaniel Greene, and Benjamin Rush accepted the promise of eventual salvation for all.

5. On European and transatlantic debates about hell, see note 4 in the Introduction. On Edwards's awareness of these debates, see Amy Plantinga Pauw, ed., *Jonathan Edwards: The "Miscellanies" (Entry Nos. 833–1152)* (New Haven: Yale University Press, 2002), 17–24. See also Peter Thuesen, ed., *Jonathan Edwards: Catalogues of Books* (New Haven: Yale University Press, 2008), 294–95. Edwards's wish-list of books contained William Whiston's *Eternity of Hell Torments Considered* (1740), which questioned hell, and William Dodwell's *The Eternity of Future Punishment Asserted and Vindicated* (1743), which, as the title suggests, defended it.

6. No. 866, "concerning the extreme and everlasting torments of ungodly men in hell," quoted in Pauw, ed., *Jonathan Edwards*, 19. Pauw writes that for Edwards, "The moral defect was not in the doctrine, but in the objector."

7. George Marsden, *Jonathan Edwards: A Life* (New Haven: Yale University Press, 2003), chap. 26 "Against an 'Almost Inconceivably Pernicious' Doctrine," and chap. 27 "Original Sin 'in This Happy Age of Light and Liberty'"; Holifield, *Theology in America*, 121–22.

8. Marsden, *Jonathan Edwards*, chaps. 26 and 27; Holifield, *Theology in America*, 121–22; also Mark A. Noll, *America's God: From Jonathan Edwards to Abraham Lincoln* (New York: Oxford University Press, 2002), 22–25.

9. Harry S. Stout, "Edwards as Revivalist," in Stephen J. Stein, ed., *The Cambridge Companion to Jonathan Edwards* (Cambridge: Cambridge University Press, 2007), 139; Pauw, *Jonathan Edwards*, 21.

10. Jonathan Edwards, "Sinners in the hands of an angry God. A sermon preached at Enfield, July 8th 1741. At a time of great awakenings; and attended with remarkable impressions on many of the hearers" (Boston: Printed and sold by S. Kneeland and T. Green. In Queen-Street over against the prison, 1741), 23. Stephen Williams (congregant) quoted in Marsden, *Jonathan Edwards*, 220.

11. Holifield, *Theology in America*, 93–101; Marsden, *Jonathan Edwards*, chap. 17 "A House Divided"; Noll, *America's God*, 44–50; Joseph Conforti, *Samuel Hopkins and the New Divinity Movement: Calvinism, the Congregational Ministry, and Reform in New England between the Great Awakenings* (Eugene, OR: Wipf & Stock Publishers, 2007; previously published by Christian College Consortium, 1981), esp. 2–3 and 71. On explanations for enthusiasm, see Ann Taves, *Fits, Trances, & Visions: Experiencing Religion and Explaining Experience from Wesley to James* (Princeton: Princeton University Press, 1999).

12. Holifield, *Theology in America*, 197; Colin Wells, *The Devil & Dr. Dwight: Satire & Theology in the Early American Republic* (Chapel Hill: University of North Carolina Press. Published for the Omohundro Institute of Early American History & Culture, Williamsburg, VA, 2002).

13. As Holifield writes in *Theology in America*, "most subsequent theological movements had to define themselves in relation to the Calvinist traditions. In a history of American theology, the Calvinists loom large" (10).

14. On Calvin: Thomas Jefferson to John Adams, April 11, 1823, quoted in James Hutson, ed., *The Founders on Religion: A Book of Quotations* (Princeton: Princeton University Press, 2005), 39; on Hopkins: Thomas Jefferson to Thomas B. Parker, May 15, 1819, quoted in ibid., 38–39.

15. Stephen West, ed., *Sketches of the Life of the Late Rev. Samuel Hopkins, D.D., Pastor of the First Congregational Church in Newport, Written by Himself; Interspersed with Notes Extracted From His Private Diary* (Hartford, 1805), 32–35, quoted in Conforti, *Samuel Hopkins*, 27.

16. Samuel Hopkins, "An Inquiry Concerning the Promises of the Gospel" (1765), excerpted in Douglas A. Sweeney and Allen C. Guelzo, eds., *The New England Theology: From Jonathan Edwards to Edwards Amasa Park* (Grand Rapids, MI: Baker Academic, 2006), 90.

17. Conforti, *Samuel Hopkins*, chaps. 7 and 8 ("Disinterested Benevolence: A Theology of Social Reform" and "True Virtue and Social Reform: Slavery and the Revolution"); Samuel Hopkins, "A Dialogue Concerning the Slavery of the Africans, Showing It to Be the Duty and Interest of the American Colonies to Emancipate All Their African Slaves" (1776), in Sweeney and Guelzo, eds., *The New England Theology*, 152, 155, 156. See also Kenneth Minkema and Harry S. Stout, "The Edwardsean Tradition and the Antislavery Debate," *Journal of American History* 92 (June 2005): 47–74.

18. Hopkins, *A Dialogue between a Calvinist and a Semi-Calvinist* (published in 1805; written in 1780s), quoted in Conforti, *Samuel Hopkins*, 120.

19. Conforti, *Samuel Hopkins*, 179–81.

20. On the emerging sense of self as individual, see Daniel Walker Howe, *Making the American Self: Jonathan Edwards to Abraham Lincoln* (New York: Oxford University Press, 1997), and Rodger M. Payne, *The Self and the Sacred: Conversion and Autobiography in Early American Protestantism* (Knoxville: University of Tennessee Press, 1998). Payne argues that conversion narratives document the transition to individualism, since the individual was the center of the story even as the narratives stressed self-renunciation. See also Marsden, *Jonathan Edwards*, chaps. 26 and 27: Edwards, Hopkins's teacher, also experienced "consternation over modern views of individual autonomy and moral agency" (439) and, as Marsden notes, "eighteenth-century Calvinists were at odds with their optimistic era" (451).

21. John Murray wrote the first six chapters of his Autobiography (to 1774); Judith Sargent Murray completed it to the point of his death in 1815. The autobiography was first published as John Murray, *Records of the Life of the Rev. John Murray... Written by Himself, to Which Is Added a Brief Continuation to the Closing Scene, by a Friend* (Boston: Munroe and Francis, 1816). The volume

went through at least five additional reprints in the nineteenth century; the version cited here is the 1833 edition with additional materials and notes by the Universalist Thomas Whittemore.

22. Murray, *Life of Rev. John Murray*, 14, 19.

23. Ibid., 64–71.

24. Holifield, *Theology in America*, 35; Noll, *America's God*, 565.

25. James Relly, *Union: Or, a Treatise on the Consanguinity and Affinity between Christ and His Church* (London; Boston: Re-printed by White and Adams, 1779), in *Readex: Early American Imprints*, Series 1, no. 16484 (American Antiquarian Society and NewsBank, Inc., 2002) (hereinafter *EAI*). This version of the pamphlet was reprinted through the efforts of Murray, who also had a hymnbook by Relly published in the United States, as well as a shorter pamphlet entitled "A Short Specimen of Apostolick Preaching."

26. Murray, *Life of Rev. John Murray*, 72.

27. Ibid., 92 (emphasis in original).

28. Ibid., 108, 115–16. This origin story appears in nearly every Universalist text that discusses John Murray.

29. Ernest Cassara, ed., *Universalism in America: A Documentary History* (Boston: Beacon Press, 1971), 10–13. According to Cassara, Murray was not an "original thinker." Still, he did not merely reprint and reiterate Relly's beliefs, but wrote texts on his own that were specific to the time and place in which he was living. He was well aware of what the orthodoxy might say about Universalism and defended it not only as better theology but also for its political and social virtues. He galled other clergy because he refused to admit that he was preaching universal salvation, instead calling his doctrine "universal redemption." To Murray, "redemption" meant the saving power of Christ's atoning sacrifice for all; "salvation" meant freedom from the worry, grief, and doubt that plagued the minds of unbelievers. Unbelievers would be redeemed in the final judgment, but in the interim, they would not experience "salvation" from their own anxieties. The distinction was subtle and, some argued, evasive. According to Richard Eddy, a nineteenth-century Universalist historian, Murray was not always consistent in using the terms. Eddy, *Universalism in America: A History*, vol. 1, *1636–1800*, (Boston: Universalist Publishing House, 1891), 160–61.

30. Chauncy espoused universalist ideas in an anonymous pamphlet, *Salvation for All Men, Illustrated and Vindicated as a Scripture Doctrine* (1782), and again in a lengthier book, *The Mystery Hid from Ages and Generations, Made Manifest by the Gospel-Revelation; or, The Salvation of All Men the Grand Thing Aimed at in the Scheme of God...* (1784). Chauncy held forth the possibility of human perfectibility and the "Pelagian idea of natural innocence" in contrast to Augustinian depravity (which the Murrays never rejected). There would be a hell for humans, Chauncy suggested, but its punishments would be temporary, according to one's sins. See Wells, *The Devil & Dr. Dwight*, 8–10. Elhanan

Winchester similarly argued for a temporary, punitive hell. Whittemore compares Murray's and Winchester's beliefs in his Appendix to the *Life*.

31. John Murray, *Some Hints Relative to the Forming of a Christian Church* (Boston: Printed by Joseph Bumstad, for Benjamin Larkin, Shakespeare's Head, Cornhill, 1791), 39–40, *EAI*, Series 1, no. 23583 (emphasis in original).

32. As even Hosea Ballou, a prominent nineteenth-century Universalist leader, put it, Murray sometimes drew "unexpected far-fetched combinations" of scripture to make his points. From the *Universalist Quarterly*, January 1848, as quoted in Eddy, *Universalism in America*, vol. 1, 153. But Olive Hoogenboom calls Murray "a powerfully effective speaker with a vigorous intellect and a retentive memory" and notes that "his preaching attracted larger and larger audiences." "Murray, John," *American National Biography Online*, Feb. 2000, http://www.anb.org/articles/08/08-01062.html.

33. The figure of twenty miles and the anecdote about Stiles come from Miller, *The Larger Hope*, 13–14. In his autobiography, Murray tells of a *"self-righteous* Calvinist" who invited him to his house, believing he was "for matter, and manner, a second Whitefield." Murray informed him of his true beliefs and conversed with him into the night. To Murray's relief, the man responded favorably (*Life of Rev. John Murray*, 152–53). On the places Murray preached, see Cassara, "John Murray and the Origins of Universalism in New England," 74; on debating with Hopkins, see Miller, *The Larger Hope*, 14; on low church adherence, see Jon Butler, *Awash in a Sea of Faith: Christianizing the American People* (Cambridge, MA: Harvard University Press, 1990), 194.

34. A. Croswell, *Mr. Murray Unmask'd. In which among other things, is shewn, that his doctrine of universal salvation, is inimical to virtue, and productive of all manner of wickedness*...(Boston: Printed and sold by J. Kneeland, in Milk-Street, 1775), 7, *EAI*, Series 1, no. 13998; John Stancliff, *An Account of the Putrid Murrinitish Plague, Lately Broke out in the City of Philadelphia; with the Causes and Symptoms. Also, the Manner of Treating the Infected, with an Infallible Cure. Humbly Offered to the Public, by John Stancliff* (Philadelphia: Sold by William Woodhouse, in Front-Street, next door to the coffee-house, 1787), 6, *EAI*, Series 1, no. 45169. Stancliff concluded the piece by explaining his tone: "Perhaps some may ask, why so satirical? I answer, because Solomon hath said, Answer a fool according to his folly" (7).

35. In an anti-Universalist address, a Rev. Chandler of Gloucester made sure to distinguish the two with the following asterisk: "*It is not the Reverend Mr. John Murray, of Boothbay.*" Not all writers were so careful to clarify which Murray they meant. Chandler's address was copied in Croswell's *Mr. Murray Unmask'd*, and Ipswich minister John Cleaveland's *An Attempt to Nip in the Bud, the Unscriptural Doctrine of Universal Salvation*...(Salem, MA: Printed by E. Russell, at his printing-office, upper-end of Main-Street, 1776), *EAI*, Series 1, no. 14684.

36. Biographical information comes from Murray's own brief description of his life in John Murray, *An Appeal to the Impartial Public, in Behalf of the Oppressed* (Portsmouth: Printed and Sold by D. and R. Fowle, 1768), *EAI*, Series 1, no. 10983. Two later sources on Murray's life include A. G. Vermilye's 1859 "Memoir of the Rev. John Murray, First Minister of the Church in Boothbay," and Euphemia Vale Blake's 1854 *History of Newburyport*, 375–76.

37. Murray's *Appeal* sought to establish his character in the face of this licensure controversy. According to Vermilye, Murray went to England to obtain his license instead of to the Presbytery of Ballymena, which should have handled the affair. His credentials were questioned upon his return and he sent his license to Edinburgh for verification. "A *certificate* was sent back to him, signed by two young friends of his, (ministers), designating themselves untruly 'moderator' and 'clerk' of presbytery. They afterwards informed him of their misdemeanor in thus counterfeiting an official document; beseeching him, however, not to ruin them, as their prospects were good in the church." Murray complied, leading to a series of accusations from the Presbytery, not only about his license but also about his integrity ("Memoir of the Rev. John Murray," 167–69).

38. See opinion letter to "Mr. Hall" from "A Lover of Impartiality," in *The Essex Gazette*, Tues. Aug. 22 to Tues. Aug. 29, 1769, Vol. II Iss. 57 pg. 20, a defense of Murray's character in the face of continued accusations surrounding the licensure controversy. It was also reprinted in *the New-Hampshire Gazette*, Sept. 15, 1769, Vol. XIII Iss. 674 pg. 1. *America's Historical Newspapers* (American Antiquarian Society and NewsBank, Inc., 2004) (hereinafter *AHN*). On "Damnation" Murray's Whitefieldian reputation, see Vermilye, "Memoir of the Rev. John Murray," 160. On Murray's popularity despite the licensure controversy, see also Blake, *History of Newburyport*, 376: "He was almost idolized by a large portion of his parishioners, but from some irregularity in his ordination papers, involving an imputation of his veracity, he never met with that cordial reception among the clerical fraternity of the town to which his talents and social qualities entitled him."

39. *Bath-Kol: A Voice from the Wilderness, Being an Humble Attempt to Support the Sinking Truths of God, Against Some of the Principal Errors, Raging at This Time* (Boston: Printed by N. Coverly, between the Sign of the Lamb and the White Horse, 1783), 67–68, 188. *Bath-Kol* was published anonymously but is attributed to Murray (1742–1793) in *EAI*, Series 1, no. 18040. Other anti-"Salvation" Murrayites similarly stressed his foreignness and lack of education. "This foreigner," the First Parish in Gloucester wrote, "through a too great indulgence, has acquired the effrontery to claim equal privileges with the learned, regular and ordained ministers of this commonwealth." *An Answer to a Piece, Entitled "An Appeal to the Impartial Publick, by an Association," Calling Themselves "Christian Independents, in Glocester"* (Salem: Printed and sold by S. Hall, 1785), 22, *EAI*, Series 1, no. 18915.

40. John Murray, *An Extract of a Letter from Mr. John Murray, Preacher of the Gospel at New-York, to the Rev. Mr. Moorhead, in Boston* (Boston?: s.n., 1764), 4, *EAI*, Series 1, no. 9745; Vermilye, "Memoir of the Rev. John Murray," 158–59.

41. John Murray, *The Last Solemn Scene. A Sermon, Preached in the Church in Back-Street, Boston, May 22nd, 1768* (Boston: Printed and Sold by William M'Alpine, about mid-way between the Governor's and Dr. Gardiner's, Marlborough Street, 1768), 24, *EAI*, Series 1, no. 10984. This sermon was reprinted three additional times before the close of the century: in 1769 and twice again in 1793, the year of "Damnation" Murray's death. In 1824, the sermon was published in Bloody-Brook, Massachusetts, by Timothy Frary. On Murray's fire and brimstone style, see also Blake, *History of Newburyport*, 375: "Mr. Murray was an orator of no ordinary abilities, and was particularly eloquent when portraying the terrors of eternal punishment, in which, in accordance with the tenets of the denomination to which he belonged, he was a firm believer."

42. Sheila Skemp, *First Lady of Letters: Judith Sargent Murray and the Struggle for Female Independence* (Philadelphia: University of Pennsylvania Press, 2009), p. xii, chap. 1 "This Remote Spot" and chap. 2 "Universal Salvation."

43. On Judith's education, see Introduction in Judith Sargent Murray, *The Gleaner*, ed. Nina Baym (Boston: I. Thomas and E. T. Andrews, 1798; reprint, Schenectady, NY: Union College Press, 1992), p. v. Baym notes that Judith's wealthy upbringing likely meant that she had access to her father's library and was exposed to the studies of a brother who attended Harvard. In her *Preface* to *The Gleaner*, Judith was unabashed about her desire for fame: "My desires are, I am free to own, aspiring—perhaps presumptuously so. I would be distinguished and respected by my contemporaries; I would be continued in grateful remembrance when I make my exit; and I would descend with celebrity to posterity" (Murray, *The Gleaner*, 13).

44. Letter 14, Judith Sargent Murray, Gloucester, to John Murray, Nov. 8, 1774; and Letter 15, Judith Sargent Murray, Gloucester, to John Murray, Dec. 6, 1774; both in Judith Sargent Murray, "Outgoing Correspondence: Letterbook Volume I/ [I]," in *The Judith Sargent Murray Papers*, Mississippi Department of Archives and History, microfilm, Roll 1, Subgroup 1, Series 2. These papers suffered extensive water damage from their years of storage in Mississippi, and the question marks and ellipses in my transcription reflect difficulties in deciphering Judith's handwriting.

45. Skemp, *First Lady of Letters*, chap. 2 "Universal Salvation"; Nina Baym, "Introduction," in Murray, *The Gleaner*, p. vi; and timeline in Sheila Skemp, *Judith Sargent Murray: A Brief Biography with Documents* (Boston: Bedford Books, 1998), 191–93.

46. Murray, *The Gleaner*, as quoted in Skemp, *Judith Sargent Murray*, 27. According to Skemp, Universalism's "egalitarian message" helped Judith to articulate her

"heretofore vague belief that men and women were intellectual and spiritual equals" (19). Of course, original sin could also be egalitarian, promising everyone equal access to hell on the basis of shared depravity.

47. "Death of an Unbeliever," in Judith Sargent Murray, "Essays Volume [1]," in *The Judith Sargent Murray Papers*, microfilm, Roll 6, Subgroup 1, Series 3.

48. Bonnie Hurd Smith, ed., *From Gloucester to Philadelphia in 1790: Observations, Anecdotes, and Thoughts from the 18th-Century Letters of Judith Sargent Murray* (Cambridge, MA: Judith Sargent Murray Society, 1998), 20.

49. Noll, *America's God*, chap. 4 "Republicanism and Religion: The American Exception." See also Amanda Porterfield, *Conceived in Doubt: Religion and Politics in the New American Nation* (Chicago: University of Chicago Press, 2012): "Painting religious skepticism as a danger to the country, advocates for religion succeeded in muting religious skepticism by equating it with moral depravity," 5. In *The Myth of American Religious Freedom* (New York: Oxford University Press, 2011), David Sehat also discusses how many saw religion as "a means of social control that acted as a check on the worst excesses of democracy"; even "moderate Enlightenment proponents such as Franklin" held "that the perpetuation of traditional institutional religious privileges was necessary to protect the state from man's inherent vice," 28. Franklin quoted in Sehat, 16.

50. Quoted in Gary Scott Smith, *Heaven in the American Imagination* (New York: Oxford University Press, 2011), 24–25.

51. Sehat, *The Myth of American Religious Freedom*, 22.

52. See Nicholas Guyatt, *Providence and the Invention of the United States* (New York: Cambridge University Press, 2007).

53. In *Redeemer Nation: The Idea of America's Millennial Role* (Chicago: University of Chicago Press, 1968), Ernest Lee Tuveson suggests that Protestant reformers saw such judgments as "definitive victories" as much as "punishments of evil" (8). "It was assumed," he writes, "that a judgment, once completed, had finished the particular form of evil on which it was passed" (207). But "Damnation" Murray listed these judgments not to reassure his readers but to warn them of much more to come if they allowed the likes of "Salvation" Murray into the new nation.

54. *Bath-Kol*, 74, 2.

55. Ibid., p. x.

56. Ibid., 338.

57. John Locke, *The Second Treatise of Government and A Letter Concerning Toleration* (Mineola, NY: Dover Publications, Inc. 2002), 145.

58. Croswell, *Mr. Murray Unmask'd*, 8–9, 10, 15.

59. First Parish of Glocester, *An Answer to a Piece*, 22–23.

60. On contrasting meanings of religious liberty, see Sehat, *The Myth of American Religious Freedom*, 25. Sehat points to legislative battles over religious liberty in the 1780s as a time when different factions—Christian and civil republicans—tested their contrasting definitions. Henry quoted in Sehat, 34.

61. BENEVOLUS, "Universalism," *The New-Hampshire Gazette; or State Journal and General Advertiser*, Oct. 9, 1784, *AHN*. The article was reprinted ten days later in *The Salem Gazette*.

62. "Universalism Indeed!" *The New-Haven Gazette, and the Connecticut Magazine*, Oct. 25, 1787, *AHN*. This poem was reprinted in multiple newspapers in New England.

63. Chauncy, *Salvation for All Men*, pp. ii–iii. See also note 30. "Damnation" Murray pointed to this factionalism in *Bath-Kol*, 188: "certain of the abettors of the tenet of Universal Salvation, have been at some pains to draw lines of distinction between their own opinions and those of Mr. Murray"—this comes right after he dubs Murray an "illiterate leader."

64. John Adams to Francis van der Kemp, July 13, 1815, Adams Papers (microfilm), reel 122, Library of Congress; Rush quote from "Travels through Life," in Corner, *Autobiography of Rush*, 163–64; both quoted in Hutson, ed., *The Founders on Religion*, 221–22.

65. Judith Sargent Murray, Jersies Mount Place, to her Father and Mother, July 24, 1790, in Smith, ed., *From Gloucester to Philadelphia in 1790*, 205–6.

66. John Murray, *Letters, and Sketches of Sermons*, vol. 1, ed. Judith Sargent Murray (Boston: Published by Joshua Belcher, 1812), 45.

67. Murray, *The Gleaner*, 34, 36.

68. Murray, *Some Hints Relative to the Forming of a Christian Church*, 3.

69. Ibid.

70. Ibid., 13.

71. Bressler, *The Universalist Movement in America*, 14.

72. Murray, *Some Hints Relative to the Forming of a Christian Church*, 46–47, 29.

73. Judith Sargent Murray, Jersies Mount Place, to Sarah Sargent Ellery, July 30th 1790, in Smith, ed., *From Gloucester to Philadelphia in 1790*, 217–19.

74. Murray, *Life of Rev. John Murray*, 165.

75. See also Bressler, *The Universalist Movement in America*: "Reason, Universalists argued, dictated that a benevolent God would redeem all of creation. The doctrine of universal salvation was God's way of influencing human affections and turning naturally self-centered human beings to the love of God and the greater creation" (9).

76. *Bath-Kol*, 348–49. Murray occasionally uses the term "Origenism" for the "tenet of Universal Salvation," after Origen (A.D. 185–232), a prominent early church figure who developed a theory of universal reconciliation. Murray's lengthy exposition of the history of Universalism in *Bath-Kol* actually grants the doctrine a greater degree of legitimacy than if it had simply been the product of Relly's and the other Murray's imagination.

77. *Bath-Kol*, 188.

78. Judith Sargent Murray, *Some Deductions from the System Promulgated in the Page of Divine Revelation, Ranged in the Order and Form of a Catechism. Intended as an*

Assistant to the Christian Parent or Teacher (Norwich: Printed by John Trumbull, 1782), pp. iii–iv, *EAI*, Series 1, No. 17729. The catechism was also printed in Portsmouth, New Hampshire, in 1782. On republican motherhood, see Linda K. Kerber, *Women of the Republic: Intellect and Ideology in Revolutionary America* (Chapel Hill: Published for the Institute of Early American History and Culture by the University of North Carolina Press, 1980).

79. *Bath-Kol*, 189. *Oxford English Dictionary*, "landlady, n.,": "'A woman who has tenants holding from her' (Johnson); *fig.* a mistress. *rare*." First Edition 1901; Second Edition, 1989, OED Online Version June 2012, http://www.oed.com/view/Entry/105479.

80. Skemp, *First Lady of Letters*, 58–59.

81. *Bath-Kol*, 257.

82. Ibid., 258.

83. Ibid., 273.

84. Ibid., 87.

85. Porterfield suggests that nostalgia for monarchy contributed to authoritarian, and in fact, monarchical, church governments in the early republic (*Conceived in Doubt*, chap. 4).

86. Quote from Christine Leigh Heyrman, *Southern Cross: The Beginnings of the Bible Belt* (New York: Alfred A. Knopf, 1997), 59–60. For evangelical/Universalist debates in the nineteenth-century awakenings, see Smith, *Heaven in the American Imagination*, 62–65. Smith downplays the earlier history of Universalism in America that this chapter considers; still, his research shows that the themes that emerged among the three Murrays were simply repeated later on. Similarly, on black Calvinist Lemuel Haynes's opposition to Universalism in the early nineteenth century, and his debates with Hosea Ballou, see Porterfield, *Conceived in Doubt*, 106–7.

87. In *Restless Souls: The Making of American Spirituality* (New York: Harper Collins, 2005; Harper San Francisco, 2006 (pb)), Leigh Schmidt notes that, "in a nation of about 150 million church members, Unitarian Universalists account for just over 150,000 of them" (14).

88. Hughes, "The Origins of New England Universalism," 37.

89. According to Ezra Stiles Ely, for instance, "Samson Occum, the Indian preacher, after a long contest with an universalist, terminated the controversy, by saying, 'Well, well, remember, if you are correct, I am safe: if you are not correct, I am safe: I have two strings to my bow; you have but one.'" *The Journal of the Stated Preacher to the Hospital and Almshouse, in the City of New-York, for the Year of Our Lord 1811* (New York: Published by Whiting and Watson, No. 96, Broadway. J. Seymour, Printer, 1812), 41. Occom was a Mohegan Presbyterian minister converted during the mid-eighteenth century revivals.

90. According to Terry Bilhartz, the idea that the "militant Calvinistic God of judgment" was replaced with "a meek and gentle Jesus who liberally granted eternal

forgiveness and temporal abundance" is overly simplistic. See T. D. Bilhartz, "Sex and the Second Great Awakening: The Feminization of American Religion Reconsidered," in Philip R. VanderMeer and Robert P. Swierenga, eds., *Belief and Behavior: Essays in the New Religious History* (New Brunswick, NJ: Rutgers University Press, 1991), 117–35. Still, the Puritan and Revolutionary-era idea of God as awe-inspiring, ineffable, and unimaginable became less popular in the nineteenth century, as an image of Christ as a personal, loving, and embodied white man began to prevail. See Edward J. Blum and Paul Harvey, *The Color of Christ: The Son of God and the Saga of Race in America* (Chapel Hill: University of North Carolina Press, 2012).

91. John Murray, *The justification of believers by imputed righteousness. Being the substance of three sermons preached in the Presbyterian Church in Newbury-Port, August, 1788, by John Murray, A. M. Pastor of said church. Published by request of the session* (Newburyport: Printed by John Mycall, 1789), *EAI*, Series 1, No. 21980.

92. Ibid., 135–36.

93. John H. Wigger, *Taking Heaven by Storm: Methodism and the Rise of Popular Christianity in America* (Urbana: University of Illinois Press, 1998; paperback 2001), 16–17. Also see chap. 4 "From Methodists to Mormons," in Peter Thuesen, *Predestination: The American Career of a Contentious Doctrine* (New York: Oxford University Press, 2009).

94. Bellamy, *True Religion Delineated* (1750), quoted in Conforti, *Samuel Hopkins*, 164. On the governmental theory of the atonement, see also Holifield, *Theology in America*, 132–33 and 147–48; and Noll, *America's God*, 134–35 and 267–68.

95. Bellamy, "The Millennium" (1758), *Works*, I, 512; Hopkins, *An Inquiry Concerning the Future State of those who die in their Sins* (Newport, 1783), 167–68; both quoted in Conforti, *Samuel Hopkins*, 164–65.

96. Although biographical information is sparse, "Damnation" Murray likely identified with the New Divinity more than with those Calvinists who tried to defend the absolute sovereignty of God and justness of election, or those who veered toward the sufficiency of moral living for salvation. Murray was a supporter of revivals like the New Divinity, had preached in Gilbert Tennent's pulpit in Philadelphia, and described a God bounded by laws of moral governance in *Bath-Kol* (though as we have seen, his depiction of God included elements of both sovereign and moral governor).

97. Jonathan Edwards the Younger, "Three Sermons on the Necessity of the Atonement, and Its Consistency with Free Grace in Forgiveness" (1785), in Sweeney and Guelzo, eds., *The New England Theology*, 141.

98. "Part 3: The Moral Government of God: Edwardseans and the Atonement," in ibid., 133–34.

99. Stephen West, "The Scripture Doctrine of Atonement, Proposed to Careful Examination" (1785), in ibid., 138.

100. The term "Second Great Awakening" simplifies the complexity of the many groups involved in antebellum revivalism and religious fervor—from Calvinists,

to "Christians," to Millerites, to Mormons. Some have used the term to refer primarily to religious excitement in the first three decades of the nineteenth century, ending with the professionalization of the clergy and the antebellum push toward respectability. Others have applied the term more loosely to the resurgent revivals of the 1790s to the 1850s, while still others have abandoned the term entirely. Despite its problems (and its assumption that there was a "First" Great Awakening, which Jon Butler has contested in "Enthusiasm Described and Decried: The Great Awakening as Interpretive Fiction," *Journal of American History* 69, no. 2 (Sept. 1982): 305–25), I take the second approach and use the term as a rough marker of periodization and shared revivalistic interests. See Catherine Brekus, *Strangers and Pilgrims: Female Preaching in America, 1740–1845* (Chapel Hill: University of North Carolina Press, 1998), 120–26.

101. On "evangelical," see Candy Gunther Brown, *The Word in the World: Evangelical Writing, Publishing, and Reading in America, 1789–1880* (Chapel Hill: The University of North Carolina Press, 2004), 2–3, 17. The blurring of doctrinal lines had political implications. By the early nineteenth century, as Porterfield puts it, "religious people on both sides of the political divide...invoked [Christ's] kingdom as a model of social order under which the unruly forces of democracy could be contained and restrained and where offenders were sent to hell where they belonged" (*Conceived in Doubt*, 145).

102. John Ffirth, *Experience and Gospel Labours of the Rev. Benjamin Abbott; to which is Annexed a Narrative of His Life and Death* (New York: Published by B. Waugh and T. Mason, For the Methodist Episcopal Church, at the Conference Office, 14 Crosby-street. J. Collord, Printer, 1832), 20. Abbott was responding to a tract by Joseph Bellamy given to him by his wife's Presbyterian pastor, who was upset at him for converting to and preaching Methodism.

CHAPTER 2

1. "An Introduction to *Sinners in the Hands of an Angry God*," *Jonathan Edwards Center at Yale University*, http://edwards.yale.edu/education/one-day.

2. Charles Finney, "Mr. Finney's Doctrinal Sermons," *New York Evangelist* 6 (36), Sept. 5, 1835.

3. On the communications revolution in antebellum America, see Daniel Walker Howe, *What Hath God Wrought: The Transformation of America, 1815–1848* (New York: Oxford University Press, 2007). See also Edward J. Blum and Paul Harvey, *The Color of Christ: The Son of God and the Saga of Race in America* (Chapel Hill: University of North Carolina Press, 2012), 79–80, on how "Information and transportation revolutions made cultural power possible." And Candy Gunther Brown notes that "shared textual practices alleviated anxieties caused by physical and social dislocations" (*The Word in the World: Evangelical Writing, Publishing, and Reading in America, 1789–1880* (Chapel Hill: The University of North Carolina Press, 2004), 12).

4. Brown, *The Word in the World*, 47–48; Paul Gutjahr, *American Popular Literature of the Nineteenth Century* (New York: Oxford University Press, 2001), p. xv.

5. See Gordon Wood, *The Radicalism of the American Revolution* (New York: Vintage Books, 1991), esp. Part 3, "Democracy"; Daniel Walker Howe, *Making the American Self: Jonathan Edwards to Abraham Lincoln* (New York: Oxford University Press, 1997); Michael Kimmel, *Manhood in America: A Cultural History* (New York: Free Press, 1996), esp. chap. 1 "The Birth of the Self-Made Man"; Nathan O. Hatch, *The Democratization of American Christianity* (New Haven: Yale University Press, 1989); and Karen Halttunen, *Confidence Men and Painted Women: A Study of Middle-Class Culture in America, 1830–1870* (New Haven: Yale University Press, 1982).

6. On the growth of denominational structures, see Amanda Porterfield, *Conceived in Doubt: Religion and Politics in the New American Nation* (Chicago: University of Chicago Press, 2012) (which complicates Hatch); Jon Butler, *Awash in a Sea of Faith: Christianizing the American People* (Cambridge, MA: Harvard University Press, 1990); and Patricia Bonomi, *Under the Cope of Heaven: Religion, Society, and Politics in Colonial America* (1988; repr. Oxford University Press, 2003). On evangelicals' disciplinary power, see also John Lardas Modern, *Secularism in Antebellum America* (Chicago: University of Chicago Press, 2011), and David Sehat, *The Myth of American Religious Freedom* (New York: Oxford University Press, 2011), which suggest that the idea of free choice in a religious marketplace obscures Protestant control.

7. Julius Rubin, *Religious Melancholy and Protestant Experience in America* (New York: Oxford University Press, 1994), 34–35, also 129–30.

8. John Ffirth, *Experience and Gospel Labours of the Rev. Benjamin Abbott; to which is Annexed a Narrative of His Life and Death* (New York: Published by B. Waugh and T. Mason, For the Methodist Episcopal Church, at the Conference Office, 14 Crosby-street. J. Collord, Printer, 1832), 6.

9. Lorenzo Dow, *The Dealings of God, Man, and the Devil; As Exemplified in the Life, Experience, and Travels of Lorenzo Dow, in a Period of over Half a Century: Together with His Polemic and Miscellaneous Writings, Complete. To which is Added The Vicissitudes of Life, by Peggy Dow. With an Introductory Essay by the Rev. John Dowling, D. D., of New York, Author of "The History of Romanism," etc. etc. Two Volumes in One* (New York: Published by Lamport, Blakeman & Law, No. 8 Park Place, 1853), 9–10.

10. Jarena Lee, *Religious Experience and Journal of Mrs. Jarena Lee, Giving an Account of Her Call to Preach the Gospel. Revised and Corrected from the Original Manuscript, Written by herself* (Philadelphia: Printed and Published for the Author, 1849), 3.

11. Charles Finney, *Memoirs of Rev. Charles G. Finney. Written by Himself* (New York: A. S. Barnes & Company, 751 Broadway, 1876), 7.

12. Ffirth, *Experience and Gospel Labours*, 7–8.

13. Dow, *The Dealings of God, Man, and the Devil*, 12.

14. Ffirth, *Experience and Gospel Labours*, 12.

15. Dow, *The Dealings of God, Man, and the Devil*, 10.

16. Lee, *Religious Experience and Journal*, 6–7, 12.

17. Finney, *Memoirs*, 9, 13, 20.

18. Ffirth, *Experience and Gospel Labours*, 20, 247 (emphasis in original).

19. Dow, *The Dealings of God, Man, and the Devil*, 16. Dow summarized the sermon as follows: "Sinner, there is a frowning providence above your head, and a burning hell beneath your feet; and nothing but the brittle thread of life prevents your soul from falling into endless perdition" (11).

20. John Dowling, "Introductory Essay," in ibid., p. vi.

21. Lee, *Religious Experience and Journal*, 17.

22. Finney, *Memoirs*, 26, 90.

23. Dow, *The Dealings of God, Man, and the Devil*, 11.

24. Allen Guelzo, "An Heir or a Rebel? Charles Grandison Finney and the New England Theology," *Journal of the Early Republic* 17, no. 1 (Spring 1997): 61–94; Charles Hambrick-Stowe, *Charles G. Finney and the Spirit of American Evangelism* (Grand Rapids, MI: W. B. Eerdmans Publishing Company, 1996).

25. Nathanael Emmons, "The Duty of Sinners to Make Themselves a New Heart," in *The Works of Nathanael Emmons, D. D.*, vol. 3, ed. Jacob Ide (Boston: Congregational Board of Publication, 1860), reprinted in Douglas A. Sweeney and Allen C. Guelzo, eds., *The New England Theology: From Jonathan Edwards to Edwards Amasa Park* (Grand Rapids, MI: Baker Academic, 2006), 121.

26. Charles Finney, "Mr. Finney's Doctrinal Sermons. Sermon II," *New York Evangelist* 6 (32), Aug. 8, 1835.

27. According to Catherine Brekus, "Women particularly emphasized the anguish they had experienced before being born again" (*Strangers and Pilgrims: Female Preaching in America, 1740–1845* (Chapel Hill: University of North Carolina Press, 1998), 174–81). Yet the memoirs of Abbott and Dow in particular, and Finney's to a lesser extent, suggest that men could be just as effusive about their anguish to the point of considering suicide. See chap. 3; see also Rubin, *Religious Melancholy in America*, esp. 133–55, "The Suicide of Benjamin Noyes."

28. George Peck, *The Life and Times of Rev. George Peck . . .* (New York, 1874), 51, quoted in Mechal Sobel, *Teach Me Dreams: The Search for Self in the Revolutionary Era* (Princeton: Princeton University Press, 2002), 13.

29. E. Brooks Holifield, "Pastoral Care and Counseling," in Charles H. Lippy and Peter W. Williams, eds., *Encyclopedia of the American Religious Experience: Studies of Traditions and Movements*, vol. 3 (New York: Charles Scribner's Sons, 1988), 1584–85.

30. Brekus notes that "female preachers were renowned for their emotional, spontaneous style." In their calls to sinners to repent and be saved, female preachers from the various sects made much the same appeals as trained male ministers,

warning that "it would be their own fault if they [sinners] were shut out of heaven" (*Strangers and Pilgrims*, 197–216).

31. See John H. Wigger, *Taking Heaven by Storm: Methodism and the Rise of Popular Christianity in America* (Urbana: University of Illinois Press, 1998; paperback 2001); Hatch, *The Democratization of American Christianity*; and Richard Bushman, *The Refinement of America: Persons, Houses, Cities* (New York: Knopf, 1992).

32. Karin Gedge, *Without Benefit of Clergy: Women and the Pastoral Relationship in Nineteenth-Century American Culture* (New York: Oxford University Press, 2003), 112–13.

33. E. Brooks Holifield, *God's Ambassadors: A History of the Christian Clergy in America* (Grand Rapids, MI: William B. Eerdmans Publishing Co., 2007), 73.

34. Timothy Merritt, "Discourse on Future Punishment," *Zion's Herald*, Nov. 19, 1823.

35. William Meade, *Lectures on the Pastoral Office, Delivered to the Students of the Theological Seminary at Alexandria, Virginia, by the Right Rev. William Meade, D. D., Bishop of the Protestant Episcopal Church of Virginia* (New York: Stanford and Swords, 137, Broadway, 1849), 12.

36. Ibid., 94–95.

37. Peter Marshall, *Beliefs and the Dead in Reformation England* (New York: Oxford University Press, 2002). The phrase "death of Purgatory" is a play off Jacques Le Goff's famous *The Birth of Purgatory* (1981; Chicago: University of Chicago Press, 1984).

38. Heman Humphrey, *Thirty-Four Letters to a Son in the Ministry* (Amherst: Published by J. S. & C. Adams; New York: Dayton & Newman; Boston: Crocker & Brewster, 1842), 66.

39. Ibid., 88–89.

40. On scholarly debates surrounding the feminization thesis, see Ann Douglas, *The Feminization of American Culture* (New York: Farrar, Straus & Giroux, 1977); Barbara Welter, "The Feminization of American Religion: 1800–1860," in Mary S. Hartman and Lois Banner, eds., *Clio's Consciousness Raised* (New York: Harper Torchbooks, 1973); T. D. Bilhartz, "Sex and the Second Great Awakening," in Philip R. VanderMeer and Robert P. Swierenga, eds., *Belief and Behavior: Essays in the New Religious History* (New Brunswick, NJ: Rutgers University Press, 1991); Harry Stout and Catherine Brekus, "Declension, Gender, and the 'New Religious History,'" in ibid.; Ann Braude, "Women's History *Is* American Religious History," in Thomas Tweed, ed., *Retelling U.S. Religious History* (Berkeley and Los Angeles: University of California Press, 1997); and Gedge, *Without Benefit of Clergy*.

41. Humphrey, *Thirty-Four Letters*, 197.

42. Finney, *Memoirs*, 83.

43. "For the American Revivalist—Revival Preaching.—No. 1. Peculiarities of Revival Preachers," *American Revivalist, and Rochester Observer. Dedicated to the Interests of Zion Generally, and Especially to Revivals of Religion*, New Series, no. 2, vol. 6, no. 40, Saturday, Oct. 6, 1832. See also "Letters on Revivals— Addressed to a Clergyman," in *New York Evangelist* 1 (23), Sept. 4, 1830: "As in preaching, so in conversation, the preacher's main object should be to bring the truth home to the sinner's conscience and heart.... When he sits down by the sinner's side, to spread out to his view the awful realities of eternity, and to persuade him to become reconciled to God through Christ, he engages in a solemn, and interesting, and responsible duty." Also Merritt, "Discourse on Future Punishment": "I know that this kind of preaching is unpopular. Many ask if 'we would frighten people to heaven?' They have persuaded themselves either that there is no future punishment or that it is not *so* painful a thing to be damned as some would represent it.... But the ambassadors of Christ must not be influenced by their views, nor terrified by opposition."

44. Humphrey, *Thirty-Four Letters*, 146–48.

45. On the gendered manners of the ideal antebellum pastor, see Gedge, *Without Benefit of Clergy*, 122–23.

46. Humphrey, *Thirty-Four Letters*, 148.

47. By the time of the Businessmen's Revival in the late 1850s, revivalists had re-fined regulation of emotions to an art, believing that emotional responses could be controlled in exchange for God's blessings. See John Corrigan, *Business of the Heart: Religion and Emotion in the Nineteenth Century* (Berkeley and Los Angeles: University of California Press, 2002).

48. Ichabod Spencer, *A Pastor's Sketches: Or, Conversations with Anxious Inquirers Respecting the Way of Salvation*, 4th ed. (New York: Published by M. W. Dodd, Brick Church Chapel, City Hall Square, (Opposite the City Hall), 1851), 143. In an-other chapter, "Waiting for the Holy Spirit," Spencer similarly wrote: "Probably the influences of the Holy Spirit are more common with impenitent sinners, than they suppose. Such persons greatly err, when, instead of fleeing at once to Christ; they wait, and think they *must* wait, for some attainment first. Their waiting for it, is but a deceptive excuse" (89).

49. Spencer himself, along with other "educated ministers ... drew on 'mental science' textbooks that taught them how to identify such states as mournfulness and melancholy, buoyancy and joy, self-centered anxiety and true conviction for sin." Some ministers even "kept notebooks on the spiritual condition of every member" (Holifield, *God's Ambassadors*, 105–6).

50. A.R.A., "Letters on Revivals—Addressed to a Clergyman. Letter IX. Means of Revivals," *New York Evangelist* 1 (25), Sept. 18, 1830.

51. Humphrey, *Thirty-Four Letters*, 215.

52. Ibid., 221–24.

53. According to Holifield, "6,000 copies were soon in circulation in a nation with 27,000 pastors" ("Pastoral Care and Counseling," 1585).

54. Humphrey, *Thirty-Four Letters*, 97.

55. Ibid., 263. "Not surprisingly, both men and women preached the majority of their sermons on the single, all-important theme of conversion," Brekus writes of preachers in denominations such as the Freewill Baptists, Christians, and Methodists on the frontiers (*Strangers and Pilgrims*, 208).

56. John Mack Faragher, Mari Jo Buhle, Daniel Czitrom, and Susan H. Armitage, *Out of Many: A History of the American People*, 5th ed. (Upper Saddle River, NJ: Pearson Prentice Hall, 2006), 258, 424.

57. The rate of 3x is from Sehat, *The Myth of American Religious Freedom*, 51; the figure of 27,000 is from Holifield, "Pastoral Care and Counseling," 1585. The average number of people per minister was obtained by dividing the mid-century population by 27,000.

58. Faragher et al., *Out of Many*, 365.

59. Gedge, *Without Benefit of Clergy*, 115.

60. On nineteenth-century evangelicals' embrace of new printing technologies and faith in the power of the printed text, see Brown, *The Word in the World*; David Paul Nord, *Faith in Reading: Religious Publishing and the Birth of Mass Media in America* (New York: Oxford University Press, 2004); John Lardas Modern, "Evangelical Secularism and the Measure of Leviathan," *Church History* 77 (Dec. 2008): 801–76; and Gregory Jackson, *The Word and Its Witness: The Spiritualization of American Realism* (Chicago: University of Chicago Press, 2009).

61. Gutjahr, *American Popular Literature*, 45.

62. See Lincoln Mullen, "Quantifying the American Tract Society: Using Library Catalog Data for Historical Research," *Religion in American History*, Aug. 1, 2013, http://usreligion.blogspot.com/2013/08/quantifying-american-tract-society.html. In the chart "Most Common Subjects of American Tract Society Publications," Mullen finds that "Salvation" was the subject of the greatest number of tracts, followed by "Christian life, Conversion, Christian education of children, Last words, Future punishment, Repentance, Temperance, Future life, Women as authors, and Death—Religious aspects." In other words, a majority of subjects in the top ten most common categories had some relation to the concept of damnation as discussed here.

63. Colin McIver, *The Southern Preacher: A Collection of Sermons, from the Manuscripts of Several Eminent Ministers of the Gospel, Residing in the Southern States....* (Philadelphia: Published by the Editor and Proprietor. William Fry, Printer, 1824), pp. x–xi; Table of Contents.

64. Adam Empie, "On the Guilt and Danger of Delaying to Keep God's Commandments," in McIver, *The Southern Preacher*, 46–48.

65. Ebenezer Porter, "The Fatal Effects of Ardent Spirits. A Sermon, by Ebenezer Porter, Pastor of the First Church in Washington, Con." (Hartford: Peter B. Gleason and Co. Printers, 1811), "ADVERTISEMENT."

66. Ibid., 5, 15–16. In *The Alcoholic Republic: An American Tradition* (New York: Oxford University Press, 1979; reprint 1981), W. J. Rorabaugh shows that the per capita consumption of hard liquor was highest between 1800 and 1830 (over 5 gallons); the rate then fell due to increased federal taxes and the temperance movement (7–8).

67. *The New-England Primer Enlarged: or, An Easy and Pleasant Guide to the Art of Reading. Adorned with cuts. To which are added, the Assembly of Divines catechism, &c.* (Newport: Printed by Oliver Farnsworth, 1800), n.p.

68. Children's Department, "Who Will Go to Heaven?" *American Revivalist, and Rochester Observer. Dedicated to the Interests of Zion Generally, and Especially to Revivals of Religion*, New Series, no. 1, vol. 6, no. 39, Saturday, Sept. 29, 1832.

69. Rubin, in *Religious Melancholy*, makes a similar observation but takes it too far: "How did evangelical child-rearing elaborate a system of beliefs, traditions, and practices that were inherently abusive to children? In the cause of the highest good—the salvation of a child's soul—evangelicals methodically injured their children's psyches" (59). The indictment of antebellum evangelicals as child abusers is indicative of Rubin's sometimes polemical tone. See note 108 in chap. 3.

70. "Reasons why there are not revivals in Sabbath Schools," *New York Evangelist* 1 (37), Dec. 11, 1830.

71. "The Living in the Pit," *New York Evangelist* 8 (46), Nov. 11, 1837.

72. Richard Baxter, *A Call to the Unconverted. By Rev. Richard Baxter. With an Introductory Essay by Rev. Thomas Chalmers, D. D.* (Published by the American Tract Society, No. 144 Nassau-Street, New-York. Fanshaw, Printer, 18–?), 56.

73. Christine Leigh Heyrman similarly notes, in *Southern Cross: The Beginnings of the Bible Belt* (New York: Alfred A. Knopf, 1997), that southern "evangelicals taught that believers fulfilled their highest duty to family by trying to convert loved ones" and "emphasized that such efforts would restore an unbroken circle of intimacy in heaven." This "spoke directly to the needs of many men and women whose closest attachments were being sundered by westward migration" (127–28).

74. "Questions for Professors of Religion," *New York Evangelist* 1 (10), June 5, 1830. Reprinted from *Western Luminary*.

75. Matthew 22:30 (KJV); Gary Scott Smith, *Heaven in the American Imagination* (New York: Oxford University Press, 2011), 53. On a nineteenth-century transition toward a heaven where relationships begun on earth could continue in the hereafter, see also Colleen McDannell and Bernard Lang, *Heaven: A History* (New Haven: Yale University Press, 1998; repr. Yale Nota Bene, 2001), esp. chaps. 7 to 9.

76. E. L. Cleaveland, *Hasting to Be Rich: A Sermon, Occasioned by the Present Excitement Respecting the Gold of California, Preached in the Cities of New Haven and Bridgeport, Jan. and Feb. 1849* (New Haven: Printed by J. H. Benham, 1849), 18, 13–14.

77. American Tract Society, "Tract No. 175: To Mothers," in Gutjahr, *American Popular Literature*, 55.

78. See Mary Ryan, *Cradle of the Middle Class: The Family in Oneida County, New York, 1790–1865* (Cambridge: Cambridge University Press, 1981); Nancy Cott, *The Bonds of Womanhood: "Woman's Sphere" in New England, 1780–1835* (New Haven: Yale University Press, 1977; 2nd ed. 1997); and Scott Stephan, *Redeeming the Southern Family: Evangelical Women and Domestic Devotion in the Antebellum South* (Athens: University of Georgia Press, 2008).

79. American Tract Society, "To Mothers," 56.

80. Ibid., 58, 56.

81. "For the Evangelist: What are the *direct and legitimate means of promoting revivals?*" *New York Evangelist* 1 (5), May 1, 1830.

82. Joshua Bradley, A.M., *Accounts of Religious Revivals in Many Parts of the United States from 1816 to 1818. Collected from numerous Publications, and Letters from Persons of piety and correct information* (Albany: Printed by G. J. Loomis & Co., State-Street, 1819), 294–95.

83. American Tract Society, "To Mothers," 53–58, esp. 56.

84. Matthew 28:19–20 (KJV): "Go ye therefore, and teach all nations, baptizing them in the name of the Father, and of the Son, and of the Holy Ghost: Teaching them to observe all things whatsoever I have commanded you: and, lo, I am with you always, even unto the end of the world."

85. John Cameron Lowrie, *A Manual of Missions, or, Sketches of the Foreign Missions of the Presbyterian Church* (New York: Anson D. F. Randolph, 1854).

86. John Scudder, *Dr. Scudder's Tales for Little Readers, about the Heathen* (American Tract Society, 1849), 177–78.

87. Ibid., 111.

88. Ibid.

89. Walter Macon Lowrie, *Sermons Preached in China, by the Rev. Walter M. Lowrie* (New York: Robert Carter & Brothers, 285 Broadway, 1851), 453–54. See also Michael C. Coleman, "Presbyterian Missionary Attitudes toward China and the Chinese, 1837–1900," *Journal of Presbyterian History* 56, no. 3 (1978): 185–200.

90. William Speer, *The Oldest and the Newest Empire: China and the United States* (Hartford: S. S. Scranton & Co., 1870), 605–6. See also Michael Hunt, "The Hierarchy of Race," in Michael L. Krenn, ed., *Race and U.S. Foreign Policy from Colonial Times through the Age of Jackson* (New York: Garland Publishing, Inc., 1998).

91. Ira Condit, "So That They Are without Excuse. Rom. 1:20," 1867, Girard, PA, MS in folder labeled "Rev. Ira Condit Sermons: 1860s, 1870s, 1880s," San Francisco Theological Seminary.

92. *The Heathen Nations: Or Duty of the Present Generation to Evangelize the World. By the Missionaries at the Sandwich Islands*, 3rd ed. (Oberlin: James M. Fitch, 1849), 34–38.

93. See, for instance, George Fredrickson, *A Short History of Racism* (Princeton: Princeton University Press, 2002): "To achieve its full potential as an ideology, racism had to be emancipated from Christian universalism" (47), which held that God had created all humans of "one blood." See also Roxann Wheeler, *The Complexion of Race: Categories of Difference in Eighteenth-Century British Culture* (Philadelphia: University of Pennsylvania Press, 2000), which points to the 1770s as the key decade in the emergence of "race" in Britain. On the reasons why racial categories never entirely replaced religious and the ways in which religion and race continue(d) to co-constitute each other, see Henry Goldschmidt and Elizabeth McAlister, eds., *Race, Nation, and Religion in the Americas* (New York: Oxford University Press, 2004); Craig Prentiss, ed., *Religion and the Creation of Race and Ethnicity: An Introduction* (New York: New York University Press, 2003); Rebecca Goetz, *The Baptism of Early Virginia: How Christianity Created Race* (Baltimore: Johns Hopkins University Press, 2012); Colin Kidd, *The Forging of Races: Race and Scripture in the Protestant Atlantic World, 1600–2000* (Cambridge: Cambridge University Press, 2006); Sylvester Johnson, *The Myth of Ham in Nineteenth-Century American Christianity: Race, Heathens, and the People of God* (New York: Palgrave Macmillan, 2004); and Judith Weisenfeld, "Post-Racial America? The Tangle of Race, Religion, and Citizenship," *Religion and Politics: Fit for Polite Company*, Oct. 24, 2012, http://religionandpolitics.org/2012/10/24/post-racial-america-the-tangle-of-race-religion-and-citizenship/.

94. *The Heathen Nations*, 35.

95. *Harper's Weekly*, Apr. 16, 1859, 249.

96. Isabella Bird, *Six Months in the Sandwich Islands among Hawai'i's Palm Groves, Coral Reefs, and Volcanoes* (1881; repr. Honolulu: Mutual Publishing, 1998), 54–55, quoted in Gary Okihiro, *Island World: A History of Hawaii and the United States* (Berkeley and Los Angeles: University of California Press, 2008), 34.

97. See Jill Lepore, *The Name of War: King Philip's War and the Origins of American Identity* (New York: Alfred A. Knopf, 1998); John Demos, *The Unredeemed Captive: A Family Story from Early America* (New York: Alfred A. Knopf, 1994); and Jorge Cañizares-Esguerra, *Puritan Conquistadors: Iberianizing the Atlantic, 1550–1700* (Stanford, CA: Stanford University Press, 2006).

98. *The Heathen Nations*, 44.

99. Ibid., 14–15.

100. Ibid., 148.

101. On changing attitudes toward poverty—from providentially ordained to a sign of individual improvidence, necessitating evangelical conversion to alleviate—see Bruce Dorsey, *Reforming Men and Women: Gender in the Antebellum City* (Ithaca, NY: Cornell University Press, 2002).

102. Ezra Stiles Ely, "A Sermon for the Rich to Buy, that They May Benefit Themselves and the Poor" (New York: Published by Williams and Whiting, at Their Theological and Classical Book-Store, No. 118, Pearl-Street. Printed by J. Seymour, 1810), 6. John Scudder offered a similar argument in his *Tales for Little Readers, about the Heathen*: "They are not as guilty before God as you are. They know not their Master's will. Still, they must perish, unless the Gospel is sent to them. But though they perish, their punishment will be lighter than the punishment of those who refuse to love and obey the Saviour.... Should it be your sad lot to perish at last, it would be far better for you to go down to hell enveloped in all the darkness of a heathen land, than to go down to hell from a land of such gospel light and privileges as you enjoy" (125).

103. Phillip Milledoler, "Prefatory Address," in Ezra Stiles Ely, *The Journal of the Stated Preacher to the Hospital and Almshouse, in the City of New-York, for the Year of Our Lord 1811* (New York: Published by Whiting and Watson, No. 96, Broadway. J. Seymour, Printer, 1812), 8–9. Porterfield finds strikingly similar language in Philadelphia, where the Presbyterian Plan of 1802 targeted the spiritual health of the impoverished: "Is not the soul of a criminal in the jail of Philadelphia as great as that of an Indian on the banks of the Ohio?" the authors asked. *Extracts from the Minutes of the General Assembly of the Presbyterian Church, in the United States of America, A.D. 1802* (Philadelphia: R. Aitken, 1802), 12–21, quoted in *Conceived in Doubt*, 87–89.

104. Samuel Irenaeus Prime, *Life in New York* (New York: Robert Carter, 58 Canal Street, and Pittsburg, 56 Market Street, 1847), preface.

105. Ibid., 10–11.

106. Ibid., 175–76.

107. Ibid., 182.

108. Ibid., 239.

109. Buntline was a "sailor and U.S. Navy officer; soldier; magazine editor; writer of several hundred 'shilling shockers,' dime novels, and other 'continuous' stories; temperance lecturer (and drunkard); superpatriot to those of Know Nothing (Buntlinite) persuasion, jingoist bigot to others; expert marksman and angler; bigamist; 'discoverer' of Buffalo Bill; playwright; proselytizer; generic showman; and occasionally outright con artist." J. Donald Crowley, "Judson, Edward Zane Carroll," *American National Biography Online*, Feb. 2000, http://www.anb.org/articles/16/16-00886.html.

110. Ned Buntline, *The Mysteries and Miseries of New York: A Story of Real Life* (New York: Berford & Co. No. 2 Astor House. 1848), Part I, 5–6.

111. Lyman Beecher, *A Plea for the West* (Cincinnati: Published by Truman & Smith; New York: Leavitt, Lord & Co., 2nd ed., 1835), 11, 20. See also Laurie Maffly-Kipp, *Religion and Society in Frontier California* (New Haven: Yale University Press, 1994).

112. In *Sin and Fear: The Emergence of a Western Guilt Culture, 13th to 18th Centuries* (1983; repr. New York: St. Martin's Press, 1990), Jean Delumeau argues that in

their deployment of fear and guilt, Catholics and Protestants were not very different. Delumeau argues that this Western guilt culture faded by the end of the eighteenth century, a finding this book complicates. On French Catholic missionaries on the frontiers, see Michael Pasquier, *Fathers on the Frontier: French Missionaries and the Roman Catholic Priesthood in the United States, 1789–1870* (New York: Oxford University Press, 2010).

113. Holifield, *God's Ambassadors*, 139.

114. François Pepin. *Narrative of the Life and Experience of François Pepin, who was for More than 40 Years a Member of the Papal Church; Embracing an Account of His Conversion, Trials, & Persecutions, in Turning to the Pure Religion of the Bible. Addressed Particularly to His Brethren of the Romish Church. With an Introduction, by Rev. Geo. Taylor, of the Michigan Annual Conference of the M. E. C.*, (Detroit: George E. Pomeroy & Co., Printers & Publishers, 32 and 34 Woodward Ave., Opposite the Post-Office, 1854), 24.

115. *Awful Disclosures, by Maria Monk, of the Hotel Dieu Nunnery of Montreal* (New York: Published by Maria Monk, and sold by booksellers generally, 1836; 1977 reprint by Arno Press), 16–17.

116. Gutjahr, *American Popular Literature*, 167, notes that thousands saw it as "a completely trustworthy exposé of Catholicism."

117. Philip M. Hanley, *History of the Catholic Ladder*, ed. Edward J. Kowrach (Fairfield, WA: Ye Galleon Press, 1993); "Catholic Ladder," *The Oregon History Project*, created by the Oregon Historical Society, http://www.ohs.org/education/oregonhistory/historical_records/dspDocument.cfm?doc_ID=1BC31EBF-ED24-1826-446AB0780892B384.

118. Pierre-Jean De Smet, *Letters and Sketches: With a Narrative of a Year's Residence among the Indian Tribes of the Rocky Mountains* (Philadelphia: Published by M. Fithian, 61 N. Second Street, 1843), 252.

119. Henry Spalding to David Greene, Feb. 12, 1846; in Narcissa Whitman and Eliza Spalding, *Where Wagons Could Go*, ed. Clifford Merrill Drury; introduction by Julie Roy Jeffrey (Arthur H. Clark Company, 1963; Lincoln, NE: University of Nebraska Press, Bison Books Edition, 1997), 223–24.

120. Mark G. Thiel, "Catholic Ladders and Native American Evangelization," *U.S. Catholic Historian* 27, no. 1 (2009): 58.

121. Ibid., 61–62.

122. See Jaime Lara, *City, Temple, Stage: Eschatological Architecture and Liturgical Theatrics in New Spain* (Notre Dame, IN: University of Notre Dame Press, 2004). The Catholic ladders of the Pacific Northwest were not the first didactic visuals in North America. Jesuit Claude Chauchetière of the Iroquois Mission of Sault St. Louis/Kahnawake wrote in an Oct. 14, 1682, letter: "One thing that helps me in my work is the drawings that I make to illustrate the truths of the gospel and the ways of virtue.... I have one book containing colored pictures of the ceremonies of the Mass as connected with the Passion of our Lord, another with illustrations of the torments of Hell, and still another on the creation of

the world. The Indians read these with pleasure and profit." From *The Jesuit Relations* 62: 166–87; quoted in Allan Greer, ed., *The Jesuit Relations: Natives and Missionaries in Seventeenth-Century North America* (Boston: Bedford/St. Martin's, 2000), 150.

123. Executive Committee of the American Home Missionary Society, *Our Country; Its Capabilities, Its Perils, and Its Hope. Being a Plea for the Early Establishment of Gospel Institutions in the Destitute Portions of the United States* (New York: Published by the Executive Committee of the American Home Missionary Society, 1842), 45.

124. "MISCELLANEOUS: A Dependent Foreign Field," *The Home Missionary* 37, no. 1 (May 1864): 19.

125. Isaac H. Brayton, "California and Home Missions," *The Home Missionary* 27, no. 3 (July 1854): 61–62.

126. Executive Committee, *Our Country*, 27–28.

127. Ibid., 15.

CHAPTER 3

1. "Minnie" to "Catherine Putnam, Yonkers, October 1854," in *Life and Letters of Mary Putnam Jacobi*, ed. Ruth Putnam (New York: G. P. Putnam's Sons, 1925), 35–38.

2. Ibid.

3. On the shift from a patriarchal household economy of producers to a domestic household of consumers kept afloat by the silent labor of women, see Mary Ryan, *Cradle of the Middle Class: The Family in Oneida County, New York, 1790–1865* (Cambridge: Cambridge University Press, 1981).

4. As Candy Gunther Brown puts it, "individual conversion marked the beginning rather than the culmination of evangelicals' day-to-day, communal pursuit of holiness, or sanctification" (*The Word in the World: Evangelical Writing, Publishing, and Reading in America, 1789–1880* (Chapel Hill: The University of North Carolina Press, 2004), 18). Similarly, Linford Fisher, who focuses on Native responses to evangelization, suggests that "Native religious engagement usually defied the more totalizing and complete notions that often frame the word 'conversion,' which too often imposes Eurocentric ideas about religion on Native populations." Fisher instead uses the words "religious engagement" and "affiliation," which allow for a focus on "what individual Natives actually did instead of speculating on interior processes." *The Indian Great Awakening: Religion and the Shaping of Native Cultures in Early America* (New York: Oxford University Press, 2012), 8, also chap. 4 "Affiliating."

5. On "inoculation theology" and didactic journeys, see Gregory Jackson, *The Word and Its Witness: The Spiritualization of American Realism* (Chicago: University of Chicago Press, 2009), esp. chap. 1 "Hell's Plot: The Hermeneutic of Fear." New

Game of Human Life quote from Jill Lepore, *The Mansion of Happiness: A History of Life and Death* (New York: Alfred A. Knopf, 2012), p. xxi.

6. David J. Voelker, "Cincinnati's Infernal Regions Exhibit and the Waning of Calvinist Authority," *American Nineteenth Century History* 9, no. 3 (Sept. 2008): 219–39. Voelker seeks to prove the "fading ability of educated Calvinist ministers to maintain rigorous doctrines of predestination and hell" (227). He asks, "Could visiting a mock hell truly set a spectator on the straight and narrow path of virtue?" (231). Voelker believes the answer is no, but Jason Bivins's *Religion of Fear: The Politics of Horror in Conservative Evangelicalism* (New York: Oxford University Press, 2008) takes seriously the didactic function of such exhibits in his study of contemporary hell houses. Voelker himself acknowledges that visitors seldom called the creators' "bluff," and even notes that some ministers exhorted visitors during the exhibit and some churches "may even have publicized" it (231–32).

7. Here I would modify Jackson's "inoculation theology" metaphor, since the notion of inoculation could imply some passivity on the part of the inoculated.

8. On the genre of memoir-as-example in evangelical print culture, see Brown, *The Word in the World*, 88–95; Catherine Brekus, "Writing as a Protestant Practice: Devotional Diaries in Early New England," in Laurie Maffly-Kipp, Leigh Schmidt, and Mark Valeri, eds., *Practicing Protestants: Histories of Christian Life in America, 1630–1965* (Baltimore: Johns Hopkins University Press, 2006); and Mechal Sobel, *Teach Me Dreams: The Search for Self in the Revolutionary Era* (Princeton: Princeton University Press, 2002). Sobel writes that "many narrators reported that their conversions were facilitated by conversions they read of, while others emulated key nonreligious activities they had learned of in narratives" (13).

Scholars have sought to determine whether conversion meant different things to antebellum women and men. They have disagreed about whether it empowered women with a sense of independence and individualism, or with a feeling of belonging and dependence on a wider peer community in an era of social instability. As for men navigating changing and highly individualistic public spaces, some have seen conversion as a renunciation of individual autonomy in favor of Christian community, while others have described it as a shrewd step granting men the perceived attributes of social control, temperance, and other advantages needed to succeed in the competitive marketplace. See Susan Juster, "'In a Different Voice': Male and Female Narratives of Religious Conversion in Post-Revolutionary America," *American Quarterly* 41, no. 1 (Mar. 1989): 34–62; Nancy Cott, "Young Women in the Second Great Awakening in New England," *Feminist Studies* 3, no. 1/2 (Autumn 1975): 15–29; Michael Kimmel, *Manhood in America: A Cultural History* (New York: Free Press, 1996); Paul Johnson, *A Shopkeeper's Millennium: Society and Revivals in Rochester, New York* (New York: Hill and Wang, 1978); and Bruce Dorsey,

Reforming Men and Women: Gender in the Antebellum City (Ithaca, NY: Cornell University Press, 2002).

Conversion could have any or all of these effects depending on context. By focusing on how both women and men pointed to the fear of hell as a major factor in their conversions, I seek to show similarities in their religious imagination rather than explain away their conversion experiences as primarily a manifestation of something "else"—whether social, political, or economic.

9. Martha Laurens Ramsay, June 2, 1795, in David Ramsay, M.D., *Memoirs of the Life of Martha Laurens Ramsay, who Died in Charleston, S.C. on the 10th of June, 1811, in the 52d Year of her Age* (America Printed; London: Re-Printed for Burton and Briggs, 156, Leadenhall Street; Sold Also by J. Hatchard, Bookseller to the Queen, 190, Picadilly. By T. Bayley, Devonshire Street, Bishopsgate, 1815), 127.

10. Julius Rubin, *Religious Melancholy and Protestant Experience in America* (New York: Oxford University Press, 1994), 12.

11. Ramsay, Aug. 3, 1795, in *Memoirs*, 146–47.

12. Rev. William T. Torrey, *Memoirs and Letters of Mrs. Mary Dexter, Late Consort of Rev. Elijah Dexter, of Plymptom* (Plymouth, MA: Allen Danforth, Printer, 1823), 27, 29.

13. See Catherine Brekus, *Strangers and Pilgrims: Female Preaching in America, 1740–1845* (Chapel Hill: University of North Carolina Press, 1998), which shows how the ability of women to exhort and preach eroded by the 1830s as populist denominations attempted to become more genteel and to appeal to a middle-class audience. See also Joanna Bowen Gillespie, *The Life and Times of Martha Laurens Ramsay* (Columbia: University of South Carolina Press, 2001), who notes that "women's memoirs as a genre had long been the accepted pattern for an assemblance of female spiritually analytic musings…. They were also a form of self-tutorial in the art of scrutinizing one's inner being" (4).

14. "A letter from the Rev. Dr. Hollinshead to Dr. David Ramsay," Charleston, S.C. July 1, 1181 [*sic*], in Ramsay, *Memoirs*, p. vii.

15. See also Amanda Porterfield, *Conceived in Doubt: Religion and Politics in the New American Nation* (Chicago: University of Chicago Press, 2012), 12–13: "Subverting religious doubt, evangelicals made admission of it a step in conversion that could be revisited to rekindle belief whenever trust in God faltered. The ritual practice of managing and manipulating doubt spilled into larger questions about American identity and the direction of American government, providing a strategy for managing concerns about America and linking idealism about America to evangelical religion."

16. Robert Abzug, *Passionate Liberator: Theodore Dwight Weld and the Dilemma of Reform* (New York: Oxford University Press, 1980), chap. 3 "Conversion," esp. 47–49.

17. Theodore Dwight Weld to Charles Finney, Apr. 22, 1828, Fabius, NY, in *The Letters of Theodore Dwight Weld, Angelina Grimké Weld and Sarah Grimké,*

1822–1844, vol. 1 (New York: D. Appleton-Century Company Incorporated, 1934. Prepared and published under the direction of the American Historical Association), 14–17.

18. On evangelical lay advice literature, see Brown, *The Word in the World*, 118–23.

19. See Richard Bushman, *The Refinement of America: Persons, Houses, Cities* (New York: Knopf, 1992).

20. Catharine Beecher, *A Treatise on Domestic Economy, for the Use of Young Ladies at Home, and at School*, Revised Edition, with Numerous Additions and Illustrative Engravings (Boston: Thomas H. Webb, & Co., 1843), 166–67, 157–58, 184.

21. John Scudder, *Dr. Scudder's Tales for Little Readers, about the Heathen* (American Tract Society, 1849), 181–82.

22. Karin Gedge, *Without Benefit of Clergy: Women and the Pastoral Relationship in Nineteenth-Century American Culture* (New York: Oxford University Press, 2003).

23. Charles Finney, *Memoirs of Rev. Charles G. Finney. Written by Himself* (New York: A. S. Barnes & Company, 751 Broadway, 1876), 173–74.

24. See Karen Halttunen, *Confidence Men and Painted Women: A Study of Middle-Class Culture in America, 1830–1870* (New Haven: Yale University Press, 1982), for a classic study of middle-class anxieties about sincerity and false appearances.

25. Henry Ward Beecher, *Seven Lectures to Young Men, on Various Important Subjects; Delivered before the Young Men of Indianapolis, Indiana, during the Winter of 1843–4* (Indianapolis: Published by Thomas B. Cutler: Charles B. Davis, Bookseller and Stationer: Cincinnati, Wm. H. Moore & Co., 1844), 146.

26. Royall Tyler, *The Contrast: A Comedy in Five Acts* (Boston: Houghton Mifflin, 1920), I, 1, p. 27, quoted in Kimmel, *Manhood in America*, 14.

27. John Todd, *The Student's Manual: Designed, by Specific Directions, to Aid in Forming and Strengthening the Intellectual and Moral Character and Habits of the Student*, 4th ed. (Northampton: Published by J. H. Butler; Boston, Crocker & Brewster and William Pierce. New-York, Leavitt, Lord & Co. Philadelphia, Wm. Marshall & Co. Buffalo, T. & M. Butler. 1835), on eating: 279; exercise: 271; teeth: 80. Kimmel notes that *The Student's Manual* went through twenty-four editions by 1854.

28. Ibid., 299–302.

29. Ibid., 293.

30. Ibid., 146.

31. Ibid., 294.

32. Ibid.

33. Ibid., 302–3 (emphasis in original).

34. American Tract Society, "Tract No. 493: Beware of Bad Books," in Paul Gutjahr, *American Popular Literature of the Nineteenth Century* (New York: Oxford University Press, 2001), 59–61.

35. Beecher, *Treatise on Domestic Economy*, 36–37.

36. Ibid., 185.

37. See John Lardas Modern, *Secularism in Antebellum America* (Chicago: University of Chicago Press, 2011).

38. Ramsay diary, Sept. 7, 1795, *Memoirs*, 148.

39. Ibid., Nov. 25, 1805, 176.

40. Dexter, *Memoirs*, 33.

41. Ibid., Dexter to "Miss S.H.," New Bedford, 1812, 137–38.

42. Elizabeth Willard diary, July 30, 1842, Oswego Indiana, Box 1, Folder 8, in Rowland Willard-Elizabeth S. Willard Papers, Yale Collection of Western Americana, Beinecke Rare Book and Manuscript Library.

43. Ibid., Sept. 18, 1842.

44. Ibid., Jan. 1, 1843.

45. Annihilationism was compatible with continued belief in a premillennial advent though not with eternal damnation. See section on Rowland Willard in chap. 4 and Elizabeth's entry dated July 11, 1863.

46. Elizabeth Willard diary, Jan. 8, 1845.

47. Newspaper clipping in ibid., Mar. 16, 1853.

48. Ibid., June 5, 1861.

49. Ibid., Apr. 18, 1862.

50. Ibid., Apr. 27, 1863.

51. Elizabeth Weld to Theodore Weld, Feb. 26, 1826, in *The Letters of Theodore Dwight Weld*, 9.

52. See Porterfield, *Conceived in Doubt*: "Stories about supernatural power at the turn of the nineteenth century highlighted the conversion of infidel men. Often taking female piety for granted, promotional accounts of revivals in cities and on the frontier focused on dramatic accounts of male conversion, leaving the impression that winning men over from skepticism was the top priority of evangelicals" (98).

53. Joshua Bradley, A.M., *Accounts of Religious Revivals in Many Parts of the United States from 1816 to 1818. Collected from numerous Publications, and Letters from Persons of piety and correct information* (Albany: Printed by G. J. Loomis & Co., State-Street, 1819), 95–98.

54. Ibid., 99–100.

55. Ibid., 103–6.

56. Diaries of Frederick G. Niles, 1858–1870, HM 70278–70281, The Huntington Library, San Marino, CA.

57. Ibid., Mar. 6, 1859.

58. Ibid., Mar. 13, 1859.

59. Ibid., Mar. 26, 1859.

60. Ibid., Dec. 11, 1859.

61. Ibid., Mar. 13, 1860.

62. Ibid., Apr. 16, 1860.

63. Ibid., Dec. 31, 1859.

64. Ibid., May 26, 1861.

65. Ibid. The underscores and periods are an attempt to replicate in typescript Niles's idiosyncratic use of lines, dashes, and dots in his handwritten diary.

66. Niles kept up a litany of similar complaints and worries in later entries, bemoaning the lack of Sabbath observance in the West and his own coldness of heart, and worrying about his own mortality as he witnessed the deaths of those near him.

67. Diaries of Frederick G. Niles, Mar. 18, 1860.

68. Ibid., Mar. 24, 1860. Niles frequently ends sentences with dashes and lines instead of periods.

69. See, for instance, Niles's entries on July 2, 1860 and Jan. 18, 1863.

70. Benedict Anderson coined the term to refer to modern nation-states in *Imagined Communities: Reflections on the Origin and Spread of Nationalism* (New York: Verso, 1983).

71. See also James Morone, *Hellfire Nation: The Politics of Sin in American History* (New Haven: Yale University Press, 2004).

72. Dec. 14, 1827, entry, and undated 1829 entry, in Eliza Fairbanks Hooper Diary and Correspondence, 1818–1830, Yale Collection of Western Americana, Beinecke Rare Book and Manuscript Library.

73. See Fisher, *The Indian Great Awakening*, esp. Introduction, 55–59, and 104–6.

74. Ibid., 209–10.

75. William Apes, *The Experiences of Five Christian Indians: or the Indian's Looking-Glass for the White Man* (Boston: Printed by James B. Dow, 1833), 44. Apess's name was occasionally rendered with one "s," as in this publication.

76. Henry Obookiah, *Memoirs of Henry Obookiah, A Native of Owhyhee, and a Member of the Foreign Mission School; Who Died at Cornwall, Conn. Feb. 17, 1818, Aged 26 Years* (New Haven: Published at the Office of the Religious Intelligencer, 1818), 26.

77. Ibid., 29.

78. Ibid., 31.

79. Ibid., 34.

80. Makaiheekona, #22, Apr. 13, 1838, Henry P. Judd, Trans., in folder labeled "Schools—Lahainaluna Seminary Student Essays. 1838-182. Translations & photocopies—Originals stored separately. TRANSLATIONS of #18, 20–25, 29, 31, 32. Photocopies of the above originals plus #34. H.E.A. Archives," Hawaiian Mission Children's Society Library, Honolulu.

81. #35, "The Result of All Things," Dorothy Barrere, Trans., in folder labeled "Schools—Lahainaluna Student Essays—Translations & photocopies—No originals. TRANSLATIONS of #35, 36 (partial), 50. Photocopies of #35, 36, 39, 40, 50. H.E.A. Archives," Hawaiian Mission Children's Society Library, Honolulu.

82. David W. Forbes, *Engraved at Lahainaluna: A History of Printmaking by Hawaiians at the Lahainaluna Seminary, 1834 to 1844 with a Descriptive Catalogue of All Known Views, Maps, and Portraits* (Honolulu: Hawaiian Mission Children's Society, 2012), 182–84.

83. Fisher asks a version of this question in *The Indian Great Awakening* (101 ff.), with reference to an earlier period and to Northeastern Native groups.

84. Apess himself experienced a "horrific childhood of being orphaned at a young age and serving under several masters (who flogged him regularly)" (ibid., 210).

85. Apes, *Experiences of Five Christian Indians*, 3, 5–6.

86. Hannah Caleb account in ibid., 38–42.

87. For similar themes in an earlier period, see Rachel Wheeler, "'Friends to Your Souls': Jonathan Edwards' Indian Pastorate and the Doctrine of Original Sin," *Church History* 72 (2003): 736–65. Wheeler suggests that Edwards's Stockbridge sermons to Native Americans emphasized the "egalitarian dimension of the Calvinist belief in universal damnation…. He preached original sin to the Indians in a way that encouraged the lowly and humbled the mighty" (765).

88. See Rodger M. Payne, *The Self and the Sacred: Conversion and Autobiography in Early American Protestantism* (Knoxville: University of Tennessee Press, 1998), on how conversions both followed established patterns subsuming the self while also celebrating it. On debates about suicide in the early republic, see Richard Bell, *We Shall Be No More: Suicide and Self-Government in the Newly United States* (Cambridge, MA: Harvard University Press, 2012).

89. As Melvin Yazawa puts it, "Rather than tracing the causes of insanity to sources outside human control, experts increasingly focused on human factors. And, in part because of the rise of an increasingly professional medical establishment, physicians came to replace ministers as the chief authorities on insanity." "The Impact of the Revolution on Social Problems: Poverty, Insanity, and Crime," in Jack P. Greene and J. R. Pole, eds., *A Companion to the American Revolution* (Blackwell Publishing, 2003), http://www.blackwellreference.com/subscriber/tocnode?id=g9781405116749_chunk_g978140511674957. Still, this shift was hardly complete by the early nineteenth century.

90. Ezra Stiles Ely, *The Journal of the Stated Preacher to the Hospital and Almshouse, in the City of New-York, for the Year of Our Lord 1811* (New York: Published by Whiting and Watson, No. 96, Broadway. J. Seymour, Printer, 1812), 77, 82–83.

91. Ibid., 235–58. Ely comments on insanity throughout the journal; he also devotes sustained attention to "INSANITY" in his last entry of the year (Dec. 31, 1811).

92. Ibid., 206.

93. Ibid., 262–69.

94. Ibid.

95. Universalists were frequently the subjects of cautionary tales about suicide. The *American Revivalist, and Rochester Observer,* for instance, suggested that consistent Universalists should commit suicide, for if they actually believed that

heaven awaited everyone, then there was no use in staying alive on earth. The newspaper included several reports of Universalists on the verge of or actually committing suicide, which it termed "a terrible gateway into Eternity." See "A Consistent Universalist," in *The American Revivalist, and Rochester Observer*, vol. 6, no. 44, Nov. 3, 1832; also "Universalist Principles Carried Out in Practice," in ibid., vol. 6, no. 42, Oct. 20, 1832.

96. See the story of "The Dying Universalist" in Ichabod Spencer's minister's manual. Although certainly dramatized, the story nevertheless suggested how the fear of hell, which the dying man's mother had tried to instill, came back at the deathbed. The dying man lamented, "But I am lost! I am lost!—You told me, father, there was no hell, and I tried to believe it. I joined you in wickedness, when I knew better. I have laughed at hell; and now hell laughs at me! God will punish sinners! He has taken hold of me, and I cannot get out of his hands!" Ichabod Spencer, *A Pastor's Sketches: Or, Conversations with Anxious Inquirers Respecting the Way of Salvation*, 4th ed. (New York: Published by M. W. Dodd, Brick Church Chapel, City Hall Square, (Opposite the City Hall), 1851), 392.

97. See William Sims Bainbridge, "Religious Insanity in America: The Official Nineteenth-Century Theory," *Sociological Analysis* 45, no. 3 (Autumn 1984): 223–39, and Rubin, *Religious Melancholy*.

98. "FIRST REPORT of the Superintendent of the State Lunatic Hospital at Worcester, Mass., from the opening of the Institution, January 19th, 1833, to November 30th," in *Reports and Other Documents Relating to the State Lunatic Hospital at Worcester, Mass. Printed by Order of the Senate* (Boston: Dutton and Wentworth, Printers to the State, Nos. 10 and 12 Exchange Street, 1837); reprinted in *The Origins of the State Mental Hospital in America* (New York: Arno Press, 1973), 49.

99. "FOURTH REPORT of the Superintendent of the State Lunatic Hospital at Worcester, Massachusetts, from December 1st, 1835, to November 30th, 1836," in ibid., 157, 160.

100. "Report of the New York State Asylum," excerpted in Appendix to Ned Buntline, *The Mysteries and Miseries of New York: A Story of Real Life* (New York: Berford & Co. No. 2 Astor House, 1848), Part V, 105. Buntline abridged the full breadth of the report's statistics, but among the causes he cited, religious anxiety was number one by a threefold factor. His book undoubtedly had a greater readership than the Report itself, thus influencing readers' perceptions of the causes of insanity more than the official document. 1849 report from Table 9, in *Sixth Annual Report of the Managers of the State Lunatic Asylum* (Albany: Weed, Parsons & Co., Public Printers, 1849), 27–29. In this report, "Religious Anxiety" was the fourth leading cause behind "Unknown," "Ill health," and "Doubtful."

101. Amariah Brigham, *Observations on the Influence of Religion upon the Health and Physical Welfare of Mankind* (Boston: Marsh, Capen & Lyon, 1835), 269.

102. Ibid., 290–91.

103. Ibid., 291.
104. Ibid., 292.
105. Ibid., 297.
106. Ibid., 295.
107. Ibid., 275, 277. Another nineteenth-century author, Pliny Earle, similarly noted that insanity from religious causes seemed much more widespread in the United States than in Europe. "In 1841, after a visit to thirteen European asylums," writes William Bainbridge, "Earle contended that religious excitement was a distinctively American cause of insanity, noting that none of 1,557 cases admitted to the Asylum at Charenton near Paris were attributed to religious excitement, compared with 53 of the 678 cases treated at the Massachusetts state hospital (Earle, 1841: 119). He suggested that the more lively and widespread religious debates in the United States promoted insanity here, while a differentiation of the French into obediently superstitious 'lower orders' and confidently unfaithful 'higher orders' left no one prey there to private indulgence in religious obsessions" (Bainbridge, "Religious Insanity in America": 228). Likewise, the 1849 New York *Sixth Annual Report* noted that "Liberty, so favorale [sic] to the development of the human intellect, multiplies the causes of derangement.... We are of the opinion, and it is an opinion formed after much inquiry, that there is more insanity in this country, especially in the northern and eastern states, than in any other, and that it is fearfully on the increase" (38).
108. Émile Durkheim suggested that suicide rates were higher in Protestant than Catholic cultures. In keeping with his view of religion as an affirmation of social bonds and norms, he explained that this was because Catholic cultures typically integrated the individual into a more cohesive social unit, whereas Protestant cultures left the individual alone with his/her feelings of guilt and repression. Émile Durkheim, *Suicide: A Study in Sociology (Le Suicide)*, ed. George Simpson, trans. John A. Spaulding and George Simpson (New York: Free Press, 1951; 1979). As this book seeks to demonstrate, though, American evangelicals were just as concerned with community: the problem for the insane was that they were left out.

A number of historians and sociologists have used economic, social, and psychological explanations to account for the rise of religious "enthusiasm." In his study of insanity and religious anxiety, Bainbridge cites several popular theories of insanity. "Freudians tend to view religious dogmas as inherently delusional, thereby being the stuff of which madness is made.... Kiev and Francis (1964) suggested that unresolved guilt aroused by deviant religious groups might undermine mental health, and other writers have emphasized the power of intense religious experiences (Allison, 1968). Psychiatrists and clinical psychologists often are among the most vehement opponents of contemporary cults, and the general public has been bombarded with pseudoscientific claims that deviant religion is psychopathological" (Bainbridge, "Religious Insanity in America": 224).

As for historical accounts, Whitney Cross suggested that women in the "burned-over district" of western New York had "suppressed desires" and "intellects" that did not develop beyond elementary school. *The Burned-over District: The Social and Intellectual History of Enthusiastic Religion in Western New York, 1800–1850* (Cornell University Press, 1950; repr. New York: Octagon Books, 1981), 89. Sean Wilentz and Paul Johnson, in the sparkling *The Kingdom of Matthias*, explain the self-proclaimed prophet Matthias's eccentricities as a result of his losses in the burgeoning antebellum market culture: particularly of economic status and of paternal authority. See *The Kingdom of Matthias* (New York: Oxford University Press, 1994). By contrast, Julius Rubin takes the theory of religious insanity very seriously. He sees evangelical religion itself as a cause of depressive disorder but in so doing, verges on the polemical in portraying evangelicals as pervasively gloomy crushers of the soul.

109. *Sixth Annual Report*, 39.

110. Bainbridge, "Religious Anxiety in America."

111. Ibid., 234; Bainbridge also refers readers to Charles Glock and Rodney Stark's *Religion and Society in Tension* (Chicago: Rand McNally, 1965), 289–306.

112. While some contend that the evolution of this "gentler" strain can be attributed to the majority of women in the pews, such an explanation is too simple. Women could welcome guilt-inducing sermons more than comforting creeds. On female preachers who held a God of mercy and justice, love and vindictiveness in creative tension, see Brekus, *Strangers and Pilgrims*, 207–16. On scholarly debates over feminization, see note 40 in chap. 2.

113. Brigham, *Observations on the Influence of Religion*, 285.

114. FOURTH REPORT, 160, 168–69. The idea that the insane were not necessarily to blame for their condition, that insanity was not a divine punishment or the earthly beginning of hell, and that some could in fact be cured also emerged in other northeastern reports. "Until a period comparatively recent," the Commissioners of New Jersey found, "Insanity has been considered an incurable disease. The universal opinion has been, that it was an awful visitation from Heaven, and that no human agency could reverse the judgment by which it was inflicted.... Even at the present day, and in communities otherwise highly enlightened, there is reason to fear that a lamentable degree of ignorance prevails upon this subject: an ignorance, which could it be once dispelled, some of the most painful records in the history of human suffering might be closed, immediately and forever" (*The Report of the Commissioners, Appointed by the Governor of New Jersey*, in *The Origins of the State Mental Hospital in America*, 15).

115. "M. C. P. to the Rev. Dr. Anderson," Apr. 19, 1863, in *Life and Letters of Mary Putnam Jacobi*, 58–59.

116. Ibid.

CHAPTER 4

1. James Richardson, Jr., "The Instinct of Progress," in *The Shekinah*, vol. 1 (New York: Partridge & Brittan, 1852), 226–27, 231 (emphasis in original).
2. Ibid., 232 (emphasis in original).
3. From the National Library of Australia's website: "The Swedish missionary was Jonas Aurén, whose letter from Conestoga of Jan. 13, 1699/1700, including the Indian speech, was printed in Latin in Grönwall, Anders, praeses.... Dissertatio gradualis, de plantatione ecclesiae Svecanae in America, quam...sistit Tobias E. Biörck. Upsaliae, [1731]," http://catalogue.nla.gov.au/Record/3372624.

   Among the many American versions of this text were reprints from 1741 (*American Magazine*), 1773 (*The Providence Gazette, and Country Journal*), 1781 (*Pennsylvania Evening Post*), 1785 (*The New-York Journal, and State Gazette*, and *The Massachusetts Spy*), 1789 (*The Daily Advertiser*, *The Independent Chronicle and the Universal Advertiser*, *The Hampshire Gazette*, and *The Berkshire Chronicle*), 1804 (a stand-alone version), 1812 (*The Herald of Gospel Liberty*), and 1818 (*The Newport Mercury*). The 1929 article comes from the Dec. 20 edition of the *Reading Eagle*, with a circulation around 45,000. The newspaper calls it a "legend" and notes that "this speech had been printed in Pennsylvania, as a genuine speech of a Conestoga chief; but whether is [sic] be really so or not, it certainly contains arguments which have been used by these people, and it may serve in part, to give some idea of their sentiments on this subject." The speech may have been the product of a European or Euro-American skeptic or Universalist assuming the posture of an "Indian chief." Still, it is not farfetched to surmise that a native person originally articulated the barbed ideas that form its essence, especially since similar arguments cropped up among other missionized peoples in later texts as well.
4. The version cited here is "An Indian Speech in Answer to a Sermon, preached by a Swedish Missionary, at Conestogo, in Pennsylvania. To which is added, Observations of a Tuscarora-Chief; and Drunkenness reproved by a Beast" (Stanford [NY]: Printed and sold by Daniel Lawrence, 1804), 4–5.
5. Ibid., 6–7.
6. Ibid., 8–9.
7. Ibid., 3–4.
8. Unlike the anonymous Indian speechmaker, Native American revitalization prophets have received considerable attention from scholars whose work informs this analysis. See Anthony F. C. Wallace, *Death and Rebirth of the Seneca* (New York: Knopf, 1970); Gregory Evans Dowd, *A Spirited Resistance: The North American Indian Struggle for Unity, 1745–1815* (Baltimore: Johns Hopkins, 1992); R. David Edmunds, *The Shawnee Prophet* (Lincoln: University of Nebraska Press, 1983); and Alfred Cave, *Prophets of the Great Spirit* (Lincoln: University of Nebraska Press, 2006).

9. John M'Cullough, "A Narrative of the Captivity of John M'Cullough, Esq., Written by Himself," in *A Selection of the Most Interesting Narratives, of Outrages, Committed by the Indians in Their Wars, with the White People*...ed. Archibald Loudon (Carlisle: From the Press of A. Loudon (*Whitehall*), 1808), 324–25.

10. On earlier visual devices, see note 122 in chap. 2.

11. *The Journal of Pontiac's Conspiracy of the Indians against the English, and of the Siege of Fort Detroit by Four Different Nations Beginning May 7*, in Milo Milton Quaife, ed., *The Siege of Detroit in 1763: The Journal of Pontiac's Conspiracy and John Rutherfurd's Narrative of a Captivity* (Chicago: Lakeside Press, 1958), 15–16. See also Dowd, *A Spirited Resistance*; Wallace, *Death and Rebirth of the Seneca*, 114–21.

12. "The Code of Handsome Lake," in *Parker on the Iroquois: Iroquois Uses of Maize and Other Food Plants; the Code of Handsome Lake, the Seneca Prophet; the Constitution of the Five Nations*, ed. William N. Fenton (Syracuse, NY: Syracuse University Press, 1968), 38, 68.

13. Ibid., 69, 58–59, 56.

14. Thomas Forsyth, St. Louis, to Gen. William Clark, Dec. 23, 1812; reprinted in Emma Helen Blair, ed., *The Indian Tribes of the Upper Mississippi Valley & Region of the Great Lakes* (Cleveland: Arthur H. Clark Co., 1911; repr. Lincoln: University of Nebraska Press, 1996; with an Introduction by Richard White), 274.

15. Thomas Jefferson to John Adams, in *Jefferson's Correspondence*, vol. 10, p. 171; cited in Benjamin Drake, *Life of Tecumseh and of His Brother the Prophet; with a Historical Sketch of the Shawanoe Indians* (Cincinnati: H. S. & J. Applegate & Co., 1852), 220; on Tenskwatawa's attacks against shamans and ritualistic practices from Catholicism, see Edmunds, *The Shawnee Prophet*.

16. Vernon Kinietz and Erminie Voegelin, eds., *Shawnese Traditions: C. C. Trowbridge's Account* (Ann Arbor: University of Michigan Press, 1939), 42.

17. "Speech by Le Maigouis, May 4, 1807," in *Letters Received by the Secretary of War: Unregistered Series, 1789–1860*, Microcopy No. 222, Roll 2: 1805–1807 (Washington, DC: National Archives and Records Service General Services Administration (microfilm publication), 1954) (emphasis in original).

18. Edmunds, *The Shawnee Prophet*, 33.

19. "All Indians who refused to follow these regulations," a white observer remembered, "were to be considered as bad people and not worthy to live, and must be put to death." Forsyth letter, in Blair, ed., *The Indian Tribes of the Upper Mississippi Valley & Region of the Great Lakes*, 277–78.

20. Edmunds, *The Shawnee Prophet*.

21. Augustus Ward Loomis, *Scenes in the Indian Country* (Philadelphia: Presbyterian Board of Publication, No. 821 Chestnut Street, 1859), 30–31.

22. Ibid., 7–8. On missionaries' attitudes to removal, see William McLoughlin, *Cherokees and Missionaries, 1789–1839* (New Haven: Yale University Press, 1984). For a newer interpretation that holds missionaries more responsible

for American imperial expansion than in earlier scholarship, see Sylvester Johnson, "Religion and American Empire in Mississippi, 1790–1833," in Michael Pasquier, ed., *Gods of the Mississippi* (Bloomington: Indiana University Press, 2013).

23. Loomis, *Scenes in the Indian Country*, 188.

24. Ibid., 188–90.

25. Ibid., 169, 171–73.

26. Ibid., 181, 183–84.

27. Ibid., 174.

28. Margaret Fuller, *Summer on the Lakes, in 1843*, in Eve Kornfeld, ed., *Margaret Fuller: A Brief Biography with Documents* (Boston: Bedford/St. Martin's, 1996), 149.

29. Amariah Brigham, *Observations on the Influence of Religion upon the Health and Physical Welfare of Mankind* (Boston: Marsh, Capen & Lyon, 1835), 186–88, esp. footnotes (z) and (b).

30. Ezra Stiles Ely and Abel C. Thomas, *A Discussion of the Conjoint Question: Is the Doctrine of Endless Punishment Taught in the Bible? Or Does the Bible Teach the Doctrine of the Final Holiness and Happiness of All Mankind? In a Series of Letters between Ezra Stiles Ely and Abel C. Thomas* (New York: P. Price, 1835).

31. Abel C. Thomas, *Autobiography of Rev. Abel C. Thomas: Including Recollections of Persons, Incidents, and Places* (Boston: Published by J. M. Usher, 37 Cornhill, 1852), 224–25.

32. On continued denominational controversies over the concept of election, see Peter Thuesen, *Predestination: The American Career of a Contentious Doctrine* (New York: Oxford University Press, 2009).

33. Herman Melville, *Typee: A Peep at Polynesian Life*, ed. A. Robert Lee (Everyman; London: J. M. Dent; Vermont: Charles E. Tuttle Co., Inc., 1998), 128. Text is from the Northwestern-Newberry edition, 1968. On the evangelical response to *Typee*, see also chap. 1 in John Lardas Modern, *Secularism in Antebellum America* (Chicago: University of Chicago Press, 2011).

34. Melville, *Typee*, 176, 130.

35. Ezra Stiles Ely, *The Journal of the Stated Preacher to the Hospital and Almshouse, in the City of New-York, for the Year of Our Lord 1811* (New York: Published by Whiting and Watson, No. 96, Broadway. J. Seymour, Printer, 1812), 109.

36. Ibid., 129.

37. Charles G. Finney to Theodore Dwight Weld, Reading [Pa.], March 30, 1829, in *The Letters of Theodore Dwight Weld*, 24.

38. By a Brother, "Attention, Fellow-Citizens to the Subject of Modern Religious 'Travelling Ministers'" (Rhode Island?: s.n., 182–?), 1–2.

39. See Karin Gedge, *Without Benefit of Clergy: Women and the Pastoral Relationship in Nineteenth-Century American Culture* (New York: Oxford University Press, 2003).

40. John Russell Kelso, "Autobiography of John Russell Kelso, 1882, Ukiah, Calif.," in *John R. Kelso's complete works in manuscript written for his beloved son John R. Kelso, Junior and his posterity, 1873–1882*, 670–77, The Huntington Library, mss HM 58109.

41. Ibid., 679.

42. Ibid., 685–86.

43. Ibid., 702.

44. Rowland Willard, Autobiography, Box 1, Folder 1, Section 1, in Rowland Willard-Elizabeth S. Willard Papers, 1825–1884, Yale Collection of Western Americana, Beinecke Rare Book and Manuscript Library. See Biographical/ Historical note, http://orbis.library.yale.edu/vwebv/holdingsInfo?searchId=911 5&recCount=50&recPointer=9&bibId=6724280.

45. Ibid., Box 1, Folder 2, Section 3.

46. Ibid., Box 1, Folder 3, Section 6.

47. For instance: "Rewards & punishments is thought by most will succeed the judgment, but the kind or amt. of corporeal or mental suffering is variously computed. The Universalian on the one extreme, and the so called orthodox comprising the popular *isms* of the day maybe considered at the other extreme." Willard, Autobiography, Box 1, Folder 3, Section 6.

48. Ibid.

49. Ibid.

50. Willard, Autobiography, Box 1, Folder 4, Section 7.

51. Ibid.

52. The organization continues to advocate complete extinction instead of eternal punishment. See Advent Christian General Conference, "Declaration of Principles": "We believe that death is a condition of unconsciousness to all persons, righteous and wicked; a condition which will remain unchanged until the resurrection at Christ's Second Coming, at which time the righteous will receive everlasting life while the wicked will be 'punished with everlasting destruction,' suffering complete *extinction of being*" (emphasis in original), http://www.adventchristian.org/Aboutus/Whatwebelieve/TheAdventChristianDeclarationofPrinciples/tabid/95/Default.aspx.

53. Membership data from the twentieth century shows 537 churches and 28,297 members in 1925; by 2007 these figures stood at 294 churches and 23,629 members. The Association of Religion Data Archives, http://www.thearda.com/Denoms/D_1101.asp.

54. Dean C. Jessee, Ronald K. Esplin, and Richard Lyman Bushman, General Editors; Dean C. Jessee, Mark Ashurst-McGee, and Richard L. Jensen, Volume Editors, *The Joseph Smith Papers. Journals*, vol. 1, *1832–1839* (Salt Lake City: The Church Historian's Press, 2008), p. xix.

55. Samuel Morris Brown, *In Heaven as It Is on Earth: Joseph Smith and the Early Mormon Conquest of Death* (New York: Oxford University Press, 2012), 9.

56. Jessee et al., *Joseph Smith Papers*, pp. xv–xvi.

57. *Doctrine and Covenants of the Church of the Latter-Day Saints: Carefully Selected from the Revelations of God, and Compiled by Joseph Smith Junior, Oliver Cowdery, Sidney Rigdon, Frederick G. Williams, Presiding Elders of said Church. Proprietors* (Kirtland, Ohio: Printed by F. G. Williams & Co. for the Proprietors, 1835), 227–28. According to an insert, this is "The first complete edition of this compilation."

58. Ibid., 227–29.

59. Ibid., 229–30.

60. Ibid., 48. See also Brown, *In Heaven as It Is on Earth*, who suggests that Smith predicted earthly corruption for the bodies of his enemies in his 1830 and 1832 visions.

61. Brown, *In Heaven as It Is on Earth*, esp. 246. See also M. Guy Bishop, "To Overcome the Last Enemy: Early Mormon Perceptions of Death," *Brigham Young University Studies* 26, no. 3 (1986): 63–79.

62. Jessee et al., *Joseph Smith Papers*, p. xvi. See also Steven C. Harper, "Infallible Proofs, Both Human and Divine: The Persuasiveness of Mormonism for Early Converts," *Religion and American Culture: A Journal of Interpretation* 10, no. 1 (Winter 2000): 99–118.

63. Parley Pratt, *The Autobiography of Parley Parker Pratt, One of the Twelve Apostles of the Church of Jesus Christ of Latter-Day Saints, Embracing the Life, Ministry and Travels, with Extracts, in Prose and Verse, from the Miscellaneous Writings, Edited by his Son, Parley P. Pratt* (New York: Published for the Editor and Proprietor by Russell Brothers, 1874), 329. On relationships in heaven, see Matthew 22:30 and note 75 in chap. 2.

64. Louise Graehl, "Story of Louise Graehl," in Carol Cornwall Madsen, ed., *Journey to Zion: Voices from the Mormon Trail* (Salt Lake City: Deseret Book Company, 1997), 508.

65. On early American debates over the porosity of the scriptural canon, see David Holland, *Sacred Borders: Continuing Revelation and Canonical Restraint in Early America* (New York: Oxford University Press, 2011).

66. This summary of Swedenborg's doctrines is culled from Sydney Ahlstrom, *A Religious History of the American People* (New Haven: Yale University Press, 1972; repr. 2004), 484–85; and Richard Kenneth Silver, "The Spiritual Kingdom in America: The Influence of Emanuel Swedenborg on American Society and Culture: 1815–1860" (PhD. diss., Stanford University, 1983), chap. 1 "Swedenborg and the Heavenly Arcana." The quote is from Ahlstrom, 484–85. See also Catherine Albanese, *A Republic of Mind and Spirit: A Cultural History of American Metaphysical Religion* (New Haven: Yale University Press, 2007). Albanese defines metaphysical religion as "turn[ing] on an individual's experience of 'mind' (instead of 'heart,' as in evangelicalism)," in which "versions of a theory of correspondence between worlds prevail" (6).

67. William Henry Holcombe, *Our Children in Heaven* (Philadelphia: J. B. Lippincott & Co., 1869), 307.

68. Ibid., 296–97.

69. Silver, "The Spiritual Kingdom in America," 44; Ahlstrom, *A Religious History of the American People*, 483; Leigh Schmidt, *Restless Souls: The Making of American Spirituality* (New York: Harper Collins, 2005; Harper San Francisco, 2006 (pb)), 45–47. On the question of influence between Mormonism and Swedenborgianism, see D. Michael Quinn, *Early Mormonism and the Magic Worldview*, revised and enlarged ed. (Salt Lake City: Signature Books, 1998), 217–19; J. B. Haws, "Joseph Smith, Emanuel Swedenborg, and Section 76: Importance of the Bible in Latter-day Revelation," in Andrew H. Hedges, J. Spencer Fluhman, and Alonzo L. Gaskill, eds., *The Doctrine and Covenants: Revelations in Context: The 37th Annual Brigham Young University Sidney B. Sperry Symposium* (Provo, UT: Religious Studies Center, Brigham Young University, and Deseret Book, 2008), 142–67; and Colleen McDannell and Bernard Lang, *Heaven: A History* (New Haven: Yale University Press, 1998; repr. Yale Nota Bene, 2001).

70. E. Brooks Holifield, *Theology in America: Christian Thought from the Age of the Puritans to the Civil War* (New Haven: Yale University Press, 2003), 205.

71. *Memoir of William Ellery Channing, with Extracts from His Correspondence and Manuscripts. In Three Volumes*, vol. 2, 4th ed. (Boston: Wm. Crosby and H. P. Nichols, 111 Washington Street; London: John Chapman, 1850), 23.

72. Quoted in Gary Scott Smith, *Heaven in the American Imagination* (New York: Oxford University Press, 2011), 55.

73. *Memoir of William Ellery Channing*, 24–25.

74. Ibid., 6.

75. S. B. Brittan, "SPIRITUALISM: ITS NATURE AND MISSIONS," in *The Shekinah*, vol. 1, 4.

76. Ibid., 8–9.

77. W. S. Courtney, "THE CELESTIAL LIFE ON EARTH," in *The Shekinah*, vol. 1, 336.

78. Ibid., 338–39.

79. Ibid., 340.

80. "Obituary. Ex-Judge Edmonds," *New York Times*, Apr. 7, 1874.

81. Hon. J. W. Edmonds, "PERSONAL EXPERIENCE," in *The Shekinah*, vol. 1, 265.

82. Ibid., 266.

83. Ibid., 269.

84. Ibid., 270–71.

85. Ibid., 271.

86. On changing attitudes toward death in Europe and America, see note 14 in the Introduction.

87. On changing burial ground styles, see Gary Laderman, *The Sacred Remains: American Attitudes Toward Death, 1799–1883* (New Haven: Yale University Press, 1996), chap. 3 "Simplicity Lost: The Urban Model of Death"; and David Charles Sloane, *The Last Great Necessity: Cemeteries in American History*

(Baltimore: Johns Hopkins University Press, 1991), esp. chap. 2 "Displacing the Dead" and chap. 3 "Mount Auburn and the Rural-Cemetery Movement." On the growing perception of death as preventable, see Charles Rosenberg, *The Cholera Years: The United States in 1832, 1849, and 1866*, 2nd ed. (Chicago: University of Chicago Press, 1987), which adopts a too-simple secularization narrative but is nonetheless a classic.

88. Henry Harbaugh, in *The Heavenly Recognition; or, An Earnest and Scriptural Discussion of the Question, Will We Know Our Friends in Heaven?* (1851) even suggested that "God might erase the saints' memories of any earthly relationships that might cause them pain"—including relationships with those who might end up in hell. Smith, *Heaven in the American Imagination*, chap. 4 "Heaven as Home," 82.

89. David L. Ogden, Oct. 5, 1852, entry, "Thoughts on Men and Things, Vol VI," General Collection, Beinecke Rare Book and Manuscript Library, Yale University.

90. Horace Bushnell, *Discourses on Christian Nurture* (Boston: Massachusetts Sabbath School Society, Depository, No. 13 Cornhill, 1847), 6–7.

91. Ibid., 55.

92. Account in Debby Applegate, *The Most Famous Man in America: The Biography of Henry Ward Beecher* (New York: Three Leaves Press, 2006), 44–46.

93. Harriet Beecher Stowe, *The Minister's Wooing* (New York: Derby and Jackson, 119 Nassau Street, 1859), 343, 346.

94. Ibid., 349.

95. Catharine Beecher, *Common Sense Applied to Religion; or, the Bible and the People* (New York: Harper & Brothers, Publishers, Franklin Square; Montreal: Benjamin Dawson, 1857), p. xii.

96. Ibid., 237.

97. Ibid., 242.

98. Here she was no different from Finney and other evangelicals who suggested that the damned would never enjoy heaven because of their "training in selfishness and sin." But for Finney, only rebirth could undo this training, whereas for Beecher, the key was right training from childhood. On Finney and other revivalists' contention that "the unredeemed would not enjoy heaven if God admitted them," see Smith, *Heaven in the American Imagination*, 67.

99. Beecher, *Common Sense*, 244.

100. Ibid., 282.

101. See also Smith, *Heaven in the American Imagination*, 79, 83; and Douglas, "Heaven Our Home: Consolation Literature in the Northern United States, 1830–1880," *American Quarterly* 26, no. 5, Special Issue: Death in America (Dec., 1974): 496–515.

102. Kelso, "Ianthus," in *John R. Kelso's complete works in manuscript*, n.d. (but likely written around the early 1860s, after his split from the church), 44.

103. McDannell and Lang, *Heaven: A History*.

104. The estimate comes from John D. Unruh, *The Plains Across: The Overland Emigrants and the Trans-Mississippi West, 1840–60* (Urbana: University of Illinois

Press, 1979), 408. The 10 percent figure comes from Ezra Meeker, *Personal Experiences on the Oregon Trail Sixty Years Ago* (St. Louis: McAdoo Printing Company, 1912), 27. In my survey of forty overland trail diaries, twenty-two kept track of graves, eleven men and eleven women. On the culture of overland migration, see John Mack Faragher, *Women and Men on the Overland Trail* (New Haven: Yale University Press, 1979).

105. "The Letter of Lucia Loraine Williams," to "Mother," "Milwaukee, [Oregon] September 16, '51," in Kenneth L. Holmes, ed., *Covered Wagon Women*, vol. 3 (Glendale, CA: Arthur H. Clark Company, 1984), 132.

106. Esther M. Lockhart Memoir, 1942, in ibid., 158–59.

107. S. Mathews to family of Benjamin F. Adams, Dec. 13, 1849, in Benjamin F. Adams Papers, Western Americana Collection, Beinecke Rare Book and Manuscript Library, Yale University.

108. See Jon Coleman, *Vicious: Wolves and Men in America* (New Haven: Yale University Press, 2004), 169–71. Lucia Williams and her husband, for instance, "had [their son's] grave covered with stones to protect it from wild beasts" (*Covered Wagon Women*, 132).

109. Peter H. Hassrick, "Prairie Burial," in *Forging an American Identity: The Art of William Ranney with a Catalogue of His Works*, by Linda Bantel and Peter H. Hassrick, with essays by Sarah E. Boehme and Mark F. Bockrath, ed. Kathleen Luhrs (Cody, WY: Buffalo Bill Historical Center, 2006), 49–51.

110. Orange Jacobs, for instance, proposed "that…we organize ourselves into a semi-military company" for protection against Native Americans. *Memoir of Orange Jacobs, Written by Himself: Containing Many Interesting, Amusing and Instructive Incidents of a Life of Eighty Years or More, Fifty-Six Years of Which Were Spent in Oregon and Washington* (Seattle: Lowman & Hanford Co., 1908), 30.

111. "Wesley Tonner's Letter in Description of the Plains Journey with the Burrel Train," in Mary Burrell's Book, 1854, Western Americana Collection, Beinecke Rare Book and Manuscript Library, Yale University.

112. Gary Laderman, in *The Sacred Remains*, shows how bodies sacralized the frontier: "Literally inserting the dead into the physical environment served to reinforce the sacrality of the 'New Israel' and contributed to the process of westward expansion. Protestants who settled the frontier believed that the ground containing the dead acquired a special significance for the young nation and therefore became the domain and responsibility of those who followed" (*The Sacred Remains*, 66–67). On preserving their memory, see David Wrobel, *Promised Lands: Promotion, Memory, and the Creation of the American West* (Lawrence: University of Kansas, 2002), esp. 99–100.

113. Meeker, *Personal Experiences*, 128, 27.

114. See Ann Fabian, *The Skull Collectors: Race, Science, and America's Unburied Dead* (Chicago: University of Chicago Press, 2010). Samuel Morris Brown, in *In Heaven as It Is on Earth*, suggests that Mormons also tapped into the antebellum grave-hunting craze, but did so to trace their sacred genealogical connections

to Native Americans, or Lamanites: "While other American Eden visions implicitly eliminated Native peoples, seeing their land as available for white colonization, Smith recovered Eden on the American frontier in part because the Indians, his remnant of Joseph, had lived and died there" (114). See also section on "Native Relics," 72–73.

115. Harriet Talcott Buckingham, "Crossing the Plains in 1851," May 5, 1851, in *Covered Wagon Women*, vol. 3, 18.

116. Diaries of Frederick G. Niles, May 23, 1860.

117. On the rise of Anglo-Saxonism in antebellum America, see Reginald Horsman, *Race and Manifest Destiny: The Origins of American Racial Anglo-Saxonism* (Cambridge, MA: Harvard University Press, 1981). See Fabian, *The Skull Collectors*, on nineteenth-century naturalists like Samuel Morton who tried to compare skull sizes to prove Anglo superiority.

118. See note 93 in chap. 2. Race was never just about supposed corporeal/physical difference; religious categories shaped assumptions about difference and continued to do so even after language of physical difference became more prominent in the late eighteenth and nineteenth centuries. On the limitations of construing race as biological, see Barnor Hesse, "Racialized Modernity: An Analytics of White Mythologies," *Ethnic and Racial Studies* 30, no. 4 (July 2007): 643–63.

119. On the evangelical underpinnings of the secular, see Modern, *Secularism in Antebellum America*, and Tracy Fessenden, *Culture and Redemption: Religion, The Secular, and American Literature* (Princeton: Princeton University Press, 2007). On an earlier move toward seeing "heathenness" as "hereditary," see Rebecca Goetz, *The Baptism of Early Virginia: How Christianity Created Race* (Baltimore: Johns Hopkins University Press, 2012). On Christianity as a source of racism, see Forrest Wood, *The Arrogance of Faith: Christianity and Race in America from the Colonial Era to the Twentieth Century* (New York: Knopf, 1990), a deeply flawed volume with some provocative ideas. For a more balanced perspective that emphasizes the importance of monogenesis in keeping racism in check, see Colin Kidd, *The Forging of Races: Race and Scripture in the Protestant Atlantic World, 1600–2000* (Cambridge: Cambridge University Press, 2006).

CHAPTER 5

1. "Anti-Slavery. From the Anti-Slavery Lecturer. Lecture XI. Religious Bearings of the Subject—Slavery versus Christianity—Duties of Christians," *The Liberator*, Dec. 20, 1839.

2. Here I disagree with Gary Scott Smith, who contends that "focus on making money, getting ahead, and the kinder, gentler aspects of heaven, including family reunions, coupled with debates over slavery, fears of disunion, and the calamity of the Civil War, combined to largely push hell from public discussion" by

mid-century (*Heaven in the American Imagination* (New York: Oxford University Press, 2011), 86).

3. See Joanne B. Freeman, *Affairs of Honor: National Politics in the New Republic* (New Haven: Yale University Press, 2001). Freeman shows how verbal (and other) insults could pack a real punch. She focuses on politicians in the early republic, but the idea that words could function as weapons of honor applies to the antislavery controversy as well.

4. See note 15 in the Introduction.

5. See Bruce Dorsey, *Reforming Men and Women: Gender in the Antebellum City* (Ithaca, NY: Cornell University Press, 2002), esp. chap. 4 "Slavery."

6. See David Brion Davis, "The Emergence of Immediatism in British and American Antislavery Thought," *Mississippi Valley Historical Review* 39, no. 2 (Sept. 1962): 209–30; and Anne C. Loveland, "Evangelicalism and 'Immediate Emancipation' in American Antislavery Thought," *Journal of Southern History* 32, no. 2 (May 1966): 172–88.

7. Theodore Dwight Weld to Arthur Tappan, Joshua Leavitt, and Elizur Wright, Jr., Lane Seminary, Walnut Hills, Ohio, Nov. 22, 1833, in *The Letters of Theodore Dwight Weld, Angelina Grimké Weld and Sarah Grimké, 1822–1844*, vol. 1 (New York: D. Appleton-Century Company Incorporated, 1934. Prepared and published under the direction of the American Historical Association), 120.

8. David W. Blight, "William Lloyd Garrison at Two Hundred: His Radicalism and His Legacy for Our Time," in James Brewer Stewart, ed., *William Lloyd Garrison at Two Hundred: History, Legacy, and Memory* (New Haven: Yale University Press, 2008), 4.

9. William Lloyd Garrison, Baltimore, to Ebenezer Dole, Hallowell, Maine, July 14, 1830, in Wendell Phillips Garrison and Francis Jackson Garrison, eds., *William Lloyd Garrison, 1805–1879: The Story of His Life Told by His Children*, vol. 1, *1805–1835* (New York: The Century Co., 1885), 194–95.

10. Amos A. Phelps, *Lectures on Slavery and Its Remedy* (Boston: Published by the New-England Anti-Slavery Society, 1834; repr. St. Clair Shores, MI: Scholarly Press, 1970), 199.

11. On the Union Missionary Society, founded in Hartford in 1841, see C. Peter Ripley, ed., *The Black Abolitionist Papers, vol. 3, The United States, 1830–1846* (Chapel Hill: University of North Carolina Press, 1991), 36.

12. Thomas Lafon, *The Great Obstruction to the Conversion of Souls at Home and Abroad* (New York: Published by the Union Missionary Society, 1843), 10.

13. Ibid., 23, 20.

14. Ibid., 16.

15. Ibid., 19.

16. Charles Colcock Jones, *Suggestions on the Religious Instruction of the Negroes in the Southern States; Together with an Appendix Containing Forms of Church Registers, Form of a Constitution, and Plans of Different Denominations of Christians* (Philadelphia: Presbyterian Board of Publication, 1847), 7.

17. On the Jones plantations, see T. Erskine Clark, *Dwelling Place: A Plantation Epic* (New Haven: Yale University Press, 2005).

18. Jones, *Suggestions*, 7, 9.

19. See Eugene Genovese, *Roll, Jordan, Roll: The World the Slaves Made* (New York: Vintage Books, 1976), 186: "A great burst of proselytizing among the slaves followed the Nat Turner revolt. Whereas previously many slaveholders had feared slaves with religion—and the example of Turner himself confirmed their fears—now they feared slaves without religion even more. They came to see Christianity primarily as a means of social control."

20. Jones, *Suggestions*, 40. 1 Timothy 6:1–8 includes such exhortations as: "They that have believing masters, let them not despise them, because they are brethren; but rather do them service, because they are faithful and beloved, partakers of the benefit"; "If any man teach otherwise, and consent not to wholesome words, even the words of our Lord Jesus Christ, and to the doctrine which is according to godliness; He is proud, knowing nothing"; "And having food and raiment let us be therewith content" (KJV).

21. Jones, *Suggestions*, 29, 40.

22. See also Smith, *Heaven in the American Imagination*, 89.

23. See Acts 5:1–10.

24. Alexander Glennie, "Sermon V," in *Sermons Preached on Plantations to Congregations of Negroes* (Charleston: Published and Sold by A. E. Miller, No. 4 Broad-street, 1844; repr. Freeport, NY: Books for Libraries Press, 1971), 31–32.

25. Glennie, "Sermon IV," in ibid., 26.

26. See Peter P. Hinks, *David Walker's Appeal to the Coloured Citizens of the World* (University Park: Pennsylvania State University Press, 2000).

27. David Walker, *Walker's Appeal, in Four Articles; Together with a Preamble, to the Coloured Citizens of the World, but in Particular, and Very Expressly, to those of the United States of America, written in Boston, state of Massachusetts, September 28, 1829. Third and Last Edition, with Additional Notes, Corrections, &c.* (Boston: Revised and Published by David Walker, 1830), 73–74.

28. Ibid., 74, 31.

29. Ibid., 40.

30. Frederick Douglass, *Narrative of the Life of Frederick Douglass, An American Slave. Written by Himself. With Related Documents*, 2nd ed., ed. David Blight (Boston: Bedford/St. Martin's, 2003), 122.

31. Ibid., 123.

32. Maria W. Stewart, *Productions of Mrs. Maria W. Stewart, Presented to the First African Baptist Church & Society, of the City of Boston* (Boston: Published by Friends of Freedom and Virtue, 1835), 3, 5.

33. Ibid., 51–52.

34. Ibid., 21.

35. Ibid., 65–66.

36. Ibid., 52–54.

37. Ibid., 8.

38. Ibid.

39. Ibid., 64–67.

40. Ibid., 6.

41. Ibid., 25.

42. Ibid., 60.

43. Henry Highland Garnet, *An Address to the Slaves of the United States of America* (Salem, NH: Arno Press, 1969; repr. ed. 1984; General Editor: William Loren Katz), 92–93.

44. On slavery as hell, hell for slavemasters, and heaven as freedom, see Lewis Baldwin, " 'A Home in Dat Rock': Afro-American Folk Sources and Slave Visions of Heaven and Hell," *Journal of Religious Thought* 41, no. 1 (Spring/Summer 1984): 38–57; and Smith, *Heaven in the American Imagination*, 93–96 (Smith draws heavily from Baldwin in his analysis). On slave converts transforming the "hell without fires" of slavery into their own "New Jerusalem," see Yolanda Pierce, *Hell without Fires: Slavery, Christianity, and the Antebellum Spiritual Narrative* (Gainesville: University Press of Florida, 2005). See also Albert J. Raboteau's classic *Slave Religion: The "Invisible Institution" in the Antebellum South* (New York: Oxford University Press, [1978] 2004).

45. "Slavery was 'Hell Without Fires,' " in George Rawick, ed., *God Struck Me Dead: Religious Conversion Experiences and Autobiographies of Negro Ex-Slaves*, Social Science Source Documents No. 2 (Nashville: Social Science Institute, Fisk University, 1945; repr. Westport, CT: Greenwood Publishing Company, 1972), 215.

46. Thomas James, *A Vision: Scene in the Nether World—Purporting to Be a Conversation between the Ghost of a Southern Slaveholding Clergyman and the Devil! In Wonderful Eventful Life of Rev. Thomas James/by Himself* (Post-Express Printing Company, 1887). In the Library of Congress, *African American Perspectives: Pamphlets from the Daniel A. P. Murray Collection, 1818–1907*, http://memory.loc.gov/cgi-bin/query/r?ammem/murray:@field(DOCID+@lit(lcrbmrptob22div4)).

47. On ironic reversal in slave religion, see Raboteau, *Slave Religion*, esp. chap. 6 "Religion, Rebellion, and Docility"; and Kathryn Gin, " 'The Heavenization of Earth': African American Visions and Uses of the Afterlife, 1863–1901," *Slavery and Abolition: A Journal of Slave and Post-Slave Studies* 31, no. 2 (2010): 207–31.

48. Ala Alryyes, trans. and ed., *A Muslim American Slave: The Life of Omar Ibn Said* (Madison: University of Wisconsin Press, 2011), 16, 8.

49. Ibid., 18.

50. Ibid., 51–53. For Alryyes's interpretation of Omar's inclusion of the *sura*, see 22–23.

51. Douglass, *Narrative of the Life*, 45.

52. Ibid., 63, 81–82, 74.

53. "Document 37: Report by the Committee on Slavery of the New England Conference of the African Methodist Episcopal Church. Presented at the Bethel African Methodist Episcopal Church. Providence, Rhode Island. 26 January 1854," in *The Black Abolitionist Papers*, vol. 4, *The United States, 1847–1858*, ed. C. Peter Ripley et al. (Chapel Hill: University of North Carolina Press, 1991), 196.

54. Theodore Dwight Weld, *American Slavery As It Is: Testimony of a Thousand Witnesses* (New York: Published by the American Anti-Slavery Society, Office, No. 143 Nassau Street, 1839), 61.

55. *The Child's Anti-Slavery Book: Containing a few Words about American Slave Children* (New York: Published by Carlton & Porter, Sunday-School Union, 200 Mulberry-Street, 1859; repr. Miami: Mnemosyne Publishing Co., Inc., 1969, from a copy in the Fisk University Library Negro Collection), 36.

56. Ibid., 62.

57. Phelps, *Lectures on Slavery and its Remedy*, 100–101.

58. Lydia Maria Child, *An Appeal in Favor of that Class of Americans Called Africans*. (New York: Published by John S. Taylor, 1836; repr. New York: Arno Press and the New York Times, 1968), 22.

59. Ibid., 31.

60. Quoted in Jack Turner, "Emerson, Slavery, and Citizenship," *Raritan: A Quarterly Review* 28, no. 2 (Fall 2008): 133.

61. William Lloyd Garrison, "Address before the Free People of Color, April 1833," in *William Lloyd Garrison, 1805–1879*, vol. 1, 336.

62. On Garrison's evolving beliefs, see William L. Van Deburg, "William Lloyd Garrison and the 'Pro-Slavery Priesthood,'" *Journal of the American Academy of Religion* 43, no. 2 (June 1975): 224–37. Van Deburg argues that Garrison's beliefs shifted as "Boston's theologically orthodox clergymen-ministers of the same stamp as those he had worshipped under as a youth in Newburyport" rejected his immediatism, while freethinkers proved more amenable to his message.

63. Reprinted in *The Liberator*, Oct. 12, 1833, and in *William Lloyd Garrison, 1805–1879*, vol. 1, 386.

64. "To Hon. Harrison Gray Otis, Letter I," *The Liberator*, Sept. 5, 1835; reprinted in *William Lloyd Garrison, 1805–1879*, vol. 1, 513.

65. "To Hon. Peleg Sprague, Letter I," *The Liberator*, Sept. 5, 1835; also in *William Lloyd Garrison, 1805–1879*, vol. 1, 505–6.

66. *William Lloyd Garrison, 1805–1879*, vol. 1, 514.

67. Ibid.; *Boston Atlas*, Oct. 22, quoted in *Right and Wrong in Boston: Report of the Boston Female Antislavery Society; with a Concise Statement of Events, Previous and Subsequent to the Annual Meeting of 1835* (Boston: Published by the Society, 1836), 57–59.

68. "To Hon. Peleg Sprague, Letter I," *The Liberator*, Sept. 5, 1835.

69. Phelps, *Lectures on Slavery and Its Remedy*, 58.

70. Walker, *Walker's Appeal*, 45.

71. Stewart, *Productions of Mrs. Maria Stewart*, 18–19.

72. Molly Oshatz, *Slavery and Sin: The Fight against Slavery and the Rise of Liberal Protestantism* (New York: Oxford University Press, 2012), 61.

73. On moderates who tried to work within the churches, see Oshatz, *Slavery and Sin*, and John R. McKivigan, *The War against Proslavery Religion: Abolitionism and the Northern Churches, 1830–1865* (Ithaca, NY: Cornell University Press, 1984); on come-outers and nonresistants, see Stewart, *Garrison at Two Hundred*, and George Fredrickson, ed., *Great Lives Observed: William Lloyd Garrison* (Englewood Cliffs, NJ: Prentice-Hall, 1968); on radical abolitionists who turned to violence in the 1850s, see John Stauffer, *The Black Hearts of Men: Radical Abolitionists and the Transformation of Race* (Cambridge, MA: Harvard University Press, 2001). See also James Brewer Stewart, *Holy Warriors: The Abolitionists and American Slavery* (New York: Hill and Wang, 1976), and John R. McKivigan, ed., *Abolitionism in American Religion* (New York: Garland Publishing, Inc., 1999).

74. Van Deburg, "Garrison and the 'Pro-Slavery Priesthood,'" 228–29.

75. *William Lloyd Garrison, 1805–1879*, vol. 1, 226–27; originally in *The Liberator*, Mar. 5, 1831; also quoted in Van Deburg, "William Lloyd Garrison and the 'Pro-Slavery Priesthood,'" 227.

76. "The Rights of God—Free Discussion—Freedom of the Press," in *The Liberator*, Jan. 30, 1846, also quoted in Van Deburg, "William Lloyd Garrison and the 'Pro-Slavery Priesthood,'" 235 n. 34.

77. William Lloyd Garrison to Elizabeth Pease, Boston, June 20, 1849, in Wendell Phillips Garrison and Francis Jackson Garrison, eds., *William Lloyd Garrison, 1805–1879: The Story of His Life Told by His Children*, vol. 3, *1841–1860* (New York: The Century Co., 1889), 263–64.

78. *The Liberator*, June 17, 1853; also in *Proceedings of the Hartford Bible Convention*; and quoted in *William Lloyd Garrison, 1805–1879*, vol. 3, 383, 386.

79. *The Liberator*, June 4, 1858; also in ibid., 473–74.

80. "The Death of President Polk, June 22, 1849," in William E. Cain, ed., *William Lloyd Garrison and the Fight against Slavery* (Boston: Bedford/St. Martin's, 1994), 121.

81. Garrison famously made this denunciation at the annual meeting of the Massachusetts Anti-Slavery Society in Faneuil Hall. *William Lloyd Garrison, 1805–1879*, vol. 3, 88.

82. *The Liberator*, June 4, 1858.

83. "'Southern Desperation,' November 16, 1860," in Cain, *William Lloyd Garrison and the Fight against Slavery*, 162.

84. See Freeman, *Affairs of Honor*.

85. "A Boston correspondent of the Picayune. . .," *Weekly Houston Telegraph*, June 26, 1844.

86. Stauffer, *The Black Hearts of Men*, 19–20.

87. John R. McKivigan, "Smith, Gerrit," *American National Biography Online*, http://www.anb.org/articles/15/15-00627.html.

88. Stauffer, *The Black Hearts of Men*.

89. Quoted in ibid., 38; see also 243–44.

90. Gerrit Smith, "The Religion of Reason," Peterboro, Feb. 21, 1858, in *Sermons and Speeches of Gerrit Smith* (New York: For Sale by Ross & Tousey, No. 121 Nassau Street, 1861; repr. New York: Arno Press and *The New York Times*, 1969), 6.

91. Smith, "The Religion of Reason," Peterboro, June 19, 1859, in ibid., 50.

92. Smith, "The Religion of Reason," Peterboro, Feb. 21, 1858, in ibid., 12.

93. Smith, "The One Test of Character," Peterboro, July 22, 1860, in ibid., 81.

94. Smith, "The Religion of Reason," Peterboro, Feb. 21, 1858, in ibid., 12–13.

95. Smith, "The Religion of Reason," Peterboro, Jan. 23, 1859, in ibid., 42.

96. Stauffer, *The Black Hearts of Men*, 243–44.

97. Ibid., 262.

98. Smith, "War Meeting in Peterboro—Speech of Gerrit Smith," Apr. 27, 1861, in *Sermons and Speeches of Gerrit Smith*, 183.

99. Theodore Parker, *Autobiography, Poems and Prayers* (Boston: American Unitarian Association, 25 Beacon Street, [1911?]), 295–96.

100. See Dean Grodzins, *American Heretic: Theodore Parker and Transcendentalism* (Chapel Hill: University of North Carolina Press, 2002), 62–73.

101. Parker, *Autobiography*, 316–17.

102. Ibid., 382.

103. Ibid., 58.

104. Ibid., 135–36.

105. *William Lloyd Garrison, 1805–1879*, vol. 3, 243; originally in the *Liberator*, Sept. 19, 1851; also quoted in Van Deburg, "William Lloyd Garrison and the 'Pro-Slavery Priesthood,'" 236.

106. Theodore Parker, "The Chief Sins of the People: A Sermon Delivered at the Melodeon, Boston, on Fast-Day, April 10, 1851" (Boston: Benjamin H. Greene, 1851), 33.

107. See Elizabeth Fox-Genovese and Eugene Genovese, *The Mind of the Master Class: History and Faith in the Southern Slaveholders' Worldview* (New York: Cambridge University Press, 2005), for elite southern views on the Bible and slavery.

108. AMOR PATRIAE, *The Blasphemy of Abolitionism Exposed: Servitude and the Rights of the South, Vindicated. A Bible Argument. Together with REFLECTIONS drawn from the premises, touching the several interests of the UNITED STATES, and the evil consequences that must result to the Northern States in case of DIVISION: the legitimate fruits of their unhallowed meddling, in violation of all principle and good faith—and above all, GOD'S HOLY WORD! which is so plain, "That a wayfaring*

man, though a fool, may not err therein" (New York: 1850. A new edition, revised, corrected and enlarged), 4.

109. Ibid., 23–24.

110. Fred Ross, *Slavery Ordained of God* (J. B. Lippincott & Co., 1859; repr. New York: Negro Universities Press, A Division of Greenwood Publishing Corp., 1969), 37.

111. Letter from Eliza Margaretta Chew Mason to Lydia Maria Child, Nov. 11, 1859, in *Letters of Lydia Maria Child with a Biographical Introduction by John G. Whittier and Appendix by Wendell Phillips* (Boston: Houghton, Mifflin & Co., 1883), 280.

112. George Fitzhugh, *Cannibals All! Or, Slaves without Masters* (Richmond, Va.: A. Morris, Publisher, 1857), chap. 26 "Christian Morality Impracticable in Free Society—but the Natural Morality of Slave Society."

113. "The Enemies of the Union," *New Hampshire Patriot* 12, no. 595 (Feb. 19, 1846): 2.

114. Quoted in the *Liberator*, Apr. 21, 1843.

115. "From the Exeter News-Letter: THE ULTRA ABOLITION REFORMERS," reprinted in the *Liberator*, June 27, 1845.

116. Frederick Douglass provides perhaps the best-known example of a slave who, upon hearing of the abolitionists, was encouraged that some people were fighting for the cause of slaves mired in the "horrible pit" of slavery (*Narrative*, 68–69).

117. Chandra Manning, in *What This Cruel War Was Over: Soldiers, Slavery, and the Civil War* (New York: Vintage, 2008), shows how slavery was central to ordinary soldiers' understanding of the war's causes on both sides.

118. Rowland Willard, Autobiography, Hammonton, Jan. 1864, Box 1, Folder 4, Section 8.

119. Richard K. Fenn and Marianne Delaporte, "Hell as Residual Category: Possibilities Excluded from the Social System," in *The Blackwell Companion to Sociology of Religion* (Blackwell Publishing, 2001; Blackwell Reference Online, 01 December 2008), http://www.blackwellreference.com/subscriber/tocnode?id=g9780631212416_chunk_g978063121241623.

120. See Martin Marty, "Hell Disappeared: No One Noticed," *Harvard Theological Review* 78, no. 3/4 (July–Oct. 1985): 381–82. Marty notes that among many scholars "the concept of hell, may raise the arcane or quaint to new levels of bizarerrie" (381–82). See also note 4 in the Introduction. In contrast to this view, scholars of African American religion have shown how the concept of hell could be invoked for radical means, a perspective with which this chapter largely agrees. See Pierce, *Hell without Fires*; Baldwin, "A Home in Dat Rock"; Raboteau, *Slave Religion*, esp. chap. 6 "Religion, Rebellion, and Docility"; and Fox-Genovese and Genovese, *The Mind of the Master Class*, esp. 558–62.

CHAPTER 6

1. Lewis N. T. Allen, "Diary of a Union Soldier," Oct. 19, 1863, in Papers of Lewis N. T. Allen, 1863–1866, The Huntington Library, San Marino, CA, mss HM 72238–72266.

2. Steven E. Woodworth acknowledges that "the writings of Civil War soldiers reveal a realization that not everyone would be going to heaven" in *While God Is Marching On: The Religious World of Civil War Soldiers* (Lawrence: University of Kansas, 2001), 46. Yet he asserts that "preachers seemed to mention hell more frequently and directly" than soldiers, since "so grim was that prospect that those who took it most seriously mentioned it very rarely in their letters" (47). While this is undoubtedly true, soldiers' private diaries sometimes reveal more than they may have wanted to write to family and friends.

3. On religious leaders hurling self-righteous rhetoric at each other, see Harry Stout, *Upon the Altar of the Nation: A Moral History of the American Civil War* (New York: Viking, 2006). Much has been written about northern and southern interpretations of the war as a cataclysmic apocalyptic event. See James Moorhead, *American Apocalypse: Yankee Protestants and the Civil War, 1860–1869* (New Haven: Yale University Press, 1978); and Terrie Dopp Aamodt, *Righteous Armies, Holy Cause* (Macon, GA: Mercer University Press, 2002).

4. By suggesting that hell mattered in the Civil War, I am departing from recent scholarship by Mark Schantz, *Awaiting the Heavenly Country: The Civil War and America's Culture of Death* (Ithaca, NY: Cornell University Press, 2008), and Drew Gilpin Faust, *This Republic of Suffering: Death and the American Civil War* (2008; New York: Vintage Civil War Library Edition, 2009). Schantz has argued that the antebellum culture of death facilitated soldiers' willingness to fight to the bone, since they expected to end up in heavenly bliss should they fall in the line of battle. Following along these lines, Faust suggests that mid-nineteenth-century Americans "denied" death "through an active and concerted work of reconceptualization that rendered it a cultural preoccupation. Redefined as eternal life, death was celebrated in mid-nineteenth century America." She also claims that "hell became less and less a subject of worry or dread" by the time of the Civil War (177–78) and that the choice most men faced was simply between death and immortality (174). But I would suggest that belief in an afterlife did not mean the denial of death—for many nineteenth-century Americans, the afterlife was central to what death meant, and the choice was not between death and immortality, but between heaven and hell.

In arguing for continuity, as well as change, I also depart from scholarship that suggests that the war marked a turning point between belief and doubt, credulousness and skepticism. Andrew Delbanco, for instance, argues that the sheer scale of violence and death challenged prevailing religious explanations for suffering, making injury and fatality seem more a result of bad luck than of God's providence (chap. 4 "The Loss of Providence," in *The Death of Satan: How*

Americans Have Lost the Sense of Evil (New York: Farrar, Straus & Giroux, 1995)). And Faust claims that "Civil War carnage transformed the mid-nineteenth century's growing sense of religious doubt into a crisis of belief that propelled many Americans to redefine or even reject their faith in a benevolent and responsive deity" (210). Faust, and to a greater extent, Delbanco, rely on the writings of literary elites to make these claims. Still, as this chapter suggests, I do see some change over time in American attitudes toward damnation as a result of the war. Here I differ from Woodworth who contends that "Very few [soldiers] gave signs of becoming embittered or losing their faith," and that "one of the most remarkable aspects of the Civil War may be how little it changed, rather than how much . . . ." (*While God Is Marching On*, 292).

My approach, which relies on the voices of ordinary people to complicate arguments that claim to be comprehensive, is sympathetic to that of George Rable, who provides a more sweeping and nuanced interpretation than in previous scholarship. In *God's Almost Chosen Peoples: A Religious History of the American Civil War* (Chapel Hill: University of North Carolina Press, 2010), Rable offers a plethora of perspectives. "Some men figured they would not likely survive the war, tried to control their anxieties, and took comfort in the promises of salvation," he notes. "For others even the fear of death paled before their fear of hell and doubts about whether they were truly ready to meet their maker; and then there were poignant stories of soldiers who had once had faith but let it slip away" (167). Rable also sees the outcome of the war as mixed, with some clinging to the faiths that had carried them through, and others questioning the bases of their beliefs.

5. Henry Breidenthal, "Civil War diary of Henry Breidenthal, 1861, Oct. 10–Nov. 12," Oct. 11, 1861, The Huntington Library, San Marino, CA, mss HM 68485–68486. See also chap. 5 "Temptations of the Camp," in Rable, *God's Almost Chosen Peoples*.

6. Breidenthal, "Civil War diary," Oct. 27, 1861.

7. Ibid., Oct. 10, 1861.

8. Ibid.

9. Ibid., Nov. 10, 1861.

10. Ibid., Nov. 12, 1861.

11. Kelso, "Speech Delivered at Mt. Vernon Mo. Apr. 23rd 1864," in *John R. Kelso's complete works in manuscript written for his beloved son John R. Kelso, Junior and his posterity, 1873–1882*, 3 (emphasis in original), The Huntington Library, mss HM 58109.

12. Kelso, "Autobiography," in *John R. Kelso's complete works*, 744.

13. Ibid., 744–45.

14. Ibid.

15. J. C. Granbery, "An Address to the Soldiers of the Southern Armies" (Richmond, Va.: Soldiers' Tract Association, M. E. Church, South, between 1861 and 1865), 8–9.

16. "Words of Counsel to Confederate Soldiers," No. 18 (Protestant Episcopal Church Publishing Association, Charlotte, N.C., 1862?), 21.

17. George Shane Phillips, "Diary, 1841, Sept. 1–1842, Aug. 13," in Papers of George S. Phillips, 1840–1904, the PHILLIPS (George Shane) COLLECTION, The Huntington Library, San Marino, CA, Huntington mss Phillips papers. Sermon notes are handwritten in the back of the diary (undated).

18. "49th Ohio Volunteer Infantry," from Whitelaw Reid, *Ohio in the War* (Cincinnati, Ohio: Moore, Wilstach, and Baldwin, 1868), http://my.ohio.voyager.net/~lstevens/49oh.html. Thanks to Peter Blodgett for his assistance in deciphering Phillips's regimental information.

19. George Phillips to "My Dear Wife," Camp Drake, Murfreesboro Tenn., June 1, 1863, and June 13, 1863, in Papers of George S. Phillips.

20. David Weston, *Among the Wounded; U.S. Christian Commission: Experiences of a Delegate* (Philadelphia: Jas. B. Rodgers, Printer, 52 & 54 North Sixth Street, 1864), 14.

21. Weston, letter to Rev. Lemuel Moss, Worcester, Mass., July 28, 1864, in ibid., 6.

22. Ibid., 7.

23. A. S. Billingsley, *Christianity in the War. Containing an Account of the Sufferings, Conversions, Prayers, Dying Requests, Last Words, and Deaths of Soldiers and Officers in the Hospital, Camp, Prison, and on the Battle-Field* (Philadelphia: Claxton, Remsen & Haffelfinger, 819 & 821 Market Street, 1872), p. vi.

24. Ibid., 33–35.

25. A. D. Betts, *Experience of a Confederate Chaplain, 1861–1864* (Greenville? S.C., 190–?), 73–74.

26. Woodworth notes that Union chaplains made more than Confederates ($145/month, comparable to a cavalry captain, versus $80/month). But on both sides "Inadequacies of pay and provision and uncertainties of privilege added to the already substantial difficulties of recruiting and keeping an adequate number of chaplains. Chaplains were always in short supply" (Woodworth, *While God Is Marching On*, chap. 8, esp. 145–47).

27. George Phillips to Mrs. Elizabeth Phillips, Camp Drake, Murfreesboro Tenn., June 20, 1863, in Papers of George S. Phillips.

28. "Books for soldiers: For the purpose of making arrangements for the systematic distribution of books and tracts among our soldiers. . ." (Boston: American Tract Society, 1861).

29. See Woodworth, *While God Is Marching On*, 163–65: "Much of the literature that was distributed was supplied by the Evangelical Tract Society of the Confederacy, which was organized in Petersburg, Virginia, in July 1861 and supported by the various denominations throughout the South. During the course of the war, it issued more than 100 different tracts with a total print run estimated at some 50 million pages.... Nor was it the only source of such literature, even in the South. The Methodist Episcopal Church, South, also established its own Soldier's Tract Society."

30. See chap. 5; also Elizabeth Fox-Genovese and Eugene Genovese, *The Mind of the Master Class: History and Faith in the Southern Slaveholders' Worldview* (New York: Cambridge University Press, 2005).

31. Rev. John E. Edwards, "A Word of Warning to an Impenitent Sinner" (Richmond, Va.: Soldiers' Tract Association, M. E. Church, South, between 1861 and 1865), 1.

32. Rev. John E. Edwards, "The Wounded Soldier" (Raleigh, NC: s.n., between 1861 and 1865), esp. 4–7. On evangelicalism coming to be associated with southern manhood (where once it had been scorned), see Christine Leigh Heyrman, *Southern Cross: The Beginnings of the Bible Belt* (New York: Alfred A. Knopf, 1997).

33. On domesticity and motherhood in the South, see Scott Stephan, *Redeeming the Southern Family: Evangelical Women and Domestic Devotion in the Antebellum South* (Athens: University of Georgia Press, 2008).

34. "Jesus, the Soldier's Friend, by a Young Lady of Virginia" (Petersburg, Va.: Printed at the Register Office, 1864), 4. The "Young Lady of Virginia" is identified as A. M. Lorraine of Abingdon, Virginia, who also authored *Donald Adair: A Novel* (Virginia: Peter Cottom, 1828—suggesting she was not so "young" after all by the 1860s!).

35. Granbery, "An Address," 3, 8, 11, 2, 12.

36. American Tract Society, *The Soldiers' Hymn-Book, with Tunes* (Published by the Boston Young Men's Christian Association. Rooms, 5 Tremont Temple. From the Press of the Am. Tract Soc., 150 Nassau-St., New York, 1861?; back cover: Presented by the United States Christian Commission), inside title page.

37. "Will You Go?" in ibid., 20–21; Wm. B. Bradbury, "Oh Say, Will You Be There?" in ibid., 21–22; "Tune, Meribah," in ibid., 23.

38. William Batchelder Bradbury, *Bradbury's Golden Chain of Sabbath School Melodies: Comprising a Great Variety of New Music and Hymns Composed and Written Expressly for the Sabbath School, Together with Many of the Best of the Well known Sabbath School Pieces* (Ivison, Phinney & Co., 1861).

39. Wm. B. Bradbury, "Safe at Home," in American Tract Society, *The Soldiers' Hymn-Book*, 63.

40. "The Expostulation," in Soldiers' Tract Society, *The Soldier's Hymn-Book: for Camp Worship* (Soldiers' Tract Society, Virginia Conference, M. E. Church South, Chas. H. Wynne, Printer, 1862), 17.

41. Isaac Watts, "God the Source of Joy," in ibid., 29.

42. "The Christian Soldier," attributed to John Leland, a Baptist Elder (1754–1841), in ibid., 52.

43. James Iredell Hall Papers, Southern Historical Collection, University of North Carolina, Chapel Hill, quoted in Woodworth, *While God Is Marching On*, 142.

44. "A Dying Soldier's Letter," in Billingsley, *Christianity in the War*, 40.

45. On communicating news of the "good death" and anxiously awaiting word of how loved ones had died, see chap. 1 "Dying," in Faust, *This Republic of Suffering*.

46. George S. Phillips to "My Dear Wife," Lookout Mountain Valley, Alabama, Sept. 15, 1863, in Papers of George S. Phillips.

47. George S. Phillips to Miss Sally L. Phillips, Hospital 3 Division 4 AC. in rear of battle line near Dallas, Georgia, June 3, 1864, in ibid.

48. George S. Phillips to Miss Fanny J. Phillips, Field Hospital of 3rd Division 4 A.C., 49th R. O.V.V.I., Acworth, GA., June 10, 1864, in ibid.

49. Steven Woodworth also discusses this issue: "What was happening was that the pressure, pain, and enthusiasm of war were leading some Northerners to create a form of civil religion, a twisted version of Christianity in which the nation was god and rewarded those who sacrificed themselves in its cause" (*While God Is Marching On*, 107). He also notes that Southerners fell sway to similar beliefs: "As a number of Southerners came to view the war more and more as a religious crusade, the temptation, as in the North, was to begin using terminology that could produce very flawed doctrine, from a Christian point of view" (141–42). Woodworth suggests that those who had "only a passing acquaintance with...Christianity" were more easily swayed by this "flawed doctrine," but as this chapter suggests, not only laypeople but also chaplains and ministers grappled with the question of what happened to the "heroic" dead, often concluding that they were in heaven because of their faithfulness to the cause/to God (i.e., Phillips, Billingsley). Woodworth's perspective is in keeping with the overall tone of his book, which is very respectful of soldiers' religiosity (as long as it complies with "orthodox Christianity"), but sees other forms as "twisted" and "flawed."

50. Benjamin Babbitt, "A Sermon on the Death of Walter L. Raymond, a Union Soldier, Delivered on Sunday, April 3, 1865" (Andover: Printed by Warren F. Draper, 1865), 9–10.

51. On civil religion in the Civil War, see also Stout, *Upon the Altar of the Nation*.

52. Babbitt, "A Sermon on the Death," 16.

53. Ibid., 21–24.

54. Ibid., 24–25.

55. Ibid., 28–29.

56. Ibid., 30.

57. Ibid., 26.

58. Billingsley, *Christianity in the War*, 152.

59. Ibid., 170–71.

60. Ibid., 157–58.

61. Ibid., 313–14.

62. See David Blight, *Race and Reunion: The Civil War in American Memory* (Cambridge, MA: Belknap Press of Harvard University Press, 2002); Eric Foner, *Reconstruction: America's Unfinished Revolution, 1863–1877* (New York: Harper & Row, 1988.

63. Christine Stansell, "Elizabeth Stuart Phelps: A Study in Female Rebellion," *Massachusetts Review* 13, no. 1–2 (1972): 242.

64. Carol Farley Kessler, *Elizabeth Stuart Phelps* (Boston: Twayne Publishers, 1982), 22.

65. Elizabeth Stuart Phelps, *Chapters from a Life* (Boston: Houghton, Mifflin and Company, 1896).

66. Elizabeth Stuart Phelps, *The Gates Ajar* (Boston: Fields, Osgood, & Co., 1869), 14.

67. Ibid., 22–23, 20.

68. Ibid., 4.

69. Ibid., 53.

70. Ibid., 199.

71. Ibid., 167–68.

72. Phelps, *Chapters from a Life*, 109.

73. Ibid., 122–23.

74. Ibid., 119.

75. "Literature of the Day: The Gates Ajar," *Hours at Home: A Popular Monthly of Instruction and Recreation* 8, no. 4 (1869): 386.

76. Ibid.: 385–86.

77. Phelps, *Chapters from a Life*, 98.

78. On postwar conceptions of heaven and hell, see James Moorhead, *World Without End: Mainstream American Protestant Visions of the Last Things, 1880–1925* (Bloomington: Indiana University Press, 1999) and Jonathan M. Butler, *Softly and Tenderly Jesus is Calling: Heaven and Hell in American Revivalism, 1870–1920* (Brooklyn, NY: Carlson Publishers, 1991).

79. The section from here to the sentence ending "and to the appeals of David Walker, Maria Stewart, and Henry Highland Garnet" is drawn from Kathryn Gin, " 'The Heavenization of Earth': African American Visions and Uses of the Afterlife, 1863–1901," *Slavery and Abolition: A Journal of Slave and Post-Slave Studies* 31, no. 2 (2010): 207–31. See also Paul Harvey, "That Was about Equalization after Freedom," esp. 85, and Edward Blum, "O God of a Godless Land," esp. 95–96, both in Edward Blum and W. Scott Poole, eds., *Vale of Tears: New Essays on Religion and Reconstruction* (Macon, GA: Mercer University Press, 2005).

80. Stephen Angell, *Bishop Henry McNeal Turner and African-American Religion in the South* (Knoxville: University of Tennessee Press, 1992); Henry McNeal Turner, "On the Eligibility of Colored Members to Seats in the Georgia Legislature" (1868), in Edwin S. Redkey, ed., *Respect Black: The Writings and Speeches of Henry McNeal Turner* (repr. New York: Arno Press and the New York Times, 1971), 14–16.

81. Angell, *Bishop Henry McNeal Turner*, 272.

82. Turner, "The Question of Race" (1884–89), in Redkey, *Respect Black*, 73, first published in *Baltimore American*, May 12, 1884; Turner, "The Democratic Victory" (1884), in ibid., 71–72, first published in the *A.M.E. Church Review* 1, no. 3 (1885); Turner, "God Is a Negro," in ibid., 176, first printed in *Voice of Missions*, Feb. 1898.

83. T. Thomas Fortune, "The Negro in Politics" (1886), in Shawn Alexander, ed., *T. Thomas Fortune, The Afro-American Agitator: A Collection of Writings, 1880–1928*

(Gainesville: University Press of Florida, 2008), 39; Fortune, "Afro-American League Convention Speech" (1890), in ibid., 148. William Montgomery notes that "Fortune demanded that ministers 'preach less about the hell beyond the Jordan and more about the one, ever present, on this side of the river'" (*Under Their Own Vine and Fig Tree: The African-American Church in the South, 1865–1960* (Baton Rouge: Louisiana State University Press, 1993), 329).

84. Kelso, "Speech Delivered at Walnut Grove Mo. Sept. 19th 1865," in *John R. Kelso's complete works*, 12.

85. Ibid., 22.

86. Kelso, "Autobiography," 708.

87. Abraham Lincoln, "Second Inaugural Address," Mar. 4, 1865, in Michael P. Johnson, ed., *Abraham Lincoln, Slavery, and the Civil War: Selected Writings and Speeches* (Boston: Bedford/St. Martin's, 2001), 320–22.

88. John Russell Kelso, "The Heaven and the Hell of the Bible," in "The Bible Analyzed," in *John R. Kelso's complete works*, 582.

EPILOGUE

1. Other titles by Peebles include *Vaccination a curse and a menace to personal liberty* (Los Angeles: Peebles Publishing Co., 1913), and *How to live a century and grow old gracefully* (New York: M. L. Holbrook & Co., 1884)—titles we might imagine gracing the shelves of contemporary bookstores.

2. J. M. Peebles, *Around the World: Or, Travels in Polynesia, China, India, Arabia, Egypt, Syria, and other "Heathen" Countries. By J. M. Peebles, Author of "Seers of the Ages," "Jesus,—Myth, Man, or God," "Spiritualism Defined and Defended," &c., &c.* (Boston: Colby and Rich, Publishers, 9 Montgomery Place, 1875), 37–38.

3. Ibid., 68.

4. William Speer, *The Oldest and the Newest Empire: China and the United States* (Hartford: S. S. Scranton & Co., 1870), 642.

5. Ibid., 654–55.

6. *The Heathen Nations: Or Duty of the Present Generation to Evangelize the World. By the Missionaries at the Sandwich Islands*, 3rd ed. (Oberlin: James M. Fitch, 1849), 144.

7. Dammitdoll.com; "**Really IS a S-=-T-=-R-=-E-=-S-=-S reliever!**," February 20, 2013 review, Amazon.com, http://www.amazon.com/review/R15QXWIM0V4ODD/ref=cm_cr_dp_title?ie=UTF8&ASIN=B007WFSGMU&nodeID=165793011&store=toys-and-games.

8. Number extrapolated from recent poll figures and current population of the United States (roughly 316 million in 2013).

9. Alan Segal, interviewed in Charles Honey, "Belief in Hell Dips, But Some Say They've Already Been There," August 14, 2008, Religion News Service, http://pewforum.org/news/display.php?NewsID=16260.

10. Albert L. Winseman, "Eternal Destinations: Americans Believe in Heaven, Hell," May 25, 2004, Religion and Social Trends Commentary, Gallup Poll, http://www.gallup.com/poll/11770/eternal-destinations-americans-believe-heaven-hell.aspx.

11. Molly Worthen, "Thou Shalt Sometimes Kill," *Foreign Policy*, May 11, 2011, http://www.foreignpolicy.com/articles/2011/05/11/thou_shalt_sometimes_kill; "CNN Poll: Majority in U.S. say bin Laden in hell," CNN, May 4, 2011, http://politicalticker.blogs.cnn.com/2011/05/04/cnn-poll-majority-in-u-s-say-bin-laden-in-hell/.

12. "Episode 304: Heretics," *This American Life*, December 16, 2005, http://www.thisamericanlife.org/radio-archives/episode/304/heretics

13. Erik Eckholm, "Pastor Stirs Wrath with His Views on Old Questions," *New York Times*, March 4, 2011, http://www.nytimes.com/2011/03/05/us/05bell.html.

14. Cited in Winseman, "Eternal Destinations."

15. Henry McNeal Turner, "The Barbarous Decision of the Supreme Court (1883)," in Edwin S. Redkey, ed., *Respect Black: The Writings and Speeches of Henry McNeal Turner* (repr. New York: Arno Press and the New York Times, 1971), 69, written in Atlanta, GA, on Jan. 4, 1889.

Index